Governance and Social Responsibility

International Perspectives

Güler Aras

Professor of Finance and Accounting and Dean of the Faculty of Economics and Business, Yildiz Technical University, Turkey

and

David Crowther

Professor of Corporate Social Responsibility and Head of the Centre for Research into Organisational Governance at Leicester Business School, De Montfort University, UK

First published 2012 by
PALGRAVE MACMILLAN

Palgrave Macmillan in the UK is an imprint of Macmillan Publishers Limited,
registered in England, company number 785998, of Houndmills, Basingstoke,
Hampshire RG21 6XS.

Palgrave Macmillan in the US is a division of St Martin's Press LLC,
175 Fifth Avenue, New York, NY 10010.

Palgrave Macmillan is the global academic imprint of the above companies
and has companies and representatives throughout the world.

Palgrave® and Macmillan® are registered trademarks in the United States,
the United Kingdom, Europe and other countries.

ISBN 978–0–230–24351–4

This book is printed on paper suitable for recycling and made from fully
managed and sustained forest sources. Logging, pulping and manufacturing
processes are expected to conform to the environmental regulations of the
country of origin.

A catalogue record for this book is available from the British Library.

A catalog record for this book is available from the Library of Congress.

10   9   8   7   6   5   4   3   2   1
21   20   19   18   17   16   15   14   13   12

Printed in China

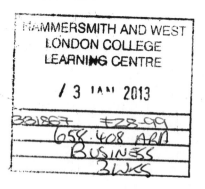

Contents

List of Tables

List of Figures

Preface

Corporate Social Responsibility and Corporate Governance are important issues in the modern business world. But they also have important implications for everyday life. Especially, they are more than theoretical subjects and they are issues which affect everyone around the world. In this book, therefore, we deliberately take an international perspective and we very deliberately relate the theory to practical implications for business and for society as a whole. The issues affect all of us. So our approach makes this a distinctive book which balances theory and practice in such a way.

At the current time it is quite noticeable how much more prominent the concepts of corporate governance (CG) and corporate social responsibility (CSR) have become – not just in the academic world or in the business world but also in everyday life. Many people have highlighted a lot of factors which have led to this interest – such things as poor business behaviour towards customers, employees and the environment. Particularly, of course, the corporate scandals of the last decade have led to a great deal of interest in governance procedures. Since then other things have also featured prominently in popular consciousness. One of these that has become more pronounced is the issue of climate change and this has given rise to fears about CSR through concern with the emission of greenhouse gases and particularly carbon dioxide. Today it is quite common for people to know and discuss the size of their carbon footprint, whereas even three years ago people in general did not even know what a carbon footprint was.

Another thing which has become prominent is a concern with the supply chain of business; in particular people are concerned with the exploitation of people in developing countries, especially the question of child labour but also such things as sweat shops and slave labour, as well as generally exploitative management. So no longer is it acceptable for a company to say that the conditions under which their suppliers operate is outside of their control and so they are not responsible. Customers have said that this is not acceptable and have called companies to account. And there have recently been a number of high-profile retail companies which have held their hands up to say *mea culpa* ('I am responsible') and taken very public steps to change this. Interestingly the popularity of companies increases after they have admitted problems and taken steps to correct these, thereby showing both that honesty is the best practice and also that customers are reasonable. The evidence suggests that individual customers are understanding and that they do not expect perfection but do expect honesty and transparency. Moreover they also expect companies to make efforts to change their behaviour and to try to solve their CSR problems. This too has raised the profile of corporate governance, particularly within organisations, as the prime mechanism for managing these problems is through a strong governance system.

Companies themselves have also changed. No longer are they concerned with greenwashing – the pretence of socially responsible behaviour through artful reporting. Now companies are taking CSR much more seriously not just because they understand that it is a key to business success and can give them a strategic advantage, but also because people in those organisations care about social responsibility. So it would be reasonable to claim that the growing importance of CSR is being driven by individuals who care – but those individual are not just customers, they are also employees, managers, owners and investors of a company. So companies are partly reacting to external pressures and partly leading the development of responsible behaviour and reporting. So accountability – one of the central principles of CSR – has become much more recognised and is being responded to by increasing transparency – another of the principles of CSR. It is not coincidental of course that these are also central principles of corporate governance and attention is being paid also in the development of governance systems and procedures.

Another issue which has come to the fore is sustainability and this is a term which has suddenly become so common as to be ubiquitous for business and for society. Every organisation mentions sustainability and most claim to have developed sustainable practices. A lot of this is just rhetoric from people who, we would claim, do not want to face the difficult issues involved in addressing sustainability. There is a danger therefore that sustainability has taken over from CSR itself as a target for greenwashing. Nevertheless although the relationship between organisations and society has been subject to much debate, often of a critical nature, evidence continues to mount that the best companies make a positive impact upon their environment. Furthermore the evidence continues to mount that such socially responsible behaviour is good for business, not just in ethical terms but also in financial terms – in other words that corporate social responsibility is good for business as well as all its stakeholders. Thus ethical behaviour and a concern for people and for the environment have been shown to have a positive correlation with corporate performance. Indeed evidence continues to mount concerning the benefit to business from socially responsible behaviour and, in the main, this benefit is no longer questioned by business managers. The nature of corporate social responsibility is therefore a topical one for business and academics. The evidence for corporate governance being actually good for business – and therefore an essential platform for sustainability – is even more overwhelming. Strong governance procedures are generally accepted to be worth a premium in the market because of the benefits which will flow therefrom.

Most people initially think that they know what CSR is and how to behave responsibly – and everyone claims to be able to recognise socially responsible or irresponsible behaviour without necessarily being able to define it. So there is general agreement what CSR is about. According to the European Commission CSR is about undertaking voluntary activity which demonstrates a concern for stakeholders. But it is here that a firm runs into problems – how to balance up the conflicting needs and expectations of various stakeholder groups whilst still being concerned with shareholders; how to practice sustainability; how to report this activity to those interested; how to decide if one activity more socially responsible that another. The situation is complex and conflicting.

Many would say that the situation for corporate governance is more simple because it is more straightforward, being merely concerned with how a corporation conducts itself whilst undertaking its business. This is overly simplistic and we have sought to show that corporate governance and corporate social responsibility and interrelated and overlapping. This is one of the distinguishing features of the book. Another is that we discuss the whole range of issues which comprise CSR rather than just the main themes and theories. And we recognise that there are a number of debates in the field at the moment – so we highlight these also. The associated website enables us to bring current information into consideration and relate it to the theoretical underpinnings of the book. Above all this book is readable and accessible to everyone and will provide a firm foundation for a detailed understanding of CSR and CG as part of any course and in preparation for a career in business based upon an understanding of the key issues.

GÜLER ARAS
DAVID CROWTHER

Every effort has been made to contact all copyright-holders, but if any have been inadvertently omitted the publishers will be pleased to make the necessary arrangement at the earliest opportunity.

Introduction to CSR

Learning objectives

After studying this chapter you should be able to:

- Outline some aspects of CSR.
- Describe the Gaia theory and its relationship to organisation theory.
- List the objectives of a firm.
- Describe the principles of the Global Compact.
- Discuss the relationship between population, population control and CSR.
- Outline the social contract.

The current interest in CSR

It is not very long ago that corporate social responsibility was a new concept and very few people understood its meaning. Certainly it was new to businesses and only a very few made any attempt to practise any aspect of it – indeed it was regarded as an extra cost for businesses, which needed to be persuaded that they should become involved. But things have changed very quickly. Now, almost everyone has heard of the concept of CSR and almost every business has a policy and a strategy for implementing aspects of CSR because they understand that the business benefits are enormous. And this is true for everywhere in the world. In this book we will examine the growth of the phenomenon of CSR and the benefits; and we will use examples from all over the world to illustrate that it is truly a global concept. We will develop our understanding of CSR in the context of its use in business and in society whilst at the same time developing our understanding of the theoretical underpinnings.

Most people initially think that they know what CSR is and how to behave responsibly – and everyone claims to be able to recognise socially responsible or irresponsible behaviour without necessarily being able to define it. So there is general agreement that CSR is about a company's concern for such things as community involvement, socially responsible products and processes, concern for the environment and socially responsible employee relations (Aras and Crowther, 2008). According to the European Commission (EC), CSR is about undertaking voluntary activity which demonstrates a concern for stakeholders. But it is here that a firm runs into problems – how to balance up the conflicting needs and expectations of various stakeholder groups whilst still being concerned with shareholders; how to practise sustainability; how to report this activity to those interested; how to decide if one activity is more socially responsible than another. The situation is complex and conflicting. In this book, therefore, we are concerned with different aspects of CSR, both with theorising and with implementing CSR in practice.

The development of CSR

Many people have traced the history of corporate social responsibility (CSR) in terms of the actions taken by firms. For some this goes back to the 1950s whilst for others it goes back to the Industrial Revolution or the Medieval Guild system. The objective of such historiographies seems to be to show that CSR activity is not new but has been ongoing – or that it is new and has had to be reinvented as corporate activity – depending upon the author's preference. We do not wish to enter this debate because any position taken is a matter of interpretation and prioritisation. Instead, we wish to make a different point in this book, and our point is concerned with research into CSR rather than about CSR itself. For a long time the research into CSR activity was dominated by academics in the Anglo-American areas of the world and slowly spread to other countries; now it can be considered to be of worldwide interest and concern. Also, for a long time the focus was upon identifying CSR activity in companies and highlighting bad practice – with greenwashing[1] being a common explanation. Now it is more generally accepted that companies are committed to CSR and accept that it is good for business and enhances economic performance.

A number of other things concerning CSR have started to feature prominently in popular consciousness. One of these which has become more pronounced is the issue of climate change and this has affected concern about CSR through a concern with the emission of greenhouse gases and particularly carbon dioxide. Today it is quite common for people to know and discuss the size of their carbon footprint whereas even a few years ago people in general did not even know what a carbon footprint was. This concern affects all businesses whatever their size.

Another thing which has become prominent is a concern with the supply chain of business; in particular people are concerned with the exploitation of people in developing countries, especially the question of child labour but also such things as sweat shops. So no longer is it acceptable for a company to say that the conditions under which their suppliers operate are outside of their control and so they are not responsible. Customers have said that this is not acceptable and have called companies to account. And there have recently been a number of high-profile retail companies which have admitted that they have had problems and have taken very public steps to change this. Interestingly, the popularity of companies increases after they have admitted the problems and publicised what they will do to correct the situation, thereby showing both that honesty is the best practice and also that customers are reasonable. The evidence suggests that individual customers are understanding and that they do not expect perfection but do expect honesty and transparency. Moreover, they also expect companies to make efforts to change their behaviour and to try to solve their CSR problems. Probably corruption and governance are also issues which are very important at the moment, and we will return to these issues in later chapters.

Companies themselves have also changed. No longer are they concerned with greenwashing – the pretence of socially responsible behaviour through artful reporting. Now, companies are taking CSR much more seriously not just because they understand that it is a key to business success and can give them a strategic advantage, but also because people in those organisations care about social responsibility. So it would be reasonable to claim that the growing importance of CSR is being driven by individuals who care – but those individual are not just customers, they are also employees, managers, owners and investors of a company. So companies are partly reacting to external pressures and partly leading the development of responsible behaviour and reporting. So accountability – one of the central principles of CSR – is much more recognised and is being responded to by increasing transparency – another of the principles of CSR.[2]

Another concern is with sustainability and sustainable development, and these are terms which have suddenly become so common as to be ubiquitous for business and for society. Now the debate is becoming concerned with durability – a stronger and more complete form of sustainability (see Aras and Crowther, 2009). Every organisation mentions sustainability and most claim to have developed sustainable practices. A lot of this is just rhetoric from people who, we would claim, do not want to face the difficult issues involved in addressing sustainability. There is a danger therefore that sustainability has taken over from CSR itself as a target for greenwashing. Nevertheless, although the relationship between organisations and society has been subject to much debate, often of a critical nature, evidence continues to mount that the best companies make a positive impact upon their environment. Furthermore, the evidence continues to mount that such socially responsible behaviour is good for business, not just in ethical terms but also in financial terms – in other words, that corporate social responsibility is good for business as well as all its stakeholders – a true win–win situation. Thus ethical behaviour and a concern for people and for the environment have been shown to have a positive correlation with corporate performance. Indeed, evidence continues to mount concerning the benefit to business from socially responsible behaviour and, in the main, this benefit is no longer questioned by business managers. The nature of corporate social responsibility is therefore a topical one for business and academics.

Another subject of great concern at the time of writing is the financial crisis of 2008–10 and how it has extended into an economic crisis affecting people and economies worldwide. What started as a problem in the USA relating to irresponsible lending by financial organisation in the subprime market has extended to reveal irresponsible lending on a global scale by banks ever seeking bigger profits without due regard for risk. This highlights failures in regulation but also failures in governance, and this problem with governance is also one of the central issues of CSR. Recently, we have also seen that corporate crime did not end with Enron and its aftermath as we now know that Madoff has lied and deceived his investors, whilst everyone has sat back and accepted the abnormal returns on offer without stopping to think that such returns are not possible on a recurring basis without taking abnormal risk. And so the financial crisis sparked a collapse of banks – helped out by governments giving them money for worthless toxic debt and buying shares. This prompted a collapse of the economy of Iceland followed by Latvia and has put severe pressure on the British economy, which has witnessed a collapse in the value of sterling. Subsequently, of course, Greece and Ireland have succumbed and Portugal is in question – with the whole Eurozone threatening to unravel. Bank irresponsibility in reckless lending has been followed by over-reaction and bank irresponsibility in lending to no one. This has resulted in the economic recession and the collapse of an increasing number of otherwise viable businesses – many of which are small and medium-sized enterprises (SMEs). So the crisis is global and affects all sectors of the economy – and hence is of concern to CSR and to the theme of this book. Some of the chapters will pick up on this issue.

These are all issues which we will consider further in later chapters.

The social purpose of organisations

A considerable number of writers over the decades have recognised that the activities of an organisation impact upon the external environment, and have suggested that such an organisation should therefore be accountable to a wider audience than simply its shareholders. Such a suggestion probably first arose in the 1970s and a concern with a wider view of company performance is taken by some writers who evince concern with the social performance of a business as a member of society at large. This concern was stated by Ackerman (1975), who argued that big business was recognising the need to adapt to a new social climate of community accountability, but that the orientation of business to financial results was inhibiting social responsiveness. McDonald and Puxty (1979), on the other hand, maintain that companies are no longer the instruments of shareholders alone but exist within society and so therefore have responsibilities to that society, and thatthere is therefore a shift towards the greater accountability of companies to all participants.

Recognition of the rights of all stakeholders and the duty of a business to be accountable in this wider context therefore has been largely a relatively recent phenomenon.[3] The economic view of accountability exclusively to owners has only recently, however, been subject to debate to any considerable extent. Some owners of businesses, however, have always recognised a responsibility to other stakeholders and this is evident from the early days of the Industrial Revolution. Thus, for example, in the nineteenth century Robert Owen (1816; 1991) demonstrated dissatisfaction with the assumption that only cost minimisation and the consequent profit maximisation was the only thing of concern to a business. Furthermore, he put his beliefs into practice through the inclusion within his sphere of industrial operations the provision of model housing for his workers at New Lanark, Scotland. Further examples of socially responsible behaviour have continued to exist since these days. Thus there is evidence from throughout the history of modernity that the self-centred approach of accounting for organisational activity only to shareholders was not universally acceptable and was unable to satisfactorily provide a basis for human activity.

Implicit in this concern with the effects of the actions of an organisation on its external environment is the recognition that it is not just the owners of the organisation who have a concern with the activities of that organisation. Additionally there are a wide variety of other stakeholders who justifiably have a concern with those activities, and are affected by those activities. Those other stakeholders have not just an interest in the activities of the firm but also a degree of influence over the shaping of those activities. This influence is so significant that it can be argued that the power and influence of these stakeholders is such that it amounts to quasi-ownership of the organisation. Indeed Gray, Owen and Maunders (1987) challenge the traditional role of accounting in reporting results and consider that, rather than an ownership approach to accountability, a stakeholder approach, recognising the wide stakeholder community, is needed.[4]

The desirability of considering the social performance of a business has not always however been accepted and has been the subject of extensive debate. Thus Hetherington (1973: 37) states:

> There is no reason to think that shareholders are willing to tolerate an amount of corporate non-profit activity which appreciably reduces either dividends or the market performance of the stock.

Conversely, and at a similar time, Dahl (1972: 18) states:

> every large corporation should be thought of as a social enterprise; that is an entity whose existence and decisions can be justified insofar as they serve public or social purposes.

Nevertheless, the performance of businesses in a wider arena than the stock market and its value to shareholders has become of increasing concern. In many respects this can be considered to be a return to the notion of the Social Contract. This is an important concept and something we will return to in Chapters 5 and 7 among others.

Social Contract theory is most often associated with the work of Hobbes (1651) and Rousseau (1762), where a contract, usually considered to be implied or hypothetical, is made between citizens for the organisation of the society and as a basis for legal and political power within that society. The idea is that for the legal and political system to be legitimate it must be one that the members of society would have rationally contracted into. Social contract theory has been applied to the question of business in society in a similar fashion by considering 'what conditions would have to be met for the members of such a society to agree to allow corporations to be formed' (Smith and Hasnas, 1999). The conclusions reached by the theorists include that the members of society would demand the benefits outweigh the detriments, implying a greater welfare for the society whilst remaining 'within the bounds of the general canons of justice' (Donaldson, 1982). This can be summarised as three basic requirements that relate to social welfare and justice. Hasnas (1998) suggests that when fully specified, the social welfare term of the social contract requires that businesses act so as to (1) benefit consumers by increasing economic efficiency, stabilising levels of output and channels of distribution, and increasing liability resources; (2) benefit employees by increasing their income potential, diffusing their personal liability, and facilitating their income allocation; whilst (3) minimising pollution and depletion of natural resources, the destruction of personal accountability, the misuse of political power, as well as worker alienation, lack of control over working conditions, and dehumanisation.

The justice term is less agreed upon but Hasnas suggests that one thing it should require as a minimum is that businesses do not 'systematically worsen the situation of a given group in society'. This obviously has a strong resonance with stakeholder ideas. Social contract theory has been criticised most usually because, as mentioned earlier, the contract is argued to be either implied or hypothetical. Therefore there is no actual contract (Kultgen, 1987), members of society have not given any formal consent to such a contract and they would be surprised to learn of its existence. Donaldson (1989) freely admits that the contract is a 'fiction' but continues that this does not undermine its underlying moral theory.

Walmart and social responsibility

Walmart has become the biggest retailer in the world. In doing so it has aroused a lot of feeling and many people claim that its growth has been founded upon exploitation rather than upon behaving in a socially responsible manner. So let us explore the reality of this.

First, the company was founded by Sam Walton with the express aim of sourcing cheap goods and passing on the savings to customers. Moreover, the stores were located where the customers were – in out-of-town locations. This made for low costs of operation but also provided what customers wanted, in contrast to other stores at the time. Many would say that this represents social responsibility.

Sam Walton had a strong commitment towards the people who worked in his store. Since then, times have changed and the main complaint against Walmart is concerned with its treatment of its staff. Claims are made that Walmart underpays them, is deeply opposed to anything resembling union organisation, and will expect total loyalty and commitment in return. It has also been claimed that the company expects staff to work in unreasonable ways: such as stacking shelves so high and without any special equipment to help them that they become injured in the process; being locked into the store at night while they clean and stack shelves, and other such bad practices. These practices are claimed to be so extreme that Walmart was named as 'Sweatshop Retailer of the Year' because of them.

Another claim made is that Walmart systematically destroys competition. When a Walmart store is established in a new location, it immediately sets up the most unequal and brutal competition with existing stores. Regardless of whether they are discounters, or traditional mom 'n pop (family-run) stores, Wal-Mart will undercut them with predatory pricing, out-advertise them, and persist until it has succeeded in driving them out of business.

Walmart is also claimed to be dictatorial with its suppliers, using its massive size and purchasing power to drive prices down to unsustainable levels.

It should be noted that these are all claims which have been made against other successful retailers – Tesco being one such example. Indeed, Tesco has aroused such fury for such similar behaviour that even books have been written about it.[5]

Walmart itself makes no claims about either CSR or sustainability. These are words which do not appear in any of its publicity material and do not feature on its website. This automatically makes Walmart different to any other major corporation – they all say something and have a policy.

On the other hand, it does take socially responsible actions at times. For example, it has said that it has asked its suppliers not to use cotton from Uzbekistan due to concerns over the use of child labour in its production. This brings Walmart in line with other major brands that have avoided the use of Uzbek cotton over recent months. The company was part of the coalition that called upon the Uzbek government to take action about child labour.

So is Walmart socially responsible? You must decide. Like all organisations it is neither totally bad nor totally good in this respect and it is the balance which matters, along with taking actions to improve.

The objectives of a business

A business manager must be concerned not just with the internal running of the business but also with the external environment in which the business operates, – that is, with his or her customers and suppliers, with competitors, and with the market for the products or services supplied by the business. Such concerns of a business manager comprise the strategic element of the manager's job and a manager must therefore be familiar with this aspect of management, and with the way in which CSR impacts upon this. Only then can we start to form an opinion concerning whether or not a company such as Walmart is socially responsible. Such an evaluation must be based upon facts and their analysis and this book will help you to achieve this.

First, however, we need to consider the various objectives which an organisation might have; the objectives of a manager need to be considered in terms of their helping to meet the objectives of the organisation in which he or she works. Whilst most business organisations aim to make a profit, this is not true of all, and the not-for-profit sector of the economy is one which is increasing in importance, whilst making a profit is not the only objective of most organisations.

Nevertheless, organisations do have objectives, and the following possible objectives of an organisation can be identified (as shown in Figure 1.1).

Profit maximisation

For organisations which exist to make a profit it seems reasonable that they should seek to make as large a profit as possible. It is not always clear, however, what course of action will lead to the greatest profit, and it is by no means clear whether profit maximisation in the short term will be in the best interests of the business and will lead to the greatest profit in the longer term. Thus, profit maximisation may not be in the best interests of a business and it certainly may conflict with other objectives which a business may have.

Maximising cash flow

Cash flow is not the same as profit, and an organisation needs cash to survive. In some circumstances this cash flow may be more important than profit because the lack of cash can threaten the survival of the organisation.

Maximising return on capital employed

This is a measure of performance of a business in terms of its operating efficiency and therefore provides a measure of how a business is performing over time. Comparative measures are useful in helping the owners and managers of a business to decide what course of action may be beneficial to the business.

Maximising service provision

This is the not-for-profit sector equivalent of maximising the return on capital employed and thus provides a similar means of evaluating decisions.

Maximising shareholder value

The value of a business depends partly upon the profits it generates and partly upon the value of the assets it possesses. These assets can partly comprise tangible assets, such as plant and machinery or land and buildings, and partly intangible assets, such as brand names. Thus the value of Coca Cola as a business far outweighs the value of its fixed assets because of the value of its brand name, which is recognised worldwide. Maximising the value of the business to shareholders therefore involves much more than maximising the profit generated.

Growth

Growth through expansion of the business, in terms of both assets and earnings, and the increase in market share which the business holds is one objective which appeals to both owners and managers. If this is an objective of the business then it will lead to different decisions to those of profit maximisation.

Long-term stability

The survival of a business is of great concern to both owners and managers and this can lead to different behaviour and a reluctance to accept risk. All decisions involve an element of risk, and seeking to reduce risk for the purpose of long-term stability can lead to performance which is less than desirable.

Sustainability

This is one of the most important objectives at the present time and always requires a review of products/services provided and also operational processes. This is considered in detail in Chapter 6.

Satisficing

It must be recognised that all objectives of an organisation are dependent upon the people who set them, and business behaviour cannot be considered without taking this into account. Satisficing is a way of reducing risk and taking multiple objectives into account by making decisions which are acceptable from several viewpoints without necessarily being the best to meet any particular objective.

Any business is likely to seek to pursue a number of these objectives at any point in time. The precise combination of them is likely to vary from one organisation to another and from one time to another, depending upon the prevailing individual circumstances of the organisation. The organisation will not, however, view all the objectives which it is pursuing at any particular time as equally important and will have more important ones to follow. These objectives will therefore tend to be viewed as a hierarchy, which may vary from time to time.

None of these conflict with socially responsible behaviour and there is growing evidence that social responsibility actually enhances the ability to achieve all of these objectives.

It can also be seen that all the accusations levelled against Walmart can be reinterpreted in the context of their seeking to achieve their objectives. This raises the question of whether the way an organisation behaves in seeking to meet its objectives is important. This, too, is an important aspect of CSR to which we will return several times in this book.

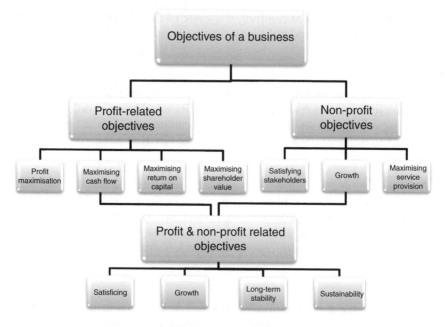

Figure 1.1 Classification of organisational objectives

The Gaia theory

Named after the Greek earth goddess, the Gaia theory[6] was created by James Lovelock in 1979. In this theory he proposed a different model of the planet Earth; in his model the whole of the ecosphere, and all living matter therein, was co-dependent upon its various facets and formed a complete system. According to the theory, this complete system and all its components were interdependent and equally necessary for maintaining the Earth as a planet capable of sustaining life. This was a radical departure from classical liberal theory,[7] which maintained that each entity was independent and could therefore concentrate upon seeking satisfaction of its own wants without regard to other entities. This classical liberal view of the world forms the basis of economic organisation, provides a justification for the existence of firms as organs of economic activity and provides the rationale behind the model of accounting adopted by society. The Gaia hypothesis, however, implied that interdependence, and a consequent recognition of the effect of one's actions upon others, was a facet of life. This consequently necessitates a different interpretation of accountability in terms of individual and organisational behaviour, activity and reporting. Initially ridiculed, the Gaia Hypothesis has gradually been accepted as true and has now become known as the Gaia theory.

Given the current constitution of the economic activity of the world into profit-seeking firms, each acting in isolation and concerned solely with profit maximisation, justified according to classical liberalism, it is inevitable that strategic planning and decision making developed as focused entirely upon the organisation rather than its environment,[8] seeking merely to measure, report and decide upon the activities of the firm insofar as they affect the firm itself. Any actions of the firm which had consequences external to the firm – as almost all do in one way or another – were held not to be the concern of the firm. Indeed, enshrined within classical liberalism, alongside the sanctity of the individual to pursue his or her own course of action, is the notion that the operation of the free-market mechanism would mediate between these individuals to allow for an equilibrium based upon the interaction of these freely acting individuals and that this equilibrium was an inevitable consequence of this interaction.[9] As a consequence, any concern of the firm about the effect of its actions upon externalities was considered to be irrelevant and not therefore a proper concern for its managerial decision making.

The Gaia theory states that all organisms are interdependent[10] and that it is necessary to recognise the actions of one organism affected other organisms and hence inevitably affected itself in ways which are not necessarily directly related to its actions – in other words, all actions may well have unintended consequences.[11] Thus the actions of an organism upon its environment and upon externalities was a matter of consequence for every organism, as everything is interdependent. This is true for humans as much as for any other living matter upon the planet. It is possible to extend this analogy to a consideration of the organisation of economic activity taking place in modern society and to consider the implications both for the organisation of and the accounting for that activity. As far as profit-seeking organisations are concerned, therefore, the logical conclusion from this is that the effect of the organisation's activities upon externalities is a matter of concern to the organisation, and hence a proper subject for accounting in terms of organisational activity.

Whilst it is not realistic to claim that the development of the Gaia theory had a significant impact upon organisational behaviour, it seems certain that there is some relationship, albeit indirect, as it seems that a social concern among business managers developed at the same time that this theory was being propounded. It is perhaps that both are symptomatic of other factors which caused a re-examination of the structures and organisation of society. Nevertheless, organisational theory has, from the 1970s, become more concerned with all the stakeholders of an organisation, whether or not such stakeholders have any legal status with respect to that organisation. At the same time, within the discourse and practice of accounting there has been a growth in concern with accounting for externalities and for the effects of the actions of the firm upon those externalities. One externality of particular concern is that of the environment; in this context the environment has been defined as including the complete ecosphere, rather than merely the human part of that ecosphere. These concepts form part of the foundations of a concern with sustainability, which we will consider in detail in a later chapter.

The original view of Lovelock was that the earth as a Gaian system would be self-healing and could therefore recover from all the actions of man. Since then there has been a lot of concern with changes that humankind has made to the earth and its constituent parts. In his latest book, therefore, he presents a somewhat different perspective. Thus, according to Lovelock (2006), climate change is inevitable, with its consequences upon the environment and therefore upon human life and economic activity. He remains positive, however, that it is possible to adapt and he is thereby more positive than some other commentators.[12]

Population

According to the pronouncements of the United States Census Bureau, the world population had increased to 6.5 billion on 25 January 2006. This was only a few years after 12 October 1999, which had been designated by the United Nations Population Fund as the approximate day on which world population would reach 6 billion. This in turn was only about twelve years after the world population had reached 5 billion, in 1987 (see Figure 1.2).

It must be noted, however, that the population of some countries, such as Nigeria or Brazil, is not known even to the nearest million, and so it can be seen that there is a considerable margin of error in such estimates. Nevertheless, it is certain that the population of the world is continuing to grow, and at a rate as quick as at present. Thus the United Nations Population Division has recently projected that the world population will be likely to exceed 9 billion by 2050. There are a number of reasons why there has been such a rapid increase in population in the last century. One factor, of course, is that of the medical advances which have been made in preventing child death and in extending the life of old people. Another factor is rising prosperity, coupled with a substantial increase in agricultural productivity, particularly in the period 1960 to 1995, which has enabled people to live more healthily and productively.

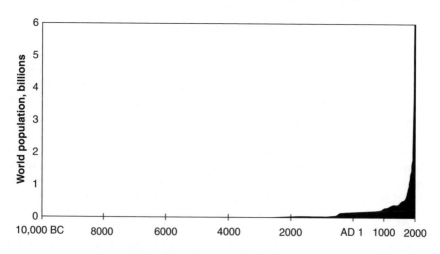

Figure 1.2   The growth in population

Source: released into the public domain by its author, El T.

An increasing population, of course, increases the requirements for goods to consume – raising a question about sustainability. This is particularly pertinent as far as the need for agricultural production to supply food in increasing quantities is concerned. When coupled with climate change and the consequent expected disruption to agriculture, this has been a cause for concern for many people, particularly in the context of sustainability. This in turn has caused Malthus and his theories to be re-examined for current relevance. Malthus, of course, was an eighteenth-century economist who developed his views primarily as a reaction to the optimistic opinions of his father and of his father's associates, notably Rousseau.[13] In his famous 'An Essay on the Principle of Populations', first published in 1798, he made his well-known prediction that food shortages would occur because population would increase at a faster rate than food supply could be increased – leading to mass starvation. He stated:

> The power of population is so superior to the power of the earth to produce subsistence for man, that premature death must in some shape or other visit the human race. The vices of mankind are active and able ministers of depopulation. They are the precursors in the great army of destruction, and often finish the dreadful work themselves. But should they fail in this war of extermination, sickly seasons, epidemics, pestilence, and plague advance in terrific array, and sweep off their thousands and tens of thousands. Should success be still incomplete, gigantic inevitable famine stalks in the rear, and with one mighty blow levels the population with the food of the world.

His argument is based on his Principle of Population. This states that population, if unchecked by such things as war or plague, increases at a geometric rate whilst the production of food will grow at only an arithmetic rate. In the optimistic years of the mid twentieth century, this argument was viewed as quaint and outdated. In recent years, it has come back into vogue somewhat and people are wondering if his ideas have current relevance.

At the same time, many people are wondering about population control. This is presently happening in China with their one child per family regulation, which has met with limited success and considerable evasion. Population control was attempted in India and was such a disaster that it is not possible politically to attempt it again. In most countries, population control is not politically possible and in quite a number the ethos is to increase population rather than limit or reduce it. Indeed, many religions[14] advocate actions which make population growth inevitable. Population, therefore, is one reason for the current concern with sustainability and therefore with CSR. Figure 1.3, however, shows that the rate of growth is decreasing.

The Global Compact

The Global Compact is an initiative developed by the United Nations with the objective of encouraging businesses worldwide to adopt policies regarding sustainable and socially responsible behaviour, and to use a common framework

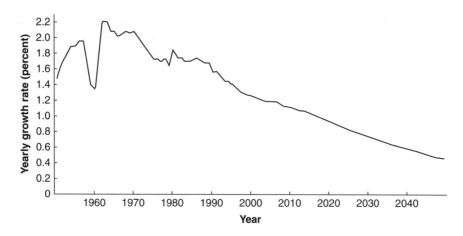

Figure 1.3 World population increase history

Source: created 2003 by Securunger from data provided by the US Census Bureau. Released under GNU Free Documentation Licence.

to report on them. The Global Compact was first announced by United Nations Secretary-General Kofi Annan in his speech to the World Economic Forum on 31 January 1999. It was officially launched at the UN headquarters in New York on 26 July 2000. The Global Compact is not a regulatory instrument, but rather a forum for discussion and a network for communication including governments, companies and labour, whose actions it seeks to influence; and NGOs and civil society organisations, representing its stakeholders.

The Compact itself says that once companies are part of the Compact, 'This does not mean that the Global Compact recognizes or certifies that these companies have fulfilled the Compact's principles.' The Compact's goals are intentionally flexible and vague, but it distinguishes the following channels

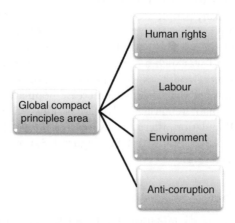

Figure 1.4 The global compact

through which it provides facilitation and encourages dialogue: *policy dialogues, learning, local networks* and *projects*. The compact is based on 10 principles (www.unglobalcompact.org/AboutTheGC/TheTenPrinciples/index.html).

The Ten Principles[15]

The Global Compact's ten principles in the areas of human rights, labour, the environment and anti-corruption enjoy universal consensus and are derived from:

The Universal Declaration of Human Rights
The International Labour Organization's Declaration on Fundamental Principles and Rights at Work
The Rio Declaration on Environment and Development
The United Nations Convention Against Corruption.

The Global Compact asks companies to embrace, support and enact, within their sphere of influence, a set of core values in the areas of human rights, labour standards, the environment, and anti-corruption:

Human rights

Principle 1: Businesses should support and respect the protection of internationally proclaimed human rights; and
Principle 2: make sure that they are not complicit in human rights abuses.

Labour standards

Principle 3: Businesses should uphold the freedom of association and the effective recognition of the right to collective bargaining;
Principle 4: the elimination of all forms of forced and compulsory labour;
Principle 5: the effective abolition of child labour; and
Principle 6: the elimination of discrimination in respect of employment and occupation.

Environment

Principle 7: Businesses should support a precautionary approach to environmental challenges;
Principle 8: undertake initiatives to promote greater environmental responsibility; and
Principle 9: encourage the development and diffusion of environmentally friendly technologies.

Anti-corruption

Principle 10: Businesses should work against corruption in all its forms, including extortion and bribery.

The Global Compact sets a standard for socially responsible behaviour for business on a worldwide basis and this is important to aid comparability as well as to set the agenda for what can be considered to be social responsibility. What is less certain, however, is whether the Compact has raised public awareness of the social responsibility agenda and helped to create a concern, or whether the Compact is merely a reflection of already-existing public concern. Certainly, many people were concerned with these issues before the announcement of the Compact by Kofi Annan, so its issue has not created public awareness, although it has probably heightened it.

Growth, welfare and sustainability

Economic rationality provides the theoretical grounding of most models of growth, with the assumption being that growth in economic terms also reflects growth in welfare terms. Increasing shareholder value is based upon growth of the firm and this implies the necessity for economic growth. Although growth for an individual firm can be achieved through competition and increased market share, at the expense of competitors, the whole concept of shareholding, and returns for risk and enterprise, is predicated upon continuing growth of the global economy. Growth is assumed to be sustainable for the economy at large and for the individual firm, something we will return to in our later chapter about sustainability (see pp. 144–66).

One way to generate growth is through demand creation, both by generating new markets and by creating a replacement market. Thus the Western European market for consumer durables is created basically by means of a replacement market through a process of adding value to products by innovation and through incorporating a fashion component. This, however, becomes increasingly expensive because of the need for ever-increasing R&D and marketing, which will inevitably change the cost function of the firm. The globalisation of markets provides a short-term opportunity for growth but also in the longer term increases competition and leads to problems of sustainability and demand creation. Economics and value added techniques do not distinguish between economic wealth and welfare, assuming that maximising wealth also maximises welfare. Thus the motor vehicle industry, for example, assumes that increasing wealth increases demand for cars which thereby increases welfare. In fact, evidence exists to suggest that welfare is reducing as wealth is increasing (Mishan, 1993) and that this situation is therefore untenable.

Conclusions

CSR is an important subject which affects all aspects of business behaviour. It also affects all aspects of society and has a significant impact upon each of us as individuals. There are many aspects to CSR and we have touched upon a sample of them in this chapter; we will cover many more in the succeeding chapters of this book. We have also touched upon a sample of theories related to

CSR; these are important to help us understand the phenomenon and in order to help us to develop strategies for CSR as well as analyse strategies which have already been developed. We will develop our skills in this respect throughout the book.

As we have seen, CSR has become central to the strategic planning of all companies. Today, virtually every company (and many other organisations) has a CSR strategy and plans. Moreover, this is a global phenomenon. In this chapter we have seen some aspects and have seen the importance of the subject. This provides a foundation for later chapters.

Summary of key points

- CSR is a global concept which almost all organisations – including not-for-profit organisations – have adopted.
- Companies recognise the commercial imperative for CSR, although this is a recent development.
- Organisations have a social purpose which is described as a social contract.
- There are a number of objectives of a business, and several of them will be followed at any one time. These, however, will be prioritised.
- The Gaia theory describes the earth and all living matter as comprising one complete interdependent system. This has implications for human behaviour.
- The growth in world population is one reason for the current concern with sustainability and therefore with CSR.
- The Global Compact is an initiative developed by the United Nations with the objective of encouraging businesses worldwide to adopt policies regarding sustainable and socially responsible behaviour, and to use a common framework to report on them. It comprises 10 principles.

Definitions of key terms and theories

Gaia theory states that the whole of the ecosphere, and all living matter therein, was co-dependent upon its various facets and formed a complete system.

The Global Compact is designed to encourage businesses worldwide to adopt policies regarding sustainable and socially responsible behaviour, and to use a common framework to report on them.

Social contract theory is where a contract is made between citizens for the organisation of the society and as a basis for legal and political power within that society.

Test your understanding

1. How does the EC describe CSR?
2. List four factors which have caused interest in CSR.
3. What are the principles of the Global Compact?

4. What is the Gaia theory?
5. List three possible objectives of a firm other than profit maximisation.
6. What is the principle of Population and why is it relevant?
7. In what way can a corporation be considered as a social enterprise?

Suggestions for further reading

Davis, K. 1973. 'The Case for and against Business Assumption of Social Responsibilities', *Academy of Management Journal*, 16: 312–22.

Friedman, M. 1970. 'The Social Responsibility of Business is to Increase its Profits', *New York Times*, 13 September.

Mintzberg, H. 1983. 'The Case for Corporate Social Responsibility', *Journal of Business Strategy*, 4, 2: S. 3–15.

Notes

1. Greenwashing is to present corporate activity in the most seemingly environmentally friendly way possible, despite different motivations driving the behaviour.
2. See Chapter 4 for a consideration of these principles.
3. Mathews (1997) traces its origins to the 1970s, although arguments (see Crowther, 2002) show that such concerns can be traced back to the Industrial Revolution.
4. The benefits of incorporating stakeholders into a model of performance measurement and accountability have, however, been extensively criticised. See for example Freedman and Reed (1983), Sternberg (1997, 1998) and Hutton (1997) for details of this ongoing discourse.
5. See *Tescopoly: how one shop came out on top and why it matters* by Andrew Sims. And also the associated campaign – <www.tescopoly.org> – against supermarket power. It is interesting to note that Tesco sells this book at a 20% discount!
6. Originally a hypothesis which was generally rejected, it has now gained general acceptance and become the Gaia Theory.
7. See the discussion of Utilitarianism later in this book and consider details of classical liberal theory.
8. We will return to this issue later in the book, as it is very relevant to an understanding of corporate social responsibility.
9. This assumption, of course, ignores the imbalances in power between the various parties seeking to enact transaction through the market – something else we will return to in a later chapter.
10. In actual fact Lovelock claimed in his hypothesis that the earth and all its constituent parts were interdependent. It is merely an extension of this hypothesis to claim the interrelationship of human activity whether enacted through organisations or not.

11. This can be considered to be related to the ideas of chaos theory. Gleick (1988) contends that Western science is founded on the idea that very small influences can be ignored; approximately accurate inputs will result in approximately accurate outputs. This is because these small influences remain small and do not escalate into much larger effects. However, since the 1960s this foundation has been questioned as there has been a realisation that in certain circumstances this is not the case. This leads to one of the cornerstones of chaos theory which considers systems that demonstrate a sensitive dependence upon initial conditions. Also it has become apparent that in certain instances this dependence is of such importance that the causal relationships are lost. Lorenz, one of the instigators of chaos theory, led us to what is known as the butterfly effect, which, as Gleick (1988) explains, is the notion that a 'butterfly stirring the air today in Peking can transform storm systems next month in New York' (1988: 35).

    Chaos theory and complexity theory are often considered to be synonymous (Hayles, 1991) and both have both been used to describe the environment within which modern organisations operate. Both are essentially concerned with the elimination of uncertainty from the environment and the representation of the future as certain, based upon the predictive ability of the theory. In this respect these theories can be likened to accounting theory in that they are concerned with the elimination of uncertainty in the prediction of the future, albeit each starts from a different base and works with a different set of assumptions.

12. See for example Reay (2005). This again will be considered in greater detail in a subsequent chapter.

13. Malthus's essay also constituted a response to the views of the Marquis de Condorcet (1743–94).

14. For example the Roman Catholic version of Christianity prohibits birth control and advocates procreation regardless of circumstances and ability to raise children.

15. <www.unglobalcompact.org/AboutTheGC/TheTenPrinciples/index>.

References

Ackerman, R. W. 1975. *The Social Challenge to Business*. Cambridge, MA: Harvard University Press.

Aras, G. and Crowther, D. 2008. 'The Social Obligation of Corporations', *Journal of Knowledge Globalisation*, 1, 1: 43–59.

Aras, G. and Crowther, D. 2009. *The Durable Corporation: Strategies for Sustainable Development*. Aldershot: Gower.

Crowther, D. 2002. *A Social Critique of Corporate Reporting*. Aldershot: Ashgate.

Dahl, R. A. 1972. 'A Prelude to Corporate Reform', *Business and Society Review*, Spring: 17–23.

Donaldson, T. (1982) *Corporations and Morality*, Englewood Cliffs, NJ: Prentice Hall.

Donaldson, T. 1989. *The Ethics of International Business.* New York: Oxford University Press.

Freedman, R. E. and Reed, D. L. 1983. 'Stockholders and Stakeholders: A New Perspective on Corporate Governance', *California Management Review*, 25, 3: 88–106.

Gleick, J. 1988. *Chaos: Making a New Science.* London: Heinemann.

Gray, R., Owen, D. and Maunders, K. 1987. *Corporate Social Reporting: Accounting and Accountability.* London: Prentice Hall.

Hasnas, J. 1998. 'The Normative Theories of Business Ethics: A Guide for the Perplexed', *Business Ethics Quarterly*, January: 19–42.

Hayles, N. 1991. *Chaos and Order: Complex Dynamics in Literature and Science.* Chicago: University of Chicago Press.

Hetherington, J. A. C. 1973. *Corporate Social Responsibility Audit: A Management Tool for Survival.* London: The Foundation for Business Responsibilities.

Hobbes, T. 1651. *Leviathan*; many editions.

Hutton, W. 1997. *Stakeholding and its Critics.* London: IEA Health and Welfare Unit.

Kultgen, J. 1987. 'Donaldson's Social Contract for Business', *Business and Professional Ethics Journal*, 5: 28–39.

Lovelock, J. 1979. *Gaia.* Oxford: Oxford University Press.

Lovelock, J. 2006. *The Revenge of Gaia.* Harmondsworth: Penguin.

McDonald, D. and Puxty, A. G. 1979. 'An Inducement – Contribution Approach to Corporate Financial Reporting', *Accounting, Organizations and Society*, 4, 1/2: 53–65.

Mathews, M. R. 1997. 'Twenty-five Years of Social and Environmental Accounting Research: Is there a Silver Jubilee to Celebrate?' *Accounting, Auditing and Accountability Journal*, 10, 4: 481–531.

Mishan, E. J. 1993. *The Costs of Economic Growth.* London: Weidenfeld & Nicolson.

Owen, R. 1816; 1991. *A New View of Society and Other Writings.* Harmondsworth: Penguin.

Reay, D. 2005. *Climate Change Begins at Home.* Basingstoke: Palgrave Macmillan.

Rousseau, J.-J. 1762. *Du Contrat Social* (trans. as *The Social Contract*); many editions.

Smith, H. J. and Hasnas, J. 1999. 'Ethics and Information Systems: The Corporate Domain', *MIS Quarterly*, March, 23, 1: 109–27.

Sternberg, E. 1997. 'The Defects of Stakeholder Theory', *Corporate Governance: An International Review*, 6, 3: 151–63.

Sternberg, E. 1998. *Corporate Governance: Accountability in the Marketplace.* London: IEA.

Defining CSR: Contested Terrain 2

Learning objectives

After studying this chapter you should be able to:

- Define CSR, based upon different approaches.
- Describe the three principles of CSR.
- Critique the Brundtland approach to sustainable development.
- Outline the stages in the development of CSR.
- Discuss the relationship between CSR and financial performance.

being the managers of other people's money than of their own, it cannot well be expected that they should watch over it with the same anxious vigilance with which partners in a private copartnery frequently watch over their own. Like the stewards of a rich man, they . . . consider attention to small matters as not for their master's honour and very easily give themselves a dispensation from having it. (Adam Smith, *The Wealth of Nations*)

Adam Smith is well known for his describing of the capitalist system. It is less well-known that he also saw the problems with the system and the lapses in ethical behaviour resulting from it. In doing so he helped explain what corporate social responsibility is all about and why it is necessary in the modern business environment.

Corporate Social Responsibility (or CSR as we will call it throughout this book) is a concept which has become dominant in business reporting. Every corporation has a policy concerning CSR and produces a report annually detailing its activity. And, of course, each of us claims to be able to recognise corporate activity which is socially responsible and that which is not. There are two interesting points about this: first, we do not necessarily agree with each other about what is socially responsible; and although we claim to recognise what it is or is not, when we are asked to define it then we find this impossibly difficult. Thus the number of different definitions is huge, and in this chapter we will look at some of these.

Definitions of CSR

The broadest definition of corporate social responsibility is concerned with what is – or should be – the relationship between global corporations, governments of countries and individual citizens. More locally, the definition is concerned with the relationship between a corporation and the local society in which it resides or operates. Another definition is concerned with the relationship between a corporation and its stakeholders.

For us, all of these definitions are pertinent and each represents a dimension of the issue. A parallel debate is taking place in the arena of ethics – should corporations be controlled through increased regulation or has the ethical base of citizenship been lost and does it need replacing before socially responsible behaviour will ensue? However this debate is represented, it seems that it is concerned with some sort of social contract between corporations and society.

This social contract implies some form of altruistic behaviour, the opposite of selfishness, whereas self-interest connotes selfishness. Self-interest is central to the Utilitarian perspective championed by such people as Bentham, Locke and J. S. Mill. The latter, for example, is generally considered to have advocated as morally right the pursuit of the greatest happiness for the greatest number – although the Utilitarian philosophy is actually based much more on selfishness than this – something which we will return to in a later chapter. Similarly, Adam Smith's free-market economics is predicated on competing self-interest.

These influential ideas put the interest of the individual above that of the collective. The central tenet of social responsibility, however, is the social contract between all the stakeholders and society, which is an essential requirement of civil society. This is alternatively described as citizenship but for either term it is important to remember that the social responsibility needs to extend beyond present members of society. Social responsibility also requires a responsibility towards the future and future members of society. Subsumed within this is, of course, a responsibility towards the environment – which we will also return to later – because of implications for other members of society both now and in the future.

There is, however, no agreed definition of CSR and so this raises the question as to what exactly can be considered to be corporate social responsibility. According to the EU Commission (2002: 347 final: 5):

> CSR is a concept whereby companies integrate social and environmental concerns in their business operations and in their interaction with their stakeholders on a voluntary basis.

We can think of CSR and the relationship between corporations and society in a number of ways.

1. Corporations are part of society

A growing number of writers, however, have recognised that the activities of an organisation impact upon the external environment and have suggested that one of the roles of accounting should be to report upon the impact of an organisation in this respect. Such a suggestion first arose in the 1970s, and a concern with a wider view of company performance is taken by some writers who evince concern with the social performance of a business, as a member of society at large.

Thus Carroll (1979), one of the early CSR theorists, states that:

> business encompasses the economic, legal, ethical and discretionary expectations that society has of organization at a given point in time (p.501).

More recently this was echoed by Balabanis, Phillips and Lyall (1998), who declared that:

> in the modern commercial area, companies and their managers are subjected to well publicised pressure to play an increasingly active role in [the welfare of] society. (p.31)

2. Profit is all that matters

Some writers have taken the view that a corporation should not be concerned with social responsibility, and you are certain to come across the statement from Milton Friedman, made in 1970:

> there is one and only one social responsibility of business – to use its resources and engage in activities designed to increase its profits so long as it stays within the rules of the game, which is to say, engages in open and free competition without deception or fraud.

Friedman was right in saying that companies must make a profit in order to survive – this is just basic common sense. He was wrong, however, – and this is a mistake that has been repeated many times by many people – in implying that social responsibility and profit are incompatible. In this book we show that the way to make a profit is by being socially responsible – indeed, it is the only way for a business to be sustainable. So all we want to say about Friedman and this quote is that it is significant that the only quote opposed to CSR that people can find is one which is 40 years old and appeared in a newspaper!

Nevertheless some people are more cynical in their view of corporate activity. So Drucker (1984) had the opinion that:

> business turns a social problem into economic opportunity and economic benefit, into productive capacity, into human competence, into well-paid jobs, and into wealth. (p.12)

3. CSR is conditional

In 1996 Robertson and Nicholson suggested that:

> a certain amount of rhetoric may be inevitable in the area of social responsibility. Managers may even believe that making statements about social responsibility insulates the firm from the necessity of taking socially responsible action. (p.1011)

Whilst Moir (2001) is more ambivalent:

> whether or not business should undertake CSR, and the forms that responsibility should take, depends upon the economic perspective of the firm that is adopted. (p.18)

So we can see that CSR is a contested topic and it is by no means certain that everybody thinks it is important or relevant to modern business.

Shell and the Brent Spar Oil Platform

The Brent oilfield is in the North Sea off the coast of the UK and is operated by Shell. It has been in·operation since 1975. Initially oil was pumped out from below the sea and stored in a floating platform – the Brent Spar – until transferred to tankers to be carried to land. Subsequently, a pipeline was built which made the Brent Spar oil-storage and tanker-loading facility surplus to requirements. With the completion of the pipeline connection to the oil terminal in Shetland, the storage facility had continued in use but was considered to be of no further value as of 1991.

Brent Spar became an issue of public concern in 1995, when the British government announced its support for Shell's application for its disposal in deep Atlantic waters at North Fenni Ridge (approximately 250 km from the west coast of Scotland, at a depth of around 2.5 km). Greenpeace organised a worldwide, high-profile media campaign against this plan. Although Greenpeace never called for a boycott of Shell service stations, thousands of people all across Western Europe, but particularly in Germany, stopped buying their petrol from Shell petrol stations. Some Shell stations in Germany reported a 50% loss of sales. Chancellor Kohl raised the issue with the UK government at a G7 meeting. But, despite the UK government's refusal to back down on plans to allow the Spar simply to be dumped into the ocean, public pressure proved too much to bear for Shell and, in a dramatic win for Greenpeace and the ocean environment, the company reversed its decision and agreed to dismantle and recycle the Spar on land.

Greenpeace activists occupied the Brent Spar for more than three weeks. In the face of public and political opposition in northern Europe (including some physical attacks – e.g. an arson attack on a petrol station in Germany), Shell abandoned its plans to dispose of Brent Spar at sea – whilst continuing to stand by its claim that this was the safest option, both from an environmental and an industrial health and safety perspective. Greenpeace hailed this as one of its most successful campaigns, and still does on its website, attempting to minimise its errors – see <http://www.greenpeace.org/international/about/history/the-brent-spar>.

Greenpeace's own reputation, however, also suffered during the campaign when it had to acknowledge that sampling errors had led to an overestimate of more than a hundredfold of the oil remaining in Brent Spar's storage tanks. Following Shell's decision to pursue only on-shore disposal options – as favoured by Greenpeace and its supporters – Brent Spar was towed to a Norwegian fjord and given temporary moorings. It was subsequently dismantled. Other subsequent calculations showed that dumping at sea was the most environmentally friendly option for this platform, although not so for other instances.

This is considered to be an important example of successful direct action changing commercial policy. It also shows, however, that evaluating the environmental implications of different courses of action is never straightforward, with valid arguments existing on both sides.

The effects of organisational activity

It is apparent, of course, that any actions which an organisation undertakes will have an effect not just upon itself but also upon the external environment within which that organisation resides. In considering the effect of the organisation upon its external environment, it must be recognised that this environment includes the business environment in which the firm is operating, the local societal environment in which the organisation is located and the wider global environment. This effect of the organisation can take many forms, such as:

- The utilisation of natural resources as a part of its production processes.
- The effects of competition between itself and other organisations in the same market.
- The enrichment of a local community through the creation of employment opportunities.
- Transformation of the landscape due to raw material extraction or waste product storage.
- The distribution of wealth created within the firm to the owners of that firm (via dividends) and the workers of that firm (through wages) and the effect of this upon the welfare of individuals.
- And, more recently, the greatest concern with climate change and the way in which the emission of greenhouse gases are exacerbating this.

It can be seen, therefore, from these examples that an organisation can have a very significant effect upon its external environment and can actually change that environment through its activities. It can also be seen that these different effects can in some circumstances be viewed as beneficial and in others as detrimental to the environment. Indeed the same actions can be viewed as beneficial by some people and detrimental by others.

Brundtland and sustainable development

In 1983 the United Nations established the World Commission on Environment and Development (WCED) under the chairmanship of Gro Harlem Brundtland. It subsequently became known as the Brundtland Commission and its report, *Our Common Future* (WCED, 1987), is normally known as the Brundtland Report. The commission was created to address a growing concern 'about the accelerating deterioration of the human environment and natural resources and the consequences of that deterioration for economic and social development'. In establishing the commission, the UN General Assembly recognised that environmental problems were global in nature and determined that it was in the common interest of all nations to establish policies for sustainable development. This commission produced its report in 1987. Whilst this report is named *Our Common Future*, as mentioned above, it is much more generally known as the Brundtland Report after its chair.

Strictly speaking, the Brundtland Report was concerned with sustainable development, which the Commission regarded as unquestionably both possible and desirable. This definition of sustainability starts from the premise that if resources are utilised in the present then they are no longer available for use in the future. This has led to the standard definition of sustainable development as:

> development which meets the needs of the present without compromising the ability of future generations to meet their own needs.

This principle has been incorporated in the Maastricht and Amsterdam Treaties of the European Union, as well as in the Rio Declaration and Agenda 21, adopted by the United Nations Conference on Environment and Development (UNCED), meeting in Rio de Janeiro on 3 to 14 June 1992. The European Community and its Member States subscribed to the Rio Declaration and Agenda 21 and committed to the rapid implementation of the principal measures agreed at UNCED.

This report is considered to be extremely important in addressing the issue of sustainability. The report described seven strategic imperatives for sustainable development:

- reviving growth;
- changing the quality of growth;
- meeting essential needs for jobs, food, energy, water and sanitation;
- ensuring a sustainable level of population;
- conserving and enhancing the resource base;
- reorienting technology and managing risk;
- merging environment and economics in decision making.

It also emphasised that the state of our technology and social organisation, particularly a lack of integrated social planning, limits the world's ability to meet human needs now and in the future.

This report made institutional and legal recommendations for change in order to confront common global problems. More and more, there is a growing consensus that firms and governments in partnership should accept moral responsibility for social welfare and for promoting individuals' interest in economic transactions.

Significantly, however, the Bruntland Report made an assumption – which has been accepted ever since – that sustainable development was possible, and the debate since has centred on how to achieve this. Thus, ever since the Bruntland Report was produced by the WCED in 1987, there has been a continual debate concerning sustainable development. Similarly, emphasis has been placed on such things as collaboration, partnerships and stakeholder involvement. It has been generally accepted, however, that development is desirable and that sustainable development is possible – with a concomitant focus on how to achieve this. Quite what is meant by such sustainable development has been much less clear, however, and a starting point for any evaluation must be to consider quite what is meant by these terms. We will consider these more extensively in Chapter 8.

Critiquing Brundtland

For more than twenty years the starting point for any discussion of sustainable corporate activity has been the Brundtland Report. Its concern with the effect which action taken in the present has upon the options available in the future has directly led to assumptions that sustainable development is both desirable and possible, and that corporation can demonstrate sustainability merely by continuing to exist into the future. Even the 2009 Copenhagen summit was based on this assumption.

It has also led to an acceptance of what must be described as the myths of sustainability:

- Sustainability is synonymous with sustainable development.
- A sustainable company will exist merely by recognising environmental and social issues and incorporating them into its strategic planning.

Both are based upon an unquestioning acceptance of market economics predicated in the need for growth and are based upon the false premise of Brundtland, to which we will return later. An almost unquestioned assumption is that growth remains possible and therefore sustainability and sustainable development are synonymous. Indeed, the economic perspective considers that growth is not just possible but also desirable and therefore the economics of development is all that needs to be addressed, and this can be dealt with through the market by clear separation of the three basic economic goals of efficient allocation, equitable distribution and sustainable scale.

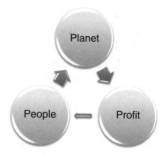

Figure 2.1   The triple bottom line

Similarly, all corporations are becoming concerned about their own sustainability and what the term really means. Such sustainability means more than environmental sustainability. As far as corporate sustainability is concerned then, the confusion is exacerbated by the fact that the term 'sustainable' has been used in the management literature over the last thirty years merely to imply continuity. Thus Zwetsloot (2003) is able to conflate corporate social responsibility with the techniques of continuous improvement and innovation to imply that sustainability is thereby ensured.

There have been various descendants of Brundtland, the best known of which is the concept of the Triple Bottom Line. This in turn has led to an assumption that addressing the three aspects of economic, social and environmental is all that is necessary in order not just to ensure sustainability but also to enable sustainable development. And all corporations imply that they have recognised the problems, addressed the issues and thereby ensured sustainable development. Let us start with the Triple Bottom Line – three aspects of performance:

- Economic
- Social
- Environmental

These are often labelled as people, planet and profit (fig 2.1) and will be referred to a number of times in subsequent chapters.

The Triple Bottom Line shown in Figure 2.1 has been widely adopted by business as a form of reporting, although it is overly simplistic. Nevertheless, it deserves full analysis and we will return to this in a later chapter.

The Dot.com boom (and bust)

In 1998, the internet was relatively new and still developing rapidly. More particularly, the idea of trading by the internet was very new. Somehow the idea came into being that any business which traded via the internet would be successful – whatever it was trading. And the Dot.com boom started – probably in 1998. As a result, a large number of new companies came into being and venture capitalists rushed to lend money to them in the belief (mass delusion) that success was assured.

The era was marked by a combination of rapidly increasing share prices, exuberant overconfidence that these companies would turn in future profits regardless of their product or business plan, individual speculation in shares, and widely available venture capital that created an environment in which many investors were willing to overlook traditional metrics such as price-to-earnings (P/E) ratios and return on capital employed (ROCE) in favour of confidence in technological advancements. Business boomed and so did speculation. So, by March 2000 the NASDAQ stood at 5048, having doubled in the previous 12 months. This was the peak and the index lost 10% within the next month and halved within the next year.

The chief marketing plan for these Dot.coms was 'the burn': the rate at which money was spent; and it was a case of the faster the better. The objective was to advertise the presence of the business and to build a customer base as quickly as possible. Returns were irrelevant and profit was almost derided. Even the biggest and subsequently most successful companies such as Google and Amazon did not see any profit in their first years. Amazon was spending on expanding customer base and letting people know that it existed, and Google was busy spending on creating more powerful machine capacity to serve its expanding search engine. The phrase 'Get large or get lost' was the wisdom of the day. At the height of the boom, it was possible for a promising dot.com to make an initial public offering (IPO) of its stock and raise a substantial amount of money even though it had never made a profit – or, in some cases, earned any revenue whatsoever. Similarly Boo.com spent $188 million in just six months in an attempt to create a global online fashion store before going bankrupt in May 2000.

In many ways the Dot.com boom was a repeat of earlier speculative frenzy and a belief that abnormal profits are there to be made by everyone. And it is not the last such frenzy – the 2008 financial crisis was caused by a similar belief, just a few years later. From a CSR perspective, one of the main lessons is to forget about greed but never to forget about finance – it will always be the cornerstone of any successful business. And transparency is paramount – it is not possible to be transparent if you do not have a business plan; would-be investors need to remember this.

A typology of CSR

It seems true that there exists a high degree of scepticism about the reality of corporate activity. Accusations of greenwashing – presenting a false picture – abound. Our opinion is that this is a legacy of past behaviour when such an accusation could reasonably be made about many organisations. Our view is that CSR is a developmental process and changes as organisations mature in their behaviour and attitude towards both their stakeholders and their ideas concerning social responsibility. Of course, we also acknowledge that there is a growing body of evidence to show that social responsibility behaviour becomes reflected positively in the financial performance of a company, thereby providing a financial imperative for changing behaviour. Moreover, we argue that there are stages of growth as far as CSR is concerned which become reflected in corporate behaviour. These can be seen as increasing levels of maturity.

In order to consider the implications for CSR then, the typology developed by Crowther (2006) provides a useful vehicle. As he argues, it would be relatively easy to develop a typology of CSR activity based upon the treatment of the various stakeholders to an organisation but, as Cooper and colleagues (2001) show, all corporations are concerned with their important stakeholders and make efforts to satisfy their expectations. Thus a concern with employees and customers is apparent in all corporations, being merely a reflection of the power of those stakeholder groupings rather than any expression of social responsibility. Similarly, in some organisations a concern for the environment is less a representation of social responsibility and more a concern for avoiding legislation or possibly a reflection of customer concern. Such factors also apply to some expressions of concern for local communities and society at large. It is therefore inappropriate to base any typology of CSR activity upon the treatment of stakeholders as this is often based upon power relationships rather than a concern for social responsibility and it is not realistic to distinguish the motivations.

A different typology was therefore proposed – one which is based upon the three principles of social responsibility outlined earlier. Moreover, it shows the way in which CSR develops in organisations as they become more experienced and more convinced of the benefits of a commitment to this form of corporate activity. The development of this typology is based upon research and interviews with CSR directors and concerned managers in a considerable number of large corporations, many of which are committed to increasing social responsibility. It demonstrates stages of increasing maturity (see Figure 2.2).

This can be explained as stages of growth reflecting increased maturity. The stages can be elaborated as follows.

Stage 1 Window dressing

The initial engagement with CSR was to change corporate reporting to indicate a concern for CSR without any actual change in corporate behaviour. This is the stage which led to accusations of greenwashing. It is also the stage which most observers of corporate activity continue to see even though, in reality, probably every organisation has progressed to a stage of greater maturity.

Stage 2 Cost containment

Corporations, of course, are always looking at their processes and seeking to operate more efficiently, thereby reducing costs. Organisations have realised that some of these can be represented as CSR activity – with things like energy efficiency or water efficiency being obvious examples. So there is a double imperative for this kind of activity – to improve financial performance and also improve

Stage of development	Dominant feature	Typical activity	Examples
1	Window dressing	Redesigning corporate reporting	Changed wording and sections to reflect CSR language (see Crowther, 2004)
2	Cost containment	Re-engineering business processes	Energy efficiency programmes
3	Stakeholder engagement	Balanced scorecard development	Customer/employee satisfaction surveys (see Cooper *et al.*, 2001)
4	Measurement and reporting	Sophisticated tailored measures	CSR reports
5	Sustainability	Defining sustainability: re-engineering processes	Sustainability reporting
6	Transparency	Concern for the supply chain: requiring CSR from suppliers	Human rights enforcement: e.g. child labour
7	Accountability	Reconfiguration of the value chain	Relocating high value added activity in developing countries

Figure 2.2   Stages of maturity of CSR activity

Source: from Crowther 2006.

the socially responsible image. Not surprisingly, therefore, corporations quickly moved from stage 1 to this stage – where action has been taken even though it is not necessarily motivated by a sense of social responsibility.

Much of this kind of activity is easy to undertake and requires very little in the way of capital investment. Naturally this activity has been undertaken first. Activity requiring capital investment has a longer payback period and tends to be undertaken more cautiously, with the threat of regulation often being needed to encourage such activity. All organisations have progressed through this stage also, although it must be recognised that the possible actions under this stage will probably never be completed by most organisations. Such cost containment therefore remains ongoing even when the easy targets have been addressed.

Stage 3 Stakeholder engagement

As stated earlier, all corporations are concerned with their important stakeholders and make efforts to satisfy their expectations. Thus a concern with employees and customers is apparent in all corporations, being merely a reflection of the power of those stakeholder groupings rather than any expression of social responsibility. Similarly, in some organisations a concern for the environment is less a representation of social responsibility and more a concern for avoiding legislation or possibly a reflection of customer concern. Such factors also apply to some expressions of concern for local communities and society at large. For CSR, though, this concern has become formalised, often through the development of a balanced scorecard and such things as customer or employee satisfaction surveys. Most organisations have progressed through this stage also, with such activity being embedded in normal ongoing business practice.

Stage 4 Measurement and reporting

Some companies have been practising social and environmental reporting for 15 years but for many it is more recent. Now most companies – certainly most large companies – provide this information in the form of a report. Over time these reports have become more extensive and more detailed, with a broader range of measures of social and environmental performance being included. So, most organisations have also reached this stage of maturity. The problem with this stage, though, is that at the moment there are no standards on what to report and so organisations tend to report different things, thereby hindering comparability. Organisations such as AccountAbility, with its AA1000 standard, and the UN Global Compact unit has sought to redress this through the introduction of a standard but none has gained universal acceptance. Consequently, it is probably true to state that this is the current stage of development for most organisations.

Stage 5 Sustainability

The discourse of sustainability has become as ubiquitous as the discourse of CSR and Aras and Crowther (2008) report that every firm in the FTSE 100, for example, mentions sustainability, with 70% of them focusing upon this. Any analysis of these statements regarding sustainability, however, quickly reveals the uncertainty regarding what is meant by this sustainability. Clearly the vast majority do not mean sustainability as defined by Aras and Crowther 2007a), or as defined by the Brundtland Report. Often it appears to mean little more than that the corporation will continue to exist in the future. A full understanding of sustainability would imply radical changes to business practice and a significant amount of process re-engineering, and there is little evidence that this is happening. So we argue that most companies are only starting to reach this stage of maturity and to grapple with the issues involved.

Stage 6 Transparency

One of the biggest issues of the moment – certainly in Europe – is the question of firms accepting responsibility for what happens further along their supply chain. This is something that has been brought about largely because of customer pressure and the revelations made about such things as child labour, slavery and other human rights abuses. So it is no longer acceptable for a firm to say that what happens in a supplying firm – or even the supplier of a supplier – is not its responsibility. Popular opinion says of companies, and so we wait for them to become sufficiently mature to enter this stage, that the firm is responsible for ensuring socially responsible behaviour among its suppliers as well as in its own company. Thus there have been examples of some very large companies – such as Gap or Nike – acknowledging responsibility and taking appropriate action to ensure change.

This is an issue which is growing in importance and is being addressed by the more mature (in CSR terms) companies. Thus it is claimed that some companies are at this stage in their maturing, but still a minority of companies.

Stage 7 Accountability

The final stage represents our wishes rather than actuality – at least so far! It is based upon the fact the multinationals can decide where to locate their operations and that all high-value added operations are located in developed countries. For many it would be relatively easy to transfer to less-developed countries and if that happened then the company would be making a real contribution towards effecting change. And we argue that there is no real cost involved.

Essentially the argument we have made (see particularly Aras and Crowther, 2007b) is that CSR must be considered as a process of development for every organisation – a process which is still taking place. Furthermore every organisation goes through the same stages in the same chronological order. Thus the leading exponents of CSR are only now beginning to address stage 6 and possibly consider stage 7. Less-developed corporations are at lower stages of development. What is significant about this, however, is our argument that sustainability starts to be recognised only once a company has reached stage 5 of its development. More significantly, stages 6 and 7 are essential for true sustainability as it is only then that an organisation recognises – and acts upon the recognition – that it is an integral part of a value chain and that sustainability depends upon the actions of the complete value chain. In others words, an organisation cannot be sustainable without its suppliers and customers. At the moment it is doubtful whether organisations recognise this and whether any organisation is (yet) truly sustainable. It is suggested, however, that all organisations go through these seven stages in the same order and will eventually arrive at stage 7, as shown in Figure 2.3.

The relationship between CSR and business financial success

Often the more significant the power that multinational corporations and some groups of stakeholders in a firm have, the more is spoken about corporate social responsibility (CSR). Thus a concept that was some kind of luxury some years ago has today reached the top of the public opinion discussion. Some steps taken

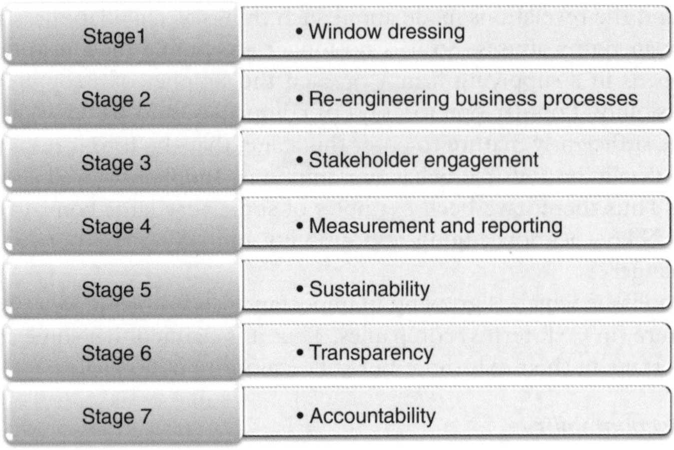

Stage 1	• Window dressing
Stage 2	• Re-engineering business processes
Stage 3	• Stakeholder engagement
Stage 4	• Measurement and reporting
Stage 5	• Sustainability
Stage 6	• Transparency
Stage 7	• Accountability

Figure 2.3   The stages of maturity

in the corporation's development, in the environment and in human values – and the consequential guilt – are probably one cause of this CSR fashion. If at the beginning firms were small and there was no distinction between ownership and management, the subsequent economic development made it a necessity to assign more capital to setting up bigger enterprises. Thus there were owners, who gave the funds, and experts in management, who managed the company and were paid by the owners. Agency theory establishes this relationship between the principal, who is the shareholder, and the agent, who is the manager, bearing in mind that the goals of the shareholders must be achieved through the management of the agents. But what are the shareholders' objectives? It is often thought that these are to increase the enterprise value through the maximisation of profits but we have discussed a broader range of objectives in Chapter 1, some of which apply to shareholders.

But a company's structure is today more complex than before and there have appeared other people, who are not owners, directly or indirectly implied in the company's operations – known as stakeholders. This complexity has, of course, increased the need for governance procedures. Multinational corporations have sometimes even more power than governments in their influence, and stakeholders have gained more power through the media and public opinion in order to require some kind of specific behaviour from companies. Within this new environment, although explained in a very simple way, the primary objective of the company has become wider. Although, generally speaking, the assumption may be that the first goal is to achieve financial performance in the company, after it the next step will be to comply with other socially responsible policies. That is because to pay attention to social objectives or to show an orientation to multiple stakeholder groups could be considered a luxury because it must have meant that the other basic company goal had been met. This argument is the basis of the first statement: 'Better performance results in greater attention to multiple stakeholders' (Greenley and Foxall, 1997: 264), whilst the other will take the opposite view: 'that orientation to multiple stakeholder groups influences performance' (Greenley and Foxall, 1997: 264), which means to 'attend' to social policies in a better way.

This double-sided relationship increases the difficulty of trying to prove any relationship empirically. Intuitively it seems as though there is a clear relationship between CSR and business success, but although the measurement of business success may be easy, through different economic and financial tools such as ratios, the measurement of a company's degree of compliance with social policies is really difficult. We can have in mind some kind of indicators such as funds donated to charitable objectives, but a company can spend immeasurable quantities of money on charitable quests and yet have problems in the relationship with labour unions because of bad working conditions or low wages, for example. In this sense there are some companies whose objectives have since times past included philanthropic aims. These may be understood as the initial values, which then the market and capitalism force the firm to change in order to survive the maelstrom of financial crises. Nevertheless, at the same time the double-sided relationship operates because socially concerned people still bear in mind these initial values and their image of the company is therefore improved, which in turn has a direct impact, of course, on economic performance. This example may be only one of those speaking about market inefficiencies[1] and the trend towards acquiring human values and ethics that must be forgotten when we are surrounded by this society and the market.

The relationship between good governance and business performance is clearer, however. Investors are increasingly willing to pay a premium for good governance in a business because of the expected improvements in sustainable performance, which will, over time, be reflected in future dividend streams. And the relationship between social responsibility and governance is similarly clear, as described by us previously (see Aras and Crowther, 2007c; 2008). In an attempt to satisfy the needs of the stakeholders, other conflicts between the interests of the different groups included in the wider concept of stakeholders can appear. Sometimes, due to this conflict of interests and the specific features of the organisation, a company tries to establish different levels among the stakeholders, paying more attention to those that are the most powerful. But are there some goals which are more socially responsible than others? In the end, the hierarchy will depend on the other goals of the company; it will give an answer to those stakeholders that can threaten the achievement of the company's economic goals.

The difficulties in measuring the social performance of a company are also due to the ownership concept. This is because the concept of corporate social responsibility is really comprehensive. There are companies whose activities are really different but all of them have to bear in mind their social responsibility, and not only companies, but also people in whatever activity they perform. From a politician to a teacher: ethics, code of conduct, human values, care for the environment, respect for minorities, and so on are values that have to be borne in mind and included in the social responsibility concept. The point of view of the concept can vary depending on the country or the region because some important problems linked to basic human values are more evident in some countries than in others. These social problems cannot be isolated because they have an important relationship with the degree of development of the country, so that in the end it is the economy that pushes the world. Capitalism allows for the differences between people, but what is not so fair is that these differences are not only due to people's effort or work but are also gained by having taken advantage of someone else's effort. Take for example multinational corporations, which sometimes abuse their power by closing factories in developed countries and moving them to developing countries where the wages are lower or security and health conditions are not so strict and so are cheaper for the company to maintain. On the other hand, the same companies obtain big amounts of profits which they may choose to expend in philanthropic ways.

The prevailing level of development of regions can determine the relationship between governance and business success. So in some developing countries, for instance, damage to the environment is allowed or there are no appropriate labour unions, and so on. Because of a lack of requirements or government attention, global players make use of these conditions to obtain a better economic performance even though they may be aware of their damaging policies. But it is not only the degree of development that has to do with governance and social responsibility; countries or regions are also deeply associated with human values disseminated through local education and culture. These values are so deep inside us that it is even said that people from different regions of the world who have shared the same education, for example ethics courses at a university, do not share the same human values because they are marked by their origins. Perhaps, conversely, the inclusion of ethics degree courses at the university could be considered useless since, finally, people will go on thinking as they have always thought, depending on the values of their original culture. However, everything is not so simple because there has been evidence of situations where different values have been imported from one culture to another and accepted as the second culture's own values without any problem. So, this shows that the questions related to CSR are more complicated than they may seem at first glance.

It could be argued that this complexity is a disadvantage to be taken into account when speaking about the creation of global standards for companies' socially responsible behaviour. There are so many different cases that to establish a general regulation may be too difficult but equally this diversity could be argued as requiring such regulation simply because there have been too many different initiatives, most of them private, which have added further diversity to the previous complications. Therefore, a common effort to tackle the problem of standards and principles is required. The latest financial scandals have proved that it is not enough to have company codes or human values and that it is necessary to reach an agreement to establish a wider, homogeneous regulation at least at the level of the global players, that is, multinational corporations which operate globally.

Summary of key points

- CSR has many definitions, according to the purpose of the definition, but all relate to a relationship between the corporation and its stakeholders.
- CSR and financial performance are related but the relationship can be difficult to understand. Certainly CSR is not a cost to business.
- An organisation has many impacts upon its external environment and all are related to CSR.
- The Brundtland Report outlined the conditions for sustainable development which have had a major impact upon organisational behaviour ever since. It has also led to Triple Bottom Line Reporting.
- It is possible to identify seven stages of increasing maturity of CSR activity.

Definitions of key terms and theories

Accountability, the actions of an organisation affect the external environment in many ways, and accountability means assuming responsibility for the effects of these actions.

Brundtland Report, the World Commission on Environment and Development (WCED) produced the report *Our Common Future* in 1987, which is normally known as the Brundtland Report.

Sustainability is concerned with the effect which action taken in the present has upon the options available in the future. (See Chapter 6 for an extended discussion.)

Transparency means that the external impact of the actions of the organisation can be ascertained from that organisation's reporting, and pertinent facts are not disguised within that reporting.

Triple Bottom Line is a form of reporting which recognises social and environmental impacts as well as economic (financial) impacts of a company's performance.

Test your understanding

1. What are the principles of CSR?
2. Should CSR be a voluntary activity?
3. What is the relationship between CSR and profit?
4. How many stages in the development of CSR can be identified, and what are they?
5. List four effects of organisational activity.
6. What is the approach of the European Community to CSR?
7. What is the Triple Bottom Line and what are the aspects included?

Suggestions for further reading

Aras, G. and Crowther, D. 2009. 'Corporate Governance and Corporate Social Responsibility in Context', in G. Aras and D. Crowther (eds), *Global Perspectives on Corporate Governance and Corporate Social Responsibility*. Aldershot: Gower, pp. 1–41.

Carroll, A. B. 1979. 'A Three-Dimensional Conceptual Model of Corporate Performance', *Academy of Management Review*, 4, 4: 497–505.

Crowther, D. and Ortiz Martinez, E. 2004. 'Corporate Social Responsibility: History and Principles', *Social Responsibility World*, Penang: Ansted University Press, pp. 102–07.

Note

1. See Baumol and Batey (1993).

References

Aras, G. and Crowther, D. 2008. 'Corporate Sustainability Reporting: A Study in Disingenuity?' *Journal of Business Ethics*, 87, supp 1: 279–88.

Aras, G. and Crowther, D. 2007a. 'What Level of Trust is Needed for Sustainability?' *Social Responsibility Journal*, 3, 3: 60–8.

Aras, G. and Crowther, D. 2007b. 'The Development of Corporate Social Responsibility', *Effective Executive*, September 2007, 10, 9: 18–21.

Aras, G. and Crowther, D. 2007c. 'Is the Global Economy Sustainable?', in S. Barber (ed.), *The Geopolitics of the City*. London: Forum Press, pp. 165–94.

Balabanis, G., Phillips, H. C. and Lyall, J. 1998. 'Corporate Social Responsibility and Economic Performance in the Top British Companies: Are they Linked?', *European Business Review*, 98, 1: 25–44.

Baumol, W. J. and Batey Blackman, S. A. 1993. *Mercados perfectos y virtud natural. La ética en los negocios y la mano invisible*. Madrid: Colegio de Economistas de Madrid, Celeste Ediciones.

Carroll, A. B. 1979. 'A Three-Dimensional Conceptual Model of Corporate Performance', *Academy of Management Review*, 4, 4: 497–505.

Cooper, S., Crowther, D., Davies, M. and Davis, E. W. 2001. *Shareholder or Stakeholder Value? The Development of Indicators for the Control and Measurement of Performance*. London: CIMA.

Crowther, D. 2006. 'Standards of Corporate Social Responsibility: Covergence within the European Union', in D. Njavro and K. Krkac (eds), *Business Ethics and Corporate Social Responsibility*. Zagreb: MATE, 17–34.

Drucker, P. 1984. 'The New Meaning of Corporate Social Responsibility', *California Management Review* 40, 2: 8–17.

European Commission (EC) 2002. *Corporate Social Responsibility: A Business Contribution to Sustainable Development*, COM (2002) 347 final, Brussels: Official publications of the European Commission, 2 July.

Friedman, M. 1970. 'The Social Responsibility of Business is to Increase its Profits', *New York Times*, 13 September.

Greenley, G. E. and Foxall, G. R. 1997. 'Multiple Stakeholders Orientation in UK Companies and the Implications for Company Performance', *Journal of Management Studies*, March, 34, 2: 259–84.

Moir, L. 2001. 'What Do we Mean by Corporate Social Responsibility?', *Corporate Governance*, 1, 2: 16–22.

Robertson, D. C. and Nicholson, N. 1996. 'Expressions of Corporate Social Responsibility in U.K. Firms', *Journal of Business Ethics*, 15, 10: 1095–106.

WCED (World Commission on Environment and Development) 1987. *Our Common Future* (The Brundtland Report). Oxford: Oxford University Press.

Zwetsloot, G. I. J. M. 2003. 'From Management Systems to Corporate Social Responsibility', *Journal of Business Ethics*, 44,2/3: 201–07.

The Context: Failure and the Need for CSR

3

Learning objectives

After studying this chapter you should be able to:

- Describe the environmental factors prompting an interest in CSR.
- Outline carbon footprinting and critique it as a methodology.
- Outline life cycle analysis.
- Describe the nature of the global village.
- Explain how the internet has changed the relationship between a business and its stakeholders.
- Discuss analysing social performance and its problems.

Introduction

For many people, particularly in the Western world, the year 2002 will be the one in which corporate misbehaviour was exposed by the collapse of some large corporations. In particular, the spectacular collapse of Enron and the subsequent fallout among the financial world – including the firm which Arthur Andersen himself founded in 1913 – will have left an indelible impression among people that all is not well with the corporate world and that there are problems which need to be addressed. This will be particularly the case among those adversely affected by this collapse, not least of whom are the former employees of the company who have lost their jobs, their life savings and their future pensions. Since then we have witnessed a large number of firms collapse through bad practice, we have seen the financial crisis of 2008–10 caused by reckless bank lending, and we have seen frauds such as the Madoff ponzi scheme. So there have been plenty of indications in the first decade of the twenty-first century that all is not right in the financial world.

The Madoff ponzi scheme

A ponzi scheme is a fraud whereby the fraudster takes in money from new investors and uses it to pay extraordinary returns to other investors. It works as long as the scheme keeps growing and not too many people want their money back. At that point the scheme collapses and the fraud is exposed. The scheme is named after Charles Ponzi, a 1920s crook who promised investors in New England a 40% return on their investment in just 90 days, compared with 5% in a savings account.

Bernard Madoff began his scheme in the early 1990s and it ran successfully until 2008. By then he had lost $65billion of his clients' money. At this point his lavish lifestyle as a 'successful' investment fund manager was replaced with a lifestyle in prison.

It is interesting to note that people believed in his success for almost twenty years during which they appeared to receive returns on their investment well in excess of the norm. This is just another example of greed blinding people to reason!

In other parts of the world it is remembered that 2009 was the twenty-fifth anniversary of the Union Carbide incident in Bhopal, India – the worst pollution incident in the world's history. This incident killed thousands, left thousands permanently injured and an even greater number living a life of misery in the area surrounding the former plant. To date, not one penny has been paid in compensation to those whose lives have been blighted by an incident caused by the lack of safety precautions that would be statutorily required in the Western world and which any socially responsible organisation would implement as a matter of course. At the same time, there are a lot of other environmental factors that are causing concern to people, as expressed in the Copenhagen summit which took place in December of that year. The principal one of these, of course, is climate change. So there are also indicators that all is not right with the world environment.

Union Carbide in Bhopal

Bhopal is a town in India where Union Carbide Corporation (a US firm) established a chemical plant in 1969 as a joint venture with various Indian investors. Primarily, it produced pesticide through various processes which involved some dangerous chemicals. In 1984 an accident occurred at the plant which resulted in a large quantity of dangerous gas being released into the atmosphere. As a result, thousands of people in Bhopal died and many more were maimed. Water and plants were also polluted, resulting in many more dying over the following years. In total, at least 20,000 people have died and a further 150,000 have been injured.

Compensation was paid by Union Carbide to the Indian government but none of this reached the Bhopal victims.

Various theories about negligence have been propounded and the case is normally cited as an example of the lack of social responsibility in exporting noxious processes to a developing country where standards are less exacting. An alternative claim from Union Carbide is that it must have been sabotage. Still another explanation is that the safety features were disabled by the Indian managers in an attempt to save costs.

The choice of explanation is yours!

These factors have provided the context in which CSR has risen up the agenda so that it is a matter of concern for businesses and for citizens also. In this chapter we will examine some of these factors.

Environmental issues

Global warming

The changes to the weather systems around the world is apparent to most people and is being manifest in such extreme weather as excessive rain or snow, droughts, heatwaves and hurricanes which have been affecting many parts of the world. Indeed, most of us remember, for example, Hurricane Katrina which devastated New Orleans. Global warming and climate change, its most noticeable effect, is a subject of discussion all over the world and it is generally, although by no means universally, accepted that global warming is taking place and therefore that climate change will continue to happen. Opinion is divided, however, as to whether the climate change which has taken place can be reversed or not. Some think that it cannot be reversed. Thus, according to Lovelock (2006) climate change is inevitable, with its consequences upon the environment and therefore upon human life and economic activity.

Although there are many factors contributing to the global warming that is taking place, it is clear that commercial and economic activity plays a significant part. Indeed, many people talk about 'greenhouse gases', with carbon dioxide being the main one, as the direct consequence of economic activity. Consequently, many people see the reduction in the emission of such gases as being fundamental to any attempt to combat climate change. This, of course, requires a change in behaviour – of people and of organisations. Such a perceived need for change is one of the factors which have caused the current concern about sustainability.

Footprinting

Another factor which is occupying the minds of people in general is that of their ecological footprint – the amount of physical area of the earth needed to provide for each person. Ecological footprint analysis compares human demand on nature with the biosphere's ability to regenerate resources and provide services. It does this by assessing the biologically productive land and marine area required to produce the resources a population consumes and absorb the corresponding waste, using prevailing technology. This approach can also be applied to an activity such as the manufacturing of a product or driving a car. A possibly more fashionable term at the moment, however, is that of carbon footprinting.

A carbon footprint can be considered to be the total amount of carbon dioxide (CO_2) and other greenhouse gases emitted over the full life cycle of a product or service. Normally a carbon footprint is usually expressed as a CO_2 equivalent (usually in kilograms or tonnes), which accounts for the same global warming effects of different greenhouse gases (UK Parliamentary Office of Science and Technology POST, 2006). There are a number of ways of calculating this footprint and a number of online resources to assist, at least as far as individuals are concerned. For a corporation it is more problematic as it involves both life cycle analysis and a detailed understanding of all stages in the supply chain.

Life cycle analysis

Life cycle analysis is concerned with all the effects of an activity over a whole lifetime. It recognises that any activity involves expenditure in the acquisition of the basis for that activity but it also involves a commitment to the future impact of its use. It is important to recognise this and to incorporate both acquisition and operating effects into the evaluation. Thus, for example, a product which has a high production cost but low operating costs may be more ecologically beneficial than one which has a low acquisition cost but high operating costs. An evaluation solely of operating effects will not take this into account and the most effective decision may not be made. The costs incurred over the full life cycle of a product are the following:

- Production or manufacturing costs – including research and development, resource consumption, energy consumption, etc.
- operating costs – e.g. maintenance, energy, spares, training
- ongoing capital costs – e.g. equipment upgrades, modifications
- disposal costs – e.g. removal and disposal of noxious substances, salvage, storage, reclamation, etc.

The objective of life cycle analysis is to measure the full range of environmental effects assignable to products and services, so as to be able to choose the least burdensome one. The term 'life cycle' refers to the notion that a fair, complete assessment requires the assessment of raw material, production, manufacture, distribution, use and disposal including all intervening transportation steps necessary to or caused by the product's existence. The sum of all those steps – or phases – is the life cycle of the product. The concept also can be used to optimise the environmental performance of a single product or to optimise the environmental performance of a company. As indicated in the preceding paragraph, however, this measurement and comparison take place in terms of cost.

For an individual the definition of carbon footprint is the total amount of carbon dioxide attributable to the actions of that individual (mainly through energy use) over a period of one year. This definition underlies the personal carbon calculators that are widely used. The term owes its origins to the idea that a footprint is what has been left behind as a result of the individual's activities. Carbon footprints can either consider only direct emissions (typically from energy used in the home and in transport, including travel by cars, aeroplanes, rail and other transport) or can also include indirect emissions (including carbon dioxide emissions as a result of goods and services consumed). Bottom-up calculations sum attributable emissions from individual actions; top-down calculations take total emissions from a country (or other high-level entity) and divide these emissions among the residents (or other participants in that entity). A number of studies have calculated the carbon footprint of organisations and nations. One of these examined age-related carbon emissions based on expenditure and consumption. The study found that on average people aged 50–65 years have a higher carbon footprint than any other age group. Individuals aged 50–65 years have a carbon footprint of approximately 13.5 tonnes per capita per year compared with the UK average of 12 tonnes.

Basically there is a relationship between the level of development and the footprint created – more development implies a larger footprint, as Figure 3.1 shows. This is also apparent from the carbon emissions shown in Figure 3.2.

It is commonly understood that the carbon dioxide emissions (and the emissions of other greenhouse gases) are almost exclusively associated with the conversion of energy carriers such as wood burning, natural gas, coal and oil. The carbon content released during the energy conversion process reaches the atmosphere and is deemed to be responsible for global warming, and therefore climate change.[1] Nevertheless, general concern has been expressed worldwide and this has led to the Kyoto Protocol.[2] The Kyoto Protocol defines legally binding targets and timetables for cutting the greenhouse-gas emissions of industrialised countries that ratified the protocol.[3]

There has been a considerable volume of criticism of the concept of a carbon footprint. All this is based on disagreement with one or more of the assumptions underlying the calculation of a carbon footprint:

- That carbon emissions are a significant cause of global warming.
- That human activity is a significant cause of these emissions.

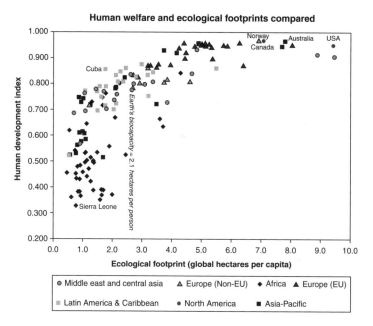

Figure 3.1   Ecological footprint for different nations compared to their Human Rights Index

Source: Global footprint network 2008 report (2005 data) UN Human development index 2007/08.

- That it is possible to attribute all or most emissions to particular individuals.
- That individual initiative is necessary because market forces or legislation will not be powerful and timely enough.
- That each individual should therefore calculate and attempt to reduce his or her share of carbon emissions.
- Sometimes, that each person should be given an equal share of emissions, or some other factor, as a target.

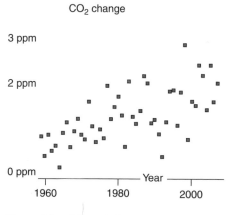

Figure 3.2 CO_2 emission per capita per year

Source: Tans (2008). Released under the GNU Free Documentation Licence.

Criticisms derived from the rejection of these assumptions therefore include:

- That other gases, such as methane, are more significant than carbon dioxide.[4]
- That human activity is not as significant a cause as natural processes like volcanic activity.
- That many emissions cannot reasonably be attributed to any individual and thus it is questionable whether it is reasonable to decide that the emissions from commuting, for example, are attributable to commuters or should be attributed to the consumers of the final products which they produce or service that they consume.
- That human activity will be changed, given sufficient time, by market forces or by political interventions.
- That population growth invalidates the calculations.
- That one cannot limit everyone to equal emissions: for example, those in urbanised societies may be unable to avoid some emissions, while less-developed countries may not have the technology to mitigate others.

Although scientific opinion has more or less reached a consensus that global warming is taking place and therefore that climate change is happening, there are still a considerable number of sceptics and people who deny that it is happening.[5] There are others who argue that the human contribution to global warming is negligible; they argue, therefore, that it is useless or even harmful to concentrate on individual contributions.

Shell in the Niger Delta

Nigeria has a population of around 140 million, with 30 million located in the Niger delta region. This is a major oil-containing part of the country but this is in conflict with the needs of the people, who rely largely upon agriculture and fishing for their livelihood. This is one source of conflict in the region. Oil is very important to the Nigerian economy: the country supplies around 3% of the world's crude oil. Nigeria depends on the oil and gas industry for 95% of export earnings and 80% of government revenue. A joint venture is a major revenue generator for the country, contributing more than $25 billion to the government over the last three years, for instance. Joint venture partners are Nigerian National Petroleum Corporation (55%), Shell (30%), Total (10%) and Agip (5%). In 2007, Shell-operated ventures produced an average of almost 934,000 barrels of oil equivalent per day: half of the country's total oil and gas production.

Another example was a well-known incident involving Kenule 'Ken' Beeson Saro Wiwa (1941–95), who was a Nigerian author, television producer and environmental activist. He led an information campaign against environmental degradation of the land and waters of Ogoniland by the operations of the oil companies, especially Shell. He was also an outspoken critic of the Nigerian government, which he viewed as reluctant to enforce environmental regulations on the foreign petroleum companies operating in the area. At the peak of his non-violent campaign, Saro-Wiwa was arrested, hastily tried by a special military tribunal, and hanged by the military government of General Sani Abacha, on charges widely viewed as entirely politically motivated and completely unfounded.

Shell as a company is deeply unpopular among Nigerians due to its environmental records in the Ogoni area of the Niger Delta. In a landmark ruling in a Nigerian court, the company was ordered to pay about £2bn in compensation to the Ogoni people. However welcoming the news might have been at the time of the ruling, it seems unlikely to be achieved as the Nigerian press have cited corruption, injustice and brutality (by the government) as major barriers that may ultimately prevent this compensation from being actually paid. As the Niger Delta saga seems to continue without end (even after the death of Ken Saro-Wiwa), Shell is also unpopular in other areas of the globe, e.g. Rossport, Ireland and British Columbia, Canada as well as a host of other areas.

The oil companies are largely castigated for their behaviour in the Niger Delta with Shell, as the largest operator, being particularly singled out. It is certainly true that the people of the delta have seen their environment degrade and few benefits from the oil revenue. If you ask the Ogoni people – who inhabit a part of the delta with major oil production – however, they mainly blame the Nigerian government, one of the most corrupt in the world, for tribal preferences which prevent them from benefiting. Shell on the other hand are quite open and most of this information can be found on their website. Such transparency, based upon full disclosure, is of course an essential feature of CSR.

Social responsibility and the free market

In 1968, Marshall McLuhan stated that we now live in a global village (McLuhan and Fiore, 1968) and that technology was connecting everyone together. Much has changed since then in terms of technology and now with access to the Internet available to everyone we truly do live in a global village in which anyone can interact with anyone else wherever they are living and whatever time zone they are residing in. The Internet has completely changed the world and this is having profound consequences for people everywhere.

Marshall McLuhan was prophetic in some of the other things which he had to say. When talking about this global village he also said that war would continue to be a feature of the world but that there would be an increasing emphasis upon economic war rather than physical war. Whilst physical war has not gone away, it might be argued that the reasons for wars in the present are economic at least in as much as they are to do with imperialistic or ideological reasons – at least as far as governments and countries are concerned. But governments, as the epitome of the nation state, are becoming less important. In Europe we have seen a number of new nation states becoming established as other countries have broken up. But this is beside the point, because what is becoming more important than both governments and nation states is the multinational company, operating in a global environment. Some of these multinationals are very large indeed – larger than many nation states and a good deal more powerful. Arguably, it is here that the economic war for the global village is taking place.

Many governments throughout the world behave as if they recognise this and respond to the veiled threats from these corporations to relocate their operations by granting concessions of various kinds. Even the government of the United States – the most powerful nation on earth – behaves in this way. For them, however, the problem is that all their politicians are funded by these corporations and so they must behave as if they are on the payroll and must do as they are told. Needless to say, these corporations are concerned with their own interests rather than with altruism and so American domestic and foreign policies are dictated by the needs of multinational corporations. And where America leads, others must follow, or suffer the consequences whether economic or physical.

One of the consequences of the acquisition of governmental influence by these corporations is the myth of the free market as being beneficial to all. It is widely accepted – almost unquestioningly – that free markets will lead to greater economic growth and that we will all benefit from this economic growth. Around the world people are arguing – and winning the argument – that restrictions upon world economic activity caused by the regulation of markets are bad for our well-being. And in one country after another, for one market after another, governments are capitulating and relaxing their regulations to allow complete freedom of economic activity. So whilst the world might not yet be a global village, it is rapidly becoming a global marketplace for these corporations.

We have witnessed the effects of the actions of some of these global corporations. Recently we have seen the effects of the actions of some of these corporations within the United States itself – the champion of the free market. We have seen the collapse of the global accounting firm Anderson; we have seen the bankruptcy of major corporations; we have seen the subprime lending scandal. Arguably, the free market has allowed this to happen. But the myth of the free market is grounded in classical liberal economic theory, as propounded by people such as John Stuart Mill (1848) in the nineteenth century, which, briefly summarised, states that anything is OK as long as the consequences are acceptable. And there is no alternative – at least, that is what many say. Indeed, Francis Fukuyama (1992) argued that, with the collapse of the Berlin Wall, liberal democracy had triumphed and the end of history had arrived. Many people are familiar with this argument of Fukuyama – and have challenged the assertion – but most are less clear that he lamented this end of history.

But it is our argument that history has not ended and that corporate social responsibility provides a way forward which cancels the negative effects of an unregulated free global market. All individuals have rights – rights to pursue their own ends and to seek to better their existence in whatever terms they define this idea of better. But with rights go responsibilities and obligations. For many corporations – and particularly for the managers of those corporations – this relationship between rights and responsibilities has been lost, with the rights maintained and the responsibilities discarded.

How did this go wrong? Crowther (2004) argues that this started to go wrong when the concept of limited liability was introduced for corporations – in the UK in the early part of the nineteenth century. The principle of limited liability was introduced to protect investors (i.e. shareholders) from the potential adverse consequences of the actions of the corporations in which they invested. One of the problems, however, must be associated with accounting and its use by organisations to record their actions.[6] The traditional view of accounting, as far as an organisation is concerned, is that the only activities with which the organisation should be concerned are those which take place within the organisation, or between the organisation and its suppliers or customers. Essentially, the only purpose of traditional accounting is to record the effects of actions upon the organisation itself; an essentially inward-looking position. Consequently, it is considered that these are the only activities for which a role for accounting exists. Here, therefore, the essential dialectic of accounting – that some results of actions taken are significant and need to be recorded whilst others are irrelevant and need to be ignored – is located. This view of accounting places the organisation at the centre of its world and the only interfaces with the external world take place at the beginning and end of its value chain.

An organisation can have a very significant effect upon its external environment and can actually change that environment through its activities. It can also be seen that these different effects can in some circumstances be viewed as beneficial and in other circumstances be viewed as detrimental to the environment. Indeed, the same actions can be viewed as beneficial by some people and detrimental by others.

A global village

It can be argued that things have not changed much in the forty years since the arguments of McLuhan and the development of a social contract approach to business management were first made, and the need for social responsibility is by no means universally accepted – or some of the things we have referred to would not have happened. But there are grounds for optimism. In the first place, ethical and socially responsible behaviour is being engaged in successfully by a number of large corporations – and this number is increasing all the time. Secondly, there is evidence that socially responsible behaviour leads to increased economic performance – at least in the longer term – and consequentially greater welfare and wealth for all involved, either actively or passively.

To return to the argument of Marshall McLuhan, however, and the way in which technology is bringing about the global village, this provides one source of optimism. The increasing availability of access to the Internet has been widely discussed and its effects upon both corporations and upon individual members of society, suggested (Rushkoff, 1997). For corporations, much has been promulgated concerning the opportunities presented through the ability to reach a global audience and to engage in electronic retailing; much less has been said about the effects of the change in accountability provided by this medium. Much of what has been said is based upon an expectation that the Internet and the World Wide Web will have a beneficial impact upon the way in which society operates (see, for example, Holmes and Grieco, 1999). Thus Sobchack (1996) argues that this technology will be more liberating, participatory and interactive than previous cultural forms, whilst Axford (1995) argues that it will lead to increasing globalisation of politics, culture and social systems. Much of this discourse is concerned at a societal level with the effects of Internet technology upon society and, only by implication, upon individuals within society. It is only at the level of the individual, however, that these changes can take place. Indeed, access to the Internet, and the ability to communicate via this technology with other individuals, without regard to time and place, can be considered to be a revolutionary redistribution of power (Russell, 1975) – a redistribution in favour of us all as individuals. Moreover, the disciplinary practices of society (Foucault, 1977) break down when the Internet is used because of the lack of spatial contiguity between communicants (see Carter and Grieco, 2000 regarding the emerging electronic ontologies) and because of the effective anonymity of the communication which prevents the normalising surveillance mechanisms of society (Clegg, 1989) from interceding in that communication. Thus the Internet provides a space for resistance to foment (Robins, 1995).

Of particular interest, however, is the way in which access to Internet technology can redefine the corporate landscape (see Crowther, 2000; 2002) and change the power relationship between large corporations and individuals. In this respect the changes in these power relationships can be profound and even revolutionary, generating new and contested arenas of control and accountability. On the one hand the communicative freedom and immediacy offered by the technology provides a potential challenge to legitimacy and can give individuals the ability to confront large corporations and to have their voice heard with equal volume within the discourse facilitated by cyberspace. In this respect the power imbalance is being equalised and we are moving from a global marketplace to a truly global village.

On the other hand, as the technological marriage of data communications (principally the Internet) and computing unfolds, old ethical issues resurface in new clothes. One such is the collection of information about individuals. Corporations, governments and their agents have been collecting information on people since the dawn of social organisation. The harnessing of computers during the last quarter of the twentieth century has enabled a significant increase in the intensity of information gathering; a development that many saw as propelling democratic society towards an Orwellian nightmare. Others acknowledged the need of institutions to collect information, but worried about how to balance that need against the individual's desire for privacy (Johnson and Nissenbaum, 1995). As the twenty-first century develops, an important feature of our modern global village is the quantum leap in the scope of this information gathering.

The application of Information and Communication Technologies (ICT) is enabling faster information transmission (within and between global corporations), involving more parties (buyer, seller, information broker, government) and new kinds of information to be collected. The cost of collecting and storing this information is often a marginal cost to the collecting organisation. For example, consider the automatic deployment of 'cookies' from host to website visitors, recording our interests, preferences and browsing behaviour. Given this scale of information gathering, we need to evaluate the moral implications of a variety of new conditions. For example, we as online consumers want information tailored to our preferences but are unhappy to divulge personal data (Rayman-Bacchus and Molina, 2001). We find ourselves in a dilemma whereby we can experience a new level of personal service, but at the price of sacrificing private information. Furthermore, giving personal information could help the tailoring, but doing so also invites spam (junk e-mail) and other possible abuses.

Shell and governance failure

On Friday 9 January 2004, a small item of news was issued alongside the plethora of other news concerning corporate activity and its possible effect upon company performance and consequently share price. It was a typical minor announcement on that day and finished with a statement that a teleconference would be held, also on that day, and hosted by Simon Henry, Head of Group Investor Relations, Mary Jo Jacobi, Vice President of Group External Affairs and John Darley, Exploration and Production Technical Director. The announcement stated that:

> The Royal Dutch/Shell Group of Companies ('Shell') announced today that, following internal reviews, some proved hydrocarbon reserves will be recategorised. The total non recurring recategorisation, relative to the proved reserves as stated at December 31st 2002, represents 3.9 billion barrels of oil equivalent ('boe') of proved reserves, or 20% of proved reserves at that date.

It also stated that:

> Reserves affected were mainly booked in the period 1996 to 2002. A significant proportion of the recategorisation relates to the current status of project maturity. The recategorisation brings the global reserve base up to a common standard of definition, consistent with the globalisation of processes within the new Exploration & Production business model.

As a standard Shell news release, of course, it also sought to reassure investors by stating that:

⟶

There is no material effect on financial statements for any year up to and including 2003. The recategorisation of proved reserves does not materially change the estimated total volume of hydrocarbons in place, nor the volumes that are expected ultimately to be recovered. It is anticipated that most of these reserves will be re-booked in the proved category over time as field developments mature.

Less than a month later the company announced its results for the last year, 2003. Highlighted by the Chairman were the following aspects of performance[7]:

- Reported net income of $12.7 billion in 2003 was 35% higher than in 2002.
- The Group's earnings on an estimated current cost of supplies (CCS) basis for the full year were a record at $13.0 billion (46% higher than last year).
- Final dividends proposed of €1.02 per share for Royal Dutch and of 9.65p per share for Shell Transport, increasing above inflation. The increase in US dollar terms, at current exchange rates, exceeds 10%, and over the past 3 years has risen by 28%.

With regard to reserves and their reclassification, the following statement was made:

The Group is continuing to discuss the implementation of the recategorisation with the staff of the SEC. The staff has advised that it appears that the 2002 Form 20-F should be amended to correct the reserve information previously reported. With regard to the financial statements, as previously advised, the Group does not believe that the recategorisation has a material impact for any year, because only a small portion affects proved developed reserves.

Within three months of this minor announcement[8] the after-tax income of the corporation for the preceding four years had been recalculated and reduced by almost $450 million and the Chairman, Sir Philip Watts, had resigned. Since that time the re-categorisation/recalculations have continued but without the newsworthiness of the original episodes.

According to the *Cautionary Note to investors* that the Shell group includes in all its documents available on its website:

The United States Securities and Exchange Commission permits oil and gas companies, in their filings with the SEC, to disclose only proved reserves that a company has demonstrated by actual production or conclusive formation tests to be economically and legally producible under existing economic and operating conditions.

It is apparent that this requirement was ignored and that the company over-stated its oil reserves over an extended period. According to the US-SEC, the company overstated proved reserves reported in its 2002 Form 20-F by 4.47 billion barrels of oil equivalent (boe), or approximately 23%. They also overstated the standardised measure of future cash flows reported in this fil-ing by approximately $6.6 billion. Shell corrected these overstatements in an amended filing on 2 July 2004, which reflected the degree of Shell's overstate-ments for the years 1997 to 2002. These amendments are included in Table 3.1. From these figures it is important to point out that to modify billions of barrels of oil equivalent (boe) in percentages ranging from 16% to 25% is a significant variation.

Table 3.1   Shell's overstatements

Year	Proved Reserves Overstatement	% Overstatement	Standardized Measure Overstatement	% Overstatement
1997	3.13 boe	16%	N/A	N/A
1998	3.78 boe	18%	N/A	N/A
1999	4.58 boe	23%	$7.0 billion	11%
2000	4.84 boe	25%	$7.2 billion	10%
2001	4.53 boe	24%	$6.5 billion	13%
2002	4.47 boe	23%	$6.6 billion	9%

Over this period it was also admitted that Shell had materially misstated its reserves replacement ratio (RRR), a key performance indicator in the oil and gas industry. If Shell had properly reported proved reserves, its RRR would have been 80% rather than the 100%[9] for the five-year period of 1998–2002. The differ-ences between the original RRR and the restated RRR are included in Table 3.2. In this case the differences are even greater than in the case of the reserves measured in boe.

Table 3.2   Shell's reserves replacement ratio (RRR)

Year	1-Year RRR		3-Year RRR	
	Original	Restated	Original	Restated
1998	182%	134%	N/A	N/A
1999	56%	−5%	N/A	N/A
2000	69%	50%	102%	60%
2001	74%	97%	66%	48%
2002	117%	121%	87%	90%
2003	N/A	63%	N/A	94%

As the US-SEC's order outlined, Shell's overstatement of proved reserves, and its delay in correcting the overstatement, arguably resulted from its desire to create and maintain the appearance of a strong RRR, the failure of its internal reserves estimation and reporting guidelines to conform to SEC requirements, and the lack of effective internal controls over the reserves estimation and reporting process. These failures led Shell to record and maintain proved reserves and to report a stronger RRR for certain years than it had actually achieved.

It is impossible to use the figures actually reported without knowing that they were incorrect. Really they should have been challenged within the company and also by the Board. The failure to do so has been attributed to poor governance within the company. Governance procedures were weak partly because of the structure of the company. Part of the problem though was the culture, which had been classed as arrogant. So, the question to consider is about the way in which culture can negate any attempts to establish sound systems of governance. This, of course, raises the issue of accountability.

Technological innovation and social change

We live in a time when technological change is generally seen as progressive, and where the enterprising exploitation of technology is credited with helping to generate economic growth and social well-being. This present time, the age of modernity, is characterised by a multitude of technological achievements that many of us take for granted: the car, aeroplane, satellite, gene therapy, embryo fertilisation, and so on. Modernity also dispensed with magic and tradition, replacing it with logic and reason, and a cultural and ethical hegemony of the developed West over the rest. In the context of a global village, many of today's social responsibility controversies revolve around the validity of this cultural and ethical hegemony. For example, corporations, such as Motorola, thinking their global strategies to be progressive have found those strategies wanting in the face of regional or national identities.

> If the confidence of the public in the integrity of accountants' reports is shaken, their value is gone. To preserve the integrity of his reports, the accountant must insist upon absolute independence of judgment and action. The necessity of preserving this position of independence indicates certain standards of conduct.
>
> (Arthur Andersen, 1932: cited in Toffler, 2003)

A historic concern with social responsibility

A concern with corporate social responsibility is not, of course, a new phenomenon. Indeed, it was a prominent feature of the 1970s where the performance of businesses in a wider arena than the stock market and its value to shareholders had become of increasing concern. Fetyko (1975) considered social accounting as an approach to reporting a firm's activities and stressed the need for identification of socially relevant behaviour, the determination of those to whom the company was accountable for its social performance and the development of appropriate measures and reporting techniques. Klein (1977) also considered social accounting and recognised that different aspects of performance are of interest to different stakeholder groupings, distinguishing, for example, among investors, community relations and philanthropy as areas of concern for accounting. He also considered various areas for measurement, including consumer surplus, rent, environmental impact and non-monetary values. Whilst these writers considered, by implication, that measuring social performance is important without giving reasons for believing so, Solomons (1974) considered the reasons for measuring the social performance of a business objectively. He suggested that whilst one reason was to aid rational decision making, another reason was of a defensive nature.

In this respect, Gray, Owen and Maunders (1987) consider social reporting in terms of responsibility and accountability, and distinguish between the internal needs of a business, catered for by management accounting, and the external needs, which are addressed for shareholders by financial reporting but largely ignored for other stakeholder interests. Social accounting is an attempt to redress this balance through a recognition that a firm affects, through its actions, its external environment (both positively and negatively) and should therefore account for these affects as part of its overall accounting for its actions.

The evaluation of the performance of an organisation is partly concerned with the measurement of performance and partly with the reporting of that performance, and, with the greater importance being given to social accountability, the changing reporting needs of an organisation are also being recognised. Thus, Birnbeg (1980) stated that accounting is attempting to supply various diverse groups, with different needs for information, and that there is a need for several distinct types of accounting to perform such a function. Similarly, Gray (1992) considers the limitations of the traditional economic base for accounting and questions some of its premises.[10] Rubenstein (1992) goes further and argues that there is a need for a new social contract between a business and the stakeholders to which it is accountable, and a business mission which recognises that some things go beyond accounting. Ogden and Bougen (1985), on the other hand, consider the disclosure of accounting information to trade unions and state that different conceptualisations of the relationship between management and employees can generate different conclusions regarding the disclosure of accounting information during industrial relations bargaining.[11]

The future of corporate social responsibility

This concern with social responsibility faded out at the end of the 1970s with the rise of the New Right politics of Thatcher and Reagan and the consequent legitimisation of selfish behaviour and greed in the acquisition of wealth. This was positively encouraged at an individual level and spilled over into the corporate world as governments facilitated free-market orientation to the provision of goods and services. Thus markets were progressively opened to competition, corporate taxes were reduced and regulations relaxed in the spirit of the times and the belief, under the 'trickle down theory', that this would lead to a benefit to all society.[12] It is only recently that any concern with social responsibility has reappeared. A question therefore remains about the extent to which any concern for corporate social responsibility may be a cyclical phenomenon that surfaces in times of economic prosperity and disappears when the economic cycle turns downwards. In other words, is the future of this concern with social responsibility one in which this cycle will be repeated and any concern for social responsibility become manifest periodically?

It is always tempting to argue that the current period is different from previous periods and any welcome changes will be sustainable this time around, even without evidence. This time, however, there is evidence that the concern with corporate social responsibility might be different because it can be seen as related to various other movements taking place around the world in the context of increased activism of citizens concerned with what is happening in the global corporate arena. Thus, evidence comes from pressure upon the accounting profession through the establishment of groups such as the Association for Integrity in Accounting[13] in the USA, the Association for Accounting and Business Affairs[14] in the UK and the Tax Justice Network,[15] providing evidence of a challenge to the hegemony of corporate activity.

Other evidence comes from such things as the feminist movement; more specifically, from the pacifist and anti-militarist strand of this movement (Liddington, 1989). Although initially started as a protest against nuclear weapons, the Greenham Common peace ideals were adopted by large numbers of women, many of whom were conventional citizens and consumers, but for some of whom the ideals of breaking with the mores of society assumed prominence. This led initially to the establishment of peace camps at Greenham Common and elsewhere but subsequently to a movement which espoused violence and sought to establish different ways of living. Further evidence comes from the various protest movements existing at present which are concerned with such things as environmental pollution, animal experimentation, road use and genetically modified crops. Such pressure groups include among their membership many members of society who express their concern not just through this membership but also through their selection of goods and services which they consume. Thus various supermarkets have suffered from a refusal to purchase goods containing genetically modified substances to such an extent that some have withdrawn such products. They have equally been affected by other campaigns such as the refusal to fish when it has been thought that dolphins have been disadvantaged. Similarly, Shell suffered from the publicity surrounding their proposed solution for the disposal of the Brent Spar oil platform.

Other activity has been more radical and illegal, and has sought to affect society at large. This has been manifest in the violent and destructive tactics of organisations such as the Animal Liberation Front, the obstructive tactics of such people as ecoprotestors in their opposition to road building programmes, and the disruptive tactics of such people as Reclaim the Streets in gaining maximum media coverage from their non-violent programme of closing major streets in London for periods of time or in affecting the 1998 G8 summit in Birmingham. Other actions of the anti-global movement have been less peaceful, such as what has become known as the battle of Seattle, but equally demonstrate a growing concern with the activities of global corporations. The discourse surrounding such environmental terrorism is one of illegitimacy, depending upon whether one considers that the ends justify the means or not. Their impact upon legitimate organisations tends to be one of increasing transaction costs for the firms targeted, or for society at large, rather than any long-term change in performance measurement and reporting. Chaliand (1987) has argued that a successful terrorist organisation needs a base in society which extends beyond its membership and needs popular support in order to exist and achieve results. Thus it can be seen that such activity enjoys an element of popular support which can become manifest in the general behaviour of individuals as consumers. This popular support can be seen particularly in the activities of the ecoprotestors (Crowther and Cooper, 2001), where such activities can be viewed as the direct action component of a popular movement that concerns large numbers of people.

Possibly a more significant activity as far as organisations are concerned is the increasing use of community-based economic activity (Brass and Koziell, 1997). Such activity is manifest in alternative modes of economic exchange and the carrying out of economic activity such as the growing number of local economic trading schemes (LETS), the growing number of economically active organisations such as workers cooperatives and activities such as community banks. Such activity reflects a disillusionment on the part of individuals in society with the current mode of organisation of society and is part of a search for alternatives. This kind of activity is relatively small in scale at present but is growing in size and can be expected to have a significant impact upon organisations, to which a response needs to be sought.

Further evidence of changes in societal mores can be gathered from the existence of the New Age Traveller movement (Earle *et al.*, 1994). The community of travellers has specific strategic objectives, not explicitly stated and not arrived at by any overt decision making but rather developed over time through an unconscious process. Nevertheless, these strategic objectives are clearly defined and openly expressed by such travellers (Crowther and Cooper, 2002). These objectives have been expressed by these travellers as seeking to achieve two distinct objectives: learning to live differently and developing a community spirit and identity.

By learning to live differently these people mean both that their relationship with nature must be different and that their ability to exist in a peaceable manner must not be driven by the normal societal motives of economic consumption and wealth creation. In this respect, therefore, they refuse to recognise the proprietary ownership mores of mainstream society as a basis for resource utilisation and this applies in particular to land, which is viewed as a common resource to be used rather than owned. This view of land and its use is, of course, one of the principal reasons why the traveller movement has so often been in conflict with conventional society and why mainstream publicity about them has been uniformly bad. As with the Leveller movement in the seventeenth century, their very existence, and possible survival, can be considered to be a threat to the economic basis of societal existence. The travellers themselves would be pleased to be perceived in this way as this provides a level of support for their ideas of existence. The other main strand of traveller philosophy, which can be seen from their way of life and their general involvement in the ecoprotest movement, is a general concern with the environment and its degradation through developments. This is particularly true when the proposed developments are for the purpose of increasing road transport, or air transport, at the expense of nature.

All of this suggests that the concern with corporate social responsibility is part of a wider social movement in which citizens are seeking to wrest power back from the global corporate world and to demand a share in the benefits of civilisation. Evidence from throughout this book suggests that these corporations are slowly responding to this pressure. So there is ground for optimism but only if the pressure from citizens and concerned stakeholders continues.

Summary of key points

- Financial misdemeanours have created a concern for CSR. This includes reckless behaviour and fraud and theft.
- Environmental issues have gained prominence in recent years. This includes climate change and resource depletion.
- The free market is a cause of problems.
- Globalisation has created a global marketplace and fostered economic competition.
- The internet has given power to stakeholders.
- A historical perspective shows that a concern for CSR is not a new phenomenon.

Definitions of key terms and theories

Global village is McLuhan's definition of the modern environment in which economic warfare has replaced physical warfare.

Global warming, climate change caused by human activity; it is creating instabilities, with various consequences.

Greenhouse gas is normally considered to be carbon dioxide but actually refers to a considerable number of gases which contribute to climate change.

Resource depletion is a term to describe the increasing rarity of various natural resources, which are therefore harder to acquire and more expensive.

Test your understanding

1. What is the Kyoto Protocol?
2. What is carbon footprinting?
3. How has the global market changed competition between nations?
4. Has the internet changed the relationship between an organisation and its stakeholders? If so, explain how this has happened.
5. What effects can an organisation have upon its external environment?
6. Name three scandals of the twenty-first century.
7. How has technology changed the relationship between individuals and organisations?

Suggestions for further reading

Aras, G. and Crowther, D. 2007. 'Is the Global Economy Sustainable?' in S. Barber (ed.), *The Geopolitics of the City.* London: Forum Press, pp. 165–94.
Aras, G. and Crowther, D. 2008. 'The Social Obligation of Corporations', *Journal of Knowledge Globalisation*, 1, 1: 43–59.
Aras, G. and Crowther, D. 2010. 'Developing Durability: A Re-examination of Sustainable Corporate Social Responsibility', in J. D. Rendtorff (ed.), *Ethics in the Economy: Power and Principle in the Market Place.* Aldershot: Ashgate.

Notes

1. This is, of course, overly simplistic, if not completely wrong. Thus people (and animals) produce carbon dioxide when breathing, cows (and other ruminants) produce methane and the process by which vegetation produces, captures and subsequently releases carbon dioxide is complex and not fully understood (see Lomborg, 2001).
2. This was agreed in 1997 and came into effect in 2005.
3. In late 2007 Australia ratified the protocol, leaving only one large developed country which has not done so. This country is, however, the USA, probably the largest producer of such greenhouse gases.
4. This is one of the arguments made in Europe by the low-cost flight air transport industry. There is evidence that cows – and therefore the dairy industry – have a more significant effect on the production of greenhouse gases.
5. The European consensus is by no means worldwide in this respect.
6. This recognition has recently led to the founding of the Association for Integrity in Accounting, the mission of which is to provide an independent forum to present and advance positions on a wide range of critical accounting and auditing issues, standards and regulations affecting the accountability and integrity of the profession and the public interest in maintaining trust and confidence in accounting. Information on the Association for Integrity in Accounting is available at <http://www.citizenworks.org<http://www.citizenworks.org>.

7. See press release 5 February 2004.

8. See report to Group Audit Committee and reserves recalculation review issued on 19 April 2004.

9. A 100% RRR means that the company is discovering as much new oil as it is pumping so that any lesser figure raises questions regarding long-term sustainability.

10. Gray in particular argues that there is a need for a new paradigm with the environment being considered as part of the firm rather than as an externality, and with sustainability and the use of primary resources being given increased weighting.

11. They argue that increased disclosure can lead to reduced opposition from employees, greater commitment and loyalty and increased legitimacy for intended action. This evidence therefore seems to suggest that greater disclosure of information can actually bring about benefits to the organisation as well as to the stakeholders involved. This is in line with the concepts of social and environmental accounting, which are concerned with greater disclosure of the activities of an organisation but with an emphasis upon disclosure of actions and the way in which they impact upon the external environment.

12. Some would argue instead that there was a callous disregard for the majority of society in the promulgation of these policies. Indeed, Thatcher is on record as stating that there is no such thing as society.

13. Information on the Association for Integrity in Accounting is available at <http://www.citizenworks.orghttp://www.citizenworks.org>.

14. See <http://visar.csustan.edu/aaba/aaba.htmhttp://visar.csustan.edu/aaba/aaba.htm>.

15. See <http://www.taxjustice.netHttp://www.taxjustice.net>. This organisation is supported by such organisations as War on Want.

References

Axford, B. 1995. *The Global System*. Cambridge: Polity Press.

Birnbeg, J. G. 1980. 'The Role of Accounting in Financial Disclosure', *Accounting, Organizations and Society*, 5, 1:, 71–80.

Brass, E. and Koziell, S. P. 1997. *Gathering Force*. London: The Big Issue Writers.

Carter, C. and Grieco, M. 2000. 'New Deals, No Wheels: Social Exclusion. Tele-options and Electronic Ontology', *Urban Studies*, 37, 10: 1735–48.

Chaliand, G. 1987. *Terrorism – From Popular Struggle to Media Spectacle*. London: Saqi.

Clegg, S. R. 1989. *Frameworks of Power*. London: Sage.

Crowther, D. 2000. 'Corporate Reporting, Stakeholders and the Internet: Mapping the New Corporate Landscape', *Urban Studies*, 37, 10: 1837–48.

Crowther, D. 2002. 'The Psychoanalysis of On-line Reporting', in L. Holmes, M. Grieco and D. Hosking (eds), *Organising in the Information Age:*

Distributed Technology, Distributed Leadership, Distributed Identity, Distributed Discourse. Aldershot: Ashgate, pp. 130–48.

Crowther, D. 2004. 'Limited Liability or Limited Responsibility?', in D. Crowther and L. Rayman Bacchus (eds), *Perspectives on Corporate Social Responsibility.* Aldershot: Ashgate, pp. 42–58.

Crowther, D. and Cooper, S. 2001. 'Innovation through Postmodern Networks: The Case of Ecoprotestors', in O. Jones and S. Conway (eds), *Networks and Innovation.* London: Imperial College Press, pp. 321–47.

Crowther, D. and Cooper, S. 2002. 'Rekindling Community Spirit and Identity: The Case of Ecoprotestors', *Management Decision,* 40, 4: 343–53.

Earle, F., Dearling, A., Whittle, H., Glasse, R. and Earle, G. 1994. *A Time to Travel?* Lyme Regis: Enabler Publications.

Fetyko, D. F. 1975. 'The Company Social Audit', *Management Accounting,* 56, 10.

Foucault, M. 1977. *Discipline and Punish,* trans. A. Sheridan, Harmondsworth: Penguin.

Fukuyama, F. 1992. *The End of History and the Last Man.* New York: The Free Press.

Gray, R. 1992. 'Accounting and Environmentalism: An Exploration of the Challenge of Gently Accounting for Accountability, Transparency and Sustainability', *Accounting, Organizations and Society,* 17, 5: 399–425.

Gray, R., Owen, D. and Maunders, K. 1987. *Corporate Social Reporting: Accounting and Accountability.* London: Prentice Hall.

Holmes, L. and Grieco, M. 1999. 'The Power of Transparency: the Internet, E-mail and the Malaysian Political Crisis', paper presented to the Asian Management in Crisis Conference, Association of South East Asian Studies, University of North London, June 1999.

Johnson, D.G. and Nissenbaum, H.F. (eds) 1995. *Computers, Ethics, and Social Values.* Englewood Cliffs, NJ: Prentice Hall.

Klein, T. A. 1977. *Social Costs and Benefits of Business.* Englewood Cliffs, NJ: Prentice Hall.

Liddington, J. 1989. *The Road to Greenham Common.* New York: Syracuse University Press.

Lomborg, B. 2001. *The Skeptical Environmentalist.* Cambridge: Cambridge University Press.

Lovelock, J. 2006. *The Revenge of Gaia.* Harmondsworth: Penguin.

McLuhan, M. and Fiore, Q. 1968. *War and Peace in the Global Village.* San Francisco: Hardwired.

Mill, J. S. 1848. *Principles of Political Economy.* London.

Ogden, S. and Bougen, P. 1985. 'A Radical Perspective on the Disclosure of Accounting Information to Trade Unions', *Accounting, Organizations and Society,* 10, 2: 211–24.

Rayman-Bacchus, L. and Molina, A. 2001. 'Internet-Based Tourism Services: Business Issues and Trends', *Futures,* 33: 589–605.

Robins, K. 1995. 'Cyberspace and the World we Live in', in M. Featherstone and R. Burrows (eds), *Cyberspace / Cyberbodies / Cyberpunk*. London: Sage.

Rubenstein, D. B. 1992. 'Bridging the Gap between Green Accounting and Black Ink', *Accounting Organizations and Society*, 17, 5: 501–08.

Rushkoff, D. 1997. *Children of Chaos*. London: HarperCollins.

Russell, B. 1975. *Power*. London: Routledge.

Sobchack, V. 1996. 'Democratic Franchise and the Electronic Frontier', in Z. Sardar and J. R. Ravetz (eds), *Cyberfutures*. London: Pluto Press.

Solomons, D. 1974. 'Corporate Social Performance: A New Dimension in Accounting Reports?', in H. Edey and B. S. Yamey (eds), *Debits, Credits, Finance and Profits*. London: Sweet & Maxwell, pp. 131–41.

Tans. 2008. en.wikipedia.org/wiki/File:C02_increase_rate.png

Toffler, B. L. 2003. *Financial Accounting: Ambition, Greed and the Fall of Arthur Anderson*. New York: Broadway Books.

The Principles of CSR

4

Learning objectives

After studying this chapter you should be able to:

- Identify the principles of CSR and explain their operation.
- Understand and explain legitimacy theory and political economy theory for CSR.
- Outline the risk factors concerning CSR.
- Consider the relationship between disclosure and stakeholders.
- Explain the relationship between CSR and environment and human rights issues.

Introduction

At the beginning of this book we have argued that the corporate excesses that have become disclosed and which are affecting large numbers of people have raised an awareness of the asocial behaviours of corporations. This is one reason why the issue of corporate social responsibility has become a much more prominent feature of the corporate landscape. There are other factors which have helped raise this issue to prominence; for example, Topal and Crowther (2004) argue that worries about the effects of bioengineering and genetic modifications of nature has become an issue which has aroused more general concern. At a different level of analysis, Crowther (2000a) has argued that the availability of the World Wide Web has facilitated the dissemination of information and has enabled more pressure to be brought upon corporations by their various stakeholders.

Such behaviour has brought the question of corporate social responsibility to prominence, and there are several theories that explain this as well as several principles on which CSR is based. In this chapter, therefore, we investigate these.

The prominence of CSR

It is quite noticeable how much more prominent corporate social responsibility (CSR) has become – not just in the academic and business worlds but also is everyday life. We can highlight a lot of factors which have led to this interest – such things as:

- Poor business behaviour towards customers
- Treating employees unfairly
- Ignoring the environment and the consequences of organisational action

Additionally, other things have also featured prominently in popular consciousness. One of these is the issue of climate change which has affected concern about CSR particularly with respect to the emission of greenhouse gases and especially carbon dioxide. Today it is qite common for people to know and discuss the size of their carbon footprint, whereas even three years ago people in general did not even know what a carbon footprint was.

Another prominent concern is with the supply chain of a business; in other words, with what is happening in other companies which that company does business with – their suppliers and the suppliers of their suppliers. In particular, people are concerned about the exploitation of people in developing countries, especially regarding the question of child labour but also such things as sweat shops.

So it is no longer acceptable for a company to say that the conditions under which their suppliers operate are outside of their control and they are not therefore responsible. Customers have said that this is not acceptable and have called companies to account. And recently a number of high-profile retail companies have admitted publicly that there are problems in their supply chain and have taken steps to correct those problems.

Interestingly, the popularity of companies increases after they have admitted problems and taken steps to correct them. In doing this they are thereby showing both that honesty is the best practice and also that customers are being reasonable. The evidence suggests that individual customers are understanding and that they do not expect perfection but do expect honesty and transparency. Moreover, they also expect companies to make efforts to change their behaviour and to try to solve their CSR problems.

Changing emphasis in companies

Companies themselves have also changed. No longer are they concerned with greenwashing – the pretence of socially responsible behaviour through artful reporting. Now companies are taking CSR much more seriously, not just because they understand that it is a key to business success and can give them a strategic advantage, but also because people in those organisations care about social responsibility.

So it would be reasonable to claim that the growing importance of CSR is being driven by individuals who care – but those individuals are not just customers; they are also employees, managers, owners and investors of a company. We can claim, therefore, that companies are partly reacting to external pressures and partly leading the development of responsible behaviour and reporting. So accountability – one of the central principles of CSR – is increasingly being recognised and responded to by much more transparency – another of the principles of CSR discussed later.

The underlying theories of CSR

Although various theories have been proposed for the underlying rationale of CSR, these have now been simplified into two theories, which support and complement each other. These are:

Legitimacy theory

This is also known as Social Contract theory because it is based upon the idea of the Social Contract.

The Social Contract

> It is impossible that such governments as have hitherto existed in the world, could have commenced by any other means than a total violation of every principle sacred and moral.
>
> (Paine, 1792, *The Rights of Man*)

In 1762, Jean-Jacques Rousseau produced his book on the Social Contract which was designed to explain – and therefore legitimate – the relationship between an individual and society and its government. In it he argued that individuals voluntarily gave up certain rights in order for the government of the state to be able to manage for the greater good of all citizens. This is, of course, a sharp contrast to the angry rhetoric of Tom Paine, shown above. Nevertheless, the idea of the Social Contract has been generally accepted.

More recently, the Social Contract has gained a new prominence as it has been used to explain the relationship between a company and society. In this view the company (or other organisation) has obligations towards other parts of society in return for its place in society. This can be depicted as shown in Figure 4.1.

This in turn led to the development of Stakeholder theory, which we consider in Chapter 7.

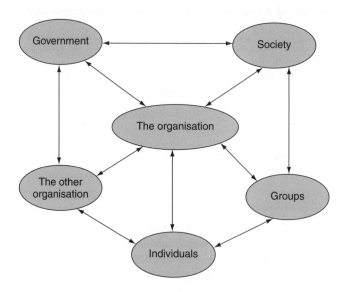

Figure 4.1   The Social Contract

Political economy theory

The theory of 'Positive Political Economy' investigates how observed differences in institutions affect economic and political outcomes in various economic, social and political systems. These institutional differences might arise in the polity of a respective economy or any other structural differences in the system. Political Economy is based on these classic works:

- Adam Smith, *An Inquiry into Nature and Causes of the Wealth of Nations* (1776).
- David Ricardo, *On the Principles of Political Economy and Taxation* (1817).
- John Stuart Mill, *Principles of Political Economy with some of the Applications to Social Philosophy* (1848).

The theory of political economy now encompasses a wide range of subjects from anthropology to history from psychology to human geography and from law to ecology. The theories of International Political Economy, if applied properly, can lead to the solution of issues such as immigration, environmental degradation, AIDS control and other developmental issues pushing developing countries into the low-level equilibrium trap. The theory can also effectively and efficiently handle the issues of Intellectual Property Rights and trade liberalisation in this globalised world.

Political economy theory is considered to be one of the most comprehensive theories in the world which can become a successful tool in combating the complex issues threatening to nullify the benefits of liberalisation and globalisation.

The principles of corporate social responsibility

It can be considered that there are three principles upon which CSR is based:

- accountability
- transparency
- sustainability

These are interrelated, as shown in Figure 4.2. Each will be considered in turn.

Accountability

Accountability is concerned with an organisation recognising that its actions affect the external environment, and therefore assuming responsibility for the effects of its actions. This concept therefore implies a quantification of the effects of actions taken, both internal to the organisation and externally. More specifically, the concept implies a reporting of those quantifications to all parties affected by those actions. This implies a reporting to external stakeholders of the effects of actions taken by the organisation and how they are affecting those stakeholders. This concept therefore implies a recognition that the organisation is part of a wider societal network and has responsibilities to all of that network rather than just to the owners of the organisation. Alongside this acceptance of

Figure 4.2   The principles of CSR

responsibility therefore must be a recognition that those external stakeholders have the power to affect the way in which those actions of the organisation are taken and a role in deciding whether or not such actions can be justified, and if so at what cost to the organisation and to other stakeholders.

Accountability therefore necessitates the development of appropriate measures of environmental performance and the reporting of the actions of the firm. This necessitates costs on the part of the organisation in developing, recording and reporting such performance and to be of value the benefits must exceed the costs. Benefits must be determined by the usefulness of the measures selected in the decision-making process and by the way in which they facilitate resource allocation, both within the organisation and between it and other stakeholders. Such reporting needs to be based upon the following characteristics:

- understandability to all parties concerned;
- relevance to the users of the information provided;
- reliability in terms of accuracy of measurement, representation of impact and freedom from bias;
- comparability, which implies consistency, both over time and between different organisations.

Inevitably, however, such reporting will involve qualitative facts and judgements as well as quantifications. This qualitativeness will inhibit comparability over time and will tend to mean that such impacts are assessed differently by different users of the information, reflecting their individual values and priorities. A lack of precise understanding of effects, coupled with the necessarily judgemental nature of relative impacts, means that few standard measures exist. This in itself restricts the inter-organisation comparison of such information. Although this limitation is problematic for the development of environmental accounting, it is in fact useful to the managers of organisations as this limitation of comparability alleviates the need to demonstrate good performance as anything other than a semiotic.

Transparency

Transparency, as a principle, means that the external impact of the actions of the organisation can be ascertained from that organisation's reporting and pertinent facts are not disguised within that reporting. Thus, all the effects of the actions of the organisation, including external impacts, should be apparent to all from using the information provided by the organisation's reporting mechanisms. Transparency is of particular importance to external users of such information as these users lack the background details and knowledge available to internal users of such information. Transparency therefore can be seen to follow from the other two principles and equally can be seen to be a part of the process of recognition of responsibility on the part of the organisation for the external effects of its actions and equally part of the process of transferring power to external stakeholders.

Sustainability

Sustainability is concerned with the effect which action taken in the present has upon the options available in the future. If resources are utilised in the present then they are no longer available for use in the future, and this is of particular concern if the resources are finite in quantity. Thus, raw materials of an extractive nature, such as coal, iron or oil, are finite in quantity and once used are not available for future use. At some point in the future therefore alternatives will be needed to fulfil the functions currently provided by these resources.

This may be at some point in the relatively distant future but of more immediate concern is the fact that as resources become depleted then the cost of acquiring the remaining resources tends to increase, and hence the operational costs of organisations tend to increase. Similarly, once an animal or plant species becomes extinct then the benefits of that species to the environment can no longer accrue. In view of the fact that many pharmaceuticals are currently being developed from plant species still being discovered, this may be significant for the future.

Sustainability therefore implies that society must use no more of a resource than can be regenerated. This can be defined in terms of the carrying capacity of the ecosystem (Hawken, 1993) and described with input–output models of resource consumption. Thus, the paper industry, for example, has a policy of replanting trees to replace those harvested and this has the effect of retaining costs in the present rather than temporally externalising them. Similarly, motor vehicle manufacturers such as Volkswagen have a policy of making their cars almost totally recyclable. Viewing an organisation as part of a wider social and economic system implies that these effects must be taken into account, not just for the measurement of costs and value created in the present but also for the future of the business itself.

Measures of sustainability would consider the rate at which resources are consumed by the organisation in relation to the rate at which resources can be regenerated. Unsustainable operations can be accommodated either by developing sustainable operations or by planning for a future lacking in resources currently required. In practice, organisations mostly tend to aim towards less unsustainability by increasing efficiency in the way in which resources are utilised. An example would be an energy efficiency programme.

Every organisation mentions sustainability and most claim to have developed sustainable practices. A lot of this is just rhetoric from people who, we would claim, do not want to face the difficult issues involved in addressing sustainability. There is a danger therefore that sustainability has taken over from CSR itself as a target for greenwashing. Nevertheless, although the relationship between organisations and society has been subject to much debate, often of a critical nature, evidence continues to mount that the best companies make a positive impact upon their environment.

Furthermore, the evidence continues to mount that such socially responsible behaviour is good for business, not just in ethical terms but also in financial terms – in other words that corporate social responsibility is good for business as well as all its stakeholders. Thus ethical behaviour and a concern for people and for the environment have been shown to have a positive correlation with corporate performance. Indeed, evidence continues to mount concerning the benefit to business from socially responsible behaviour and, in the main, this benefit is no longer questioned by business managers. The nature of corporate social responsibility is therefore a topical one for business and academics.

Sustainability has become one of the most important topics for businesses – and for society – in recent times and is dealt with in detail in Chapter 8.

Disclosure in corporate reporting

These principles affect not just the behaviour of an organisation but also the reporting of its activities. Thus disclosure is also important and can be expected to increase as corporations engage more in socially responsible activity. An examination of the external reporting of organisations, however, does demonstrate an increasing recognition of the need to include social and environmental information – the triple bottom line reporting mentioned in several chapters – and an increasing number of annual reports of companies include some information in this respect. This trend is gathering momentum as more organisations perceive the importance of providing such information to external stakeholders. It has been suggested, however, (Till and Symes, 1999) that the inclusion of such information does not demonstrate an increasing concern with the environment but rather some benefits to the company itself.[1] One trend which is also apparent, however, is the tendency of companies to produce separate environmental reports. In this context such reports are generally termed environmental reports although in reality they include reporting upon both environmental and social impact. Thus the terms 'social accounting' and 'environmental accounting' tend to have been conflated within the practice of corporate reporting and the two terms used interchangeably for the form of performance measurement and reporting which recognises and reports the effects of the organisation's actions upon its external environment.

Whilst these reports tend to contain much more detailed environmental information than is contained in the annual report, the implication of this trend is that such information rather than the information contained in the annual report is required by a separate constituency of stakeholders. This gives an impression, therefore, that environmental information is not necessary for the owners and investors in a business but is needed by other stakeholders. This therefore leads to a further suggestion that organisations view environmental issues as separate from the economic performance of the business rather than as integral to it. This highlights the problematic nature of environmental accounting and some of the problems associated with environmental impact measurement.

Accounting and accountability

Alongside this recognition that corporations are accountable to their stakeholders is a development of the principles upon which this demonstration of accountability should be based. Inevitably this is based in accounting as a mechanism by which such action can be measured and reported. In general terms this has come to be called either social or environmental accounting[2] or triple bottom line accounting. The objective of environmental accounting is to measure the effects of the actions of the organisation upon the environment and to report upon those effects. In other words, the objective is to incorporate the effect of the activities of the firm upon externalities and to view the firm as a network which extends beyond the internal environment to include the whole environment (see Crowther, 2000b; 2002).

In this view of the organisation the accounting for the firm does not stop at the organisational boundary but extends beyond to include not just the business environment in which it operates but also the whole social environment. Environmental accounting therefore adds a new dimension to the role of accounting for an organisation because of its emphasis upon accounting for external effects of the organisation's activities. In doing so, this provides a recognition that the organisation is an integral part of society, rather than a self-contained entity which has only an indirect relationship with society at large. This self-containment has been the traditional view taken by an organisation as far as their relationship with society at large is concerned, with interaction being only by means of resource acquisition and sales of finished products or services. Recognition of this closely intertwined relationship of mutual interdependency between the organisation and society at large, when reflected in the accounting of the organisation, can help bring about a closer, and possibly more harmonious, relationship between the organisation and society. Given that the managers and workers of an organisation are also stakeholders in that society in other capacities, such as consumers, citizens and inhabitants, this reinforces the mutual interdependency.

Environmental accounting also provides an explicit recognition that stakeholders other than the legal owners of the organisation have power and influence over that organisation and also have a right to extend their influence to affect the organisation's activities.[3] This includes the managers and workers of the organisation who are also stakeholders in other capacities. Environmental accounting therefore provides a mechanism for transferring some of the power from the organisation to these stakeholders, and this voluntary surrender of such power by the organisation can actually provide benefits to the organisation. Benefits from increased disclosure and the adoption of environmental accounting can provide further benefits to the organisation in its operational performance, beyond this enhanced relationship with society at large. These benefits can include:

- an improved image for the organisation which can translate into additional sales;
- the development of environmentally friendly or sustainable methods of operation which can lead to the development of new markets;
- reduced future operational costs through the anticipation of future regulation and hence a cost advantage over competitors;
- decreased future liabilities brought about through temporal externalisation;

- better relationships with suppliers and customers which can lead to reduced operational costs as well as increased sales;
- easier recruitment of labour and lowered costs of staff turnover.

It needs to be recognised, however, that there are increased costs of instituting a regime of environmental accounting and that these additional costs need to be offset against the possible benefits that mayaccrue. These increased costs are concerned with the development of appropriate measures of environmental performance and the necessary alterations to the management information and accounting information systems to incorporate these measures into the reporting system. This is particularly problematical for the organisation in terms of justification because the increased costs are readily quantifiable but the benefits are much more difficult to quantify.

This leads to one of the main problems with the accounting for externalities through social and environmental accounting. This problem is the quantification of the effects of the activities of the organisation upon its external environment and it revolves around four main areas:

- determining the effects upon the external environment of the activities of the organisation;
- developing appropriate measures for those effects;
- quantifying those effects in order to provide a comparative yardstick for the evaluation of alternative courses of action, particularly in terms of an accounting-based quantification;
- determining the form and extent of disclosure of those quantifications so as to maximise the benefits of that disclosure while minimising the costs of the disclosure and minimising the possibility of knowledge of the firms' operational activities being given to competitors.

These are problems which have been addressed by proponents of this form of accounting but it is fair to say that these problems have primarily been recognised to exist rather than being satisfactorily resolved. Those that argue in favour of an increased extent of disclosure in this area tend to consider the advantages of the disclosure from the point of view of external stakeholders rather than from the point of view of the organisation itself. Indeed, one of the features of the environmental accounting discourse is the polarisation of views between those concerned with the firm, and its owners and managers, and those concerned with the environmental, and thereby certain external stakeholders. The management of stakeholders, and the business on behalf of all stakeholders, is one mechanism for reinforcing the organisational boundary, which becomes less important under a social accounting perspective. Indeed, it will be argued that this polarisation of perspectives is an important component of organisational performance reporting. Accordingly, it is increasingly apparent that these environmental issues are recognised by organisations as being of importance and the extent of environmental reporting by organisations is increasing and seems likely to increase further in the future.[4]

Before the development of any appropriate measures can be considered, it is first necessary for the organisation to develop an understanding of the effects of its activities upon the external environment. The starting point for the development of such an understanding, therefore, is the undertaking of an environmental audit. An environmental audit is merely an investigation and recording of the activities of the organisation in order to develop this understanding (Kinnersley, 1994). Indeed, BS7750 is concerned with such audits in the context of the development of environmental management systems. Such an audit will address, *inter alia*, the following issues:

- the extent of compliance with regulations and possible future regulations;
- the extent and effectiveness of pollution control procedures;
- the extent of energy usage and possibilities increasing for energy efficiency;
- the extent of waste produced in the production processes and the possibilities for reducing such waste or finding uses for the waste necessarily produced;
- the extent of usage of sustainable resources and possibilities for the development of renewable resources;
- the extent of usage of recycled materials and possibilities for increasing recycling;
- life cycle analysis of products and processes;
- the possibilities of increasing capital investment to affect these issues;
- the existence of or potential for environmental management procedures to be implemented.

Once this audit has been completed then it is possible to consider the development of appropriate measures and reporting mechanisms to provide the necessary information for both internal and external consumption. These measures need to be based upon the principles of environmental accounting, as outlined below. It is important to recognise, however, that such an environmental audit, whilst the essential starting point for the development of such accounting and reporting, should not be viewed as a discrete isolated event in the developmental process. Environmental auditing needs to be carried out on a recurrent basis, much as is financial or systems auditing, in order to both review progress through a comparative analysis and to establish where further improvement can be made in the light of progress to date and changing operational procedures.

Oil in the Mexican Gulf

The US search for oil has become more intense as Hubbert's Peak for land-based oil in the USA passed long ago and other sources of oil have proved to be located in countries which are both volatile and not particularly friendly to

→

the USA. As a consequence, attention turned to the Mexican Gulf which was considered to have significant quantities of oil beneath it. Thus, in March 2008, the mineral rights to drill for oil at the Maconda well, located in Mississippi Canyon Block 252 in the United States sector of the Gulf of Mexico about 41 miles (66 km) off the Louisiana coast, were purchased by BP, the third largest global oil-producing company. In February 2009, BP filed a 52-page exploration and environmental impact plan for the well with the US Minerals Management Service (MMS). The plan stated that it was 'unlikely that an accidental surface or subsurface oil spill would occur from the proposed activities'. In the event that an accident did take place, the plan stated that, due to the well being 77 km from shore and the response capabilities that would be implemented, no significant adverse impacts would be expected. The Department of the Interior agreed and exempted BP's Gulf of Mexico drilling operation from a detailed environmental impact study after concluding that a massive oil spill was unlikely.

In February 2010, the Deepwater Horizon drilling rig, owned by Transocean but leased to BP, began drilling on the Maconda Prospect. The planned well was to be drilled to 5 500 m below sea level. In April BP drilled the last section with the bore 5 600 m below sea level but the last 360 m needed casing. Halliburton recommended liner/tieback casing to provide four redundant barriers to flow but BP chose a single liner with fewer barriers that was faster and cheaper to install. Various recommendations about best practice and possible dangers had previously been ignored by BP – with the full approval of the MMS. It is perhaps pertinent to note that BP had a track record of cutting costs, and therefore safety, in the pursuit of shareholder returns with some disastrous consequences such as in Alaska. It should also be noted that the US regulatory regime has been progressively weakened during the previous decade – also in the interests of cost saving and facilitating the creation of shareholder returns.

On 20 April 2010, an explosion occurred killing 11 people and causing oil to pour out of the borehole without restraint. It was estimated that oil was escaping at the rate of 8 000 barrels per day but this estimate was progressively increased to 70,000 barrels per day – leading to accusations of dishonesty by BP. The leak was described by Tony Hayward, BP CEO, as relatively tiny compared with the size of the ocean, although he did promise that the company would meet all clean-up costs. The company made many unsuccessful attempts to stem the flow (including the interesting tactic of using golf balls!) before successfully drilling another borehole four months later.

The incident shows that the company violated all sensible safety precautions as well as all the principles of CSR. It reflects equally badly, however, on the US administration which appears equally guilty and complicit in profit-enhancing shortcuts.

Recognising CSR

Most people initially think that they know what CSR is and how to behave responsibly – and everyone claims to be able to recognise socially responsible or irresponsible behaviour without necessarily being able to define it. So there is general agreement that CSR is about a company's concern for such things as community involvement, socially responsible products and processes, concern for the environment and socially responsible employee relations (Ortiz-Martinez and Crowther, 2006).

Issues of socially responsible behaviour are not new, of course, and examples can be found from throughout the world and at least from the earliest days of the Industrial Revolution, the concomitant founding of large business entities (Crowther, 2002) and the divorce between ownership and management – or the divorcing of risk from rewards (Crowther, 2004). According to the European Commission, CSR is about undertaking voluntary activity which demonstrates a concern for stakeholders.

But it is here that a firm runs into problems – how to balance up the conflicting needs and expectations of various stakeholder groups whilst still being concerned with shareholders; how to practise sustainability; how to report this activity to those interested; how to decide if one activity is more socially responsible than another. The situation is complex and conflicting. In this book therefore the contributors are concerned with different aspects of CSR, both with theorising and with implementing CSR in practice.

Environmental issues and their effects and implications

When an organisation undertakes an activity which impacts upon the external environment then this affects that environment in ways which are not reflected in the traditional accounting of that organisation. The environment can be affected either positively, through, for example, a landscaping project, or negatively, through, for example, the creation of heaps of waste from a mining operation.

These actions of an organisation impose costs and benefits upon the external environment. These costs and benefits are imposed by the organisation without consultation, and in reality form part of the operational activities of the organisation. These actions are, however, excluded from traditional accounting of the firm,[5] and by implication from its area of responsibility. Thus we can say that such costs and benefits have been externalised. The concept of externality therefore is concerned with the way in which these costs and benefits are externalised from the organisation and imposed upon others.

Such externalised costs and benefits have traditionally been considered to be not the concern of the organisation and its managers, and hence have been excluded from its accounting. It must be recognised, however, that the quantification of the effect of such externalisation, particularly from an accounting viewpoint, is problematical and not easy to measure,[6] and this is perhaps one reason for the exclusion of such effects from the organisation's accounting.

It is probably fair to state, however, that more costs have been externalised by organisation than benefits.

Hence a typical organisation has gained from such externalisation and the reported value creation of such an organisation has been overstated by this failure to account for all costs and benefits. This is achieved by restricting the accounting evaluation of the organisation to the internal effects. Indeed, one way in which an organisation can report, through its accounting, the creation of value is by an externalisation of costs, which are thereby excluded from the accounting of the organisation's activities. As far as the externalisation of costs is concerned it is important to recognise that these can be externalised both spatially and temporally.

Spatial externalisation

Spatial externalisation describes the way in which costs can be transferred to other entities in the current time period. Examples of such spatial externalisation include:

- Environmental degradation though such things as polluted – and therefore dead – rivers or through increased traffic imposes costs upon the local community through reduced quality of life.
- Causing pollution imposes costs upon society at large.
- Waste disposal problems impose costs upon whoever is tasked with such disposal.
- Removing staff from shops imposes costs upon customers who must queue for service.
- Just-in-time manufacturing imposes costs upon suppliers by transferring stockholding costs to them.

In an increasingly global market then, one favourite way of externalising costs is through transfer of those costs to a developing country. This can be effected by a transfer of operational activities, or at least those with environmental impacts, to such a country where the regulatory regime is less exacting. In this respect it should be noted that the arguments regarding reducing labour costs are generally used for such a transfer of operational activities but at the same time less exacting regulatory regimes also exist.

Temporal externalisation

The temporal externalisation of costs describes the way in which costs are transferred from the current time period into another – the future. This thereby enables reported value creation, through accounting, to be recorded in the present. Examples of temporal externalisation include:

- Deferring investment to a future time period and so increasing reported value in the present.
- Failing to provide for asset disposal costs in capital investment appraisal and leaving such costs for future owners to incur.

- Failure to dispose of waste material as it originates and leaving this as a problem for the future.
- Causing pollution which must then be cleaned up in the future.
- Depletion of finite natural resources or failure to provide renewable sources of raw material will cause problems for the future viability of the organisation.
- Lack of research and development and product development will also cause problems for the future viability of the organisation.
- Eliminating staff training may save costs in the present but at the expense of future competitiveness.

It can be seen that such actions have the effect of deferring dealing with problems to the future but not of alleviating the need to deal with such problems. In this respect it must be recognised that it is not always apparent in the present that such costs are being temporally externalised, as they may not be recognised as a problem at the present time. For example, the widespread use of asbestos in the 1930s to 1960s was considered to be beneficial at the time and was only later found to be problematic.

This temporal externalisation of costs, through causing the clean-up problems and costs to be deferred to a later period, was therefore incurred unintentionally. Equally, such costs may at the present time be in course of being transferred into the future through actions taken in the present which will have unanticipated consequences in the future. Nevertheless, it is reasonable to suggest that such actions may be taken in the present for cost-minimisation purposes with little regard for possible future costs.

For example, considering the nuclear power generation industry we can see it is now generally accepted that if the full costs of generating power by this means, which would include the costs of disposing of nuclear waste and the costs of decommissioning nuclear generators at the end of their working life, had been taken into account initially then the idea of power generation by this means would never have been put into operation. Nevertheless, nuclear power is again being considered in a lot of countries as the only realistic solution to global warming. Nuclear power stations emit minimal amounts of greenhouse gases and so are attractive for that reason. Of course, their future costs are again being ignored and so temporarily externalised.

We can see, therefore, that if we take externalities into account the decisions made and actions taken by firms may be very different. We can equally see that the recognition of the effect upon these externalities of actions taken by an organisation can have significant impact upon the activities of the organisation, and also the way in which an organisation chooses to internalise or externalise its costs can have a significant impact upon its operational performance.

Environmental issues and their effects

Many organisations can be seen as becoming more proactive in the setting of their own agendas for environmental performance improvement because of the perceived benefits from such a course of action. Much criticism, however, has been levelled at the internal drivers of environmental performance, both from environmental pressure groups and from academics. Common criticisms have been concerned with the following:

- Many companies are driven by the need to comply with existing or anticipated legislation rather than by any real concern with the environment.
- Much corporate environmental action is concerned with publicity and image rather than any concern with the actual environment, and is therefore little more than a public relations exercise.
- Internal motivations for environmental improvement are often prevented or diluted by budgetary and other business constraints which prevent significant action being taken; consequently external compulsion, through legislation or regulation, is necessary to bring about effective action by a company.
- Measures of environmental performance tend to be selectively chosen to demonstrate improvement rather than to provide a balanced picture of environmental performance.
- A concern with measurement and quantification can, in itself, be symptomatic of a managerialist discourse which seeks to impose its own limits on the environmental debate and thereby to effectively silence alternative points of view.

Whilst any action by companies is open to such interpretation, and there is an element of truth in such interpretations, there is nevertheless sufficient evidence to show that companies are to a large extent genuinely concerned with their environmental performance. This is not just because such companies recognise their social duties as corporate citizens but also because they recognise the business benefits that can follow an improving environmental performance. These business benefits inevitably feed through into the bottom-line performance of the organisation.

Cotton from Uzbekistan

Uzbekistan is a largely arid country but the Soviets decided that it would be a good place to grow cotton. They therefore commenced large-scale irrigation projects by diverting river water which previously flowed into the Aral Sea. Canals were built to use this water but built so inefficiently that between 30% and 75% of the water is wasted. This has had serious consequences for the Aral Sea, which was once the fourth largest inland sea in the world but has been shrinking so steadily since the 1960s that it now consists of a couple of small lakes. This has devastated the fishing and other industries which were dependent on it. The northern lake is in Kazakhstan, which has instituted conservation measures to attempt to restore the sea, with some success. The southern lake is in Uzbekistan, a much poorer country, which is dependent upon cotton for 20% of its exports – it is the second largest exporter of cotton in the world, exporting most of its production to Europe. No action has been taken about the sea or about increasing the efficiency of the irrigation.

There are much greater problems, however, with the production of Uzbek cotton. The first is related to its harvesting: most countries make use of machines to harvest cotton – Uzbekistan uses manual labour. Specifically child labour is used. Every autumn, state officials shut down schools and send students, together with their teachers, to the cotton fields. University students and public officials are also sent. Many thousands of children, some as young as seven, are forced to undertake weeks of this labour – which is very arduous – for no financial reward. Cotton quotas teachers are made to ensure that students pick the required daily amount. Children who fail to pick their target of cotton are reportedly punished with detentions and told that their grades will suffer. Those who refuse to take part can face academic expulsion.

Uzbekistan's cotton farmers do not benefit from this system. Officially they receive the market price for their crops. In practice they are forced to sell their cotton to the state agency and receive less than one third of the world market price, so that, effectively, they are barely receiving subsistence-level returns for their hard work. The government, however, sells the cotton on commodity exchanges at the market price – thereby guaranteeing huge profits primarily for President Karimov and his associates. Uzbekistan is rated as one of the most corrupt countries in the world.

There are therefore serious environmental issues and serious human rights issues associated with the production of Uzbek cotton. Indeed, the production methods make it clear that it is not sustainable as a crop. Nevertheless, it is bought extensively by European cotton manufacturers, who do not disclose the sources of their cotton in the goods manufactured from it and sold to domestic consumers. Nevertheless, pressure has mounted on manufacturers who are gradually refusing to use Uzbek cotton, thereby exerting pressure for reform upon the Uzbek government and thus demonstrating the pressures towards socially responsible behaviour.

Conclusions

There are a number of important issues relating to CSR which we have covered in this chapter. We have looked at the theories behind CSR as well as the principles. We have also considered some of the implications mainly in terms of environmental effects. This is very important when considering corporate behaviour and performance, so we will return to some of those issues in later chapters (see pp. 219–24).

Risk management is also a very important topic for a modern corporation and CSR can have a big impact upon the identification, management and control of various aspects of risk, as we have explored. These are all important issues in the area of strategic management as well as for CSR.

Definitions of key terms and theories

Accountability is central to CSR and means that a company is responsible for all of the effects of its actions.

Legitimacy theory is one of the key theories for CSR and is based upon the social contract.

Political economy theory is one of the key theories for CSR and is based upon the work of Adam Smith and John Stuart Mill.

Risk management has become an important aspect of business management and CSR has a role to play in this.

The Social Contract is an explanation of the relationship between all citizens in society.

Spatial externalisation describes the way in which costs can be transferred to other entities in the current time period.

Sustainability is one of the most important concepts for business at the present. It is a central principle of CSR.

Temporal externalisation describes the way in which costs are transferred from the current time period into another.

Transparency is one of the principles of CSR and requires the company to give sufficient information about its activities to satisfy stakeholders.

Test your understanding

1. What has led to the current interest in CSR?
2. What is greenwashing?
3. What is cost externalisation? Why does it happen?
4. What is the Social Contract? Why has it become prominent in CSR?
5. Describe the possible attitudes to risk.
6. What is political economy theory and why is it relevant to CSR?
7. What is the relationship between accountability and transparency?

Suggestions for further reading

Aras, G. and Crowther, D. 2009. *The Durable Corporation: Strategies for Sustainable Development*. Farnham: Gower.
Carroll, A. B. 1979. 'A Three-Dimensional Conceptual Model of Corporate performance', *Academy of Management Review*, 4, 4: 497–505.
Crowther, D. and Ortiz-Martinez, E. 2004. 'Corporate Social Responsibility: History and Principles', in *Social Responsibility World*, Penang: Ansted University Press, pp. 102–7.

Notes

1. Till and Symes consider Australian companies where there are tax effects of environmental actions and disclosure benefit companies with increased disclosure. The cultural and legal environments differ from country to country and in the UK such benefits do not accrue. Nevertheless, the lack of altruism, or concern for stakeholders, needs to be borne in mind when considering such increased environmental reporting.
2. Although among academics the terms social accounting and environmental accounting are deemed to denote different aspects of responsibility accounting, among practitioners the terms tend to be treated as synonymous and generally called environmental accounting. This approach has been followed here.
3. See Rubenstein (1992) for fuller details of this argument.
4. But see Deegan and Rankin (1999) for a consideration of the deficiencies of current environmental reporting.
5. They are, of course, included in the costs of the firm's activities and thereby in its accounting but all the costs and benefits resulting from such action are not fully recognised through traditional accounting.
6. This will be dealt with more fully in Chapter 11.

References

Crowther, D. 2000a. 'Corporate Reporting, Stakeholders and the Internet: Mapping the New Corporate Landscape', *Urban Studies*, 37, 10: 1837–48.

Crowther, D. 2000b. *Social and Environmental Accounting.* London: Financial Times/Prentice Hall.

Crowther, D. 2002. *A Social Critique of Corporate Reporting.* Aldershot: Ashgate.

Crowther, D. 2004. 'Limited Liability or Limited Responsibility', in D. Crowther and L. Rayman-Bacchus (eds), *Perspectives on Corporate Social Responsibility.* Aldershot: Ashgate, pp. 42–58.

Deegan, C. and Rankin, M. 1999. 'The Environmental Reporting Expectations Gap: Australian Evidence', *British Accounting Review*, 31, 3: 313–46.

Hawken, P. 1993. *The Ecology of Commerce.* London: Weidenfeld & Nicolson.

Kinnersley, D. 1994. *Coming Clean: The Politics of Water and the Environment.* London: Penguin.

Ortiz-Martinez, E. and Crowther, D. 2006. '¿Son compatibles la responsabilidad económica y la responsabilidad social corporativa?', *Harvard Deusto Finanzas y Contabilidad*, No. 71: 2–12.

Paine, T. 1792. *The Rights of Man* (many editions).

Rousseau, J.-J. 1762. *The Social Contract, Or Principles of Political Right* (many editions).

Rubenstein, D. B. 1992. 'Bridging the Gap between Green Accounting and Black Ink', *Accounting, Organizations and Society*, 17, 5: 501–08.

Till, C. A. and Symes, C. F. 1999. 'Environmental Disclosure by Australian Mining Companies: Environmental Conscience or Commercial Reality?' *Accounting Forum*, 28, 3: 137–54.

Topal, R. S. and Crowther, D. 2004. 'Bioengineering and Corporate Social Responsibility', in D. Crowther and L. Rayman Bacchus (eds), *Perspectives on Corporate Social Responsibility*. Aldershot: Ashgate, pp. 186–202.

The Social Contract: Moral Obligation or Regulation

5

Learning objectives

After studying this chapter you should be able to:

- Define and explain Utilitarianism and Classical Liberalism.
- Explain the basics of the agency problem.
- Critique the free market system and underlying theories.
- Describe the End of History thesis.
- Distinguish between wealth and welfare.
- Explain the Organisational Failure Framework.

Introduction

The Social Contract, as we have seen previously, is a legitimating theory for CSR and describes the extent to which people and corporations surrender power for the benefit of a better functioning society. One of the perennial debates in CSR is the extent to which this should happen due to the ethical principles of those involved and the extent to which government regulation is required. In other words, there is a debate about the relative merits of ethics and regulation, which has been heightened by the recent finical crisis. All the argument is situated in the debates about the free market system and its strengths and weaknesses, so we must start by examining this and the philosophical underpinnings of it. The starting point needs to be Classical Liberal theory and then Utilitarianism which was developed from it.

Classical liberalism

Classical Liberal theory started to be developed in the seventeenth century by such writers as John Locke as a means of explaining how society operated, and should operate, in an era in which the Divine Right of Kings to rule and to run society for their own benefit had been challenged and was generally considered to be inappropriate for the society which then existed. Classical Liberalism is founded upon the two principles of reason and rationality: reason in that everything had a logic which could be understood and agreed with by all, and rationality in that every decision made was made by a person in the light of what their evaluation had shown them to be for their greatest benefit. Classical Liberalism therefore is centred upon the individual, who is assumed to be rational and would make a rational decision, and is based upon the need to give freedom to every individual to pursue his or her own ends. It is therefore a philosophy of the pursuance of self-interest. Society, insofar as it existed and was considered to be needed, was therefore merely an aggregation of these individual self-interests. This aggregation was considered to be a sufficient explanation for the need for society. Indeed, Locke argued that the whole purpose of society was to protect the rights of each individual and to safeguard these private rights.

There is, however, a problem with this allowing of every individual the complete freedom to follow his or her own ends and to maximise his or her own welfare. This problem is that in some circumstances this welfare can be created only at the expense of other individuals. It is through this conflict between the rights and freedoms of individuals that problems occur in society. It is for this reason therefore that de Tocqueville argued there was a necessary function for government within society. He argued that the function of government therefore was the regulation of individual transactions so as to safeguard the rights of all individuals as far as possible.

Although this philosophy of individual freedom was developed as the philosophy of Liberalism, it can be seen that this philosophy has been adopted by Conservative governments throughout the world, as led by the UK government in the 1980s. This philosophy has led increasingly to the reduction of state involvement in society and the giving of freedom to individuals to pursue their own ends, with regulation providing a mediating mechanism where deemed necessary. It will be apparent, however, that there is a further problem with Liberalism and this is that the mediation of rights between different individuals works satisfactorily only when the power of individuals is roughly equal. Plainly this situation never arises between all individuals and this is the cause of one of the problems in society.

Whilst this philosophy of Liberalism was developed to explain the position of individuals in society and the need for government and regulation of that society, the philosophy applies equally to organisations. Indeed, Liberalism considers that organisations arise within society as a mechanism whereby individuals can pursue their individual self-interests more effectively that they can alone. Thus firms exist because it is a more efficient means of individuals maximising their self-interests through collaboration than is possible through each individual acting alone. This argument provides the basis for the Theory of the Firm, which argues that through this combination between individuals the costs of individual transactions are thereby reduced.

Utilitarianism

The concept of Utilitarianism was developed as an extension of Liberalism in order to account for the need to regulate society in terms of each individual pursuing, independently, his or her own ends. It was developed by people such as Bentham (1789) and John Stuart Mill (1863) who defined the optimal position for society as being the greatest good of the greatest number. They argued that it was government's role to mediate between individuals to ensure this societal end. In Utilitarianism it is not actions which are deemed to be good or bad but merely outcomes. Thus, any means of securing a desired outcome was deemed to be acceptable and if the same outcomes ensued then there was no difference, in value terms, between different means of securing those outcomes. Thus actions are value neutral and only outcomes matter. This is, of course, problematical when the actions of firms are concerned because firms consider outcomes only from the point of view of the firm itself. Indeed, accounting, as we know, captures the actions of a firm only insofar as they affect the firm itself and it ignores other consequences of the actions of a firm. Under Utilitarianism, however, if the outcomes for the firm were considered to be desirable then any means of achieving these outcomes was considered acceptable. In the nineteenth and early twentieth centuries this was the way in which firms were managed[1] and it is only in more recent times that it has become accepted that all the outcomes from the actions of the firm are important and need to be taken into account.

The development of Utilitarianism led to the development of Economic theory as a means of explaining the actions of firms. Indeed, the concept of Perfect Competition is predicated in the assumptions of Classical Liberal theory – and the arguments for the unregulated Free Market are based upon the concept of such Perfect Competition.[2] From Economic theory, of course, both Finance theory and accounting developed as tools for analysis to aid the rational decision making assumed in Economic theory. This is a problem because it encourages selfish and exploitative behaviour. So we can either believe that the market will mediate in an optimal way – which is complete nonsense – or we can suggest that ethical understanding will compensate – also nonsense. Or we must look for an alternative.

In 1762, Jean-Jacques Rousseau produced his book on the Social Contract which was designed to explain – and therefore legitimate – the relationship between an individual and society and its government. In it he argued that individuals voluntarily gave up certain rights in order for the government of the state to be able to manage for the greater good of all citizens. Thus the idea of the Social Contract has been generally accepted. More recently the Social Contract has gained a new prominence as it has been used to explain the relationship between a company and society. In this view the company (or other organisation) has obligations towards other parts of society in return for its place in society.

Most people would argue that the extension of the Social Contract to corporations provides an answer through a voluntary giving up of some autonomy for the greater good and the subjection to regulation.

Classical liberal philosophy is important for the situating of debates concerning corporate social responsibility within the discourse of both the social contract and of the globalisation phenomenon. As a philosophy it places an emphasis upon rationality and reason, with society being an artificial creation resulting from an aggregation of individual self-interest, and with organisations being an inevitable result of such aggregations for business purposes. Thus Locke (1690) viewed societies as existing in order to protect innate natural private rights, whilst Bentham (1789) and J. S. Mill (1863) emphasised the pursuit of human need. Of paramount importance to all was the freedom of the individual to pursue his[3] own ends, with a tacit assumption that maximising individual benefits would lead to the maximisation of organisational benefits and also societal benefits. In other words, societal benefits can be determined by a simple summation of all individual benefits. Classical liberal economic theory extended this view of society to the treatment of organisations as entities in their own right with the freedom to pursue their own ends. Such theory requires little restriction of organisational activity because of the assumption that the market, when completely free from regulation, will act as a mediating mechanism which will ensure that, by and large, the interests of all stakeholders of the organisation will be attended to by the need to meet these free market requirements. This view, however, resulted in a dilemma in reconciling collective needs with individual freedom. De Tocqueville (1840) reconciled these aims by suggesting that government institutions, as regulating agencies, were both inevitable and necessary in order to allow freedom to individuals and the protection of those freedoms.

Thus classical liberal arguments recognise a limitation in the freedom of an organisation to follow its own ends without any form of regulation. Similarly, Fukuyama (1992) developed his End of History Thesis and argued that liberalism is not in itself sufficient for continuity and that traditional organisations have a tendency to atomise in the pursuance of the ends of the individuals who have aggregated for the purpose for which the organisation was formed to fulfil. He argued that liberal economic principles provide no support for the traditional concept of an organisation as a community of common interest, which is only sustainable if individuals within that community give up some of their rights to the community as an entity and accept a certain degree of intolerance. On the other hand, Fukuyama considered the triumph of liberal democracy as the final state of history, citing evidence of the break-up of the eastern bloc as symbolising the triumph of classical liberalism.[4]

The free market system

Although this classical liberal/economic rationality view of organisations can be viewed as one paradigm representing the structure and behaviour of organisations, it is by no means the only such paradigm. An alternative paradigm, predicated in the stakeholder view of organisations and the dynamic disequilibrium existing within organisations, and brought about by the conflicting needs of the various stakeholders, is a pluralistic paradigm.[5] Such a paradigm views organisations not as entities acting for a particular purpose but rather as a coalition of various interest groups acting in concert, through the resolution or subsumption of their convergent interests, for a particular purpose at a particular point in time. This purpose changes over time as the power of the various stakeholders changes and as various stakeholders join, and influence, the dominant coalition whilst other stakeholders leave that coalition.

These and a lot of other factors have led to the current interest in corporate social responsibility – such things as poor business behaviour towards customers, employees and the environment. A lot of other things have also featured prominently in popular consciousness. One of these, which has become more pronounced, is the issue of climate change and this has affected concern about CSR through a concern with the emission of greenhouse gases and particularly carbon dioxide. Another thing which has become prominent is a concern with the supply chain of business; in particular, people are concerned with the exploitation of people in developing countries, especially the questions of child labour and slavery.

An important principle of CSR is that of sustainability and this is a term which has suddenly become so common as to be ubiquitous for business and for society. Every organisation mentions sustainability and the concept is applied in the press to just about everything, whether appropriate or not. Nevertheless, it is of major concern to businesses, and to academics concerned with businesses, and is therefore of great relevance to a study of corporate social responsibility. Governance and the ethics of corporate behaviour also are items of considerable interest and importance, especially given the unfolding of events surrounding the 2008–10 economic crisis and the claims made about individual, corporate and state behaviour – or more accurately misbehaviour. There are therefore many issues worthy of investigation which fall within the realm of corporate social responsibility.

The financial and consequent economic crises which we have experienced are a direct consequence of preceding activity. They have been discussed frequently and have been depicted as representative of systemic failures of the market system and the lax application of systems of governance and regulation, as depicted in Figure 5.1. Thus, many people are arguing for improved systems to combat this. Others have been more concerned to allocate blame – to the banks, the financial markets, the regulators or to governments – according to their personal prejudices. Still others would say that it is an inevitable consequence of greed, ignorance and irresponsibility.

Where we differ from the majority, however, is that we hold the view that this greed, ignorance and irresponsibility is not among the bankers, regulators and governmental representatives – or at least not among them alone. It is among society at large – affecting and infecting each one of us. All the evidence shows that most individuals are ready and willing to believe that abnormal rewards are

Figure 5.1   Causes of the financial crisis

possible for them personally without the need to take abnormal risks and that this situation can be perpetuated. And the evidence also shows that as long as we are personally benefiting like this then we are happy not to ask questions and to accept lax regulation – after all, that regulation is to protect others rather than us...

The lesson is, of course, readily apparent although not really being talked about. This is that it is not sufficient to blame others when we are personally culpable; and it is not sufficient to look for social responsibility in organisations. Before we can demand that we must also accept that it must be practised by us also as individuals. In other words, social responsibility demands individual responsibility.

The Bretton Woods legacy

By July 1944 it was obvious who would win the war and attention was turning to what would happen afterwards. Consequently, in that month over 400 delegates representing 44 countries met at Mount Washington Hotel, Bretton Woods, New Hampshire, USA to make plans to ensure that such a war would never again happen. It was described by J. M. Keynes as 'the most monstrous monkey-house assembled for years'.

The belief was that a stable international economic environment, based upon a capitalism and market mechanism. would provide this. US Secretary of State Cordell Hull believed that the fundamental causes of the two world wars lay in economic discrimination and trade warfare. Specifically, he had in mind the trade and exchange controls (bilateral arrangements) of Nazi Germany and the imperial preference system practised by Britain, by which members or former members of the British Empire were accorded special trade status, itself provoked by German, French, and American protectionist policies. Consequently, a vision for the future was laid out by US President Harry Truman. It was based upon fostering capital investment, making available to peace-loving people the benefits of the US store of technical knowledge and helping them realise their aspirations for a better life.

The outcome of the conference was a set of economic institutions:

- The International Monetary Fund (IMF).
- The International Bank for Reconstruction and Development which is now known as The World Bank.
- The International Trade Organization, which in 1995 became the World Trade Organization (WTO).
- A fixed exchange-rate mechanism, which was later abandoned.

The altruistic and idealistic intentions of the founders worked well for post-war reconstruction and for economic development until the great betrayal of 1981. At that time, US President Ronald Reagan said that these institutions as '... organs of international aid and so-called Third World development were invested with socialist error'. The subsequent US investigation reported in 1982 that 'the Bank usually acts in support of American political and strategic interests' but the antipathy of Reagan continued and was continued by others, culminating in the actions of George Bush.

The IMF developed a model of reconstruction for countries in difficulties, which was applied to all countries in the belief that this model would work everywhere. Despite overwhelming evidence of its failure, it is still being applied. Basically, loans are dependent upon Structural Adjustment and Economic Reform. This involves an austerity programme, cutting public services, privatisation and devaluation. The failures of this programme have led to claims such as:

> We know that the IMF and World Bank programs have greatly exacerbated poverty and undermined the basic human and democratic rights on people in Southern countries to determine our own destiny. (Jubilee South Africa, 1999)
>
> The three leading causes of death in Zambia today include AIDS, malnutrition and malaria. Each of these is related to the slavish pursuit by the Zambian Government of the IMF imposed structural adjustment programs. (Africa Faith and Justice Network)
>
> We denounce and reject the globalization of the Neo-liberal model as exclusive, undemocratic, exploitative, pillaging and genocidal, imposed on the world ... (Declaration of the South-North Exchange, Chiapas, Mexico, October 2000)

Such claims are supported by many in the developed world.

We can conclude that good intentions do not necessarily survive unless constantly renewed.

A solution is needed

One of the most important issues arising recently is the financial crisis, which has become a global economic recession. As such a recession develops then many people are being severely affected, both in developed and developing countries, despite the situation that they have never had any involvement in financial market speculation and would be economically unable to do so even if they wished to. Such is the power of finance that it causes this contagious effect which can devastate lives at a distance, much as a butterfly flapping its wings in the Amazon can cause a hurricane in Wall Street – to paraphrase a basic principle of chaos theory (Gleick, 1988). Although it is generally accepted that the crisis was instigated by the subprime lending debacle which was one of the features of the deregulation of the US financial economy, the effects of the global financial crisis have been felt around the world.

The financial and economic crisis has shown that there are failures in governance and problems with the market system. In the main these have been depicted as representative of systemic failures of the market system and the lax application of systems of governance and regulation. Thus, many people are arguing for improved systems to combat this. Naturally many people have discussed these failures and the consequent problems and will continue to do so into the future. It is not, of course, the first such crisis and the market economy has been proceeding on a course of boom and bust for the last twenty years, which is not dissimilar to that of the 1960s and 70s which the neo-conservatives claimed to have stopped. The main differences are that recent cycles are driven by the financial markets and the era of globalisation means that no country is immune from the effects felt in other countries.

This globalisation should stifle one of the debates concerning the crisis: this is the one concerning the prevention of future occurrences through the introduction of an enhanced regulatory regime. Regulators are bounded by their terms and areas of reference whereas finance and trade is increasingly boundary-less. So the only form of regulation which would be effective would be a global system of regulation (Aras and Crowther, 2009a). At present this does not appear to be a viable option because of vested interests in other forms of control.

Of vital concern to all forms of business, however, and also to leaders in governments, NGOs and financial institutions is the question of sustainability and the conditions under which sustainable development become possible. Although environmental effects are an important part of sustainability for businesses and for economic or financial activity mediated through the markets, sustainability is actually much more complex than this and requires the balancing of a variety of different factors (Aras and Crowther, 2009a). Nevertheless, sustainable economic activity is dependent upon sustainable businesses whilst sustainable businesses are equally dependent upon stable and sustainable markets; equally the sustainability of national economies is dependent upon both, as is the global economy – a truly complex and symbiotic relationship! If regulatory control of these interrelationships is problematic then this means that governance is also problematic – possibly one cause of the current crisis.

The cause of the financial crisis

With such powerful effects it is naturally a newsworthy topic – and certainly one for which we should strive to understand the causes in order to develop mechanisms which will alleviate its effects and more importantly prevent its reoccurrence. First, of course, we need to recognise that this is not the first such crisis – and that it is not very long since the last one. It seems therefore that the memories of the people buying and selling in financial markets are very short. This can be explained as a feature of the quick turnover of these people coupled with the enormous bonuses which they receive, which gives a very short-term focus to their decision making – surely a very significant factor in the cause of the crisis and recognised as such by most people even though no one is willing to take action.

Many people have commented upon the current financial crisis, its causes and consequences and there have been many attempts to theorise the problem in terms of market failure or governance failure. For some it is even the failure of capitalism. These people tend to advocate a change to the system – generally to another of their personal preference. Others have been more concerned to allocate blame – to the banks, the financial markets, the regulators or to governments – again according to their personal prejudices. Still others would say that it is an inevitable consequence of greed, ignorance and irresponsibility. And the solutions all seem to involve government rescue, sometimes coupled with penalties for those in the financial sector who are deemed to be responsible. And an important aspect seems to be the need to apportion blame rather than consider remedies for the future.

One thing which is apparent, however, is that the current financial crisis, much as previous ones, has highlighted failures in governance and failures in regulation. Indeed, some writers, in their desire for scapegoating, have argued that the regulators are more guilty even than the perpetrators and should be sanctioned accordingly. There is, of course, one flaw in this argument and one problem with managing the prevention of future financial crisis and this is concerned with the recognition of and regulation of a truly global financial market. The liberalisation of financial markets instigated by the Washington consensus has made the free movement of funds a fact of financial life and has encouraged the parcelling together of doubtful debts into mystery parcels to be sold around the world. And, of course, the operators in all financial markets, always ready to accept a gamble in the hope of ever larger profits and bonuses, have been quick to respond. We therefore need to probe deeper in order to understand the causes of the crisis.

Thomas Hobbes (1651) is well known for discussing the concept of the social contract. In his work citizens would agree to vest absolute power in a sovereign power as the only way to avoid anarchy. In doing so, citizens give up their individual rights, including control of liberty and property, and possibly even life. He argued that human self-interest is such that we would be willing to wage war on each other, the end result being a short and unpleasant life for all. This tradition accords with a utilitarian position: the pursuit of maximum welfare, and this can be considered to provide the basis for the capitalist system and its reliance upon the market and individual endeavour. This therefore provides the test for whether corporate behaviour is morally right or wrong. Utilitarianism regards corporate activity as morally good if it maximises human welfare, and collective welfare may override individual welfare.

There are, however, problems with Utilitarianism which need to be considered. The first problem is that the philosophy states that it is only outcomes which matter – not how those outcomes are arrived at. In other words, it states that unethical behaviour is acceptable if the outcome is beneficial overall – many people cannot subscribe to such a philosophy. The second problem is that it believes that net outcome can be arrived at by adding together all the individual outcomes; if the sum is positive then this is beneficial. Thus one person (or corporation) can benefit greatly and a million people can be disadvantaged to a small amount and the philosophy will view this as beneficial and therefore desirable. Thus, the philosophy actually legitimates exploitation and the abuse of power. There is surely a problem with a philosophy like this but it is the underlying philosophy of our free market system. So we need to consider what alternatives are available.

During the era of individualism in the 1980s a theoretical alternative was developed in the USA, which became known as Communitarianism, although the concept goes back to the earlier work of such people as Tonnies (1957) and Plant (1974). Communitarianism is based upon the argument that it is not the individual, or even the state, which should be the basis of our value system. Thus the social nature of life is emphasised alongside public goods and services. The argument is that all individuals, including corporations, have an obligation to contribute towards the public nature of life rather than pursuing their own self-interests. Underpinning the theories of communitarianism is the assumption that ethical behaviour must proceed from an understanding of a community's traditions and cultural understanding. Exponents argue that the exclusive pursuit of private interest erodes the network of social environments on which we all depend, and is destructive of our shared experiment in democratic self-government. A communitarian perspective recognises both individual human dignity and the social dimension of human existence and that the preservation of individual liberty depends on the active maintenance of the institutions of civil society where citizens learn respect for others as well as self-respect and where we acquire a lively sense of our personal and civic responsibilities, along with an appreciation of our own rights and the rights of others.

The twenty-first century has seen an explosion of interest in the concept of corporate social responsibility as a means of conducting business. Corporate social responsibility is based upon the concepts of transparency and accountability and the adoption of these concepts into business practice has led to an increasing level of disclosure and a more firmly defined basis for the governance of organisations. Hence the concept of corporate governance has become as ubiquitous as the concept of corporate social responsibility within both business practice and academic investigation. Early work was concerned with the critique of business practice but more recently the concern has been with finding a theoretical basis to underpin this current concern. The theories which have been adopted primarily consist of stakeholder theory, social contract theory and political economy theory. Other theories have also been used which provide valuable insights. One striking feature of the discourse concerning CSR, however, is its relative homogeneity concerning its application to corporate behaviour. Initial concern has been with large firms, especially multinationals. Only relatively recently has attention been turned towards SMEs, despite the fact that they account for 99% of all forms of business activity throughout the world.

Agency and economic activity

The basic assumption of economic activity is that it should be organised into profit-seeking firms, each acting in isolation and concerned solely with profit maximisation, and justified according to classical liberalism and the Utilitarian philosophy of John Stuart Mill. This inevitably results in management which is organisation-centric, seeking merely to measure and report upon the activities of the firm insofar as they affected the firm. Any actions of the firm which had consequences external to the firm were held not to be the concern of the firm (Aras and Crowther, 2009b; 2009c). Indeed, enshrined within classical liberalism, alongside the sanctity of the individual to pursue his own course of action, was the notion that the operation of the free market mechanism would mediate between these individuals to allow for an equilibrium based upon the interaction of these freely acting individuals and that this equilibrium was an inevitable consequence of this interaction.[6] As a consequence, any concern of the firm with the effect of its actions upon externalities was irrelevant and not therefore a proper concern for its management.

One issue of relevance to all organisations is the governance problem caused by the agency problem (Becker and Westbrook, 1998); for financial organisations, however, this problem is particularly profound. The general agency problem can be characterised as a situation in which a principal (or group of principals) seeks to establish incentives for an agent (or group of agents) which takes decisions that affect the principal to act in ways that contribute maximally to the principal's own objectives. In business this means the relationship between the owner of the business and other investors – as principal – and the managers of the business – as agents. The difficulties in establishing such an incentive structure arise from either divergence of the objectives of principals and agents or the asymmetric information between principals and agents (Vickers and Yarrow, 1988), and very often from both of these factors.

When financial companies are considered then there are significant implications from the agency problem. The first of these is that there are considerably more stakeholders than for an ordinary company. Every borrower and lender is a stakeholder with a continuing relationship with the company. This relationship is much stronger than that with customers who are suppliers of an ordinary company due to the ongoing financial commitment by both parties. The second implication is concerned with information asymmetry because the level of risk taken in financial transactions is often much higher but more importantly cannot be assessed by the stakeholders to the financial company even though the managers have sophisticated methodologies for doing so. Thus, stakeholders need to rely upon rating agencies to eliminate – or significantly reduce – this information asymmetry. It is significant to note, however, that the current crisis has shown that the methodologies of financial organisations have been proved to be inadequate[7] and rating agencies have failed to demonstrate any ability to compensate for the information asymmetry.

Market failure

Regulators inevitably, according to their requirements, must focus upon local market whilst finance escapes them through its ability to migrate around the world. Effectively this means that any realistic form of regulation does not and cannot exist. One consequence of this regulatory failure, of course, is that contamination spreads and the dubious practices developed in one financial market become the norm in other markets. When the inevitable crisis appears this too spreads from one country to another as all economies are affected by both the consequences of dubious lending practices and by the ensuing crisis of confidence.

The only barriers to financial transactions are national regulations (Tobin, 2000). However, it can be seen that regulation is not enough to regulate and control for international transactions and capital flows in developing countries and transitional economies – or to effectively regulate global financial companies. Risk has been effectively ignored and corporate governance principles (see Aras and Crowther, 2008; 2009d) flouted. The principles of governance and the principles of sustainability are inextricably interrelated and the ignoring of governance principles shows that such firms have scant regard for sustainability; indeed, the behaviour of financial institutions still continues to show no regard for sustainability – for themselves, for national economies and for the global economic system. It seems that they have learned nothing from previous crises, which have been a regular occurrence in the Western economic system. The only difference this time is the global nature of the effects from the local American cause. The financial crisis has, of course, expanded into an economic crisis and many sound businesses are perishing in this climate. Others are, however, prospering and it is our argument that a large part of the difference between survival and failure in the current climate of economic downturn is a proper understanding and assessment of risk, based upon an understanding of the principles of sustainability (see Aras and Crowther, 2009e). The evidence to support this assertion is still accumulating as the crisis continues to unfold.

Organisational failure

It is often stated that two features can be considered to describe the modern world – namely globalisation and the free market. It has been widely accepted – almost unquestioningly – that free markets will lead to greater economic growth and that we will all benefit from this economic growth. Around the world people – especially politicians and business leaders – have argued that restrictions upon world economic activity caused by the regulation of markets are bad for our well-being. And in one country after another, for one market after another, governments have been seen to capitulate and relax their regulations to allow complete freedom of economic activity. So the world is rapidly becoming a global marketplace for global corporations, increasingly unfettered by regulation. Whilst this argument was unchallenged, we have seen the effects of the actions of some of these corporations within the United States itself – the champion of the free market. We have seen the collapse of the global accounting firm Andersen; we have seen the bankruptcy of major corporations such as Enron and World.com with thousands of people being thrown out of work and many people losing the savings for their old age which they have worked so long and hard to gain. More recently we have seen the devastating effects of untrammelled and unregulated free market behaviour – best described as greed, corruption and the kind of plundering most commonly associated with pirates in an earlier age. The economic collapse triggered as a direct consequence of this behaviour has caused some rethinking and so perhaps the free market model might not become so ubiquitous.

In considering why this situation has arisen we must acknowledge that basically there are problems with accounting, with auditing, and with peoples' expectations. We must remember that the myth of the free market is grounded in classical liberal economic theory – subsequently developed into Utilitarianism and the foundation of the capitalist economic system, and as propounded by people such as John Stuart Mill (1863) in the nineteenth century, which, briefly summarised, states that anything is OK as long as the consequences are acceptable. The regulatory regime of accounting has been increasingly changed over time to serve the interests of businesses rather than their owners or society. Thus it is no longer expected that the accounting of a business should be undertaken conservatively by recognising potential future liabilities whilst at the same time not recognising future profit. Instead, profit can be brought forward into the accounts before it has been earned, whilst liabilities (such as the replacement of an aging electricity distribution network) can be ignored if they reduce current profitability. A study of the changes made in accounting standards over the years (Aras and Crowther, 2009a) shows a gradual relaxation of this requirement for conservatism in accounting as these standards have been changed to allow firms to show increased profits in the present. This, of course, makes the need for strong governance procedures even more paramount.

The management of an organisation tends to be treated as a discrete entity[8] but it is important to remember that this entity actually comprises a set of individuals with their own drives, motivations and desires. Thus, every individual has a desire to fulfil his or her needs and one of these is self-actualisation (Maslow, 1954). This need is the one at the top of Maslow's hierarchy of needs and consequently perhaps the one most considered in terms of motivation. The next two most important needs – the need for esteem (as reflected in self-respect and the respect of others) and the need for love and belonging (as reflected in the need for being an integral part of a community) – are, however, more important for the understanding of the behaviour of the members of the dominant coalition of management within an organisation. These two needs help explain why managers, in common with other individuals, need to feel important, skilled and essential to organisational performance.

Whilst the Theory of the Firm explains why firms come into existence and the role of accounting in firms as a tool to aid rational decision making, it does not sufficiently explain the workings of a firm. Thus the role of accounting within a firm cannot be considered without a consideration of the people involved in that firm as a firm, of course, consists of a collection of people who are involved. The people involved in the firm are affected by the accounting systems of that firm as well as affecting those accounting systems, and this will be considered in greater details in future chapters. The main people involved in the control of a firm are, of course, its managers and Williamson (1970) argues that because in any large organisation the management of the firm is normally divorced from its ownership then this is a factor which hinders its control and decision making. This leads to internal efficiencies within the firm and conflicts of interests, which mean that organisations do not operate efficiently as a means of transaction cost-minimisation and value-creating maximisation. From this analysis Williamson developed what is known as the Organisational Failure Framework.

Thus Williamson (1975) develops this analysis and considers organisations to be complex due to their size, which leads to uncertainty, bounded rationality and information impactedness. He argues that the extent of these factors determines the likelihood of organisational failure from organisations becoming the principal means of resource allocation and decision making. Thus, he argues that there are organisational limits to the size of a firm brought about by such factors as diseconomies of scale, communication distortion and bureaucratic insularity. Furthermore, he argues that the market as a mediating mechanism cannot itself overcome these inefficiencies brought about through the organisation of productive activity into firms. He states that multidivisionalism is a method of overcoming this but that there are still limits to size because of difficulties of communication, resource allocation and lack of entrepreneurial opportunities. He argues, therefore, that organic growth beyond a certain size leads to failure, thereby limiting the size of a firm. Whilst this theory has a certain logic to it, practical examples of such activity are lacking and there do appear to be some very large firms in existence in the world. Perhaps, however, current trends towards downsizing and returning to core business aims is evidence of the validity of this theory, but some empirical testing seems to be needed which is beyond the scope of this chapter. These factors together are described as the Organisational Failure Framework, which describes how firms collapse through becoming too big; arguably this is what has happened to some of the major financial institutions currently having problems.

Who is responsible?

The current crisis is not the first such crisis affecting economies and cause within the financial sector. Such crises have been a recurrent feature for at least the last century – or even since the time when John Stuart Mill legitimated the activities of the market system through the development of his Utilitarian philosophy, which has become the legitimating principle of the Free Market approach to economic activity. It is no coincidence that the result has been that risk has been ignored and responsibility flouted through the adoption of a Utilitarian rationale for business behaviour. There are many problems with Utilitarianism – both as a philosophy and as a basis for economic activity – which are documented elsewhere. The problem which we want to focus upon here is its amorality, which we regard as one of the root causes of the financial crisis. This is especially the case when it is coupled with the assumption that a summative approach to welfare, when negotiated through the unequal power relationships of the free (but most certainly not perfect in economics terms) market. The very nature of the Utilitarian philosophy is that exploitation is sanctioned as it is only outcomes which matter.

Thus, risk has been largely ignored and information asymmetry has simply been accepted. Perhaps this demonstrates prescience (or arrogance) as the failed financial organisations have just been supported by individual citizens (via government loans), thereby demonstrating that the risk to the agents at least is nonexistent! Indeed, the US bank managers are so self-congratulatory about this that they paid themselves large bonuses, much to the disgust of President Obama!

At the same time these financial companies have been making large[9] profits: for example, HSBC made profits of 114% from borrowing and lending and adding fees into the process during the first half of 2008 and of 102% for 2007, and this is typical of all similar institutions. With (abnormal) returns at this level coupled with low levels of risk it is perhaps unsurprising that investors in financial organisations have been happy to leave the management of the business to their agents and to pay them very large sums of money as remuneration. No one wished to question this performance and risk killing the golden goose. Even governments have been complicit in this by gradually relaxing the regulatory regime, *in the interests of competing in the global market*. It is only when the crisis unfolds and these financial transactions unravel that anyone has started to question the behaviour of these financial organisations and their managers (Spence, 2008).

Most people consider that the financial crisis was caused by unsustainable activity in the US housing finance market – commonly known as subprime lending. It quickly became apparent, however, that the banking sector around the world had been engaged in what can only be described as gambling. Supposed assets had been packaged together into parcels for which even the most sophisticated models available could not calculate the risk; consequently risk was ignored in the naïve assumption that these packages were safe investments. When it was discovered that they were actually worthless then they were quickly relabelled as toxic assets and governments were persuaded to buy them from the banks. Surprisingly, even the US government complied. For some – such as Madoff with his hedge fund – even this gambling was insufficient; outright theft was required.

Risk and responsibility

As the economic recession worsened, the revelations of misbehaviour continued unabated, each instance more believable than the previous one. After the Madoff debacle it has become apparent that a number of others were also committing fraud in order to cover up their unsuccessful gambling with other people's money, with the objective of keeping their sinking financial operations afloat. Indeed, Sir Allen Stanford – already vilified and forced to apologise for inappropriate behaviour towards cricketers' wives – has been charged with fraud and the violation of US securities laws. More revelations will doubtless follow.

In the UK the whistleblowers, such as Paul Moore of HBOS, who have announced that the level of risk taken in the financial world was unsustainable, have been sacked, although subsequent revelations resulted in the resignation of government ministers. In the US the new saviour President Barack Obama has seen some of his chosen assistants withdraw after revelations that they did not bother to pay some of the taxes which they owed. Equally, one of the first things that happened to the 2010 coalition government in the UK was the resignation of David Laws, Chief Secretary to the Treasury and Cabinet Minister, who did not seem to understand that the rules about expenses applied to him also, despite wholesale resignations from the last Parliament and some impending criminal prosecutions. And everywhere we have witnessed bankers and others failing to show contrition or even to acknowledge that the recklessness of their behaviour has been the cause of the current global economic problems.

The question which needs to be addressed is not that of who is to blame for the current problems – plainly many people are partly culpable. Instead, the important question – which is not yet being addressed – is whether there is an underlying malaise which is causing all of these problems. And if so then what might it be?

For us the answer is plain: it is concerned with a lack of understanding of risk and the rewards associated with the taking of risk. Elementary financial theory teaches us that returns are a reward which is related to the level of risk undertaken. This means that in order to earn higher-than-average levels of reward it is necessary to accept higher-than-average levels of risk. This basic principle has been ignored and there has been a general acceptance that higher-than-normal rewards are available for lower-than-normal levels of risk – and that this is a situation which will continue *ad infinitem*. Indeed, it has been so generally accepted that such good times are here forever that the regulations enacted to protect investors from misdeeds have been relaxed or more generally not enforced – thereby enabling some of the frauds revealed to continue over long periods of time.

What is constantly surprising is that this simple lesson of the relationship between risk and rewards is taught so often but is so readily forgotten, or at best ignored. So it is only a few years since the collapse of Enron in 2001 – a company built upon fraud and a general acceptance that abnormal profits could be made and abnormal growth achieved in a power supply company. This in turn was only just after the Dot.Com Bubble had shown that spectacular growth and profitability from Internet trading was not achievable. Slightly earlier, in 1995, the collapse of Barings Bank had shown that continued abnormal profits from gambling in financial markets were not achievable on a continuing basis. This collapse also highlighted the need for ensuring satisfactory regulatory oversight. This was something which had been repeated from 1991 when the collapse of the Bank of Credit and Commerce International – also founded upon fraud and misbehaviour – had shown that abnormal profit and returns were not possible in the long term and that regulatory oversight needed to be firmly and consistently enforced. Similar examples can be cited tracing all the way back in history to the English South Sea Bubble of the early eighteenth century and the Dutch tulip bulb speculation of the seventeenth century.

What is apparent from this continual re-enactment of the same events is that nothing has been learned from any of these happenings. Another way of looking at this is to suggest that memories are short and that attribution theory applies to convince people that they will not repeat the same mistakes as others – even though all the evidence shows otherwise.

Further actions have been taken since to alleviate corporations (and hence shareholders) from the risk associated with their investments. Buckminster Fuller (1981) describes lucidly the actions of successive US governments during the twentieth century which had the effects of transferring all risk to society in general through taxation, reduced regulation and through acting to bail out failed enterprises. Examples can be found in the actions of most other governments. So, without risk, corporations were able increasingly to do whatever they wished – and without responsibility anything became possible, even the lies of the present as no one was accountable for their actions as long as economic growth – and profitability – continued. Thus we arrive at the present excesses. The link between rights and responsibilities had been severed and forgotten.

Conclusion

It is at this point that we must summarise our arguments, which have shown both the causes of the crises and our belief that they are an inevitable consequence of the current economic system, predicated as it is in Utilitarian philosophy. In particular, we have sought to show that although failures in regulation exist, they are not the main cause of the crises. Instead, we have argued that the severance of responsibility from risk – through allowing abnormal returns to not just be made but also allowing the expectation that these have become the norm – is clearly an unrealistic belief.

The concepts of risk and responsibility are actually inseparable, and elementary finance theory teaches us that arbitrage will quickly eliminate abnormal returns. Equally, elementary economic theory teaches us that perfect competition cannot exist and thereby destroys the very foundations of free market legitimisation. So there is a need to reconnect these elementary pieces of knowledge with our understanding of the economic system and there is a need to remind all of those involved of this elementary theory which they surely must have learned and subsequently forgotten. So is it here that bridges are needed. And finally there is a need to introduce morality into the marketplace and into the economic system. Only then can we ensure that crises such as we have witnessed will not recur.

Summary of key points

- Financial misdemeanours have created a concern for CSR. This includes reckless behaviour and fraud and theft.
- Utilitarianism, based upon Classical Liberalism, is the underlying philosophy of the market system.
- The Free Market is a cause of problems.
- Globalisation has limited the ability of regulators to control the financial markets.
- The agency problem means that all information is not known to potential investors.
- The Organisational Failure Framework explains inefficiencies in firm behaviour.

Definitions of key terms and theories

The agency problem is that there is information asymmetry so that investors do not have complete information.

Classical liberal theory states that individuals are rational and seek to pursue their own self-interest, which benefits everyone.

Communitarianism is based upon the argument that it the public good which is at the centre of social life.

Organisation failure framework explains that size leads to inefficiencies in a firm.

Utilitarianism as a philosophy defines good as the maximum benefit.

Test your understanding

1. What is the philosophical basis of the free market system?
2. What is the role of government in protecting individuals?
3. What is the problem with regulating global markets?
4. How has the global market changed competition between nations?
5. What is contamination in financial markets?
6. What is the relationship between governance of a firm and its external environment?

Suggestions for further reading

Aras, G. and Crowther, D. 2010. 'Developing Durability: A Re-examination of Sustainable Corporate Social Responsibility', in J. D. Rendtorff (ed.), *Ethics in the Economy: Power and Principle in the Market Place*. Farnham: Ashgate.
Cassidy, J. 2009. *How Markets Fail*. Harmondsworth: Penguin.
Crowther, D. 2008. 'Stakeholder Perspectives on Social Responsibility', in D. Crowther and N. Capaldi (eds), *Research Companion to Corporate Social Responsibility*. Aldershot: Ashgate, pp. 47–64.
Crowther, D. and Davila Gomez, A.-M. 2011. 'Governance, Dignity and Responsibility: Towards a Symbiosis', in A.-M. Davila Gomez and D. Crowther (eds), *Human Dignity and Managerial Responsibility: A Sustainability Perspective*. Farnham: Gower.

Notes

1. It is arguably the way that the Russian plutarchs have usurped economic power in that country, and legitimated that usurption.
2. This is despite the fact that the concept of Perfect Competition is an elementary assumption in foundation-level economics which is recognised as never existing, and is an assumption that is speedily relaxed in more advanced economics.
3. The use of the term *his* here is intentional as these writers were concerned with only a certain section of society, who were, of course, all male and relatively prosperous and priveleged.
4. Fukuyama presents these arguments as the end of history, which he does not celebrate. In actual fact it is his critique of classical liberalism which is the most significant contribution of his work. This aspect of his work is almost universally ignored in favour of his end-of-history argument.
5. Pluralism was of, course, one of the strands of classical liberalism which was written out of the discourse of liberalism during the late nineteenth century.
6. This assumption, of course, ignores the imbalances in power among the various parties seeking to enact transaction through the market.
7. Or possibly ignored in the search for greater profits.
8. Or rather a coalition which acts in unison.

9. Many would describe these profits as exorbitant and unjustifiably large – exploiting their oligopolistic positions.

References

Aras, G. and Crowther, D. 2008. 'Exploring Frameworks of Corporate Governance', in G. Aras and D. Crowther (eds), *Culture and Corporate Governance*. Leicester: SRRNet, pp. 3–16.

Aras, G. and Crowther, D. 2009a. *The Durable Corporation: Strategies for Sustainable Development*. Aldershot: Gower.

Aras, G. and Crowther, D. 2009b. 'Towards Truly Global Markets', SRRNet Discussion Papers in Social Responsibility 0901: www.socialresponsibility.biz/discuss1.pdf.

Aras, G. and Crowther, D. 2009c. 'Corporate Governance and Corporate Social Responsibility in Context', in G. Aras and D. Crowther (eds), *Global Perspectives on Corporate Governance and Social Responsibility* (forthcoming). Aldershot: Gower.

Aras, G. and Crowther, D. 2009d. 'Corporate Sustainability Reporting: A Study in Disingenuity?' *Journal of Business Ethics*, 87 (supp 1): 279–88.

Aras, G. and Crowther, D. 2010. 'Analysing Social Responsibility in Financial Companies', *International Journal of Banking Accounting and Finance*, 2(3): 295–308

Becker, B. and Westbrook, D. A. 1998. 'Confronting Asymmetry: Global Financial Markets and National Regulation', *International Finance*, 1, 2: 339–55.

Bentham, J. 1789. *An Introduction to the Principles of Morals and Legislation*. many editions.

Buckminster Fuller, R. 1981. *Critical Path*. New York: St Martin's Press.

Fukuyama, F. 1992. *The End of History and the Last Man*. New York: The Free Press.

Gleick, J. 1988. *Chaos: Making a New Science*. London: Heinemann.

Hobbes, T. 1651. *Leviathan*. many editions.

Locke, J. 1690. *Two Treatises of Government*. many editions.

Mill, J. S. 1863. *Utilitarianism, Liberty and Representative Government*. many editions.

Maslow, A. H. 1954. *Motivation and Personality*. New York: Harper & Row.

Plant, R. 1974. *Community and Ideology*; London: Routledge & Kegan Paul.

Rousseau, J.-J. 1762. *Du Contrat Social*. Trans. 'The Social Contract'. many editions.

Spence, M. 2008. 'Agenda for the Next Few Months', in B. Eichengreen and R. Baldwin (eds), *What G20 Leaders Must Do to Stabilise our Economy and Fix the Financial System*. London: CEPR, pp. 11–14

Tobin, J. 2000. 'Financial Globalisation', *World Development*, 28, 6: 1101–04.

Tocqueville, A. de 1840. *Democracy in America*;. many editions.

Tonnies, F. 1957. *Community and Society*. Trans. C. P. Loomis. New York: Harper & Row.

Vickers, J. S. and Yarrow, G. K. 1988. *Privatization*. Cambridge, MA.: MIT Press.

Williamson, O. E. 1970. *Corporate Control and Business Behavior*. New York: Prentice Hall.

Williamson, O. E. 1975. *Markets and Hierarchies: Analysis and Anti-trust Implications*. New York: The Free Press.

Ethics, CSR and Corporate Behaviour

6

Learning objectives

After studying this chapter you should be able to:

- Describe different ethical philosophies.
- Distinguish between legal responsibility and ethical responsibility.
- Describe alternative approaches to creating value.
- Explain the role of stakeholders in the value-creation process.
- Explain the concept of shareholder value.
- Discuss the relationship between corporate mission and value creation.

Introduction

Ethics is not new for people in business. The corporate world has always had some rules, standards and norms for doing business. However, these generally change according to their social and cultural basis, which can vary from country to country, even though we might expect universal rules. When the company applies these standards or norms as a part of its responsibility we can call them an ethical code for conduct of business. Moreover, ethics is also inevitably part of business responsibility. Corporate behaviour should be ethical and responsible; that is why corporate promises made to shareholders and stakeholders are to behave in a fair, ethical and equitable manner.

What is ethics? The why

Ethics shows a corporation how to behave properly in all business dealings and operations. However, business ethics is characterised by conflicts of interests. Businesses attempt to maximise profits as a primary goal on one hand whilst they face issues of social responsibility and social service on the other. Ethics is the set of rules prescribing what is good or evil, or what is right or wrong for people. In other words, ethics is the values that form the basis of human relations, and the quality and essence of being morally good or evil, or right or wrong. Business Ethics means honesty, confidence, respect and fair acting in all circumstances. However, such values as honesty, respect and confidence are rather general concepts without definite boundaries. Ethics can also be defined as overall fundamental principles and practices for improving the level of well-being of humanity.

Ethics is the natural and structural process of acting in line with moral judgements, standards and rules. Because it is a concrete and subjective concept, 'business ethics' can be discussed with differing approaches and in varying degrees of importance in different fields. Indeed, it is highly difficult to define ethics and identify its limits and criteria. Accordingly, there are difficulties in discussing this concept in literature as it is ubiquitous in business life, at the business level, and in human life. According to what, how, how much and for whom ethics is or should be are important questions. It is not always easy to find answers to these questions (Aras, 2006).

A business which does not respect ethical criteria and fails to improve them will disrupt its integrity and unity, i.e., its capacity to achieve its goal, and this will lead to internal or external conflicts. Business ethics is the honest, respectful and fair conduct of a business and its representatives in all of its relations (Aras, 2006). An important question concerning the role of ethics in business is the question of why businesses should and do engage in ethical practices. Some authors, notably Milton Friedman (1962), would strongly deny that a business has a fiduciary responsibility to any group but the firm's stockholders.

To initiate corporate giving, for example, would be a fiduciary breach of management in Friedman's opinion: an agent for a principal is neither legally nor morally permitted to give away or 'waste' the principal's capital (Joyner and Payne, 2002). Milton Friedman also argued that 'there is only one social responsibility of business – use its resources and engage in activities designed to increase its profits so long as it . . . engages in open and free competition without deception and fraud' (Friedman, 1962).

However, ethical behaviour and ethical business has effects not only on stakeholders and shareholders but also on the entire economy. We believe that when we act ethically in the business decision-making process this will ensure more effective and productive utilisation of economic resources.

Ethical philosophies

One component of the change to a concern with social responsibility and accountability has been the recognition (or reinstatement) of the importance of ethics in organisational activity and behaviour. In part this can be considered to be a recognition of the changing societal environment of the present time and in part a recognition of the problems brought about through corporate activity taken without any account of ethical implications. Among such activity can be seen the many examples of pollution (e.g. Union Carbide at Bhopal, India or the Exxon Valdiz oil spill) and greed (such as the Enron incident). These have caused a rethinking of the role of ethics in organisation theory.

Ethics is, however, a problematical area as there is no absolute agreement as to what constitutes ethical (or unethical) behaviour. For each of us there is a need to consider our own ethical position as a starting point because that will affect our own view of ethical behaviour. The opposition provided by deontological ethics and teleological ethics (regarding the link between actions and outcomes; see below), and by ethical relativism and ethical objectivism (regarding the universality of a given set of ethical principles) represents key areas of debate and contention in the philosophy of ethics. This provides a starting point for our consideration of ethics.

Deontological ethics

According to deontologists, certain actions are right or wrong in themselves and so there are absolute ethical standards which need to be upheld. The problems with this position are questions of how to recognise which acts are wrong and how to distinguish between a wrong act and an omission. Philosophers such as Nagel argue that there is an underlying notion of right which constrains our actions, although this might be overridden in certain circumstances. Thus, there may be an absolute moral constraint against killing someone, which in time of war can be overridden.

Teleological ethics

Teleological theory distinguishes between 'the right' and 'the good', with 'the right' encompassing those actions which maximise 'the good'. Thus, it is outcomes which determine what is right, rather than the inputs (i.e. our actions), in terms of ethical standards. This is the viewpoint which is promoted by Rawls in his *A Theory of Justice*. Under this perspective, one's duty is to promote certain ends, and the principles of right and wrong organise and direct our efforts towards these ends.

Utilitarianism

We have discussed this extensively previously in Chapter 5 so you will remember that Utilitarianism is based upon the premise that outcomes are all that matter in determining what is good and that the way in which a society achieves its ultimate good is through each person pursuing his or her own self-interest. The philosophy states that the aggregation of all these self-interests will automatically lead to the maximum good for society at large. Some Utilitarians have amended this theory to suggest that there is a role for government in mediating between these individual actions to allow for the fact that some needs can best be met communally.

Ethical relativism

Relativism is the denial that there are certain universal truths. Thus, ethical relativism posits that there are no universally valid moral principles. Ethical relativism may be further subdivided into: 'conventionalism', which argues that a given set of ethics or moral principles are only valid within a given culture at a particular time; and 'subjectivism', which sees individual choice as the key determinant of the validity of moral principles.

According to the 'conventional' ethical relativism it is the mores and standards of a society which define what is moral behaviour and ethical standards are set, not absolutely, but according to the dictates of a given society at a given time. Thus, if we conform to the standards of our society then we are behaving ethically. We can see, however, that ethical standards change over time within one society and vary from one society to another; thus the attitudes and practices of the nineteenth century are different to our own, as are the standards of other countries.

A further problem with this view of ethics is that of how we decide upon the societal ethics to which we seek to conform. Thus there are the standards of society at large, the standards of our chosen profession and the standards of the peer group to which we belong. For example, the standards of society at large tend to be enshrined within the laws of that society. But how many of us rigorously abide by the speed limits of this country, for example.?

Different groupings within society tend to have different moral standards of acceptable behaviour and we have a tendency to behave differently at different times and when we are with different groups of people. Equally, when we travel to a foreign country we tend to take with us the ethical standards of our own country rather than changing to the different standards of the country which we are visiting. Thus, it becomes very difficult to hold to a position of ethical relativism because of the difficulty of determining the grouping to which we are seeking to conform.

Ethical objectivism

This philosophical position is in direct opposition to ethical relativism; it asserts that although moral principles may differ between cultures, some moral principles have universal validity whether or not they are universally recognised. There are two key variants of ethical objectivism: 'strong' and 'weak'. Strong ethical objectivism or 'absolutism' argues that there is one true moral system. Weak ethical objectivism holds that there is a 'core morality' of universally valid moral principles, but also accepts an indeterminate area where relativism is accepted.

There is no single theory of ethics because there is no single view about what is ethical. Each of us can identify ethical and unethical behaviour but only contextually in relation to our own beliefs. We can see, therefore, that each of these theories of ethics is problematical and that there is no overarching principle which determines either what is ethical or what is not. Nevertheless, a concern with ethics has been introduced explicitly into organisation theory and strategy in recent years. This has led to an increased interest in Corporate Social Responsibility.

Corporate behaviour

Corporate behaviour is important for company success both financially and concerning the relationship between corporate and business interests (stakeholders). We cannot define corporate behaviour without an ethical and CSR base in order to refer to that behavioural aspect. Corporate behaviour involves legal rules, ethical codes of conduct and social responsibility principles (Figure 6.1). In other words, corporate behaviour is based on all of these components and involves law, ethics and CSR. It is important to recognise also that this behaviour must be ethical but must also be seen to be ethical – perceptions are very important.

Corporate behaviour has effects not only on stakeholders and shareholders but also on the entire economy. When a corporation acts ethically and socially responsibly in its business decisions and strategic planning then that corporation will be more sustainable. As we have seen, socially responsible corporate behaviour is increasingly seen as essential to the long-term survival of companies.

CSR, ethics and corporate behaviour

Carroll (1979: 500) describes CSR in these terms: 'the social responsibility of business encompasses the economic, legal, ethical, and discretionary expectations that society has of organizations at a given point in time'. After his definition, in 2002 Whetten and colleagues defined CSR as 'societal expectations of corporate behaviour; a behaviour that is alleged by a stakeholder to be

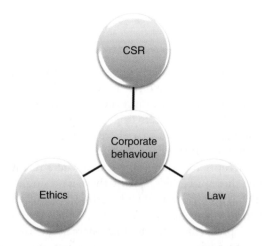

Figure 6.1   The components of corporate behaviour

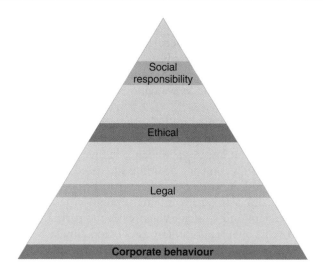

Figure 6.2   The corporate behaviour pyramid

expected by society or morally required and is therefore justifiably demanded of a business' (2002: 374). After the first definition, the CSR definition on the one hand expanded and covered more corporate behaviour and stakeholder expectation. On the other hand, some broad terms – especially society – have been narrowed to stakeholders.

Corporate behaviour towards the stakeholders is becoming a much more important concept in every definition. Corporate behaviour is an important concept because it has to be ethical, legal and responsible behaviour for organisations, stakeholders and society alike. This aspect of the corporate behaviour has more benefit for society also and so that is why it is more closely related to ethics and CSR. We have referred to stakeholders in other chapters, of course, and this is an increasingly important aspect of CSR.

To be a socially responsible corporation, a company must be more than a legal and ethical person also. CSR is not always a legal necessity; increasingly it is an obligation. However, a company has to be socially responsible even though it is not a legal obligation (Aras and Crowther, 2008) – which is one of the most important characteristics of CSR. These provide the platform (see Figure 6.2) upon which social responsibility is built.

Corporate reputation

One concept which is of growing importance for business management is that of corporate reputation. The beginning of the twenty-first century creates a new challenge for corporations – realising the potential of their corporate brands. In today's markets organisations focus on intangible factors in order to compete and differentiate their services/products in an environment that is characterised by rapid changes. The reputation of the corporation is often the most important factor in gaining a competitive advantage as well as building financial and social success.

Corporations are realising that possessing a well-known name, such as Johnson & Johnson, can help them secure a good position in the marketplace. Businesses are faced with not only sophisticated and informed stakeholders but also by rigorous regulation and evolving standards as well as by independent associations and agencies that act as watchdogs guarding the interests of their publics.

There are many benefits claimed for being perceived as having a good corporate reputation. One of the main benefits is that it improves shareholder value; a strong corporate reputation inspires confidence in investors, which in turn leads to a higher stock price for a company. It brings increased customer loyalty to the products of the company. A positive customer perception of a company extends to its products. Equally, a strong corporate reputation is an influential factor for forming partnerships and strategic alliances as the partner company has the potential to improve its own reputation by association. Similarly, a company with a solid reputation is more influential on legislative and regulatory governmental decision making.

Employee morale and commitment are higher at corporations with a good corporate reputation. At a time of crisis a good corporate reputation can shield the company from criticism and even blame, and can help it communicate its own point of view more easily to audiences that are willing to listen. A good example is the Pepsi Cola tampering case according to which products on sale were found to contain hypodermic syringes. Pepsi dealt effectively with the crisis by defusing public alarm with a public relations campaign that highlighted the integrity of its manufacturing process and its corporate credibility.

Marks & Spencer: a question of ethics

Marks & Spencer was probably the most successful retailer in the UK during the 1980s and early 1990s, and had expanded to many other countries throughout the world – then it all went wrong. After a variable period, things seemed to be going well again with prospects looking good. Then during the Spring of 2004 Philip Green, the Bhs and Arcadia owner, made a potential takeover offer for M&S which turned into one of the most extraordinary and dramatic business battles of the last few years. The bid from Green was based upon a value of 400p per share. From the moment Green's plans were first revealed, during the spring, the M&S Board was thrown into turmoil and there was a management shake-up which led to the ousting of the incumbent chief executive and chairman and the appointment of Stuart Rose. A vigorous campaign was mounted by the Board to claim that this offer substantially undervalued the company and its potential. The shareholders overwhelmingly agreed and the takeover offer was rejected.

It was only three months later, however, that the Board announced its intention of a share buyback – but at a price of 350p per share. This was of course significantly below the supposedly undervaluing offer of 400p per share. How had so much value been destroyed in such a short time?

Marks & Spencer chairman Paul Myners continued to insist that the earlier potential bid from Philip Green had undervalued the high street retailer. Myners was speaking to enable shareholders to vote on the retailer's £2.3 billion share buyback, designed to return proceeds from the sale of the M&S Money business, one of the initiatives implemented by new chief executive Stuart Rose.

M&S shareholders voted 99.56% in favour of the buyback plan. A 'yes' vote does not commit then to sell all or any shares, with some analysts expecting more institutional shareholders to take up the offer, whilst smaller investors are more likely to hold onto their stake to give Rose's strategy time to have an impact. The final take-up will set the exact price.

Responding to criticism that the buyback is priced at 350p a share, significantly below the final 400p a share Bhs and Arcadia owner Green was willing to offer, Myners said: 'A potential offer for all the company's shares is one thing. A move to repurchase a significant proportion of equity, leaving the rest in your hands, is entirely different.'

As far as the possible bid was concerned, the board concluded that the proposal of no more than 400p a share was a significant undervaluation of your business.

He said the rejection of Green's potential offer 'was not a promise to return the share price to 400p in a matter of months. No responsible board could make such a promise. The rejection was about the value of your investment over the longer term – as our plan begins to bear fruit.'

The question which this poses is the perennial one about whose interests the Board should be serving and whether it did so in this case. The evidence which exists does not suggest that the Board acted in the best interests of the owners of the business. This raises the issue of accountability. Of course, there might be much more evidence than we know about – which would raise the question of transparency. Unfortunately, all of this raises the question of ethics in relation to the Board's behaviour.

Creating value

The managers of most companies recognise that their function is to serve the needs of the owners of that business – in other words their shareholders. Thus the concept of creating shareholder value, as an objective for the business, appears to be widely accepted within the business community. Indeed, the creation of value for shareholders is frequently seen to be one of the objectives of the company which is stated in its annual report. What is much less frequently stated, however, is the means by which the managers of the business ensure that such value is created; indeed, the use of techniques as a quantified evaluation is less often found in practice.

The idea that the purpose of managing a business is to create value for the shareholders of that business is not, of course, a new idea. It has been commonly accepted that the arguments of Agency theory are not subject to questioning. Agency theory suggests that the management of an organisation is undertaken on behalf of the owners of that organisation – in other words the shareholders of the organisation. Consequently, the only concern surrounding the creation of value within an organisation is that it should accrue to the shareholders of that organisation, and that the purpose of the managers of the organisation is to find ways to increase that value. Thus, the managers of a company are expected to manage on behalf of the shareholders in order to increase the value of the company for the benefit of shareholders. As a reward, of course, they can be expected to benefit from that value created by means of the executive reward scheme. Implicit within this view of the management of the firm is that society at large, and consequently all other stakeholders to the organisation, will also benefit as a result of managing the performance of the organisation in this manner. From this perspective, therefore, the concerns are focused upon how to manage performance for the shareholders and how to report upon that performance.

This view of an organisation has, however, been extensively challenged by many writers over the last twenty years; such writers argue that the way to maximise performance for society at large is to both manage on behalf of all stakeholders and ensure that the value thereby created is not appropriated by the shareholders but is distributed to all stakeholders. At the same time, others argue that this debate is sterile and that organisations maximise value creation not by a concern with either shareholders or stakeholders but by focusing upon the operational objectives of the firm and assuming that value creation and equitable distribution will thereby follow.

Adherents to each of these conflicting philosophies regarding the method of managing a business in order to secure maximum value creation have a tendency to adopt different perspectives on the management and evaluation of performance. Thus, for one school of thought the correct way of managing and deciding upon priorities is assumed to be incorrect for the other schools of thought. For those concerned with managing on behalf of shareholders then one of the most important techniques for doing so has become known as Value-Based Management (VBM).

Value for shareholders

There has been a revival of interest in economic techniques to measure the value of a firm through the use of economic value added as a technique for measuring such value to shareholders. This technique, based upon the concept of economic value equating to total value, is founded upon the assumptions of classical liberal economic theory. Such techniques have been subject to criticism both from the point of view of the level of adjustment to published accounts needed to make the technique work and from the point of view of the validity of such techniques in actually measuring value in a meaningful context. Thus in this chapter we contrast this approach to managing the creation of value with more traditional techniques of measuring value created. We consider the merits of the respective techniques in explaining shareholder and managerial behaviour and the problems with using such techniques in considering the wider stakeholder concept of value.

The nature of the debate concerning the measurement and evaluation of corporate performance has broadened in recent years with the adoption of different perspectives and this has been reflected in the changing nature of corporate reporting. Thus, there has been a shift from an economic view of corporate performance measurement to an informational perspective with a recognition of the social implications of an organisation's activities. This has resulted in a shift from treating financial figures as the foundation of corporate performance measurement to treating them as part of a broader range of measures. At the same time, it has been argued that companies are no longer the instruments of shareholders alone but exist within society and so have responsibilities to that society.

The debate therefore seems to have moved away from the concerns of shareholders in the firm and away from the economic rationale for accounting towards a consideration of the wider stakeholder environment. At the same time, however, these concerns cannot be ignored and part of the debate has seen a return to economic values in assessing the performance of the firm. Thus some of the problems with accounting, such as the exclusion of risk and investment policies from the analysis, have been recognised and the concept of shareholder value and how this can be created and sustained has been addressed. Rappaport (1986) has developed a methodology of shareholder value, in which he argues that a shareholder value approach is the correct way of evaluating alternative company strategies, stating that the ultimate test of a corporate plan is whether it creates value for the shareholders, and that this is the sole method of evaluating performance. He identifies a conflict between the achievement of competitive advantage and creating shareholder value when he states:

> Increasingly, companies are becoming polarised into two camps: those who consider shareholder value the key to managing the company and those who put their faith in gaining competitive advantage. (1986: 85)

but argues that both are based upon long-term productivity.

The return to a consideration of the importance of economic value to the theory of the firm therefore is based upon the assumption that maximising the value of a firm to its shareholders also maximises the value of that firm to society at large. Within the debate, therefore, the concept of shareholder value is frequently mentioned and there is acceptance of the need to account for shareholder value within the practitioner community. Indeed, the annual reports of companies regularly show the creation of value for shareholders and it is frequently cited as a corporate objective. What is less clear, however, from an examination of such annual reports is precisely what is meant by this creation of shareholder value, which often seems to be used in a nebulous manner to indicate some desirable but unidentifiable objective.

This, it is argued, is because the managers of a firm are preoccupied with other objectives such as growth in size, turnover, market share or accounting returns, which are more easily measured. The achievement of these objectives is also often correlated with managerial rewards but less so with increasing shareholder value. Indeed, agency theory can be used to demonstrate how following managerial interests can lead to higher rewards for those managers at the expense of a reduction in the value of the company.

Value-based management

In recent years an alternative approach to managing an organisation has developed which is known as value-based management (VBM). In comparison with stakeholder management, VBM techniques have the advantage that they propose the use of a single metric to measure performance as well as set objectives and reward executives, and therefore appear far simpler and more appealing. There is, however, more to the VBM approach to managing an organisation than mere simplicity. Although there seems to have been a move away from the concerns of shareholders in the firm and the economic rationale for accounting towards a consideration of the wider stakeholder environment, this has not been universal. At the same time, there has been a recognition that the concerns of shareholders cannot be ignored and another argument has seen a return to economic values in assessing the performance of the firm. Broadly speaking this approach is known as value-based management – or, alternatively, shareholder value management. This approach is based upon a simple premise that the ultimate test of a corporate plan is whether it creates value for the shareholders, and that this is the sole method of evaluating performance.

This approach to managing an organisation is based upon the assumption that maximising the value of a firm to its shareholders also maximises the value of that firm to society at large. The concept of shareholder value as an objective appears to be widely accepted within the accounting community but its use as a quantified evaluation is less often found in practice. The central argument is based upon the inadequacy of traditional accounting and financial information to provide adequate information for corporate decision making.

Thus, it is argued that problems arise from the use of accounting measures as a means of evaluating company performance. Many people consider how the use of earnings per share can be of doubtful value in achieving this end, both because of the different calculations used for the same accounting measure and because of the adoption of different accounting measures. Equally, others argue that return on investment (ROI), return on assets (ROA) and return on equity (ROE) suffer from the same problem. The techniques of VBM are claimed to provide a solution to these problems through their different approach to using financial information for strategic decision making.

If that is the case then the techniques are important to understand and so we must start by considering exactly what it is that we are considering. Perhaps the most succinct definition of VBM has been provided by Copeland, Koller and Murrin (1996: 12), who state that it is:

> an approach to management whereby the company's overall aspiration, analytical techniques and management processes are all aligned to help the company maximise its value by focusing on the key drivers of value.

This definition implies a different approach to management but concomitantly a differing use made of accounting information. VBM therefore goes further than merely using accounting information differently as it also requires the application of appropriate measures of value to provide a 'shareholder value' perspective for all key internal planning and control systems – that is, strategic decision making, resource allocation, performance measurement and control, and managerial compensation. This is an important distinction between these techniques and other approaches to managing an organisation and this distinction and the implications arising from it need to be clearly understood. An important, if not fundamental, feature of all VBM approaches is this alignment of objectives, measures and rewards intended to promote shareholder value creation at all levels of the business.

In addition, VBM theoretically involves a shift away from the use of traditional accounting measures such as earnings per share and net profit, which are argued, by the proponents of VBM, to offer an unreliable guide to 'shareholder value creation'. In the place of such accounting measures, a number of alternative measures have been proposed which are intended to provide a 'calculating machine consistent with the principles of economic income'. The use of VBM techniques does not remove any concern for accounting measures. Instead, it replaces a concern with such measures as earning per share with a concern for maximising the net present value of the company. This can be achieved by improving the economic returns achieved on existing assets employed and by seeking new investments giving positive net present values. A recent development in the quest for a tool to measure shareholder value has been the concept of economic value added,[1] which has been developed by Stewart as a better measure to assess corporate performance and the creation of shareholder value than conventional accounting measures. Indeed, Stewart states that:

> Economic value added is an estimate, however simple or precise, of a business's true economic profit. (1995: 73)

Economic value added is claimed to have a number of important advantages over traditional accounting measures, the chief one being that economic performance is determined only after the making of a risk-adjusted charge for the capital employed in the business. Critics, however, argue that whilst this may be theoretically sound, the need to make arbitrary adjustments to standard accounting numbers in order to put the technique into practice makes the technique of doubtful validity.

The AA1000 reporting standard

The Institute of Social and Ethical Accountability (probably better known as AccountAbility) was established in London in 1995 with the stated aim to 'develop new tools, thinking and connections that enable individuals, institutions and alliances to respond better to global challenges'. The organisation has grown considerably and now has bases in Beijing, London, São Paulo and Washington, DC and Country Representatives in Brazil, Canada, China, Jordan, Spain, Sweden and the US. AccountAbility's work is closely related but not limited to the CSR field. The organisation is often labelled as a global think-tank, and has undertaken work in the areas of Responsible Competitiveness, Partnership Effectiveness, Collaborative Governance, Stakeholder Engagement and Sustainability Assurance and Reporting.

AccountAbility is a global network of leading business, public and civil institutions 'working to build and demonstrate the possibilities for tomorrow's global markets and governance through thought leadership and advisory services'. They work to:

- Enable open, fair and effective approaches to stakeholder engagement.
- Develop and reward strategies for responsible competitiveness in companies, sectors, regions and nations.
- Create and develop effective collaborative governance strategies for partnerships and multilateral organisations that are delivering innovation and value.
- Set and influence sustainability standards.

In 1999, AccountAbility published the AA1000 Assurance Standard with the aim of fostering greater transparency in corporate reporting. AccountAbility, an international, not-for-profit, professional institute has launched the world's first-ever assurance standard for social and sustainability reporting. The AA1000 framework (http://www.accountability.org.uk) is designed to improve accountability and performance by learning through stakeholder engagement. It was developed to address the need for organisations to integrate their stakeholder engagement processes into daily activities. It has been used worldwide by leading businesses, non-profit organisations and public bodies. The Framework is designed to help users establish a systematic stakeholder engagement process that generates the indicators, targets and reporting systems needed to ensure its effectiveness in overall organisational performance. The principle underpinning AA1000 is inclusivity. The building blocks of the process framework are planning, accounting and auditing, and reporting. It does not prescribe what should be reported on but rather the 'how'.

According to AccountAbility, the AA1000 Assurance Standard is the first initiative offering a non-proprietary, open-source Assurance standard covering the full range of an organisation's disclosure and associated performance (i.e., sustainability reporting and performance). It draws from and builds on mainstream financial, environmental and quality-related assurance, and integrates key learning with the emerging practice of sustainability management and accountability, as well as associated reporting and assurance practices.

AA1000 provides a set of tools to help organisations manage, measure and communicate their overall sustainability performance: social, environmental and economic. Together, they draw on a wide range of stakeholders and interests to increase the legitimacy of decision making and improve performance. Individually, each initiative supports the application of the other – at least this is the claim of both organisations concerned; AA1000 provides a rigorous process of stakeholder engagement in support of sustainable development.

Management for stakeholders

The competing basis for managing performance in an organisation is based upon stakeholder management theory. A stakeholder approach to managing the performance of an organisation is based upon the idea that all stakeholders are important and their objectives need taking into consideration. Numerous definitions of a stakeholder have been provided by various people, as we discussed earlier.

A stakeholder approach to managing an organisation can be considered to exist when the management of that organisation considers the impact of its operations on its stakeholders before making its decision. Due to the diverse nature and conflicting needs of the relevant stakeholders, it is necessary for this type of management to involve some form of trade-off. This implies that all stakeholders are taken into consideration before any decision is made but in reality when stakeholder theory is used as a managerial tool it is specifically concerned with identifying which stakeholders are more important and, as a result, should receive a greater proportion of management's time.

It has been suggested that there are three reasons for the importance of stakeholder theory:

- The first is that it is an accurate description of how management works. This implies that all management is a form of stakeholder management where the interests of different stakeholders are actually considered.
- The second argues that it is more morally and ethically correct for organisations to consider wider needs than purely concentrating on the needs of one group, usually taken to be shareholders. Thus, by adopting a stakeholder approach the objective of the firm is to be become a more ethical and more socially responsible organisation.
- The third view suggests that the reason for managing your stakeholders is to create shareholder wealth. This view suggests that shareholder wealth can be

created through the correct management of the other stakeholders and in this respect it is considered to have instrumental power.

The link between stakeholder performance and financial performance, its instrumental power, has been argued to exist for a number of reasons. Some suggest that a balance between the different stakeholder groups' interests is essential in ensuring that the organisation continues to be viable and achieves other performance goals. Others suggest that stakeholder management is a source of competitive advantage, as contracts between organisations and stakeholders will be on the basis of trust and cooperation and therefore less expense will be required in monitoring and enforcing such contracts. In a similar vein, numerous empirical studies have been performed in an attempt to find links between corporate social responsibility and financial performance.

An underlying assumption, which is not always explicitly recognised, is that an organisation should be operating for shareholders – that is they should be shareholder wealth maximising. Therefore stakeholder management, or corporate social responsibility, is not an end in itself but is simply seen as a means for improving economic performance. A fundamental aspect of stakeholder theory, in any of its aspects, is that it attempts to identify numerous different factions within a society to whom an organisation may have some responsibility. It has been criticised for failing to identify these factions satisfactorily although some attempts have been made. Indeed, attempts have been made by stakeholder theorists to provide frameworks by which the relevant stakeholders of an organisation can be identified. One suggestion is that a stakeholder is relevant if it has invested something in the organisation and is therefore subject to some risk from that organisation's activities. These stakeholders can be separated into two groups: the voluntary stakeholders, who choose to deal with an organisation, and the involuntary stakeholders, who do not choose to enter into – nor can they withdraw from – a relationship with the organisation.

Irrespective of which model is used, it is not controversial to suggest that there are some generic stakeholder groups that will be relevant to most organisations. Most people would recognise that the voluntary stakeholders include shareholders, investors, employees, managers, customers and suppliers, and each will require some value added or otherwise they can withdraw their stake and choose not to invest in that organisation again. Equally, most people would accept that involuntary stakeholders such as individuals, communities, ecological environments or future generations do not choose to deal with the organisation and therefore may need some form of protection, maybe through government legislation or regulation.

Stakeholder management has significant requirements for, often complex, informational to meet the needs of the various stakeholders. It is extremely difficult to manage on behalf of a variety of stakeholders if there is no measurement of how the organisation has performed for those stakeholders. Thus, for each stakeholder identified it is necessary to have a performance measure by which the stakeholder performance can be considered. Due to the nature of the stakeholders, and their relationship with the organisation, this will not necessarily be easy, nor will it necessarily be possible in monetary terms. Therefore non-financial measures will be of great importance but this information is often considered more subjective than financial information. Therefore measures of customer satisfaction are sometimes based on surveys and sometimes on statistical performance measures such as numbers of complaints or returns, or market share or customer retention. Recently there have been a number of multidimensional performance measurement frameworks that can be argued to have some level of stakeholder orientation.

Multidimensional performance management

Probably the best known of the multidimensional performance measurement frameworks is the 'balanced scorecard' (see Figure 6.3). Another example is the 'service profit chain' which specifically considers three stakeholders – namely employees, customers and shareholders. Again, this model specifically considers the first two stakeholders as means to achieving superior financial results. Thus it is argued that satisfied and motivated employees are essential if service quality is to be of a high standard and hence customers are to be satisfied. Further, it is then argued that satisfied customers provide the base for superior financial results. Both of these models acknowledge the needs of stakeholder groups and thus deem it necessary to measure performance for these groups but still target financial performance as the ultimate goal.

A stakeholder-managed organisation therefore attempts to consider the diverse and conflicting interests of its stakeholders and balance these interests equitably. The motivations for organisations to use stakeholder management may be in order to improve financial performance or social or ethical performance, however these may be measured. In order to be able to manage stakeholder interests adequately, it is necessary to measure the organisation's performance to these stakeholders and this can prove complicated and time-consuming.

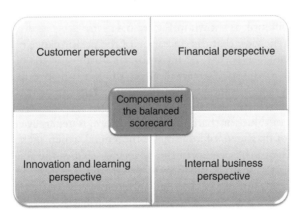

Figure 6.3   The balanced scorecard

Value creation and performance

We have already noted that there is considerable debate concerning the extent to which a firm should be either shareholder- or stakeholder-oriented, yet there is little evidence of how firms themselves regard this issue, or indeed whether and how firms currently identify and manage the needs and interests of their various stakeholder communities. One of the perennial debates surrounding shareholder value techniques and their implementation concerns the effect of such techniques upon other stakeholders to an organisation. One strand of the debate suggests that the maximisation of shareholder value automatically maximises, as a corollary, the value created in a business for other stakeholders. An opposing strand of the debate, however, suggests that this shareholder value is not necessarily created but instead is merely maximised through an expropriation of value from other stakeholders to the business.

It has been argued therefore by different parties that each of the following mutually exclusive hypotheses holds true:

(i) Value attributable to other stakeholders is sacrificed by companies in order to create higher levels of performance when judged in terms of stakeholder value.

(ii) Creating value for shareholders through the management process automatically creates value for other stakeholders.

For our purposes, there is little need to make this distinction and adopting the principles of VBM will resolve this issue. The creation of shareholder value, however, requires the management of the processes of the firm in an appropriate and consistent manner in order to achieve this end. This requires an understanding of the relationship between the various aspects of the management of that performance. In this respect it is possible to construct a three-part model to explore the relationship between the mission of the organisation, the techniques it employs in managing this mission and the outcomes in terms of reported performance. Such a model will look as shown in Figure 6.4.

Here we take the view that the operation of the performance management system of an organisation is that the intention of a firm in terms of its stakeholder priorities and its own aspirations will affect the performance management systems of the firm as well as its actual performance. This can be modelled as shown in Figure 6.5.

The creation of value for shareholders, therefore, is generally considered to be the prime task of managers of a business. In general, when such value is created then it will accrue to the owners of the business – that is, the shareholders – and either be returned to them in the form of dividends or invested in order to create further value in the future. Traditionally, therefore, the question of whether or not value has been created – or how much value has been created – has been measured in accounting terms by such measures as earnings per share or return on capital employed. These measures give a calculation of the value which has

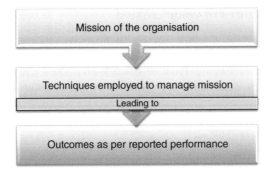

Figure 6.4   The relationship between mission and performance
Source: Adapted from Crowther, 2002.

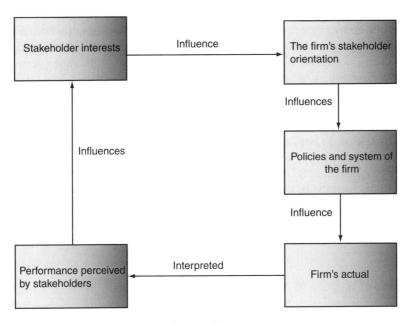

Figure 6.5   Operation of the performance management system
Source: Adapted from Crowther, 2002.

been created by shareholders but it is argued by those who propose the techniques of VBM that they do not give a correct calculation. Moreover, they give a calculation after the event whereas VBM techniques also give a means of evaluating the strategies which might be adopted by the managers of a business in order to create this value. Thus, VBM provides a means of managing a business and making decisions as well as a measure of what value has been created.

Traditional measures of value created

Managers make use of a whole variety of financial ratios in order to understand and calculate the performance of a business. You will remember from your study of the Managing Finance module that these can be classified into four different types, depending upon what they tell us about a company. These four classes are:

(1) Measures of profitability
(2) Measures of efficiency
(3) Measures of liquidity
(4) Measures of risk

In order to calculate the value which has been created for shareholders in a business, however, we need only concern ourselves with the first of these – measures of profitability. Profitability (revenues less expenses over a reporting period) ratios measure how efficiently a firm appears to be using its fixed assets – the more efficiently a company uses its assets the greater the profit it can get from their use and therefore the more value is created. The operating results are the most important for most private businesses and therefore it is the trading, profit and loss account (or income statement) that is of primary importance in providing the data for measuring profitability.

Such ratios include return on the capital employed in the business, return on total assets and on net assets, return on equity (net profits available to ordinary shareholders divided by common equity), return on sales and asset turnover, and the earnings per share. Interpreting calculations of financial ratios for profitability requires identifying the major factors we believe to be responsible for these changes. This usually requires us to extend our analysis to focus on management strategies to remedy or improve efficiency, productivity and thus profitability. We will return to this in Chapter 11.

Conclusion

Ethical behaviour and ethical business has effects not only on stakeholders and shareholders but also on the entire economy. We believe that when acting ethically in the business decision-making process this will ensure more effective and productive utilisation of economic resources. Corporate behaviour affects responsible and proper economic and institutional improvement. It will also be an influence on all society and a common benefit.

Additionally we can make the following points:

• Organisations affect the external environment – businesses and the wider global environment.
• The Gaia theory (see pp. 10–11) shows that the whole ecosphere forms a complete system, unlike classical liberal theory which postulates the independence of each entity.

- From 1970 there have developed theories and regulations to include all stakeholders inside and outside the organisation.
- Corporate reputation is an increasingly important factor for organisations.
- Ethics has been reinstated as a standard for organisational activity.
- Corporate Social Responsibility (CSR) as a subject indicates concern with social and environmental effects of organisational behaviour.

Summary of key points

- Ethical understanding differs according to the philosophy we follow.
- The social responsibility of business covers a number of issues and is dependent upon what is considered important at that time.
- Corporate reputation is increasingly important.
- Managing according to shareholder expectations or stakeholder expectations are alternatives which are subject to debate.
- VBM techniques have the advantage that they propose the use of a single metric to measure performance as well as set objectives and reward executives.
- Ethical behaviour and ethical business has effects not only for stakeholders and shareholders but also for the entire economy.

Definitions of key terms and theories

Deontological ethics holds that there are absolute ethical standards which need to be upheld.

Ethical objectivism asserts that some moral principles have universal validity whether or not they are universally recognised.

Ethical relativism is the denial that there are certain universal truths.

Ethics is the natural and structural process of acting in line with moral judgements, standards and rules.

A **stakeholder management** approach is based upon the idea that all stakeholders are important and their objectives need taking into consideration.

Teleological ethics distinguishes between right and good.

Value-based management (VBM) is a technique for managing on behalf of shareholders.

Test your understanding

1. Why are there different ethical philosophies?
2. Why does a company have to be ethical?
3. What is the relationship between corporate mission and performance?
4. List three measures of performance.
5. What is the opposite approach to stakeholder management?
6. What is the difference between ethical objectivism and ethical relativism?

Suggestions for further reading

Bhattacharya, C. B. and Sen, S. 2004. 'Doing Better at Doing Good: When, Why and How Consumers Respond to Corporate Social Initiatives', *California Management Review*, 47, 1: 9–24.

Clarkson, M. B. E. 1995. 'A Stakeholder Framework for Analysing and Evaluating Corporate Social Performance', *Academy of Management Review*, 20, 1: 92–117.

Joyner, B. E. and Payne, D. 2002. 'Evolution and Implementation: A study of Values, Business Ethics and Corporate Social Responsibility', *Journal of Business Ethics*, 41: 297–311.

Kell, G. 2003. 'The Global Compact: Origins, Operations, Progress, Challenge', *Journal of Corporate Citizenship*, 11: 35–49.

Simms, A. and Boyle, D. 2010. *Eminent Corporations*. London: Constable.

Note

1. The term Economic Value Added (EVA) is copyrighted as the property of Stern Stewart & Co.

References

Aras, G. 2006. 'The Ethical Issues in the Finance and Financial Markets', in David Crowther and Kıymet Caliyurt (eds), *Globalization and Social Responsibility*. Cambridge: Scholars Press.

Aras, G. and Crowther, D. 2008. 'The Social Obligation of Corporations', *Journal of Knowledge Globalisation*, 1, 1: 43–59.

Carroll, A. B. 1979. 'A Three-Dimensional Conceptual Model of Corporate Social Performance; *Academy of Management Review*, 4: 497–505.

Copeland, T., Koller, T. and Murrin, J. 1996. *Valuation: Measuring and Managing the Value of Companies*. New York: John Wiley & Sons.

Crowther, D. 2002. *Creating Shareholder Value*. London: Spiro.

Friedman, M. 1962. *Capitalism and Freedom*. Chicago: University of Chicago Press.

Joyner, B. E. and D. Payne 2002. 'Evolution and Implementation: A Study of Values, Business Ethics and Corporate Social Responsibility', *Journal of Business Ethics*, 41: 297–311, 2002.

Rappaport, A. 1986. *Creating Shareholder Value*. New York: The Free Press.

Stern Stewart and Co. 1995. *The EVA Company*. New York: The Free Press.

Whetten, D. A., Rands, G. and Godfrey, P. 2002. 'What Are the Responsibilities of Business to Society?' in A. Pettigrew, H. Thomas,and R. Whittington (eds), *Handbook of Strategy and Management*. London: Sage, pp. 373–408.

Stakeholders

7

Learning objectives

After studying this chapter you should be able to:

- Identify a range of stakeholders and describe their interests in the organisation.
- Understand and explain proxy stakeholders.
- Outline a typology of pressure groups.
- Consider the relationship between stakeholders.
- Explain the environment as a stakeholder.
- Discuss analysing stakeholder relationships.

Introduction

In the first chapter we considered the social contract as a way of explaining the relationship between corporations and individual and society. We now need to expand upon that and consider it in relationship to stakeholders and to Stakeholder theory. This theory[1] is one of the major influences on CSR. It was created by Freeman in his 1984 book.

So we need to start by describing exactly what a stakeholder is. There are several definitions. The most common ones are:

- Those groups without whose support the organisation would cease to exist.
- Any group or individual who can affect or is affected by the achievement of the organisation's objectives.

We can see from these definitions that a lot of people can be a stakeholder to an organisation. The most common groups who we consider to be stakeholders include:

- Managers
- Employees
- Customers
- Investors
- Shareholders
- Suppliers

Then there are also some more generic groups who are often included:

- Government
- Society at large
- The local community

Many people consider that only people can be stakeholders to an organisation. Some people extend this and say that the environment can be affected by organisational activity. These effects of the organisation's activities can take many forms, such as:

- the utilisation of natural resources as a part of its production processes;
- the effects of competition between itself and other organisations in the same market;
- the enrichment of a local community through the creation of employment opportunities;
- transformation of the landscape due to raw material extraction or waste product storage;
- the distribution of wealth created within the firm to the owners of that firm (via dividends) and the workers of that firm (through wages) and the effect of this upon the welfare of individuals;
- pollution caused by increased volumes of traffic and increased journey times because of those increased volumes of traffic.

Thus, many people also consider that there is an additional stakeholder to an organisation, namely:

The environment

and we consider some of the implications of this later in the chapter. As we will see in forthcoming chapters, the actions of an organisation can also have a big effect upon future possibilities. It is for this reason that we also add one extra stakeholder:

The future.

It should be noted, however, that others do not generally include the future as a stakeholder.

So it is possible to describe the stakeholders in terms of their distance from the organisation:

Figure 7.1   Stakeholders of the organisation

And it should be noted that the purposes of the corporation have been subject to debate for a considerable period of time.

> There is no reason to think that shareholders are willing to tolerate an amount of corporate non-profit activity which appreciably reduces either dividends or the market performance of the stock. (Hetherington, 1973: 37)
>
> every large corporation should be thought of as a social enterprise; that is an entity whose existence and decisions can be justified insofar as they serve public or social purposes. (Dahl, 1972: 18)

Multiple stakeholding

It is normal to consider all of these stakeholder groups separately. It should be noted, however, that each person will belong to several stakeholder groups at the same time. For example, a single person might be a customer of an organisation and also an employee and a member of the local community and of society at large. He or she may also be a shareholder and a member of a local environmental association and therefore concerned about the environment. Most probably that person will also be concerned about the future, on their own behalf or on behalf of their children.

We can therefore see that it is often not helpful to consider each stakeholder group in isolation and to separate their objectives. Reality is more complex and often there are conflicting pressures upon people because they belong to different stakeholder groupings.

The classification of stakeholders

There are two main ways to classify stakeholders:

Internal v. external

Internal stakeholders are those included within the organisation such as employees or managers whereas external stakeholders are such groups as suppliers or customers who are not generally considered to be a part of the organisation. Although this classification is fine it becomes increasingly difficult in a modern organisation to distinguish the two types when employees might be subcontractors and suppliers might be another organisation within the same group.

Voluntary v. involuntary

Voluntary stakeholders can choose whether or not to be a stakeholder to an organisation whereas involuntary stakeholders cannot. For example, an employee can choose to leave the employment of the organisation and therefore is a voluntary stakeholder. The local society or the environment are not able to make this choice and must therefore be considered to be involuntary stakeholders.

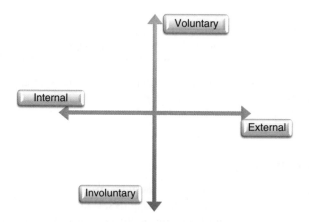

Figure 7.2   Dimensions of stakeholders

Stakeholder theory

The argument for Stakeholder theory is based upon the assertion that maximising wealth for shareholders fails to maximise wealth for society and all its members and that only a concern with managing all stakeholder interests achieves this.

Stakeholder theory states that all stakeholders must be considered in the decision-making process of the organisation. The theory states that there are three reasons why this should happen:

(1) It is the morally and ethically correct way to behave.
(2) Doing so actually also benefits the shareholders.
(3) It reflects what actually happens in an organisation.

As far as this third point is concerned then this is supported by research from Cooper and colleagues (2001) into large firms. This research shows that the majority of firms are concerned with a range of stakeholders in their decision-making process (see Figure 7.3).

According to this theory, stakeholder management, or corporate social responsibility, is not an end in itself but is simply seen as a means for improving economic performance. This assumption is often implicit although it is clearly stated by Atkinson, Waterhouse and Wells (1997) and is actually inconsistent with the ethical reasons for adopting stakeholder theory. Instead of stakeholder management improving economic, or financial, performance, therefore, it is argued that a broader aim of corporate social performance should be used (Jones and Wicks, 1999).

Furthermore, Jones and Wicks note that certain ethicists need no instrumental justification as moral behaviour 'is, and must be, its own reward'. Waddock and Graves (1997) consider whether stakeholder management enhances corporate social performance, as opposed to financial performance, and they find a positive relationship.

A fundamental aspect of stakeholder theory, in any of its aspects, is that it attempts to identify numerous different factions within a society to whom an

	Concerned with	Very concerned with
Stakeholder	%	%
Customers	89	57
Employees	89	51
Shareholders	100	78
Suppliers	70	3
The environment	62	5
Society	73	3

Figure 7.3   Stakeholder inclusion in decision making

organisation may have some responsibility. It has been criticised for failing to identify these factions (Argenti, 1993), although some attempts have been made. Indeed, Sternberg (1997) suggests that the second of Freeman's definitions of stakeholder, which is now the more commonly used, has increased the number of stakeholders to be considered by management adopting a stakeholder approach; in fact this definition includes virtually everything whether alive or not.

However, attempts have been made by stakeholder theorists to provide frameworks by which the relevant stakeholders of an organisation can be identified. Clarkson (1995) suggests that a stakeholder is relevant if they have invested something in the organisation and are therefore subject to some risk from that organisation's activities. He separated these into two groups: the voluntary stakeholders, who choose to deal with an organisation, and the involuntary stakeholders, who do not choose to enter into – nor can they withdraw from – a relationship with the organisation. Mitchell, Agle and Wood (1997) develop a framework for identifying and ranking stakeholders in terms of their power, legitimacy and urgency. If a stakeholder is powerful, legitimate and urgent then its needs will require immediate attention and be given primacy.

Irrespective of which model is used, it is not controversial to suggest that there are some generic stakeholder groups that will be relevant to all organisations. Clarkson (1995) suggests that the voluntary stakeholders include shareholders, investors, employees, managers, customers and suppliers and they will require some value added or otherwise they can withdraw their stake and choose not to invest in that organisation again. It is argued that involuntary stakeholders such as individuals, communities, ecological environments or future generations do not choose to deal with the organisation and therefore may need some form of protection, maybe through government legislation or regulation. Other more specific interest groups may be relevant for certain industries due to the nature of the industry or the specific activities of the organisation.

For example, utility industries have been regulated by a regulator since privatisation and thus the regulator is a stakeholder of these organisations. Similarly, certain industries are more environmentally, politically or socially sensitive than others and therefore attract more attention from these stakeholder groups; again the water or nuclear industries provide examples here.

Mount Eyjafjallajökull

There are a considerable number of dormant volcanoes in the world and an even greater number of volcanoes which only erupt occasionally. They potentially cause a great threat to the local residents – with perhaps Vesuvius being the best known example. In AD79 it erupted and buried Pompeii and its sister city, Herculaneum. Since then it has erupted at least 50 times but today 2 million people live within its vicinity.

Sometimes, however, these volcanoes have a much more dramatic effect. So, in early 2010, Mount Eyjafjallajökull in Iceland erupted and expelled a large quantity of volcanic ash into the atmosphere. This went on for some days, and intermittently for several weeks causing large clouds of volcanic ash to spread over much of Europe and parts of North America, depending upon where the prevailing winds blew it. As a consequence, flying was deemed to be unsafe and much airspace was closed to flights for considerable periods of time, causing much disruption to passengers and commerce. The airspace was closed because of safety fears. This was largely based upon an incident which happened in 1982 when a British Airways flight over Indonesia suffered engine problems whilst flying over a volcano. Since then operational procedures have been changed to prevent similar incidents but manufacturers issued no information about the safety of their engines in such circumstances.

The general approach taken by airspace regulators was that if the ash concentration rose above zero, then the airspace was considered unsafe and was consequently closed. The April 2010 eruption of this volcano caused considerable disruption and economic difficulties. As a consequence, pressure from various stakeholders – including the airlines, businesses and passengers/customers – was intense and so aircraft manufacturers were forced to define specific limits on how much ash is considered acceptable for a jet engine to ingest without damage. Initially, the Civil Aviation Authority, in conjunction with engine manufacturers, set new guidelines which allowed aircraft to fly when there are levels of volcanic ash between 200 and 2000 microgrammes of ash per cubic metre. These levels were declared by governments, aircraft manufacturers and airlines not to have safety implications if appropriate maintenance and ash inspection procedures were followed. A few weeks later – after further disruptions – the limits were further revised and the safe limit was increased to 4mg per cubic metre of air space. Subsequently, new technology is also under testing.

It is generally accepted that the problem with Eyjafjallajökull was caused by global warming melting the glacier around it. This shows the power of the environment as a stakeholder to business whereas the response to the problems illustrates the power of the various stakeholders involved to make changes and the necessity for corporations to be responsive to stakeholder demands.

Informational needs

Stakeholder management has significant informational needs. It is extremely difficult to manage for a variety of stakeholders if there is no measurement of how the organisation has performed for those stakeholders. Thus, for each stakeholder identified it is necessary to have a performance measure by which the stakeholder performance can be considered. Due to the nature of the stakeholders and their relationship with the organisation, this will not necessarily be easy nor will it necessarily be possible in monetary terms.

Therefore non-financial measures will be of great importance, but this information is often considered more subjective than financial information. Therefore measures of customer satisfaction are sometimes based on surveys and sometimes on statistical performance measures such as numbers of complaints or returns, or market share or customer retention. Recently there have been a number of multidimensional performance measurement frameworks that can be argued to have some level of stakeholder orientation.

Probably the best known of the multidimensional performance measurement frameworks is the 'balanced scorecard' (Kaplan and Norton, 1992; 1993; 1996a; 1996b). Another example is the service profit chain (Heskett *et al.*, 1994) that specifically considers three stakeholders: namely, employees, customers and shareholders. Again this model specifically considers the first two stakeholders as means to achieving superior financial results.

Thus they argue that satisfied and motivated employees are essential if service quality is to be of a high standard and hence customers are to be satisfied. Further, it is then argued that satisfied customers provide the base for superior financial results. Both of these models acknowledge the needs of stakeholder groups and thus deem it necessary to measure performance for these groups but still target financial performance as the ultimate goal. A stakeholder-managed organisation therefore attempts to consider the diverse and conflicting interests of its stakeholders and balance these interests equitably.

Recently the Centre for Business Performance, Cranfield University, UK, has set up a 'Catalogue of measures' related to their Performance Prism that contains measures of each of the 'dimensions of performance' – stakeholder satisfaction; strategies; processes; capabilities; and stakeholder contributions. The stakeholders identified were customer, employee, investor, regulator and community, and suppliers, and in total the catalogue includes over 200 relevant measures.

This shows the vast number of stakeholder measures that could be used to evaluate any organisation, although it is not expected that all of these will be relevant for an individual organisation. This again highlights the potential complexity of measuring performance for stakeholders as these numerous measures will provide conflicting evidence on performance that somehow must be reconciled. In comparison, VBM techniques that propose the use of a single metric to measure performance as well as set objectives and reward executives appear far simpler.

Regulation and its implications

As we will see later in the book, the disclosure of the actions of the firm in terms of their impact upon the external environment is essentially voluntary in nature – but this does not necessarily mean that the actions themselves are always voluntary. Nor does it mean that all such disclosure is necessarily voluntary.

The regulatory regime which operates in any particular country means that certain actions must be taken by firms which affect their influence upon the external environment. Equally certain actions are prevented from being taken. These actions and prohibitions are controlled by means of regulation imposed by the government of that country – both the national government and local government.

For example, those regulations probably govern the type of discharges which can be made by organisations, particularly when these are considered to cause pollution. Such regulations govern the way in which waste must be disposed of and the level of pollutants allowed for discharges into rivers, as well as restricting the amount of water which can be extracted from rivers.

The regulatory regime which operates in every country is continuing to change and become more restrictive as far as the actions of an organisation and its relationship with the external environment are concerned.[2] It seems reasonable to expect these changes to continue into the future and concern for the environmental impact of the activities of organisations to increase. These regulations tend to require reporting on the activities of organisations and such reporting also involves an accounting connotation.

This accounting need is to satisfy regulatory requirements but also to meet the internal needs of the organisation. This is because the managers of that organisation, in both controlling current operations and planning future business activities, must have accounting data to help manage the organisational activities in this respect. The growth of environmental data, as part of the management information systems of organisations, therefore can be seen to be, at least in part, driven by the needs of society at large. In this way it is reflected in the regulations imposed upon the activities of organisations.

Environmental impact reporting

As the extent of regulation of such activities can be expected to increase in the future, therefore, the more forward-looking and proactive organisations might be expected to have a tendency to extend their environmental impact reporting in anticipation of future regulation, rather than merely reacting to existing regulation.

It should not be thought, however, that the increase in stature and prominence accorded to environmental accounting and reporting among organisations is driven entirely by present and anticipated regulations. To a large extent the external reporting of such environmental impact is not determined by regulations – these merely require reporting to the appropriate regulatory body. Nor can it be argued that the increasing multinational aspect of organisational activity, and the consequent need to satisfy regulatory regimes from different countries, has alone driven the increased importance of environmental accounting.

Organisations which choose to report externally upon the impact of their activities on the external environment tend to do so voluntarily. In doing so, they expect to derive some benefit from this kind of accounting and reporting. The kind of benefits which organisations can expect to accrue through this kind of disclosure will be considered later. At this point, however, we should remember the influence of stakeholders upon the organisation and it can be suggested that increased disclosure of the activities of the organisation is a reflection of the growing power and influence of stakeholders, without any form of legal ownership, and the recognition of this influence by the organisation and its managers.

When the UK government, for example, initiated its process of the privatisation of nationally owned utilities it was felt necessary to compensate for the inadequacy of the market mechanism for mediating between the conflicting needs of the stakeholders to these industries. Thus the concept of regulation was devised, with appropriate bodies formed, to compensate for the imperfections of competition in the quasi-markets that came into being.

One of the functions of the regulators created in this manner was to control the prices charged by these privatised utilities in order to ensure that the benefits and efficiencies gains vaunted as a benefit of privatisation were shared between shareholders and other stakeholders, principally the customers. Thus, the regulators were to act as the very visible, 'invisible' hand of the market. The main mechanism for this has been achieved by means of a periodic review of pricing policy. For other industries, however, the effects of regulation vary in extent but in general terms can be stated to be increasing over time, and this increase can be expected to continue into the future.

Environmental issues and stakeholders

There are, of course, a number of important issues concerning the environment which are affecting companies and there are a wide variety of stakeholders who are involved and representing – or claiming to represent – the environment. It is obvious, of course, that the environment is not able to speak for itself and thus these other groups are representing the environment. This is known as proxy stakeholding and can be quite important in a wide variety of contexts. It should be noted, however, that all proxy stakeholders claim to represent the environment but have different opinions and this is one of the dangers of proxies – they do not necessarily represent what they claim to represent. We will return to this in Chapter 11 in the context of performance measurement. At this point, therefore, let us proceed to look at some of the topical environmental issues.

Water

In many parts of the world, water is becoming a serious problem. Irrigation has led to serious problems in such parts of the world as California whilst in Uzbekistan it has led to the shrinking of the Aral Sea to a fraction of its previous size. And many rivers, in all parts of the world, have so much water extracted from them that they no longer reach the sea. At the same time, millions of people do not have access to safe drinking water. And countries are entering into disputes with each other for access to water that they share between them. Indeed, access to water is forecast to become a major source of conflict in the twenty-first century.

Resource depletion

Obviously the resources of the planet are finite and this is a limiting factor to growth and development which we will consider to a considerable extent in this book. The depletion of the resources of the planet, however, is one of the actors which has helped create the current interest in sustainability. Of particular concern are the extractive industries and such things as aluminium are becoming in short supply. In the UK the mineral resources such as tin and lead were fully extracted long ago and the thriving industries based around them are long gone. As other resources – such as coal – are extracted in total then the companies based upon them disappear, as do the jobs in those industries. This is an obvious source of concern for people.

Of particular concern is the extinguishing of supplies of oil, because much economic activity is only possible because of energy created by the use of oil. Indeed, many would argue that the wars in the Middle East,[3] particularly the problems in Iraq and Iran, are caused by oil shortages, actual or impending, and the problems thereby caused rather than by any concern for political issues. Most people have now heard of Hubbert's Peak and engaged with the debate as to whether or not it has been reached. Certainly it has in parts of the world such as the USA and the North Sea but it is less certain whether it has been reached for the world as a whole. Nevertheless, the whole crux of sustainability – and sustainable development – is based upon the need for energy and there are insufficient alternative sources of energy to compensate for the elimination of oil as a source of fuel. Consequently, resource depletion, real or imagined, and particularly as it relates to energy resources, is one of the most significant causes of the current interest in sustainability.

Hubbert's Peak

In 1956 Dr King Hubbert, a geologist working for Shell Oil, developed his theory about the depletion of finite resources like fossil fuels. Now commonly known as Hubbert's peak, his theory explains that production rates of oil and gas will

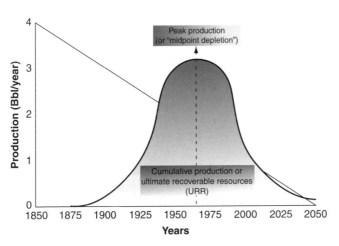

Figure 7.4   Hubbert's Peak

increase to a peak and then rapidly taper off as reserves are depleted. He developed his theory to explain the coming reduction in production of oil in the USA and it is generally accepted that his theory was correct about this. It is now generally accepted that in the world this peak has either already arisen or is on the point of arising – hence the current concern regarding energy production.

Competition

As resources become more obviously finite then the competition for the use of them necessarily increases. Globalisation, of course, necessarily increases the scale of the competition, which has become worldwide rather than local. The drive for growth, of course, exacerbates this as each company thereby requires more of the finite resources, and competition therefore increases. The advent of China into the global economy with its double-digit growth rate has highlighted this issue about the increased competition for finite resources. These are all issues which we will return to at various times in this book because they are very significant for any analysis of sustainability. They are also all things with which most people are familiar and therefore are some of the factors which have caused the current interest in sustainability and the possibilities or limitations for sustainable development.

A typology of environmental pressures

As we stated, there are a number of proxy stakeholders for the environment. They can be considered to have different objectives and a typology can be constructed which is based upon the aims of the particular types of pressure groupings. However, six different categories of pressure group can be identified, as shown in Figure 7.5.

International environmental organisations

This grouping naturally contains the largest organisations and also those organisations which tend to have the greatest public profile. This profile is achieved partly because they have the resources to generate such a profile through campaigning and partly because they have the skills to exploit the media to ensure maximal coverage. The declared aim of such groups is the protection of the global environment in its broadest context and probably the most familiar of such organisations would be Greenpeace and Friends of the Earth. Such organisations operate at all levels from the global, when considering issues such as nuclear testing by the French or whaling by anyone, to a national level when dealing with such issues as the disposal of North Sea oil platforms, and also to a local level when dealing with community issues such as the provision of cycle paths for a local community.

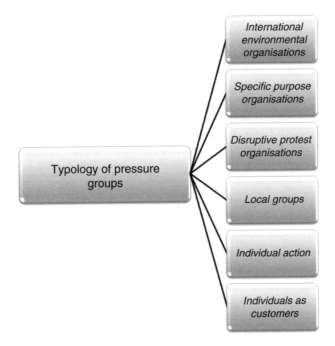

Figure 7.5   Categories of pressure group

The *modus operandi* of these organisations is to target specific organisations through specific campaigns and to use their resources, even illegitimately if this increases their impact, for specific ends. These campaigns have the effect of polarising opinion about the specific issues they are concerned with and using the emotional power of 'the environment' to achieve success. This is sometimes regardless of whether or not the scientific arguments can withstand scrutiny, as in the case of the disposal of the Brent Spar oil platform. Nevertheless, such organisations have had a significant impact upon the operating procedures of certain businesses, and hence their performance reporting systems, whilst leaving other businesses untouched.

Specific purpose organisations

These organisations tend to be organised on either an international basis or a national basis, depending upon their objectives, but the distinguishing feature is the limitation of their purpose to the achieving of a particular objective. Thus, an international organisation such as the World Wildlife Fund is concerned with the protection of wildlife globally whilst a national group such as the Royal Society for the Protection of Birds is concerned solely with bird life in the UK, extending its operation overseas only to the extent that what happens to migratory birds overseas can impact upon their welfare in the UK. Other organisations are UK-based but concerned with issues overseas, such as the Woodland Trust, which is concerned with the preservation, through acquisition, of forest. Still other organisations purport to be international whilst being totally UK-based. An example of such an organisation is Compassion in World Farming which, despite its name, is concerned primarily with farm animal welfare in the UK and to a lesser extent the EC. These organisations all tend to operate through the mobilising of mass opinion and only seek to exert influence on business organisations when these organisations have a direct impact upon the issue with which they are concerned. Such issues tend to be discrete issues of limited temporal extent, such as the construction of a new reservoir or mine. Their impact upon organisational performance and reporting systems therefore is likely to be limited in extent.

Disruptive protest organisations

The use of disruptive techniques as a means of securing political ends has an extensive history and some record of effectiveness.[4] Success has a tendency to change the discourse surrounding such activity from one of illegitimacy to one of legitimacy. The use of terrorist organisation and methods has been extended in recent years to the arena of environmental issues. This has been manifest in the violent and destructive tactics of organisations such as the Animal Liberation Front, the obstructive tactics of such people as Ecoprotestors in their opposition to road-building programmes,[5] and the disruptive tactics of such people as Reclaim the Streets in gaining maximum media coverage from their non-violent programme of closing major streets in London for periods of time. The Anti-Globalisation Movement has made extensive use of such tactics in its protesting. The discourse surrounding environmental terrorism is one of illegitimacy, depending upon whether one considers that the ends justify the means or not. Their impact upon legitimate organisations tends to be one of increasing transaction costs for the firms targeted, or for society at large, rather than any long-term change in behaviour. Chaliand (1987) has argued that a successful terrorist organisation needs a base in society which extends beyond its membership and needs popular support in order to exist and achieve results. One way to negate the power base of such an organisation is to subsume the aims of the organisation within popular discourse and thereby negate its impact. The environmental impact reporting of an organisation is one way of achieving this subsumption and perhaps is one reason why such protest groups have had little impact upon organisational behaviour.

Local groups

Large numbers of local groupings exist for the purpose of exerting pressure on organisations because of concern about a particular environmental issue. Such groups tend to have a purely local interest in a particular environmental issue and to be concerned with a particular locality. Examples would include groups concerned with the protection of a particular site from use in the building or extractive industries. Other examples include both groups concerned with pressure for reducing traffic congestion through the construction of a bypass and conversely groups concerned with preventing the construction of a bypass because of its environmental impact.[6] The essential feature of such groups is their temporary nature due to their concern with a specific aim; once their objective is past and their pressure group has met with either success or failure then the reason for their existence ceases. At this time the grouping tends to disintegrate, although individuals active within such a group may well feel motivated to become involved in further environmental issues through joining or starting another pressure group. Due to the ephemeral nature of these local issues groups and the fact that they tend be concerned with purely local issues, the impact which they have upon organisational performance reporting systems tends to be minimal, unless the issues can be brought to general public attention and gain the involvement of some larger group.

Individual action

Large numbers of people, as individuals, are concerned about environmental issues, either in general or about specific issues, but do not associate with others in a pressure group. This does not necessarily mean that such people do not take any action but rather that the action taken is not in concert with others. Thus, individuals acting alone often take action in the form of lobbying by writing to influential people, writing to the organisation concerned and writing to members of parliament asking for action to be taken, or not taken, depending upon the issues in hand and the institution which they are contacting. Equally, individuals acting alone often ignore the dominant economic rationality[7] and act in a non-price discriminatory manner in selecting the goods and services which they choose to consume because of their concern about the environmental impact of certain organisations as opposed to others. Thus, the debate concerning genetically modified foods available in supermarkets has been affected by individuals choosing not to purchase such foods.[8] This has had the effect of some supermarkets (e.g. Sainsbury's) making alternatives available and other supermarkets (e.g. Somerfield) excluding such foods from their stores.

Individuals as customers

Individuals acting alone are customers of some organisations and their actions can affect the behaviour of those organisations. Indeed, this is one course of action selected by some of the larger pressure groups through attempting a boycott of the services of particular organisations. Thus, for example, Europe-wide boycotts of Shell petrol stations by individuals had some affect upon the company changing its mind about its proposed disposal of the Brent Spar oil platform. Equally, campaigns exist from time to time to boycott the purchase of the goods of certain food producers because of concern regarding fishing policy for some of the food products used by that producer – e.g. catching tuna by line rather than net because of the adverse impact upon dolphins caused by the use of nets. Such campaigns can influence the organisations concerned and change their operating procedures, and hence their performance reporting, but in doing so it needs to be recognised that the power relationship is significant. Individual customers acting alone have little power to influence large organisations and it requires significant numbers of individuals acting in the same way to exert suffi-cient influence to bring about a change in policy. It is for this reason that success through acting in this way tends to be limited and to be focused upon one issue at a time.

Not all customers of organisations, however, are individuals, and many organi-sations have other organisations – often large and hence powerful organisations – as their customers. Pressure from such customers can provide a very powerful motive for changing operating procedures and reporting systems. Thus, for example, retailing companies can take decisions not to stock certain goods – such as British beef, tuna caught by nets rather than lines, or goods which are excessively packaged – and affect the policies of the producers of these products very directly. These retailers may be responding to pressure brought upon them by individuals acting as customers or may be taking a proactive stance because of the expectation of longer-term competitive advantage. Whatever the reason, such organisations are in a position to affect the performance of their supplying organisations. Customer power can therefore vary from low to high depending upon the power of the individual customer.

Cyrus and human rights

In 1879, during the excavations of the ruins of Babylon (in what is now Iran), a clay cylinder was uncovered which proved to be extraordinarily important. After translation it proved to be a copy of an edict issued by Kourosh (better known in the UK as Cyrus the Great) and has become known as the Kourosh Cylinder, which can be found in the British Museum. The translation of the cylinder starts:

> I am Kourosh, King of the world, great king, mighty king, king of Babylon, king of the land of Sumer and Akkad, king of the four quarters . . .

And continues:

> I announce that I will respect the traditions, customs and religions of the nations of my empire and never let any of my governors and subordinates look down on or insult them until I am alive. From now on, till (Ahura) Mazda grants me the kingdom favour, I will impose my monarchy on no nation. Each is free to accept it, and if any one of them rejects it, I never resolve on war to reign. Until I am the king of Iran, Babylon, and the nations of the four directions, I never let anyone oppress any others, and if it occurs, I will take his or her right back and penalize the oppressor.

> And until I am the monarch, I will never let anyone take possession of mov-able and landed properties of the others by force or without compensation.

Until I am alive, I prevent unpaid, forced labour. To day, I announce that everyone is free to choose a religion. People are free to live in all regions and take up a job provided that they never violate other's rights.

No one could be penalized for his or her relatives' faults. I prevent slavery and my governors and subordinates are obliged to prohibit exchanging men and women as slaves within their own ruling domains. Such traditions should be exterminated the world over.

This declaration dates from around 2 500 years ago and is accepted as the first declaration of human rights. It guarantees more rights to ordinary people than any subsequent declaration including the US constitution and the United Nations Universal Declaration of Human Rights – and certainly more rights than many people still have. Many people do not have freedom to choose their own religion and unpaid forced labour is still a problem in many parts of the world. And even globalisation (see Chapter 13) has not allowed the free movement of labour. So it can be asserted that stakeholders were more powerful 2 500 years ago and the social contract was stronger.

Risk reducing

One thing which is of particular importance for all corporations, and is becoming more important, is the matter of risk and the managing of that risk. A stakeholder approach to decision making and managing the organisation is likely to identify more risks and to manage them better. Risk is also closely related to sustainability (see Chapter 6) and we will show that the lack of a full understanding of what is meant by sustainability, and particularly by sustainable development, means that the issue is confused in corporate planning and reporting (Aras and Crowther, 2008).

This allows for the kind of confusion which is taking place. We do not necessarily claim that such obfuscation is deliberate but we do suggest that it indicates a certain amount of disingenuity, which it is convenient for corporations to exhibit. Moreover, we suggest that methodologies for the evaluation of risk are deceived by this rhetoric and are deficient in their evaluation of risk – particularly environmental risk. In order to fully recognise and incorporate environmental costs and benefits into the investment analysis process, the starting point needs to be the identification of the types of costs and revenues which need to be incorporated into the evaluation process.

Once these types of costs have been identified then it becomes possible to quantify such costs and to incorporate qualitative data concerning those less tangible benefits which are not easily subject to quantification. The completion of an environmental audit will enhance the understanding of the processes involved and will make this easier. In considering environmental benefits, as distinct from financial benefits, it is important that an appropriate time horizon is selected which will enable those benefits to be recognised and accrued. This may imply a very different time horizon from one which is determined purely by the needs of financial analysis.

Once all the data have been recognised, collected and quantified it then becomes possible to incorporate these data, in financial terms, into an evaluation which incorporates risk in a more consistent manner. It is important to recognise benefits as well as costs, and it is perhaps worth reiterating that many of these benefits are less subject to quantification and are of the less tangible and image-related kind. Examples include:

- enhanced company or product image – this in itself can lead to increased sales;
- health and safety benefits;
- ease of attracting investment and lowered cost of such investment;
- better community relationships – this can lead to easier and quicker approval of plans through the planning process;
- improved relationship with regulators, where relevant;
- improved morale among workers, leading to higher productivity, lower staff turnover and consequently lower recruitment and training costs;
- general improved image and relationship with stakeholders.

Many of these benefits are not just intangible but will take some time to realise, hence the need to select an appropriate time horizon for the evaluation of the risk and associated effects. This time horizon will very likely be a longer one than under a traditional financially based evaluation. Obviously cash flows need to be considered over that period and an appropriate method of evaluation (e.g. a discounted cash flow technique) needs to be used in the evaluation.

None of this will change with the incorporation of environmental accounting information, except for assessment of risk and its associated impact upon the cost of capital, which can be expected to rise as the true extent of the environmental impact is fed into the calculation.

The steps involved in the incorporation of environmental accounting into the risk evaluation system can therefore be summarised as follow:

- identify environmental implications in term of costs and benefits;
- quantify those costs and incorporate qualitative data regarding less tangible benefits;
- use appropriate financial indicators;
- set an appropriate time horizon which allows environmental effects to be fully realised.

Conclusions

Stakeholder theory is one approach to the managing of an organisation. It is particularly important for an understanding of CSR and its incorporation into organisational activity. There are various aspects to this which we have considered in this chapter. At the same time we have introduced a variety of other aspects which are related. Our purpose is to show that all of these concepts are interrelated in the management of an organisation and that CSR cannot be considered in isolation from the rest of organisational activity. We will see this more clearly throughout this book.

Definitions of key terms and theories

Carbon footprint is the amount of carbon dioxide consumed in the production of a product or the completion of an activity.

Embedded water is the amount of water required to manufacture a product.

Hubbert's Peak is the point at which maximum production of oil is reached and output cannot be increased by any means.

Life cycle analysis is concerned with all the effects of an activity over the whole of its life. It is also known as terotechnology.

Stakeholder is any group which has an interest in the activities of an organisation; it can be voluntary or involuntary.

Stakeholder theory is a way of managing an organisation and one of the core theories explaining CSR.

Test your understanding

1. What justification does Stakeholder theory use for considering stakeholders?
2. How can we classify stakeholders?
3. What are the steps involved in the incorporation of environmental accounting into the risk evaluation system of an organisation?
4. What is a proxy stakeholder?
5. Why is the future a stakeholder?
6. How can pressure groups be described as categories?
7. Why is Hubbert's Peak significant for businesses?

Suggestions for further reading

Bhattacharya, C. B. and Sen, S. (2004); 'Doing Better at Doing Good: When, Why and How Consumers Respond to Corporate Social Initiatives', *California Management Review*, 47, 1: 9–24.

Donaldson, T. and Preston, L. E. (1995); 'The Stakeholder Theory of the Corporation: Concepts, Evidence, and Implications', *Academy of Management Review*, 20(1): 65–91.

Jensen, M. C. and Meckling, M. H. (1976); 'Theory of the Firm: Managerial Behaviour, Agency Costs and Ownership Structure', *Journal of Financial Economics*, 3, 4: 305–60.

Kell, G. (2003); 'The Global Compact: Origins, Operations, Progress, Challenge', *Journal of Corporate Citizenship*, 11: 35–49.

Notes

1. It is generally described as a theory and we do so here but some people would argue that it is not a theory at all – merely a useful tool of analysis. They would argue that in order to be a theory it must be testable and must have predictive power. That is an argument for elsewhere – in this book we describe it as a theory because most others do so.
2. In other words, the extent of regulation in this area has increased in recent years and is continuing to increase.
3. And most probably any other parts of the world also – it would be instructive to correlate the presence of oil with conflicts.
4. Consider for example the protest against the Poll Tax.
5. See Crowther and Cooper (2001) for a consideration of the tactics of ecoprotestors.
6. See Crowther and Cooper (2001) for a consideration of the role of ecoprotest in local community activity opposing the building of roads.
7. Thus they focus upon their own utility and select their purchase and consumption patterns accordingly, rather than purely upon price. This is in perfect accord with the arguments of Marshall (1947) and earlier economists.
8. A particularly good example is the debate concerning genetically modified foods which has led several supermarket chains to announce that they will stop using such foods in their own-label products.

References

Aras, G. and Crowther, D. 2008. 'Corporate Sustainability Reporting: A Study in Disingenuity?', *Journal of Business Ethics*, 87 (supp.1): 279–88.
Argenti, J. 1993. *Your Organization: What Is it for?* London: McGraw-Hill.
Atkinson, A. A., Waterhouse, J. H., and Wells, R. B. 1997. 'A Stakeholder Approach to Strategic Performance Management', *Sloan Management Review*, Spring.
Chaliand, G. 1987. *Terrorism: From Popular Struggle to Media Spectacle.* London: Saqi.
Clarkson, M. E. 1995. 'A Stakeholder Framework for Analysing and Evaluating Corporate Social Performance', *Academy of Management Review*, 20, 1: 92–117.
Cooper, S., Crowther, D., Davies, M. and Davis, E. W. 2001. *Shareholder or Stakeholder Value? The Development of Indicators for the Control and Measurement of Performance.* London: CIMA.
Crowther, D. and Cooper, S. 2001. 'Innovation through Postmodern Networks: The Case of Ecoprotestors', in O. Jones, S. Conway and F. Steward (eds), *Social Interaction and Organisational Change.* London: Imperial College Press.
Dahl, R. A. 1972. 'A Prelude to Corporate Reform', *Business and Society Review*, Spring: 17–23.

Freeman, R. Edward 1984. *Strategic Management: A Stakeholder Approach.* Boston, MA: Pitman.

Heskett, J. L., Jones, T. O., Loverman, G.W., Sasser, Jr W.E. and Schlesinger, L. A. 1994. 'Putting the Service-Profit Chain to Work', *Harvard Business Review*, March–April: 164–74.

Hetherington, J. A. C. 1973. *Corporate Social Responsibility Audit: A Management Tool for Survival.* London: The Foundation for Business Responsibilities.

Jones, T. M. and Wicks, A. C. 1999. 'Convergent Stakeholder Theory', *The Academy of Management Review*, April, 24, 2: 206–21.

Kaplan, R. S. and Norton, D. P. 1992. 'The Balanced Scorecard – Measures that Drive Performance', *Harvard Business Review*, Jan/Feb: 71–9.

Kaplan, R. S. and Norton, D. P. 1993. 'Putting the Balanced Scorecard to Work', *Harvard Business Review*, Sept/Oct: 134–47.

Kaplan, R. S. and Norton, D. P. 1996a. 'Using the Balanced Scorecard as a Strategic Management System', *Harvard Business Review*, January/February: 75–85.

Kaplan, R. S. and Norton, D. P. 1996b. *The Balanced Scorecard: Translating Strategy into Action.* Harvard: Harvard Business School Press.

Lovelock, J. 2006. *The Revenge of Gaia.* Harmondsworth: Penguin.

Marshal, A. 1947. *Principles of Economics.* London: Macmillan.

Mitchell, R. K., Agle, B. R. and Wood, D. J. 1997. 'Toward a Theory of Stakeholder Identification and Salience: Defining the Principle of Who Really Counts', *The Academy of Management Review*, October: 853–86.

Sternberg, E. 1997. 'The Defects of Stakeholder Theory', *Corporate Governance: An International Review*, 5, 1: 3–10.

Waddock, S. A. and Graves, S. B. 1997. 'Quality of Management and Quality of Stakeholder Relations', *Business and Society*, 36, 3: 250–79.

Issues Concerning Sustainability

8

Learning objectives

After studying this chapter you should be able to:

- Describe the meaning of sustainability and sustainable development.
- Outline the three pillars of the Brundtland Report.
- Describe the factors involved in an analysis of social performance.
- Explain how corporate sustainability operates in a global environment.
- Discuss analysing social performance and its problems.
- Critique the four-factor model of durability.

Introduction

One of the most used words relating to corporate activity at present is the word 'sustainability'. Indeed, some would argue that it has been so heavily overused and with so many different meanings applied to it that it is effectively meaningless. Thus, the term 'sustainability' currently has a high profile within the field of corporate activity. Indeed, it is frequently mentioned as central to corporate activity without any attempt to define exactly what sustainable activity entails. This is understandable as the concept is problematic and subject to many varying definitions – ranging from platitudes concerning sustainable development to the deep green concept of returning to the 'golden era' before industrialisation – although often it is used by corporations merely to signify that they intend to continue their existence into the future.

The ubiquity of the concept and the vagueness of its use mean that it is necessary to re-examine the concept and to consider how it applies to corporate activity. In this chapter, therefore, we do just this – examining what is meant by sustainability – and looking at the various aspects of sustainability. For us there are two aspects: corporate actions and their consequences; and the distribution of the benefits accruing from such corporate activity. Furthermore, both have to be set not just within the sphere of the corporation itself or even the wider context of its stakeholders but also within the widest geospatial context: that of the global environment.

There is a considerable degree of confusion surrounding the concept of sustainability; for the purist, sustainability implies nothing more than stasis – the ability to continue in an unchanged manner – but often it is taken to imply development in a sustainable manner (Marsden, 2000; Hart and Milstein, 2003) and the terms 'sustainability' and 'sustainable development' are viewed as synonymous by many. On our part, we take the definition as being concerned with stasis (Aras and Crowther, 2008a); at the corporate level if development is possible without jeopardising that stasis then this is a bonus rather than a constituent part of that sustainability. Moreover, sustainable development is often misinterpreted as focusing solely on environmental issues. In reality, it is a much broader concept. Sustainable development policies encompass three general policy areas: *economic, environmental* and *social.* In support of this, several United Nations texts, most recently the 2005 World Summit Outcome Document, refer to the '*interdependent and mutually reinforcing pillars*' of *sustainable development* as *economic development, social development, and environmental protection.*

The Brundtland Report and after . . .

The starting point must be taken as the Brundtland Report (WCED, 1987) because there is general acceptance of the contents of that Report and because the definition of sustainability contained in it is pertinent and widely accepted. Equally, the Brundtland Report is part of a policy landscape being explicitly debated by the nation states and their agencies, big business supra-national bodies such as the United Nations through the vehicles of the WBCSD[1] and ICC[2] (see, for example, Beder, 1997; Gray and Bebbington, 2001). Its concern with the effect which action taken in the present has upon the options available in the future has directly led to glib assumptions that sustainable development is both desirable and possible, and that corporation can demonstrate sustainability merely by continuing to exist into the future (Aras and Crowther, 2008a). It is important, therefore, to remember the Brundtland Commission's (WCED, 1987: 1) definition of sustainable development that is the most accepted by everyone and used as the standard definition of sustainable development:

> development that meets the needs of the present without compromising the ability of future generations to meet their own needs.

This is the standard definition of sustainable development which has been taken up by everyone subsequently. This report makes institutional and legal recommendations for change in order to confront common global problems. More and more, there is a growing consensus that firms and governments in partnership should accept moral responsibility for social welfare and for promoting individuals' interest in economic transactions (Amba-Rao, 1993).

Brundtland and sustainability

At a similar time all corporations are becoming concerned about their own sustainability and what the term really means. Such sustainability means more than environmental sustainability. As far as corporate sustainability is concerned then the confusion is exacerbated by the fact that the term 'sustainable' has been used in the management literature over the last thirty years (see, for example, Reed and DeFillippi, 1990) merely to imply continuity. Thus, Zwetsloot (2003) is able to conflate corporate social responsibility with the techniques of continuous improvement and innovation to imply that sustainability is thereby ensured. Consequently the trajectory of all of these effects is increasingly being focused upon the same issue.

One of the most used words relating to corporate activity at present is the word sustainability. Indeed, it can be argued that it has been so heavily overused, and with so many different meanings applied, to it that it is effectively meaningless. It is therefore time to re-examine the legacy of Bruntland and to redefine what is meant by sustainable activity. Thus, we argue sustainable development has assumed such significance in the lexicon of corporate behaviour that it is in effect a strategic imperative, despite there being little understanding of the term and its implications (see Aras and Crowther, 2008b). It is part of our argument that the current fashionably ubiquitous use of the term has obfuscated any consideration of a real understanding of sustainability. This is unfortunate as we consider that sustainability must be an integral part of the strategic development of a company, but a complete understanding of sustainability is necessary before sustainable development can be countenanced.

Sustainability is, of course, fundamental to a business and its continuing existence. It is equally fundamental to the continuing existence not just of current economic activity but also of the planet itself – at least in a way which we currently understand. It is a complex process, as we have discussed. Moreover, it is a process which must recognise not just the decision being made in the operational activity of the organisation but also the distributional decisions which are made. Only then can an organisation be considered to be sustainable.

Some have tended to assume that a sustainable company will exist merely by recognising environmental and social issues and incorporating them into its strategic planning. According to Marrewijk and Werre (2003) there is no specific definition of corporate sustainability and each organisation needs to devise its own definition to suit its purpose and objectives, although they seem to assume that corporate sustainability and corporate social responsibility are synonymous and based upon voluntary activity which includes environmental and social concern.

Sustainability therefore implies that society must use no more of a resource than can be regenerated. This can be defined in terms of the carrying capacity of the ecosystem (Hawken, 1993) and described with input–output models of resource consumption. Thus the paper industry, for example, has a policy of replanting trees to replace those harvested and this has the effect of retaining costs in the present rather than temporally externalising them. Similarly, motor vehicle manufacturers have a policy of making their cars almost totally recyclable. Viewing an organisation as part of a wider social and economic system implies that these effects must be taken into account, not just for the measurement of costs and value created in the present but also for the future of the business itself.

Such concerns are pertinent at a macro-level of society as a whole or at the level of the nation state but are equally relevant at the micro-level of the corporation, the aspect of sustainability with which we are concerned in this work. At this level, measures of sustainability would consider the rate at which resources are consumed by the organisation in relation to the rate at which resources can be regenerated. Unsustainable operations can be accommodated for either by developing sustainable operations or by planning for a future lacking in resources currently required. In practice, organisations mostly tend to aim towards less unsustainability by increasing efficiency in the way in which resources are utilised. An example would be an energy efficiency programme.

The descendants of Brundtland

There have been various descendants of Brundtland, including the concept of the Triple Bottom Line (Aras and Crowther, 2008d). This in turn has led to an assumption that addressing the three aspects of economic, social and environmental is all that is necessary in order to ensure not just sustainability but also sustainable development (see Figure 8.1). Indeed, the implicit assumption is one of business as usual – add some information about environmental performance and social performance to conventional financial reporting (the economic performance) and that equates to triple bottom line reporting. And all corporations imply that they have recognised the problems, addressed the issues and thereby ensured sustainable development. This implication is generally accepted without questioning – certainly without any rigorous questioning. One descendant is the Triple Bottom Line – the three aspects of performance:

Sustainability and the cost of capital

It is recognised in the financial world that the cost of capital which any company incurs is related to the perceived risk associated with investing in that company – in other words, there is a direct correlation between the risk involved in an investment and the rewards which are expected to accrue from a successful investment. Therefore it is generally recognised that the larger, more established companies are a more certain investment and therefore have a lower cost of capital. This is all established fact as far as finance theory is concerned and is

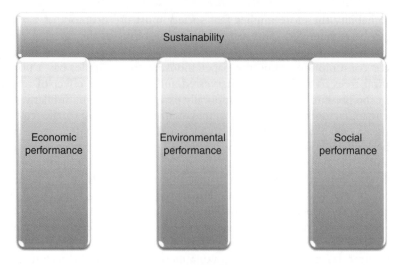

Figure 8.1   The three pillars of sustainability

recognised in the operating of the financial markets around the world. Naturally a company which is sustainable will be less risky than one which is not. Consequently, most large companies mention sustainability in their reporting and frequently it features prominently. Indeed, it is noticeable that extractive industries – which by their very nature cannot be sustainable in the long term – make sustainability a very prominent issue. The prime example of this can be seen in oil companies – BP being a very good example – which make much of sustainability and are busy redesignating themselves as energy companies, with a feature being made of renewable energy even though this is a very small part[3] of their actual operations.

All businesses recognise the business benefits of sustainability activity in their reporting. Equally, all businesses recognise that sustainability is important and they feature it prominently in their reporting. For example, an investigation of the FTSE 100 companies (see Aras and Crowther, 2007a) reveals the following:

Mention on corporate website	% of companies
Sustainability	100
Sustainable development	35
Expressly link sustainability to CSR policy	70

Although, as we have said, industries such as the extractive industry cannot be sustainable, they continue to make a feature of this in their reporting. Any analysis of these statements regarding sustainability, however, quickly reveals the uncertainty regarding what is meant by sustainability. Clearly the vast majority do not mean sustainability as defined by the Brundtland Report. Often it appears to mean little more than that the corporation will continue to exist in the future. It is therefore time to re-examine the legacy of Brundtland and to redefine what is meant by sustainable activity.

Just as a company which is sustainable is less risky than one which is not then one which can claim sustainable development is even less risky and many companies mention this concept and imply that it relates to their operations. Such a company has a rosy future of continued growth, with an expectation of continued growth in profitability. An investigation of the FTSE 100, for example, shows that 70% make a feature of sustainability whilst 35% make a feature of sustainable development. So the cost of capital becomes lower as the certainty of returns becomes higher. We have shown in this chapter that the concept of sustainability is complex and problematic and that the idea of sustainable development is even more problematic. It is our argument that companies are not really addressing these issues but are merely creating an image of sustainability.[4] The language of the statements made by corporations tends therefore to be used as a device for corrupting thought (Orwell, 1970), that is, as an instrument to prevent thought about the various alternative realities of organisational reality. Significantly, it creates an image of safety for investors and thereby reduces the cost of capital for such corporations.

Shell: responding to criticisms

Shell's response to problems such as Brent Spar and Nigeria was to launch an internal review of processes and an external communications campaign to persuade stakeholders of their commitment to corporate social responsibility. In response to criticism of its track record on environmental matters, Shell published its unequivocal commitment to sustainable development, supported by executive speeches reinforcing this commitment. At the same time, Shell was one of the first companies to leave the Global Climate Coalition. The Shell Chairman, Philip Watts, gave a speech in Houston in 2003 calling for sceptics to get off the fence and take action before it is too late. Shell was also a founding member of the World Business Council for Sustainable Development.

When delivering the annual business lecture hosted by Greenpeace in 2005, Shell chairman Lord Oxburgh said that we must act now on global warming or face a disaster, and he encouraged governments to provide a regulatory framework to encourage the reduction of greenhouse gas emissions. He stated that 'our job is to respond in a positive way to a regulatory environment that has to be determined by government ... given the urgency, we have to start now'. Shell's commitment to CSR also includes its well-respected *Live*WIRE Programme. This programme has over twenty years' experience of encouraging young people to start and develop their own businesses in the UK and elsewhere in the world (26 countries). Shell has said that it is committed to listening to stakeholders: 'Your opinions are important to us and we want to listen and

→

respond as best we can to your comments and concerns.' This included the setting up of a global internet-based facility for whistleblowers to report alleged violations of the law or of Shell General Business Principles (the SGBP): a voluntary code of ethics which promised transparency, integrity and honesty in all of Shell's business dealings. Whistleblowers are asked to provide identity details but anonymous reports are also accepted. The Helpline is available to 'customers, suppliers, partners, advisers and employees of Shell'.

Much of Shell's reputation-building advertising has concentrated on the embryonic renewables business despite the fact that this remains a very small business compared to the core hydrocarbon extraction, processing and marketing operations. The corporate advertising campaign has been described as *greenwash* by some NGO critics, but praised by other commentators. In response to questions which focused on the small percentage of its capital investment programme that was directed towards alternative energy solutions, Shell said that it would be pointless to say exactly how much of capital expenditure was going into renewable energy schemes. CEO Jeroen van der Veer indicated that the investment in renewables was small, saying it would be 'throwing money away' to invest in alternative energy projects that were non-commercial and people could not afford to buy.

Then in November 2004, following a period of turmoil caused by the revelation it had been overstating its oil reserves, it was announced that the Shell Group would move to a single capital structure, creating a new parent company to be named Royal Dutch Shell plc, with its principal listing on the London Stock Exchange and the Amsterdam Stock Exchange and with its headquarters in The Hague in the Netherlands. The unification was completed on 20 July 2005.

Shell's image suffered further blows recently because problems have arisen with the massive Sakhalin II project in Russia and the controversial Corrib Gas Field development in Ireland. Shell's social investment initiative – the Shell Foundation – has also run into some controversy. In 2007, Friends of the Earth alleged that the damage to local communities and the wider environment caused by Shell's oil activities could be assessed at $20 billion.

As an oil producer, Shell will always be under particular scrutiny regarding its environmental behaviour, and problems will continue to arise. A socially responsible company, whilst it will still have problems, does not try to pretend otherwise; instead it recognises the need to be accountable and tries to be transparent. Visit the website (www.shell.com) and judge for yourself.

Redefining sustainability

Most analysis of sustainability (e.g. Dyllick and Hockerts, 2002) recognises only a two-dimensional approach, of the environmental and the social. A few (e.g. Spangenberg, 2004) recognise a third dimension which is related to organisational behaviour. We argue that restricting analysis to such dimensions is deficient. One problem is the fact that the dominant assumption by researchers is based upon the incompatibility of optimising, for a corporation, both financial performance and social/environmental performance. In other words, financial performance and social/environmental performance are seen as being in conflict with each other through this dichotomisation (see Crowther, 2002). Consequently, most work in the area of corporate sustainability does not recognise the need for acknowledging the importance of financial performance as an essential aspect of sustainability and therefore fails to undertake financial analysis alongside – and integrated with – other forms of analysis for this research. This is an essential aspect of corporate sustainability and therefore adds a further dimension to the analysis of sustainability. Furthermore, the third dimension sometimes recognised as organisational behaviour needs actually to comprise a much broader concept of corporate culture. There are therefore four aspects of sustainability which need to be recognised and analysed, namely:

(1) *Societal influence*, which we define as a measure of the impact that society makes upon the corporation in terms of the social contract and stakeholder influence.

(2) *Environmental Impact*, which we define as the effect of the actions of the corporation upon its geophysical environment.

(3) *Organisational culture*, which we define as the relationship between the corporation and its internal stakeholders, particularly employees, and all aspects of that relationship.

(4) *Finance*, which we define in terms of an adequate return for the level of risk undertaken.

These four must be considered as the key dimensions of sustainability, all of which are equally important. Our analysis is therefore considerably broader – and more complete – than that of others. Furthermore, we consider that these four aspects can be resolved into a two-dimensional matrix along the polarities of internal *v* external focus and short-term *v* long-term focus, which together form a complete representation of organisational performance, which can be represented as the model in Figure 8.2 below.

This model provides both a representation of organisation performance and a basis for any evaluation of corporate sustainability.

In order to achieve sustainable development[5] it is first necessary to achieve sustainability and there are a number of elements to this. What is important for sustainability is not just addressing each of these elements individually but also paying attention to maintaining the balance between them. It is the maintenance of this balance which is the most challenging – but also the most essential – aspect of managing sustainability. There are a number of elements which must be addressed but these can be grouped together into four major elements, which map exactly onto the model for evaluating sustainability outlined earlier. These four major elements of sustainability therefore are:

(1) *Maintaining economic activity*, which must be the central *raison d'être* of corporate activity and the principal reason for organising corporate activity; this, of course, maps onto the finance aspect.

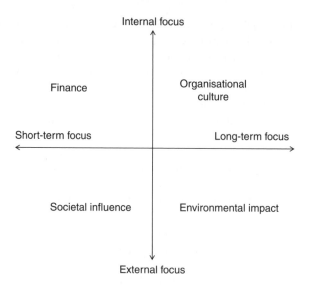

Figure 8.2   Model of sustainability

(2) *Conservation of the environment*, which is essential for maintaining the options available to future generations; this maps onto the environmental impact aspect.

(3) *Ensuring social justice*, which will include such activities as the elimination of poverty, the ensuring of human rights, the promotion of universal education and the facilitation of world peace; this maps onto the societal influence aspect.

(4) *Developing spiritual and cultural values*, which is where corporate and societal values align in the individual and where all of the other elements are promoted or negated; sadly at present they are mostly negated (see Davila Gomez and Crowther, 2007; Crowther and Davila-Gomez, 2006a; 2006b; 2006c); this maps onto the organisational culture aspect.

Often theorists attempt to prioritise these but it is the balancing of them equitably which is essential to developing sustainability, and hence we maintain that most considerations of the concept are unworkably simplistic. It can therefore be seen that the representation of corporate activity is considerably more complex than simply managing the stakeholder *v* shareholder dichotomisation which is ever present in organisational theory.

Financial, social and environmental performance

One view of good corporate performance is that of stewardship and thus, just as the management of an organisation is concerned with the stewardship of the financial resources of the organisation so too would management of the organisation be concerned with the stewardship of environmental resources. The difference, however, is that environmental resources are mostly located externally to the organisation. Stewardship in this context therefore is concerned with the resources of society as well as the resources of the organisation. As far as stewardship of external environmental resources is concerned then the central tenet of such stewardship is that of ensuring sustainability. Sustainability is focused on the future and is concerned with ensuring that the choices of resource utilisation in the future are not constrained by decisions taken in the present. This necessarily implies such concepts as generating and utilising renewable resources, minimising pollution and using new techniques of manufacture and distribution. It also implies the acceptance of any costs involved in the present as an investment for the future.

Not only does such sustainable activity impact upon society in the future, however; it also impacts upon the organisation itself in the future. Thus, good environmental performance by an organisation in the present is in reality an investment in the future of the organisation itself. This is achieved through the ensuring of supplies and production techniques which will enable the organisation to operate in the future in a similar way to its operations in the present and so to undertake value creation activity in the future much as it does in the present. Financial management, however, is also concerned with the management of the organisation's resources in the present so that management will be possible in a value creation way in the future. Thus, the internal management of the firm, from a financial perspective, and its external environmental management coincide in this common concern for management for the future.

Good performance in the financial dimension leads to good future performance in the environmental dimension and vice versa. Thus there is no dichotomy (Crowther, 2002) between environmental performance and financial performance and the two concepts conflate into one concern. This concern is, of course, the management of the future as far as the firm is concerned.[6] The role of social and environmental accounting and reporting and the role of financial accounting and reporting therefore can be seen to be coincidental. Thus, the work required needs to be concerned not with arguments about resource distribution but rather with the development of measures which truly reflect the activities of the organisation upon its environment. These techniques of measurement, and consequently of reporting, are a necessary precursor to the concern with management for the future – and hence with sustainability.

Similarly, the creation of value within the firm is followed by the distribution of value to the stakeholders of that firm, whether these stakeholders are shareholders or others. Value, however, must be taken in its widest definition to include more than economic value as it is possible that economic value can be created at the expense of other constituent components of welfare such as spiritual or emotional welfare.[7] This creation of value by the firm adds to welfare for society at large, although this welfare is targeted at particular members of society rather than treating all as equals. This has led to arguments by Tinker (1988), Herremans and colleagues (1992) and Gray (1992), among others, concerning the distribution of value created and as to whether value is created for one set of stakeholders at the expense of others. Nevertheless, if, when summed, value is created then this adds to welfare for society at large, however distributed. Similarly, good environmental performance leads to increased welfare for society at large, although this will tend to be expressed in emotional and community terms rather than being capable of being expressed in quantitative terms. This will be expressed in a feeling of well-being, which of course will lead to increased motivation. Such increased motivation will inevitably lead to increased productivity, some of which will benefit the organisations, and also a desire to maintain a pleasant environment, which will in turn lead to a further enhanced environment, a further increase in welfare and the reduction of destructive aspects of societal engagement by individuals.

Thus, increased welfare leads to its own self-perpetuation. In the context of welfare, therefore, financial performance and environmental performance also conflate into a general concern with an increase in welfare.

The ownership of performance

Agency theory suggests that the management of an organisation should be undertaken on behalf of the owners of that organisation, in other words, the shareholders. Consequently the management of value created by the organisation is only pertinent insofar as that value accrues to the shareholders of the firm. Implicit within this view of the management of the firm, as espoused by Rappaport (1986) and Stewart (1991) among many others, is that society at large, and consequently all stakeholders to the organisation, will also benefit as a result of managing the performance of the organisation in this manner. From this perspective, therefore, the concerns are focused upon how to manage performance for the shareholders and how to report upon that performance (Myners, 1998).

This view of an organisation, however, has been extensively challenged by many writers (e.g. Tinker, 1985) who argue that the way to maximise performance for society at large is both to manage on behalf of all stakeholders and ensure that the value thereby created is not appropriated by the shareholders but is distributed to all stakeholders. Others argue that this debate is sterile and that organisations maximise value creation not by a concern with either shareholders or stakeholders but by focusing upon the operational objectives of the firm and assuming that value creation and equitable distribution will thereby follow.

Adherents to each of these conflicting philosophies have a tendency to adopt different perspectives on the evaluation of performance. Thus, good performance for one school of thought is assumed to be poor performance for the others. Thus, performance-maximising philosophies are polarised in the discourse and this leads to a polarisation of performance reporting and the creation of the dialectic considered earlier. Almost unquestioned within the discourse, however, is the assumption that good performance from one aspect necessitates the sacrificing of performance from the other, despite the ensuing distributional conflicts being hidden within the discourse. Indeed, Kimberley and colleagues (1983) have argued that some areas of performance which are important to the future of the business are not even recognised let alone evaluated. It is argued in this chapter that the future orientation of performance management necessitates the creation of value over the longer term for all stakeholders and, moreover, that this value creation must be manifested in the way in which the value created in the organisation is distributed among the various stakeholders. It is only in this way that the continuing temporal existence of the organisation can be ensured.

It can readily be seen that the differing needs of different parties in the evaluation process cause tensions within the organisation as it seeks to meet its internal control, strategy formulation and accountability functions, and produce a reporting structure to meet these needs. Whilst the basic information required to satisfy these needs is the same organisational information, or at least derives from the same source data, the way in which it is analysed and used is different, which can lead to conflict within the organisation. Such conflict is exacerbated when a measure is adapted for one need but only at the expense of a deterioration in its appropriateness for another purpose. It is for this reason that accounting and information systems in organisations are in a constant state of development and enhancement as the systems are designed to meet perceived needs and adapted to meet newly identified needs. One such source of conflict in an organisation, therefore, is caused by the different stakeholders seeking to access and use information differently, and this conflict tends to have a dysfunctional impact upon organisational cohesiveness and, ultimately, performance. Performance therefore can also be viewed deterministically in that it can be considered to be as good as it is evaluated to be.

One factor of importance in performance evaluation is the concept of sustainability as far as performance is concerned. It is therefore important for all stakeholders to be able to ascertain, or at least project, not just current performance but also its implications for the future. Performance evaluation must therefore necessarily have a future orientation for all evaluations. The appropriate measures are likely to facilitate a better projection of the sustainability of performance levels and the future impact of current performance. This is because the addressing of the needs of all stakeholders is likely to reveal factors which will impact upon future performance and might not be considered if a more traditional approach to performance evaluation were taken. An example might be the degree to which raw materials from renewable resources have become significant to many industries recently but were not considered at all until recently by any stakeholders of an organisation other than community and environmental pressure groups.

Sustainability reporting

There have been many claims (see Crowther, 2000) that the quantification of environmental costs and the inclusion of such costs into business strategies can significantly reduce operating costs by firms; indeed this was one of the main themes of the 1996 Global Environmental Management Initiative Conference. Little evidence exists that this is the case but Pava and Krausz (1996) demonstrate empirically that companies which they define as 'socially responsible' perform in financial terms at least as well as companies which are not socially responsible. It is accepted, however, that different definitions of socially responsible organisations exist and that different definitions lead to different evaluations of performance between those deemed responsible and others. Similarly, in other countries efforts are being made to provide a framework for certification of accountants who wish to be considered as environmental practitioners and auditors. For example, the Canadian Institute of Chartered Accountants has been heavily involved in the creation of such a national framework. Azzone, Manzini and Noel (1996), however, suggest that, despite the lack of any regulatory framework in this area, a degree of standardisation, at least as far as reporting is concerned, is beginning to emerge at an international level, one of the central arguments of this chapter.

Growth in the techniques offered for measuring social impact, and reporting thereon, has continued throughout the last twenty-five years, during which the concept of this form of accounting has existed. However, the ability to discuss the fact that firms, through their actions, affect their external environment and that this should be accounted for has often exceeded within the discourse any practical suggestions for measuring such impact. At the same time as the technical implementation of social accounting and reporting has been developing, the philosophical basis for such accounting – predicated in the transparency and accountability principles – has also been developed. Thus, some people consider the extent to which accountants should be involved in this accounting and argue that such accounting can be justified by means of the social contract as benefiting society at large. Others have argued that sustainability is the cornerstone of social and environmental accounting and that auditing should be given prominence.

An examination of the external reporting of organisations gives an indication of the extent of socially responsible activity. Such an examination does indeed demonstrate an increasing recognition of the need to include information about this and an increasing number of annual reports of companies include some information in this respect. This trend is gathering momentum as more organisations perceive the importance of providing such information to external stakeholders. It has been suggested, however, that the inclusion of such information does not demonstrate an increasing concern with the environment but rather some benefits – for example, tax breaks – to the company itself. One trend which is also apparent in many parts of the world, however, is the tendency of companies to produce separate social and environmental reports. In this context such reports have been generally redefined as CSR reports or Sustainability reports, depending upon the development of the corporation concerned. This trend is gathering momentum as more organisations realise that stakeholders are both demanding more information and demanding accountability for actions undertaken. Equally, the more enlightened of these corporations are realising that socially responsible activity makes business sense and actually assists improved economic performance.

This realisation obviates any need for regulation and calls into question the standards suggested by such bodies as accountability. The more progressive corporations have made considerable progress in what they often describe as their journey towards being fully socially responsible. In doing so they have developed an understanding of the priorities for their own business – recognising that CSR has many facets and needs to be interpreted differently for each organisation – and made significant steps towards both appropriate activity and appropriate reporting of such activity. The steps towards CSR can be likened to increasing maturity as all organisations progress towards that maturity by passing through the same stages (see below), although at different paces. The most mature are indeed recognising that nature of globalisation by recognising that the organisational boundary is permeable and that they are accountable also for the behaviour of other organisations in their value chain.

Risk reducing

Sometimes the methodologies for the evaluation of risk are deceived by this rhetoric and are deficient in their evaluation of risk – particularly environmental risk. In order to fully recognise and incorporate environmental costs and benefits into the investment analysis process, the starting point needs to be the identification of the types of costs and revenues which ought to be incorporated into the evaluation process. Once these types of costs have been identified then it becomes possible to quantify such costs and to incorporate qualitative data concerning those less tangible benefits which are not easily subject to quantification. The completion of an environmental audit will enhance the understanding of the processes involved and will make this easier. In considering environmental benefits, as distinct from financial benefits, it is important that an appropriate time horizon is selected which will enable those benefits to be recognised and to accrue. This may imply a very different time horizon from one which is determined purely by the needs of financial analysis.

Once all the data have been recognised, collected and quantified it then becomes possible to incorporate these data, in financial terms, into an evaluation which incorporates risk in a more consistent manner. It is important to recognise benefits as well as costs, and it is perhaps worth reiterating that many of these benefits are less subject to quantification and are of the less tangible and image-related kind. Many benefits are not just intangible but will take some time to realise, hence the need to select an appropriate time horizon for the evaluation of the risk and associated effects. This time horizon will very likely be a longer one than under a traditional financially based evaluation. Obviously cash flows should be considered over that period and an appropriate method of evaluation (e.g. a discounted cash flow technique) needs to be used in the evaluation. None of this will change with the incorporation of environmental accounting information except for assessment of risk and its associated impact upon the cost

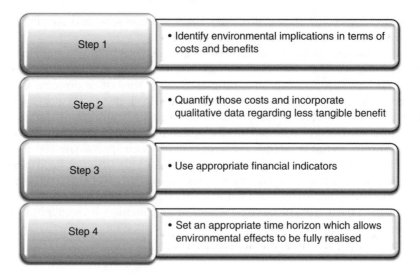

Step 1
- Identify environmental implications in terms of costs and benefits

Step 2
- Quantify those costs and incorporate qualitative data regarding less tangible benefit

Step 3
- Use appropriate financial indicators

Step 4
- Set an appropriate time horizon which allows environmental effects to be fully realised

Figure 8.3   The risk evaluation process

of capital, which can be expected to rise as the true extent of the environmental impact is fed into the calculation.

The steps involved in the incorporation of environmental accounting into the risk evaluation system can therefore be summarised as shown in Figure 8.3.

The distributional problem

An organisation is completely embedded in its environment as the actions it takes have wide-ranging effects. Thus, one of the key aspects of sustainability is concerned with distribution of the effects of its actions. The traditional approach to this was recording profit as internal to the organisation and treating everything else as an externality to be ignored. Thus, the sole discussion was concerned with the distribution of the profit resulting from corporate activity: to owners as their return for bearing risk; to managers as their reward for creating profit; and to be retained for future profitability enhancement.

Such an approach, of course, ignores two aspects of corporate activity:

(i) it is possible to earn an increase in profit (as recorded by accounting) simply by externalising costs;
(ii) it is not realistically possible to earn profit without the cooperation – active or passive – of the other stakeholders to the organisation.

Thus, the social accounting approach is to recognise all costs and benefits resulting from an organisation's activities and to focus upon a distribution of these to ensure that all stakeholders are satisfied – a satisficing approach common within the social accounting literature. The underlying principle is that if all stakeholders are satisfied then conflict between them will cease and all will cooperate for mutual benefit.

Thus, the performance of businesses in a wider arena than the stock market and its value to shareholders has become of increasing concern. Fetyko (1975) considered social accounting as an approach to reporting a firm's activities and stressed the need for identification of socially relevant behaviour, the determination of those to whom the company is accountable for its social performance and the development of appropriate measures and reporting techniques. Klein (1977) also considered social accounting and recognised that different aspects of performance are of interest to different stakeholder groupings, distinguishing, for example, between investors, community relations and philanthropy as areas of concern for accounting. He also considered various areas for measurement, including consumer surplus, rent, environmental impact and non-monetary values. Whilst these writers considered, by implication, that measuring social performance is important without giving reasons for believing so, Solomons (1974) considered the reasons for objectively measuring the social performance of a business. He suggested that whilst one reason is to aid rational decision making, another reason was of a defensive nature.

Unlike other writers, Solomons not only argued for the need to account for the activities of an organisation in terms of its social performance but also suggested a model for doing this, in terms of a statement of social income. His model for the analysis of social performance is shown in Figure 8.4.

This approach, however, still fails to recognise the realities of the global environment (see Aras and Crowther, 2007a; 2007b) insofar as the company is firmly embedded in a global environment which necessarily takes into account the past and the future as well as the present. This effectively makes a stakeholder out of everything and everybody both in the present and in the future.

Sustainability therefore requires a distribution of effects – positive and negative – in a way which eliminates conflict between all of these and pays attention to the future as well as the present. Thus, a short-term approach is no longer acceptable for sustainability (see Figure 8.5, which represents such an approach to sustainability).

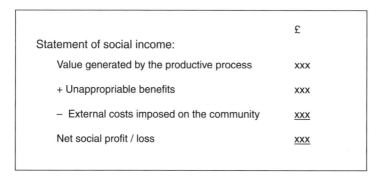

Figure 8.4 Analysis of social performance

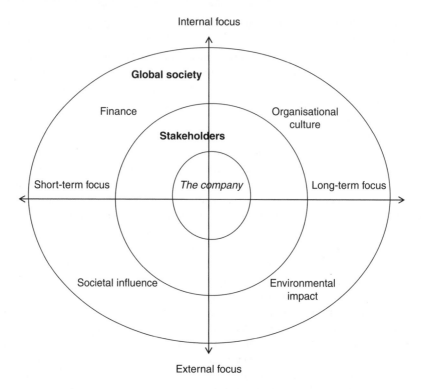

Figure 8.5   Model of sustainable distribution

Marks & Spencer and Plan A

In 2007 M&S set out to establish its reputation as one of the high street's most ethical retailers. It did this with its Plan A project, which sets out public commitments with concrete targets that are intended to achieve this. It is a five-year plan to address the issue of the sustainable development of the company – with the slogan 'because there is no Plan B'. It is a 100-point plan which includes, among other things, the intention to make the company carbon neutral within this period. At the heart of Plan A are the five pillars of Climate Change, Waste, Sustainable Raw Materials, Fair Partner and Health. It also extends to a commitment to ethical trading standards as well as addressing human rights and environmental issues. There has been an extensive marketing campaign and it is proving very popular with its customers.

Plan A is all about sustainability and sustainable development and it makes great marketing. But it is also subject to much cynical evaluation as greenwashing; hence the press report about recycling. This, of course, raises questions of the reality of this plan and how much of it is about greenwashing and cheap marketing – except that it is not cheap! So it raises questions concerning what is meant by sustainable development or being carbon neutral. And it raises questions as to whether it is actually possible to be brilliant at every aspect of CSR or is some prioritising essential, and whether there must always be a trade-off between conflicting desires.

Despite all the publicity for its Plan A (there is no Plan B), however, Marks & Spencer was, in 2007, rated as worse than all other UK supermarkets in terms of the ability to recycle its packaging of food products. Only 60% was recyclable compared with 70% for Asda or Sainsburys and 79% for local retailers. However, M&S has taken some action. This is what it says:

> Between April 2007 and May 2008, we managed to save 12%, or 1 402 tonnes, of packaging. In some cases we also managed to make a change for the better by adding recycled content to our packaging, whilst still maintaining 90% recyclability. Since October 2007, we've increased the amount of widely recyclable food packaging from 68% to 74%. And a further 17% of our food packaging is recyclable where the local facilities are available.

As a result, they won the Retail Leadership award at the 2009 Greener Package Awards for their industry-leading approach to reducing packaging and addressing sustainability.

Moreover, they remain firmly committed to Plan A despite difficult conditions during the recession starting in 2009. In 2010 they stated:

> Every aspect of our business has a carbon footprint, but we are aiming to reduce our emissions across the board. Our goal is to become carbon neutral by 2012 in our UK and Republic of Ireland operations. We're doing this by both reducing our energy consumption and increasing our use of renewable electricity, only using offsetting as a last resort.

This plan can therefore be viewed as great marketing. Or it can be viewed as a firm commitment to sustainability which, as an aside, creates great marketing. There is nothing wrong with gaining publicity from being socially responsible. Indeed the Department of Trade & Industry of the UK government openly states: 'Make the most of your corporate social responsibility (CSR) activities by publicising them. Ensure that customers, suppliers and the local community know what you are doing. CSR lends itself to good news stories.'

Distributable sustainability

At this point we introduce the term 'distributable sustainability' in order to reflect one of our key points. This is that true sustainability depends not just upon the way actions affect choices in the future but also upon the way the effects of those actions – both positive and negative – are distributed among the stakeholders involved. A central tenet of our argument is that corporate activity, to be sustainable, must not simply utilise resources to give benefit to owners but must recognise all effects upon all stakeholders, and distribute these in a manner which is acceptable to all of these – both in the present and in the future. This is, in effect, a radical reinterpretation of corporate activity.

Manageable (strategic)	Measurable (financial)
Equitable (distributional)	Efficient (technological)

Figure 8.6   Distributable sustainability
Source: from Aras and Crowther, 2009.

It is necessary to consider the operationalisation of this view of sustainability. Our argument has been that sustainability must involve greater efficiency in the use of resources and greater equity in the distribution of the effects of corporate activity. To be operationalised then, of course, the effects must be measurable and the combination, of course, must be manageable.

This can be depicted as a model of sustainability as shown in Figure 8.6.

This model acts as a balanced scorecard to provide a form of evaluation for the operation of sustainability within an organisation. It concentrates upon the four key aspects, namely:

  (i) Strategy
 (ii) Finance
(iii) Distribution
 (iv) Technological development

Moreover, the model recognises the balance between these factors, which is the most significant aspect of sustainability. From this model a plan of action for an organisation is possible that will reflect priorities and provide a basis for performance evaluation.

Summarising sustainability

To summarise, sustainability requires a radical rethink and a move aware from the cosy security of the Brundtland definition. We therefore reject the accepted terms of 'sustainability' and 'sustainable development', preferring instead to use the term 'durability' to emphasise the change in focus.

The essential features of durability can be described as follows:

• Efficiency is concerned with the best use of scarce resources. This requires a redefinition of inputs to the transformational process and a focus upon environmental resources as the scarce resource.

- Efficiency is concerned with optimising the use of the scarce resources (i.e. environmental resources) rather than with cost reduction.
- Value is added through technology and innovation rather than through expropriation.
- Outputs are redefined to include distributional effects to all stakeholders.

Conclusions

The two key components of durability – or durable sustainability – therefore are efficiency and equity. But efficiency needs to be redefined to prioritise the efficient use of environmental resources rather than the efficient use of financial resources. And equity requires as a minimum the satisficing of all stakeholders, and not merely the provision of returns to owners and investors. These are the prerequisites for sustainable development.

Sustainability is, of course, fundamental to a business and its continuing existence. It is equally fundamental to the continuing existence not just of current economic activity but also of the planet in a way which we currently understand. It is a complex process, as we have discussed. Moreover, it is a process which must recognise not just the decision being made in the operational activity of the organisation but also the distributional decisions which are made. Only then can an organisation be considered to be sustainable.

Summary of key points

- Brundtland defined the three pillars of sustainable development which led to triple bottom line reporting.
- We can actually identify four factors for sustainability.
- Managing sustainable performance is a complicated process, as is reporting upon that performance.
- Risk is related to sustainability and sustainable performance reduces risk.
- All companies are concerned about sustainability but do not necessarily understand the concept or its implications.

Definitions of key terms and theories

Durability is a strong form of sustainability addressing efficiency and equity.

Satisficing means making sure that all parties are sufficiently content not to protest.

Social performance also recognises externalities in its calculation of benefit.

Sustainable development is development that meets the needs of the present without compromising the ability of future generations to meet their own needs.

The Triple Bottom Line is economic (financial), environmental and social performance.

Test your understanding

1. What does the Triple Bottom Line consist of?
2. What are the four factors of sustainability?
3. What are the factors of distributable sustainability?
4. What are the factors in an analysis of social performance?
5. How does social justice relate to sustainability?
6. What is the difference between sustainability and continuing existence?
7. How important is the concept of sustainability for a business?

Suggestions for further reading

Aras, G. and Crowther, D. 2010. 'Sustainability', in *The Gower Handbook of Corporate Governance and Social Responsibility.*

Aras, G. and Crowther, D. 2009. *Durable Corporation: Strategies for Sustainable Development.* Aldershot: Gower.

Hart, S. L. 1997. 'Beyond Greening: Strategies for a Sustainable World', *Harvard Business Review*, January–February: 67–76.

WCED (World Commission on Environment and Development) 1987. *Our Common Future* (The Brundtland Report). Oxford: Oxford University Press.

Notes

1. World Business Council for Sustainable Development.
2. International Chamber of Commerce.
3. It needs a very careful reading of the annual report to discover this.
4. See Crowther (2002) for a full discussion of image creating in corporate reporting.
5. Many authors continue to assume both the possibility and desirability of sustainable development, hence our mentioning of it. For us, however, the achievement of sustainability is both a necessary precondition and sufficient in itself.
6. Financial reporting is premised, of course, upon the continuing of the company – the going concern principle.
7. See for example Mishan (1967) and Ormerod (1994). This can be equated to the concept of utility from the discourse of classical liberalism.

References

Amba-Rao, S. C. 1993. 'Multinational Corporate Social Responsibility, Ethics, Interactions and Third World Governments: An Agenda for the 1990s', *Journal of Business Ethics*, 12: 553–72.

Aras, G. and Crowther, D. 2007a. 'Is the Global Economy Sustainable?' in S. Barber (ed.), *The Geopolitics of the City*. London: Forum Press, 165–94.

Aras, G. and Crowther, D. 2007b. 'Sustainable Corporate Social Responsibility and the Value Chain', in D. Crowther and M. M. Zain (eds), *New Perspectives on Corporate Social Responsibility*, 109–28.

Aras, G. and Crowther, D. 2008a. 'Corporate Sustainability Reporting: A Study in Disingenuity?' *Journal of Business Ethics*, 87 (supp 1): 279–88.

Aras, G. and Crowther, D. 2008b. 'Governance and Sustainability: An Investigation into the Relationship between Corporate Governance and Corporate Sustainability', *Management Decision*, 46, 3: 433–48.

Aras, G. and Crowther, D. 2008c. 'The Social Obligation of Corporations', *Journal of Knowledge Globalisation*, 1, 1: 43–59.

Aras, G. and Crowther, D. 2008d. 'Evaluating Sustainability: A Need for Standards', *International Journal of Social and Environmental Accounting*, 2, 1: 19–35.

Aras, G. and Crowther, D. 2009. *Durable Corporation: Strategies for Sustainable Development*. Aldershot: Gower.

Azzone, G., Manzini, R. and Noel, G. 1996. 'Evolutionary Trends in Environmental Reporting', *Business Strategy and Environment*, 5, 4: 219–30.

Beder, S. 1997. *Global Spin: The Corporate Assault on Environmentalism*. London: Green Books.

Crowther, D. 2000. *Social and Environmental Accounting*. London: Financial Times Prentice Hall.

Crowther, D. 2002. *A Social Critique of Corporate Reporting*. Aldershot: Ashgate.

Crowther, D. and Davila-Gomez, A. M. 2006a. 'Is Lying the Best Way of Telling the Truth?', *Social Responsibility Journal*, 1, 3 and 4: 128–41.

Crowther, D. and Davila-Gomez, A. M. 2006b. 'Stress in the Back Office', in *Proceedings of India – the Processing Office of the World*, Kochi, January: 27–38.

Crowther, D. and Davila-Gomez, A. M. 2006c. 'I Will if You Will: Risk, Feelings and Emotion in the Workplace', in D. Crowther and K. T. Caliyurt (eds), *Globalization and Social Responsibility*. Newcastle: Cambridge Scholars Press, pp. 163–84.

Davila Gomez, A. M. and Crowther, D. 2007. 'Psychological Violence at Work: Where Does the Human Dignity Lie?' in A. M. Davila Gomez and D. Crowther (eds), *Ethics, Psyche and Social Responsibility*. Aldershot: Ashgate, pp 15–34.

Dyllick, T. and Hockerts, K. 2002. 'Beyond the Business Case for Corporate Sustainability', *Business Strategy and the Environment*. 11: 130–41.

Fetyko, D. F. 1975. 'The Company Social Audit', *Management Accounting*, 56 (10): 645–7.

Gray, R. 1992. 'Accounting and Environmentalism: An Exploration of the Challenge of Gently Accounting for Accountability, Transparency and Sustainability', *Accounting, Organizations and Society*, 17, 5: 399–425.

Gray, R. and Bebbington, J. 2001. *Accounting for the Environment*. London: Sage.

Hart, S. L. and Milstein, M. B. 2003. 'Creating Sustainable Value', *Academy of Management Executive*, 17, 2: 56–67.

Hawken, P. 1993. *The Ecology of Commerce*. London: Weidenfeld & Nicolson.

Herremans, I. M., Akathaparn, P. and McInnes, M. 1992. 'An Investigation of Corporate Social Responsibility, Reputation and Economic Performance', *Accounting, Organizations and Society*, 18, 7/8: 587–604.

Kimberley, J., Norling, R. and Weiss, J. A. 1983. 'Pondering the Performance Puzzle: Effectiveness in Interorganizational Settings', in R. H. Hall and R. E. Quinn (eds), *Organizational Theory and Public Practice*. Beverly Hills: Sage, pp. 249–64.

Klein, T. A. 1977. *Social Costs and Benefits of Business*. Englewood Cliffs, NJ: Prentice Hall.

Marrewijk, M. van and Werre, M. 2003. 'Multiple Levels of Corporate Sustainability', *Journal of Business Ethics*, 44, 2/3: 107–19.

Marsden, C. 2000. 'The New Corporate Citizenship of Big Business: Part of the Solution to Sustainability', *Business and Society Review*, 105, 1: 9–25.

Mishan, E. J. 1967. *The Costs of Economic Growth*. Harmondsworth: Pelican.

Myners, P. 1998. Improving Performance Reporting to the Market', in A. Carey and J. Sancto (eds), *Performance Measurement in the Digital Age*. London: ICAEW, pp. 27–33.

Ormerod, P. 1994. *The Death of Economics*. London: Faber & Faber.

Pava, M. L. and Krausz, J. 1996. 'The Association between Corporate Social Responsibility and Financial Performance: The Paradox of Social Cost', *Journal of Business Ethics*, 15, 3: 321–57.

Rappaport, A. 1986. *Creating Shareholder Value*. New York: The Free Press.

Reed, R. and DeFillippi, R. J. 1990. 'Causal Ambiguity, Barriers to Imitation, and Sustainable Competitive Advantage', *Academy of Management Review*, 15, 1: 88–102.

Solomons, D. 1974. 'Corporate Social Performance: A New Dimension in Accounting Reports?, in H. Edey and B. S. Yamey (eds), *Debits, Credits, Finance and Profits*. London: Sweet & Maxwell, pp. 131–41.

Spangenberg, J. H. 2004. 'Reconciling Sustainability and Growth: Criteria, Indicators, Policies', *Sustainable Development*, 12: 74–86.

Stewart, G. B. III 1991. *The Quest for Value*. New York: HarperCollins.

Tinker, T. 1985. *Paper Prophets: A Social Critique of Accounting*. London: Holt, Rinehart & Winston.

Tinker, T. 1988. 'Panglossian Accounting Theories: The Science of Apologising in Style', *Accounting, Organizations and Society*, 13, 2: 165–89.

Zwetsloot, G. I. J. M. 2003. 'From Management Systems to Corporate Social Responsibility', *Journal of Business Ethics*, 44, 2/3: 201–07.

Corporate and Managerial Behaviour

9

Introduction

Often our understanding of corporate behaviour in the context of CSR assumes that the firm acts as if it is a person in its own right. So we talk about corporate activity. In actual fact, of course, such activity is based upon the decision taken by the managerial team of the organisation. So it is effectively the actions of individual people acting alone or as part of a small group. Consequently we need to spend some time understanding such behaviour.

The theory of the firm

The theory of the firm explains why firms come into existence and the role of accounting in firms as a tool to aid rational decision making. It does not, however, sufficiently explain the workings of a firm. Thus, the role of accounting within a firm cannot be considered without a consideration of the people involved in that firm since a firm, of course, consists of a collection of people involved in that firm's undertakings. Those involved are affected by the accounting systems of that firm as well as, in turn, affecting those accounting systems, and this will be considered in greater detail in Chapter 11. The main people involved in the control of a firm are, of course, its managers, and Williamson (1970) argues that because in any large organisation the management of the firm is normally divorced from its ownership then this is a factor which hinders its control and decision making. This leads to internal efficiencies within the firm and conflicts of interests, which mean that organisations do not operate efficiently as a means of transaction cost-minimisation and value-creating maximisation. From this analysis Williamson developed what is known as the Organisational Failure Framework.

In its simplest form this framework can be summarised as follows:

- people are not perfect and managers are unlikely to ignore their own self-interest in pursuing the interests of the owners of the firm;
- organisations as resources allocation mechanisms are not perfect and inefficiencies arise as the size of firms increases;
- markets are not perfect and cannot by themselves compensate for the other inefficiencies inherent in the organising of productive activity into firms.

The first problem, concerning the people within organisations, has been tackled through the development of Agency theory, whilst the other two problems have been addressed through the development of Transaction Cost theory.

Introduction to transaction cost theory

As far as the activities of a firm are concerned, accounting adopts an entirely internal perspective and fails to recognise that the effects of the actions of the firm have effects outside the organisation; as we stated earlier these are considered to be irrelevant to the firm operating under the assumptions of Classical Liberalism. Moreover, accounting as practised by firms is based upon the product or service provided by the firm as the basic unit of cost. In working in this manner, accounting has been designed to capture the costs that are incurred in the provision of these products or services and simply to measure the costs that are accumulated in the production process. These cost accumulations form the basis of accounting information which is used for the multiple purposes of management accounting within the firm. These uses, of course, will include:

- operational planning and control
- decision making
- performance measurement and reporting
- the evaluation and rewarding of managerial performance

The implications from the use by firms of accounting in this way is that the key to successful management of the firm is the understanding of cost behaviour, so that extensive techniques have been developed to understand the behaviour

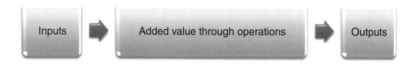

Figure 9.1   The transformational process

of costs in the operational processes of the firm. Equally, many techniques have been developed for the allocation of costs and their absorption into the product costs which are the outcome of the accounting process. There is an implicit assumption, therefore, that cost minimisation is the key to operational success for a firm. This is untrue, of course, and the key to the sustainable success of a firm is the maximisation of value creation. This is achieved through an understanding of the transformational process of the firm, which can be depicted as shown in Figure 9.1.

Transaction Cost theory adds to this theory through an understanding of the transformational process (as in Figure 9.1). The starting point for the theory is that all activities of the firm are transactions. This is true whether these activities are carried out within the firm or are carried out by an interaction between the firm and a part of its external environment. Thus, there is no difference in principle between internal activities and external activities as far as the firm is concerned because they are all transactions. The only actual difference is that when these transactions take place externally to the firm then a price can be determined for the transactions through the operation of the market mechanism. When they occur entirely within the firm, the no-market mechanism exists to set a price for the transactions and hence we have to develop accounting techniques to compensate for this deficiency and to simulate the operation of the market mechanism. Such techniques would include, for example, the transfer pricing systems used by firms.

As well as a price for the exchange, all transactions have a cost associated with them. This is the cost of engaging in the transaction itself and examples include the cost of acquiring raw materials, which is included in the accounting cost of those raw materials, or the cost of creating a Pareto optimal principal–agent contract. In theory, firms exist because the cost of engaging in these transactions is reduced when they are carried out within the firm rather than through the market as mediated through the price mechanism. In practice, all firms carry out some transactions entirely within the firm and some through the market mechanism. This is theoretically because the cost of each individual transaction can be minimised by either internalising it within the firm or externalising it to the market. For optimal value creation in the transformational process these transaction costs need to be minimised and therefore this theory turns the focus of organisational activity upon the transaction costs associated with the transformational process. Minimising the costs of all transactions will inevitably achieve the following:

- the maximising of the efficiency of operational activity through optimising the source of all transactions;

- the maximising of the profitability of the firm through the minimising of the costs of the products or services provided;
- the minimising of the costs of the transformations undertaken and hence the maximising of value created within the firm.

If a firm understands the transaction costs associated with its transformational process then it will be able to decide whether transactions are more efficiently accommodated within the firm or through the market. If transactions are reduced in cost through accommodating them within the firm then they should be carried out within the firm and this could imply a firm engaging in vertical integration as a means of reducing its transaction costs. Another way of reducing the cost of any particular type of transaction is by ensuring that economies of scale lead to a reduction in unit transaction costs and this could lead to horizontal integration. On the other hand, an understanding of these transaction costs may lead to a firm externalising transactions and engaging in them through the market; this would lead to a firm downsizing and divesting certain activities whilst engaging in the outsourcing of such transactions as the need arises. In such a way the performance of any individual firm would be optimised and this implies that there is an optimal size for any particular firm and an optimal set of activities in which it should engage.

An observation of the economy of any country will show that firms are engaged in changing the source of their transactions through both integration and divestment at all times. The assumption to be drawn from this is that the managers of these organisations understand their transaction costs and are reacting accordingly. The Organisational Failure Framework, however, argues that this is not the case and that communication distortions and bureaucratic mechanisms prevent this from happening efficiently. One problem which firms face, however, that interferes with this process is the use of accounting information itself. Accounting as cost accumulation does not, however, measure these transaction costs and so does not provide a means of measurement that will facilitate transaction cost minimisation. This therefore reveals one problem with the use of accounting information to manage the value creation process of the firm and this is that accounting does not even measure this key determinant of operational performance.

Transaction Cost theory therefore provides a different perspective on the operation of a firm and shows that accounting fails the managers of the firm in determining its transaction costs. It argues that accounting differently would help a firm optimise its performance.

The problems of transaction cost theory

This sounds intuitively logical and these arguments accord with those of strategic management which focus upon the value chain. There are problems, however, with putting this theory into practice. These problems stem from the points made earlier in this chapter, stemming from the Organisational Failure

Framework, which are that firms are not efficient allocators of resources and that markets themselves do not operate efficiently. It is to these points that we now turn.

Organisations as resource allocators

Traditionally organisations base their resource allocation decision on the information available to them from their accounting systems. We have already identified, however, that accounting information does not provide the information necessary to base decisions concerning the allocation of resources upon the transaction costs associated with individual transactions in the transformational process. Thus, such decisions tend to be based upon incomplete information and it is logical therefore to accept that the optimum allocation of resources within a firm will not be achieved through the use of traditional accounting information as a decision-making tool. Furthermore, we have considered the behaviour of managers in the context of Agency theory and this makes it apparent that these managers do not necessarily have the incentive to allocate resources in a way which is optimum for the organisation itself. The behaviour of managers in organisations is further complicated by the way in which accounting information is used to motivate managers and reward them for performance as well as the way in which the accounting information is shaped in its use by the managers of the organisation themselves. In this respect it becomes impossible to separate accounting information from the decision-making process and both of these from the power relationships which exist in all organisations. These are all points which we will be considering in greater details in subsequent chapters.

It is therefore apparent that both the behaviour of managers and the way in which accounting information is used in organisations are factors which prevent organisations operating efficiently as resource allocators. These arguments support the problems of organisations which have been identified in the Organisational Failure Framework itself.

Inefficiencies in the market

Economic theory focuses upon the market as a means of exchange between different individuals or organisations, with the assumption that one party to the exchange offers goods or services whilst the other offers money in payment. These exchanges take place in the market. The market therefore is a shorthand expression for the process by which consumers of goods and services decide upon their needs and the suppliers of those goods and services decide upon what to provide. The mediating mechanism which reconciles the demand and supply for any particular good or service is that of price. There is an implicit assumption that each party to a transaction will behave rationally in seeking to maximise his or her utility and that in the long term the free operation of the price mechanism will be sufficient to determine a price at which supply and demand are brought into equilibrium. These assumptions, however, only apply in a situation of perfect competition and in reality such competition never exists. In reality, therefore, the market is affected by the respective power of various competitors in the market, the actions of the firm itself in the market, government regulation of the market, and the expectations of the various actors in the market concerning both the present and the future. Thus, it can be argued that an equilibrium price never actually exists, or at least never exists for more than a brief period of time.

Thus, one of the basic assumptions of economic theory, as far as the operations of markets is concerned, that equilibrium is a natural state can be seen not to apply and this is the basic problem with market efficiency and the price mechanism for transaction mediation. The actions of the firm in determining its operational processes and seeking to minimise its transaction costs depend, however, upon a stable equilibrium in the market to make the necessary planning for operational activities. It therefore follows that the market too is problematical as far as the allocation of resources for the minimisation of transaction costs is concerned.

Thus, although it seems that Transaction Cost theory provides a means for focusing upon the transformation process within the firm as a basis for managerial decision making and upon transaction cost-minimising as a basis for profit-maximisation, it can be seen that this would imply a restructuring of the way in which accounting information is collected and utilised within organisations. We can see, however, that there are practical problems with the application of the theory as far as ongoing decision making within organisations is concerned. Unfortunately, therefore, we must conclude that the theory has little practical application for organisations other than to provide a means to focus upon different aspects of the organisations transformational and operations processes.

Bernard Madoff and abnormal profits

On 29 June 2009 Bernard Madoff was sentenced to 150 years in prison with restitution of $170 billion. According to the original federal charges, Madoff said that his firm had liabilities of approximately $50 billion whereas the state prosecutors estimated the size of the fraud to be $64.8 billion, based on the amounts in the accounts of Madoff's 4 800 clients as of 30 November 2008. This made it the biggest fraud in financial history although, interestingly, after ignoring opportunity costs and taxes paid on fictitious profits, half of Madoff's direct investors lost no money at all.

The Madoff investment scandal was what is known as a Ponzi scheme, whereby dividends were made out of new investments. Obviously such a scheme cannot be maintained forever but Madoff managed for almost twenty years whilst funding a lavish lifestyle and acquiring a reputation as an investment guru. He founded his firm Bernard L. Madoff Investment Securities LLC in 1960, and was its chairman until his arrest. Alerted by his sons, federal authorities arrested Madoff on 11 December 2008. On 12 March 2009, Madoff pleaded guilty to 11 federal crimes and admitted to operating what has been called the largest investor fraud ever committed by an individual. Madoff started his firm in 1960 as a penny stock trader with $5 000 (about $35,000 in 2008 dollars), earned from working as a lifeguard and sprinkler installer. His business began to grow with the assistance of his father-in-law, accountant Saul Alpern, who referred a circle of friends and their families. Initially, the firm made markets via the National Quotation Bureau's Pink Sheets. In order to compete with firms that were members of the New York Stock Exchange trading on the stock exchange's floor, his firm began using innovative computer information technology to disseminate its quotes. After a trial run, the technology that the firm helped develop became the NASDAQ. At one point, Madoff Securities was the largest market maker at the NASDAQ.

In 1992, *The Wall Street Journal* described him as 'one of the masters of the off-exchange third market and the bane of the New York Stock Exchange'. Madoff explained his purported strategy to *The Wall Street Journal*. He said the returns were really nothing special, given that the Standard and Poors 500-stock index generated an average annual return of 16.3% between November 1982 and November 1992. 'I would be surprised if anybody thought that matching the S&P over 10 years was anything outstanding.' The majority of money managers actually trailed the S&P 500 during the 1980s. The *Journal* concluded Madoff's use of futures and options helped cushion the returns against the market's ups and downs. Madoff said he made up for the cost of the hedges, which could have caused him to trail the stock market's returns, with stock-picking and market timing. In March 2009, Madoff admitted that since the mid 1990s he stopped trading and his returns had been fabricated.

It might seem strange that so many people allowed this to continue but history shows that people are willing to accept abnormally large profits on a continuing basis even though history also shows that this is not possible.

The motivation of managers

In considering the way in which corporate reporting impacts upon managerial accountability, it is essential to consider the motivations of managers (Crowther, 2002b). This section therefore considers the motivations of managers in terms of psychoanalytic theory from the Freudian and Lacanian perspectives to consider the implications for managerial needs for individuation. It has been argued (Crowther, 2002a) that this drive for individuation leads to the managerial motivation for the usurpation of primacy.

The management of an organisation is often treated as a discrete entity but it is important to remember that this entity actually comprises a set of individuals with their own drives, motivations and desires. Thus, every individual has a desire to fulfil his or her needs and one of these is self-actualisation (Maslow, 1954). This need is the one at the top of Maslow's hierarchy of needs and consequently perhaps the one most considered in terms of motivation. The next two most important needs – the need for esteem (as reflected in self-respect and the respect of others) and the need for love and belonging (as reflected in the need for being an integral part of a community) – are, however, more important for the understanding of the behaviour of the members of the dominant coalition of management within an organisation. These two needs help explain why managers, in common with other individuals, need to feel important, skilled and essential to organisational performance.

A more suitable basis for arriving at a deeper understanding of the drivers of management behaviour, when considered from the point of view of the behaviour and motivations of individual managers of the organisation, is, however, based upon a psychoanalytic interpretation. Psychoanalytic theory was created initially by Freud but has been widely adapted by others. In a general sense, such theory can be considered to be a theory of human emotional behaviour. An investigation of some of the major perspectives is necessary in order to understand the implications for managerial behaviour.

Sigmund Freud: the father of psychoanalysis

Most people know that psychoanalytic theory was created initially by Freud but has been widely adapted by others. In a general sense, such theory can be considered to be a theory of human emotional behaviour. Freud was concerned with the role of childhood experiences in the development of a person and argued that early childhood experience, particularly during the first year of life, were critical to the formation of personality. These experiences resulted in unconscious motivations that govern the way in which we all behave for the rest of life. In particular, these early experiences led to feelings of guilt and insecurity brought about by our desire to please our parents but failing to do so. Thus, according to Freud the rest of our life is devoted to assuaging these feeling of guilt and insecurity.

According to Freud, the personality consists of three elements: the conscious, the preconscious and the unconscious. The conscious consists of our current perceptions whilst the preconscious contains our memory. The largest element, however, consists of the unconscious which contains repressed memories. It is these which largely govern our behaviour although we cannot consciously remember them. Thus, we are acting without actually knowing why we do so. The structure of the personality is based upon three aspects which must be maintained in balance. These are the Id, known as the pleasure principle, which seeks to allow us to do whatever will give us maximum satisfaction; the Ego, known as the reality principle, which enables us to compromise with the demands of the world; and the Superego which acts as a conscience.

In his psychoanalytic theory, Freud (1984) argues that the real motivation for any act undertaken by a person may be disguised and not apparent even to the person who performs that act. Thus, for Freud the underlying basis for identity, and therefore for an explanation of individual behaviour, was in the unconscious. He argued that an individual's identity was based upon past experience which was largely unconscious and that behaviour was largely dependent upon an attempt to resolve the conflicts and motivations inherent in the unconscious (Freud, 1975). Furthermore, he stated (1976, 1977) that most aspects of identity are laid down in early childhood and that it is an attempt to integrate the various facets of childhood experience which leads a person to act in particular ways. Part of this conflict is based upon parental influence, which leads to the development within the child of the concept of the ideal self as the perfect being to strive to become in order to win parental approval. This ideal self is, of course, unattainable but adult life, and the actions undertaken by adults, is based upon an unconscious motivation to achieve this ideal self and thereby secure respect. This motivation has been expressed by psychoanalysts as the drive towards individuation and explains the continual need for reassurance and the gaining of both self-respect and the respect of others.

For psychoanalysts this drive for individuation is the means by which we express our identity as an individual. This is manifested in the way we dress, the signs and symbols which we choose to display, and in the way we behave. Sometimes these are expressed in the way we seek to be different from others and sometimes in the way we seek to blend in by looking like others. Either way, it has obvious implications for our buying behaviour.

All these arguments naturally have consequences for an individual which affect the behaviour of that individual. They also naturally have implications for others affected by this behaviour and Sievers (1994) has described this as leading to psychotic behaviour. These interpretations of individual behaviour naturally apply to all people and the implication of these Freudian arguments is that we are motivated by unconscious conflicts and desires, which we seek to reconcile through acting out these conflicts as part of our desire for individuation. Furthermore, these arguments imply that all individuals are anxious and insecure and seek to reduce anxiety and increase security through their actions. Thus, the drive to reduce anxiety is manifested in the desire to seek confirmation of worth from others in order to increase self-esteem. One way to raise our self-esteem is through our buying behaviour and this is recognised by marketing people, who play upon our sense of insecurity in seeking to suggest that the purchase of particular goods or services will increase our self-esteem.

Carl Jung: analytic psychology

Further understanding of the psychoanalytic motivation of behaviour can be derived from a consideration of the Jungian interpretation of behaviour. Although based initially upon the work of Freud, Jung deviated from this interpretation significantly by focusing his concentration upon understanding individual behaviour through an understanding of societal behaviour and through the development of his concept of the collective unconscious (Jung, 1972). This determines the way in which all people act and, according to Jung, provides a way of acting which is universal in nature and is inherited by all individuals. This way of behaving has existed from time immemorial and can be seen equally in the myths of primitive society[1] and in the behaviour of individuals in our current society.

Many of the concepts which Jung developed in his work have become part of everyday speech to such an extent that people use the concepts without being aware of their origins. An example of this is Jung's work in the development and identification of personality types. In this work he laid the foundations of psychometric testing as developed by Eysenck, and his concepts of extroversion and introversion have entered common vocabulary. Other work led to his formulation of the concept of the collective unconscious as an impersonal substratum of memory underlying the personal unconscious that is common to everyone. In this respect it can be likened to a form of racial memory which is independent of an individual's own experiences. An example of the operation of the collective unconscious is that of the urban myth.

An essential part of the motivation provided by the collective unconscious is concerned with the drive for belonging to a society or to a group within that society. This is manifested in such features of society as tribalism, the concept of the nation state, and the existence of a multitude of diverse groups such as local football supporters clubs, the Mothers Union and the Sealed Knot. It also explains the need for identification with and belonging to the organisation by which one is employed as well as the importance of family ties. This belonging (to whatever group or groups one chooses to identify with) is an essential part of the constitution of an individual's sense of identity and is vital in an individual's search for meaning in life. This sense of belonging through identification is naturally enhanced if one can have a significant, and preferably an essential, role in the group to which one belongs. This search for belonging and being needed is a part of every person's search for meaning in life, which we will explore in more detail in later chapters.

This need for meaning and belonging is manifested in the mythopoeic imagination (Jung, 1953; 1954), and one manifestation of this need leads to the need for the creation of myth (May, 1991) and the constitution of self as hero (or saviour) within the group to which one belongs (Jung, 1953; Campbell, 1949). In its extreme manifestation within a group situation this need for myth creation and the constitution of oneself as hero leads to a situation of groupthink (Janis, 1972) and the notion of invulnerability. At a lesser level of intensity it leads the managers of an organisation both to portray themselves to the outside world as essential to the well-being of the organisation, and to believe this portrayal themselves. These unconscious motivations driving our behaviour are present in all of us and consequently form one of the underlying themes of individual existence and behaviour (Mitroff, 1983).

Alfred Adler: individual psychology

Adler was born and grew up in Vienna. In his adult life he first trained and practised as an ophthalmologist before turning his attention to mental disease and psychiatry. It is difficult to consider the work of Adler without setting it in the context of his dispute with Freud concerning the driving force behind a person's sense of self. Whilst he agreed with Freud that early childhood was significant in personality development in addition to the influences of heredity and the environment, Adler argued that each person is endowed with an individual creative power which combines with innate potentialities and environmental influences to help that person overcome the obstacles in the path of life and self-development. Adler's Individual Psychology theory is built around the fact that, although a person is born with this free creative power, the interaction of this power with hereditary and environmental influences leads an individual to choose a lifestyle. As a consequence the creative power becomes the main determinant of individual personality and through interaction with the other influences no longer remains free.

His psychology is built upon the following principles:

- Teleology, in which he argues that the final goal provides sufficient explanatory reasons for everything a person thinks, feels or does. He therefore rejects causality and determinism.
- The aggressive drive, which Adler believed to be the main force for self-assertion in a person.

The inferiority complex, which is the major concept in Adler's work that has entered common parlance and found a place in current culture, is, according to Adler, based on a deficiency in a physical organ or sense, which leads to the deficit in this area being compensated for by action to it. Thus, a great orator, Demosthenes, had a stutter, Beethoven had hearing problems and many artists (e.g. Turner) had optical disorders which they sought to overcome. He refined this concept to argue that each person is driven to overcome feelings of inferiority, stating that 'to be human means to be inferior' and that every child bases his or her development on attempting to overcome feelings of inferiority. This attempt to overcome inferiority therefore led to a striving for superiority over nature and one's fellows and this explains the conflicts within and between different societies. Each person, however, strives towards superiority in a different way and this he termed 'style of life' which provides an explanation of individual differences. Thus, our style of life is, according to Adler, concerned with the desire to overcome our innate sense of inferiority.

The Lacanian view: the reassertion of the individual

Since the development of psychoanalysis by Freud, critiques of this theory have been common in social theory and in Marxism. Indeed, the intertwining of Marxist and Freudian theory as a means of understanding organisational behaviour and the distribution of power within society is a recurrent theme. Thus, for example, Marcuse (1956) argues that rather than the foundations of civilisation being built upon the subjugation of human instincts in the assuagement of guilt, instead it is built upon the way in which power is distributed and the consequent suppression of labour. Similarly, Habermas (1971) argues that Freudian psychoanalysis is based upon the voluntary self-deception of individuals as part of their anxiety-reducing mechanisms; moreover, he argues that corporate organisations are also involved in this deception. Baudrillard (1993, 1999) is equally critical of psychoanalysis.

Possibly the most significant critique of psychoanalysis has been undertaken by Lacan, who developed an alternative interpretation of Freudian theory which has permeated popular culture, whilst at the same time providing a basis for an understanding of the role of managers as individuals in the development of the semiology of corporate reporting. Lacanian interpretations can be encapsulated in the work of Harris (1979), who stated that the Freudian attempts to understand pan-human psychodynamic processes were sufficient to understand and explain the similarities but not the differences in such processes.

Lacan argues that the formation of the ego is concerned with a fascination with one's own image. For him the external world merely represents a mirror upon which the self is displayed and the concern of the individual is to create a reflection in this mirror. This reflection must, of course, support that person's desire to see the most flattering reflection, but in such a way that it appears as reality. This is brought about by every person's inherent insecurity and seeking for the ideal self (Lacan, 1977; 1991) and thus every action which a person undertakes is derived from this motivation. It is accepted, however, that this motivation may not be overt and may not even be recognised by the individual him- or herself. Like Freud, therefore, Lacan accepts that an individual's motivation may not be transparent even to him- or herself but nevertheless that motivation becomes inseparable from the actions undertaken, and those actions have a motivation which is based upon the seeking of personal individuation.

Lacan uses the work of Saussure (1966) to argue that language is a system of signs which refer, not to objects themselves but rather to the psychic representation created by their interplay. According to Lacan, therefore, the human subject is inserted into the symbolic order of language, attempting the impossible task of representing itself whilst being at the same time an effect of the Saussurian signifier. Saussure (1966) identified a sign as dyadic, having two sides – the signifier and the signified: the signifier being the material object and the signified being its associated mental concept. The inseparability of these two aspects of the sign led to his diagrammatic representation, depicted in Figure 9.2.

Thus Saussure's understanding of the process of communication is based upon an assumption of the transfer of mental concepts through the signs produced. One significant analysis of Saussure's work has been undertaken by Lacan (1977), who argued that human beings are entirely enmeshed within the sign and its subjectivity, thereby making the separation of the signifier and the signified impossible.

This leads to the division of the subject in language because for Lacan the unconscious is not a realm within the subject but rather an intersubjective space between people. Thus, Lacan argues that the unconscious is essentially outside the subject and is produced by the subject's insertion into the symbolic order. For him the unconscious is structured like language (Lacan, 1988) and therefore

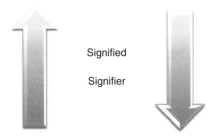

Figure 9.2   The Saussurian Dyadic

operates in accordance with the relationships which are inherent in language. It therefore is not possible to state that the unconscious belongs to the individual but rather it is correct to say that it comes to the individual from outside and is an effect of signification on the subject.

Lacan bases upon this argument his understanding of unconscious desire by arguing that because the subject is divided from itself in language it is continually aware of a sense of absence. By this he means an awareness that as a subject (s)he is not fully present, and he refers to this as the 'Thing' of the 'lost object'. He considers that this sense of the 'lost object' produces in the subject a desire for something which will make good this loss, thereby creating the unconscious desire. For Lacan this unconscious desire is doomed to be unfulfilled because it is a fantasy and there is no position of completeness to which it is possible to return. Thus the subject is forever seeking to recapture an impossible position and it is this which motivates its continual identification with the subject positions which the symbolic order make available to it. Thus, according to Lacan, we are continually motivated to invest in the various subject positions of language, in our attempts to recover from our absence from them and to recover a state of completeness in self-presence.

Lacan's work is complex but important in the context of psychoanalysis. It is concerned primarily with the ego and with the fascination with one's own image. Lacan argues that the external world is merely a mirror to reflect the self. This reflection becomes reality and therefore we are each seeking to see reality in the most flattering reflection and behaving in such a way as to achieve this. In this respect Lacan concurs with the other psychoanalysts we have considered in suggesting that we all suffer from inherent insecurity which drives us to search for ideal self.

Al Gore, environmental crusader

In December 2000 – more than two weeks after the election – it was decided that Al Gore had not been elected as President of the USA. Opinion is still divided as to whether he was actually elected and the result was stolen by George Bush jnr. Certainly, the world is less safe because of subsequent events.

Nevertheless, Gore accepted defeat and turned his back on politics, refusing to stand again in 2004. Beginning in late 2002, Gore began publicly to criticise the Bush administration and its policies. In a speech given in 2004, during the presidential election, Gore accused Bush of betraying the country by using the 9/11 attacks as a justification for the invasion of Iraq. The next year, Gore gave a speech which covered many topics including what he called 'religious zealots' who claim special knowledge of God's will in American politics. After Hurricane Katrina in 2005, Gore chartered two planes to evacuate 270 people from New Orleans and criticised the Bush administration's response to the hurricane. In 2006, Gore criticised President Bush's use of domestic wiretaps without a warrant. One month later he criticised the treatment of Arabs in the United States after 9/11 stating, 'Unfortunately there have been terrible abuses and it's wrong...I do want you to know that it does not represent the desires or wishes or feelings of the majority of the citizens of my country.' Gore's 2007 book, *The Assault on Reason*, is an analysis of what Gore refers to as the 'emptying out of the marketplace of ideas' in civic discourse during the Bush administration. He attributes this phenomenon to the influence of television and argues that it endangers American democracy. By contrast, Gore argues, the internet can revitalise and ultimately 'redeem the integrity of representative democracy'.

Gore has received a number of awards, the most prestigous being the Nobel Peace Prize (joint award with the Intergovernmental Panel on Climate Change (2007), an Emmy for Current TV (2007), and a Webby Award (2005). In 2007 he was named a runner-up for *Time Magazine*'s Person of the Year. Gore is also known for popularising the term 'information superhighway'.He is currently the founder and chair of the Alliance for Climate Protection, the co-founder and chair of Generation Investment Management, the co-founder and chair of Current TV, a member of the Board of Directors of Apple Inc, and a senior advisor to Google. Gore is also a partner in a venture capital firm, heading that firm's climate change solutions group. He is also visiting professor at a number of universities.

Gore is a committed and visible environmental campaigner. He is also criticised because his Tennessee mansion consumes 20 times as much power as the average US home and 400 times as much as an average African home. An inconvenient truth?

Language and power

Swales and Rogers (1995) consider that the language used in business affairs is important as it provides a framing context for the communication of decisions in terms of the history and culture of that organisation. The language used by the dominant coalition therefore becomes part of the institutional behaviour of the organisation but also gives power to the coalition as they set the agenda of communication. Indeed, Hanna and Wilson (1984: 21) argue that language is inextricably entwined in power relationships, stating:

Communication is almost always an attempt to control change, either by causing it or preventing it.

It has been argued that information places power in the hands of the dominant coalition. It is also argued, however, that although this enables the decision agenda to be set by them, they are in fact constrained by these data and by the institutional rituals that determine which decisions can be made and how they are implemented. Williamson (1970) states that the divorce of ownership and management hinders decision making and leads to inefficiencies in the decisional process. An alternative explanation is that the decisions made are grounded in the needs and desires of the dominant coalition rather than in the needs of the business as far as the owners are concerned. Monks and Minow (1991) illustrate the way in which the power in the decision-making domain is divorced from accountability for the implementation of those decisions, and how this is deleterious to corporate performance. This too can be interpreted as an illustration of the effects of the ownership of decision making being in the hands of the dominant coalition rather than of all the stakeholders of the organisation.

It has been argued (Dermer, 1988) that organisations consist of a sustained set of beliefs and behaviours and that the existence of organisational rules, beliefs and rituals limit the extent of the control which it is possible for managers to exert in the organisation. Thus, the control of the decision-making domain, as exercised by the dominant coalition of the management team, is constrained by the institutional nature of the organisation and the need to transfer ownership of decisions from the decision makers to the organisation as a whole for the implementation of those decisions. In this context, Covalenski and Dirsmith (1986) state that organisational politics play a key role in the construction of reality as far as members of the organisation are concerned. Thus, although the decision agenda is set by the decision makers, this agenda is in reality constrained by the nature of organisational behaviour. Thus, rather than having a free choice as to decisions to be made, the management team actually have a limited choice of decisions. These decisions are limited by the following factors:

- the available information and the way in which it is presented and interpreted, and accounting information is crucial in this respect;
- the organisational rules and rituals which determine the way decisions are put into effect;
- the need to transfer decision ownership into the public domain within the organisation.

Accounting has often been described as the language of business (Davidson, Schindler and Weil, 1974) and, as such, provides the technology by which an organisation may be represented by and to its stakeholders. The technology of this accounting language also provides a means by which the owners and managers of a business can communicate with each other, plan for the future, control the implementation of that planning and report upon the subsequent performance. This consideration of accounting as the language of business has been extended by Belkaoui (1978), who argues that accounting is not just the language of business but is actually a language in its own right, satisfying the grammatical and lexical characteristics of a language. On the basis of this argument that accounting is a language rests some of the problems of interpretation of accounting information. This is because accounting is not the native language of any person and so all users of the accounting language suffer from the interpretation problems of all users of a second language.

The acceptance of accounting as a language explains some of the interpretative difficulties with accounting data, but these difficulties can also be explained by the way in which accounting is used. Thus, accounting as a language is capable of being studied linguistically in order to understand its use in practice. Language is a means of communication between people sharing a common culture, or at least sufficient commonality to enable communication to take place. This cultural commonality can be in terms of a societal culture or, as in the case of corporate reporting, in terms of a business culture. Thus, accounting as the universal language of business enables this communication to take place regardless of the original native language of the parties to the communication process. In this communication such language provides not merely a representation of objects and events which the communicator of information has in mind but also a representation of the desires, intentions and goals of the communicator. These are either consciously embedded in the communication according to the communicator's intentions or unconsciously embedded despite the communicator's intentions. As such these intentions are subject to analysis and interpretation.

Linguistic studies have shown that language is used to identify social class (e.g. Labov, 1966; Klein, 1965; Hewitt, 1989) but that language also defines identity much more narrowly in terms of the social group to which one belongs. This view has been identified by Le Page (1968: 194), who stated:

> Each individual creates the systems for his verbal behaviour so that they shall resemble those of the group or groups with which from time to time he may wish to be identified.

Thus, this view suggests that language acts like a membership card and assumes that language usage and behaviour is adopted to gain membership. A contrary argument from feminist discourse, however, suggests that language is used as a source of power and dominance, and is used in this manner by the dominant group in order to exclude others. Thus Lakoff (1975: 136) considers language in the context of power and dominance, stating:

> The language of the favoured group, the group that holds the power, along with its non-linguistic behaviour, is generally adopted by the other group, not vice versa.

Thus the power of accounting in organisations can be based upon the argument that accounting is a language and therefore that knowledge of the language, and acceptance of the precepts upon which it is based, can be used to give or with-hold power within the organisation. Decisions are made in an organisation by those with the information necessary to make the decisions (or at least by those who perceive themselves to be in possession of that information) and the power necessary to enforce that decision. Thus, Finkelstein (1992) argues that strategic choice in an organisation is dependent upon the power of the top management team. Accounting information provides a mechanism for giving power to that team, or enabling the team to take power, as it provides a source of expert and referent power.

The precision of accounting as a language, together with its existence only in terms of the elaborate code of its written form, suggest that there should be little problem in the interpretation of information conveyed through the use of accounting language. It must be recognised, however, that accounting language is rarely used for communication solely through that language, except between one accountant and another. When the communication is intended to be between non-accountants then the use of accounting language is normally accompanied with the use of another language, being the native language of at least one party to the communication. Thus, accounting information for organisations is normally communicated partly in the language of accounting and partly in another language.

Accounting and other measurements

Traditionally, performance has been measured in accounting terms using the annual report as the reporting mechanism for external reporting and management accounting reports for internal reporting. To some extent this has been determined by legal requirements and to some extent by the easily quantitative nature of accounting information. It has been increasingly argued, however, that accounting information does not provide a full picture of the performance of an organisation, and does not necessarily provide an accurate picture for those areas in which it does not report performance. One problem with accounting is that it lends itself to comparative analysis and has tended to be used for control purposes to track performance against budget. The purpose of doing so is to highlight problem areas for corrective action rather than to highlight areas of significance. Its use therefore has been essentially defensive rather than strategic. This use has been highlighted by Drucker (1985: 36–7), who argues that strategic opportunities for organisational benefit are missed because accounting information is used defensively. He states:

> Far more often, the unexpected success is simply not seen at all. Nobody pays any attention to it. Hence nobody exploits it... One reason for this blindness to the unexpected success is that our existing reporting systems do not as a rule report it, let alone clamour for management attention. Practically every company ... has a monthly or quarterly report. The first sheet lists the areas in which performance is below expectations: it lists the problems and the shortfalls. At the meetings of the management group ... everybody therefore

focuses on the problem areas. No one even looks at the areas where the company has done better than expected. And if the unexpected success is not quantitative but qualitative ... the figures will not even show the unexpected success as a rule.

This illustrates that the evaluation of performance is dependent not just upon the perspective of those evaluating performance but also upon the measurement and reporting system. It also illustrates the danger of accepting the presentation of accounting information as truth, rather than an interpretation of the situation. The increasing dissatisfaction with accounting as the sole means of measuring performance has led to the use of other measures in addition to accounting measures. Such measures include qualitative measures as well as quantitative measures. The development of new measures of performance has largely therefore, in recent times, taken place outside the arena of accounting and has reflected the increasing concerns of both organisations and society with such issues as quality and environmental impact. There is a need, however, to view accounting, other quantitative measures and qualitative measures not as separate systems for measuring performance but as parts of an integrated system, and attention has turned to this.

At the same time, the means by which an organisation has reported upon performance have undergone considerable change (Eccles, 1991) and the extent of disclosure of performance has changed from an emphasis upon minimisation to one of maximisation of disclosure. This is reflected in changes to corporate reports but also in the publication of environmental impact reports, the increasing use of press releases and general informative publicity. It is possible to track these changes over time to reveal changes in the extent of disclosure and also changes in the parties to whom disclosure is made. This arguably reflects a change from an ownership reporting stance to one of a stakeholder stance.

Greenwashing

Many people are cynical about corporate activity and regard any CSR activity as little more than greenwashing – the presentation of activities to look as though they are socially responsible. In the main this is the stage which most observers of corporate activity continue to see even though in reality probably every organisation has progressed to a stage of greater maturity.

Corporations are always, of course, looking at their processes and seeking to operate more efficiently, thereby reducing costs. Organisations have realised that some of these can be represented as CSR activity – with things like energy efficiency or water efficiency being obvious examples. So there is a double imperative for this kind of activity – to improve financial performance and also improve the social responsible image. Not surprisingly, therefore, corporations quickly moved from stage 1 to this stage – where action has been taken even though it is not necessarily motivated by a sense of social responsibility.

Much of this kind of activity is easy to undertake and requires very little in the way of capital investment. Naturally this activity has been undertaken first – it has been described as picking the low hanging fruit. Activity requiring capital investment has a longer payback period and tends to be undertaken more cautiously, with the threat of regulation often being needed to encourage such activity. All organisations have progressed through this stage also, although it must be recognised that the possible actions under this stage will probably never be completed by most organisations. Such cost containment, of course, remains ongoing even when the easy targets have been addressed.

Conclusions

A lot of issues have been mentioned in this chapter; understanding management behaviour is a complicated process and we will continue in the next chapter with a review of agency theory. In this chapter we have looked at psychoanalysis which helps us to understand the motivations of individuals and we have looked at transaction costs theory which helps explain the priorities adopted by a firm. And we have considered the use of language in corporate communication. Together these are important issues for understanding the operation of CSR within an organisation.

Summary of key points

- Transaction cost theory explains when it is better for a firm to undertake activities itself and when to undertake them through the market.
- Personality consists of three elements: the conscious, the preconscious and the unconscious. There are three aspects to the structure of personality: the Id, the Ego and the Superego.
- Motivation is often unconscious but is concerned with the drive towards individuation.
- Jung developed the concepts of the collective unconscious and of archetypes, both of which affect our personality and our behaviour.
- Adler developed the concept of the inferiority complex
- For Lacan the world is a mirror in which we seek to enhance our reflection. He is concerned with signs and symbols and the relationship of the self to others through language. This is the only way to become complete personalities.
- Language represents power and can be used to represent different realities.
- Many people expect greenwashing from a firm but this expectation is normally unjustified.

Definitions of key terms and theories

Archetype is a type of personality present in each of us.

Collective unconscious provides a way of acting which is universal in nature and is inherited by all individuals.

Greenwashing is representing actions as social responsible without amending practice.

Individuation is the process of becoming a whole individual self.

Inferiority complex is a deficiency in a physical organ or sense which leads to the deficit in this area being compensated for by action to overcome this deficiency.

Superego: this acts as a conscience.

Transaction cost theory explains a firm's behaviour with respect to the market.

Test your understanding

1. Why do firms sometimes perform actions themselves and sometimes use others to do so?
2. How do the five stages of development identified by Freud relate to characteristics of consumer behaviour?
3. How does the drive for individuation manifest itself (according to Freud) in our behaviour?
4. How do the anxieties of childhood affect our adult existence?
5. How does the collective unconscious affect our patterns of consumption?
6. What is the relationship between aggression and the inferiority complex?
7. How are the concepts of psychoanalysis useful for understanding CSR?
8. According to Lacan, how do we seek for the ideal self?
9. Why is accounting known as the language of business?

Suggestions for further reading

Aoki, M., Gustoffson, B. and Williamson, O. E. (eds), 1989. 'The Firm as a Nexus of Treaties', *Journal of the Japanese and International Economies*, 3, 4: 345–66.

Crowther, D. 2002. 'Psychoanalysis and Auditing', in S. Clegg (ed.), *Paradoxical New Directions in Management and Organization Theory*. Amsterdam: J. Benjamins, pp. 227–46.

Gellner, E. 1985. *The Psychoanalytic Movement*. London: Paladin.

Note

1. See also Campbell (1949, 1972, 1993).

References

Baudrillard, J. 1993. *Symbolic Exchange and Death*; trans I. H. Grant. London: Sage.

Baudrillard, J. 1999. *Fatal Strategies*; trans P. Beitchman and W. G. J. Niesluchowski. London: Pluto Press.

Belkaoui, A. 1978. 'Linguistic Relativity in Accounting', *Accounting, Organizations and Society*, 3, 2: 97–104.

Campbell, J. 1949. *The Hero with a Thousand Faces*. Princeton, NJ: Princeton University Press.

Campbell, J. 1972. *Myths to Live By*. London: Souvenir Press.

Campbell, J. 1993. *The Mythic Dimension: Selected Essays 1959–1987*. New York: HarperCollins.

Covalenski, M. A. and Dirsmith, M. W. 1986. 'The Budgetary Process of Power and Politics', *Accounting, Organizations and Society*, 11, 3: 193–214.

Crowther, D. 2002a. 'The Psychoanalysis of On-line Reporting', in L. Holmes, M. Grieco and D. Hosking (eds), *Organising in the Information Age*. Aldershot: Ashgate, pp. 130–48.

Crowther, D. 2002b. 'Psychoanalysis and Auditing' in S. Clegg (ed.), *Paradoxical New Directions in Management and Organization Theory*. Amsterdam: J. Benjamins, pp. 227–46.

Davidson, S., Schindler, J. S. and Weil, R. L. 1974. *Accounting: the Language of Business*. New York: Thomas Horton & Daughters.

Dermer, J. 1988. 'Control and Organisational Order', *Accounting, Organizations and Society*, 13, 1: 25–36.

Drucker, P. F. 1985. *Innovation and Entrepreneurship*. Oxford: Butterworth-Heinemann.

Eccles, R. G. 1991. 'The Performance Evaluation Manifesto', *Harvard Business Review*, 69, 1: 131–7.

Finkelstein, S. 1992. 'power in Top Management Teams: Dimensions, Measurements and Validation', *Academy of Management Journal*, 35 (3): 505–38.

Freud, S. 1975. *The Psychopathology of Everday Life*, trans A. Tyson. Harmondsworth: Pelican.

Freud, S. 1976. *Jokes and their Relation to the Unconscious*, trans A. Richards. Harmondsworth: Pelican.

Freud, S. 1977. *On Sexuality*, trans A. Richards. Harmondsworth: Pelican.

Freud, S. 1984. *On Metapsychology*, trans A. Richards. Harmondsworth: Penguin.

Habermas, J. 1971. *Knowledge and Human Interests*, trans J. J. Shapiro. Boston, MA: Beacon Press.

Hanna, M. S. and Wilson, G. L. 1984. *Communication in Business and Professional Settings*. New York: Random House.

Harris, M. 1979. *Cultural Materialism*. New York: Random House.

Hewitt, J. 1989. 'White Adolescent Creole Users and the Politics of Friendship', *Journal of Multicultural and Multilingual Education*, 3, 3: 340–57.

Janis, I. L. 1972. *Victims of Groupthink*. Boston, MA: Houghton Mifflin.

Jung, C. G. 1953. *Psychology and Alchemy*, trans R. F. C. Hull. London: Routledge.

Jung, C. G. 1954. *The Development of Personality*, trans R. F. C. Hull. London: Routledge.

Jung, C. G. 1972. *Four Archetypes*, trans C. F. Baynes. London: Routledge.

Klein, J. 1965. *Samples from English Cultures.* London: Routledge & Kegan Paul.

Labov, W. 1966. 'The Linguistic Stratification of "r" in New York City Department Stores', in W. Labov (ed.), *Sociolinguistic Patterns.* Philadelphia: Pennsylvania University Press.

Lacan, J. 1977. *Ecrits: A Selection,* trans A. Sheridan. London: Tavistock.

Lacan, J. 1988. *The Seminar of Jacques Lacan Book III The Psychoses 1955–56,* trans R. Grigg. London: Routledge.

Lacan, J. 1991. *The Seminars of Jacques Lacan Book I: Freud's papers on Technique 1953–1954,* trans J. Forrester. New York; W. W. Norton & Co.

Lakoff, R. 1975. *Language and Woman's Place.* Cambridge: Harper & Row.

Le Page, R. 1968. 'Problems of Description in Multilingual Communities', *Transactions of the Philological Society,* 189–212.

Marcuse, H. 1956. *Eros and Civilisation.* London: Routledge & Kegan Paul.

Maslow, A. H. 1954. *Motivation and Personality.* New York: Harper & Row.

May, R. 1991. *The Cry for Myth.* New York; W. W. Norton & Co.

Mitroff, I. I. 1983. *Stakeholders of the Organisational Mind.* San Francisco: Jossey-Bass.

Monks, R. A. G. and Minow, N. 1991. *Power and Accountability.* Glasgow: HarperCollins.

Saussure, F. de 1966. *Course in General Linguistics,* trans W. Baskin. New York: McGraw-Hill.

Sievers, B. 1994. *Work Death and Life Itself. Essays on Management and Organization.* Berlin: de Gruyter.

Swales, J. M. and Rogers, P. S. 1995. 'Discourse and the Projection of Corporate Culture: The Mission Statement', *Discourse and Society,* 6, 2: 223–42.

Williamson, O. E. 1970. *Corporate Control and Business Behavior.* Englewood Cliffs, NJ: Prentice Hall.

Agency Theory and Governance

10

Learning objectives

After studying this chapter you should be able to:

- Describe the basic principles of agency theory.
- Outline what is meant by information asymmetry.
- Explain what is meant by corporate governance.
- Critique agency theory.
- Explain how the various approaches to corporate governance differ.

Introduction

One of the most important factors for any company is the relationship between it and its various stakeholders. This is important for the general management of the company and not just for its approach to CSR. Many factors affect these relationships, as we can see in many of the chapters in this book. Two factors in particular determine the relationship between the managers of the organisation and its stakeholders but particularly its owners and investors. These two factors are the agency relationship and the governance arrangements, the subject of this chapter.

Agency theory and asymmetric power

Agency theory argues that managers merely act as custodians of the organisation and its operational activities[1] and places upon them the burden of managing in the best interest of the owners of that business.[2] According to agency theory all other stakeholders of the business are largely irrelevant and if they benefit from the business then this is coincidental to the activities of management in running the business to serve shareholders.[3] This focus upon shareholders alone as the intended beneficiaries of a business has been questioned considerably from many perspectives, arguing that it is either not the way in which a business is actually run or that it is a view which does not meet the needs of society in general. Conversely, stakeholder theory argues that there are a whole variety of stakeholders involved in the organisation and each deserves some return for involvement. According to stakeholder theory, therefore, benefit is maximised if the business is operated by its management on behalf of all stakeholders and returns are divided appropriately among those stakeholders, in some way which is acceptable to all. Unfortunately, a mechanism for dividing returns among all stakeholders[4] which has universal acceptance does not exist, and stakeholder theory is significantly lacking in suggestions in this respect. Nevertheless, this theory has some acceptance and is based upon the premise that operating a business in this manner achieves as one of its outcomes the maximisation of returns to shareholders, as part of the process of maximising returns to all other stakeholders. This maximisation of returns is achieved in the long run through the optimisation of performance for the business to achieve maximal returns to all stakeholders.[5] Consequently, the role of management is to optimise the long-term performance of the business in order to achieve this end and thereby reward all stakeholders, including themselves as one stakeholder community, appropriately.

These two theories can be regarded as competing explanations of the operations of a firm, which lead to different operational foci and to different implications for the measurement, and reporting of performance. It is significant, however, that both theories have one feature in common. This is that the management of the firm is believed to be acting on behalf of others, either shareholders or stakeholders more generally. They do so, not because they are the kind of people who behave altruistically, but because they are rewarded appropriately, and much effort is therefore devoted to the creation of reward schemes which motivate these managers to achieve the desired ends. Similarly, much literature is devoted to the consideration of the effects of reward schemes on managerial behaviour (see Briers and Hirst, 1990; Child, 1974; 1975; Coates *et al.*, 1993; Fitzgerald *et al.*, 1991) and suggestions for improvements.

The simplest model of Agency theory assumes one principal and one agent (see Crowther, 2004), and a modernist view of the world merely assumes that the addition of more principals and more agents makes for a more complex model without negating any of the assumptions. In the corporate world, this is problematic as the theory depends upon a relationship between the parties and a shared understanding of the context in which agreements are made. With one principal and one agent, this is not a problem, as the two parties know each other. In the corporate world, the principals are equated to the shareholders of the company. For any large corporation, however, those shareholders are an amorphous mass of people who are unknown to the managers of the business. Indeed, there is no requirement, or even expectation, that anyone will remain a shareholder for an extended period of time. Thus, there can be no relationship between shareholders – as principals – and managers – as agents – because the principals are merely those holding the shares – as property being invested in – at a particular point in time. So, shareholders do not invest in a company and in the future of that company; rather they invest for capital growth and/or a future dividend stream, and shares are just one way of doing this which can be moved into or out of at will. This problem is exacerbated, particularly in the UK, by the fact that a significant proportion of shares are actually bought and sold by fund managers of financial institutions acting on behalf of their investors. These fund managers are rewarded according to the growth (or otherwise) of the value of the fund. Thus, shares are bought and sold as commodities rather than as part ownership of a business enterprise. In another perspective of the same problem, as Scherrer and Greven (2001) explain, almost 10% of the total value of the commodities in the world market are produced in violation of the fundamental rights of workers. Consequently, agency theory fails as a mechanism for directing managerial behaviour (see Crowther and Ortiz-Martinez, 2007).

Agency theory

It is important to recognise that the firm is assumed to exist for the benefit of its owners, who are assumed to be solely interested in the maximisation of their wealth. Managers, on the other hand, are the decision makers in an organisation and they are implicitly assumed to automatically act in the best interests of owners, either because they are also the owners, or because they share the same interests. In other words, managers are assumed to make the same decisions that owners would make, irrespective of the effect on their personal interests.

Managers are therefore assumed to assess objectively alternative actions, and always select the option favoured by the owners of the firm. The management accountant, therefore, is then concerned with providing the 'right' information combined with the 'right' decision-model which will help the manager make the 'right' decision. An obvious criticism of this approach, however, is that it fails to recognise managers may not share the same interests as owners, and this is likely to impact upon real-world decision making. Agency theory attempts to address this problem by providing a more realistic representation of decision making.

Agency theory therefore recognises that people are unlikely to ignore their own self-interest in making decisions; in other words, people do not behave altruistically. It is a relatively new approach to analysing decision making that provides a framework within which the political and behavioural aspects of decision making can be considered as part of the decision-making process. The theory is therefore positive rather than normative as it seeks to understand and explain what happens in practice rather than seeking to prescribe what ought to happen. It recognises that the manager is an agent of the owners of the firm, whose actions the management accounting system seeks to influence.

An agency relationship exists whenever one party, the principal (P), hires another party, the agent (A), to perform some task. This relationship applies to many superior–subordinate relationships in business and elsewhere, and in a management accounting context, agency relationships can be seen to exist between shareholders and directors, between directors and managers (including divisional managers), and between managers and other employees. In this chapter, we will concentrate on the relationship between the owners of the firm and its managers – in other words the owner–manager principal–agent relationship.

Under Agency theory both P and A are assumed to be rational economic persons: in other words, they know what they are doing and they act consistently and rationally. They are both assumed to be motivated by self-interest alone, although the theory recognises that they possess different preferences, beliefs and information. Both wish to maximise their own 'utility' (the value or benefit they place on any economic good they receive). P and A may also have different attitudes to risk, an issue to which we return later. Agency theory is concerned with the design of effective contracts between the P and A, which specify the combination of incentives, risk-sharing and information system that maximise the utility of P subject to the constraints imposed by ensuring that A's self-interest will also be served through his or her actions. Thus Agency theory provides a means of establishing a contract between the principal and the agent which will lead to optimal performance by the agent on behalf of the principal. This can be depicted by the diagram in Figure 10.1.

Focusing on the shareholder–manager agency relationship, the key elements of agency theory will now be examined.

The owners of the firm provide capital to the firm, and are assumed to be interested solely in the returns to be derived from their use of capital in the firm – in other words, the expected monetary value of their investment. Managers, on the other hand, derive utility from not only their wealth, provided through their employment in the firm, but also their leisure time, when they are not employed by the firm. Thus managers derive utility from all their activities, whether or not these activities are associated with the firm by which they are employed. It is important to appreciate this distinction between 'utility' and 'monetary wealth' in this context, as utility applies to well-being in general rather than simply to wealth.

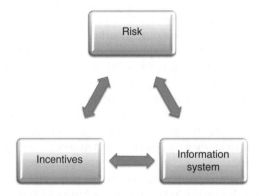

Figure 10.1   Optimal contracts: balancing risk, incentives and choice of information system

Whilst it is certainly true that managers derive utility from additional wealth, it must be recognised that this is unlikely to be in the form of a linear relationship whereby each increment to wealth results in the same addition to utility. Managers will derive greater incremental utility from additions to wealth from lower levels of wealth, but as wealth increases the extra amount of utility gained from each unit, addition to wealth will diminish. In other words, the utility which managers derive from wealth is subject to decreasing marginal returns.

For example, a manager who is paid £100,000 per annum derives greater utility from the first £10,000 of pay then he or she who takes pay from £90,000 to £100,000. At higher levels of pay, non-financial factors associated with employment such as status, job-related pressure, and so on take on greater significance.

The manager's utility function in relation to income received from employment can thus be shown by the graph in Figure 10.2.

In addition, however, managers are assumed to value their own leisure time, which means that they attach disutility to effort. The extra utility which is derived from higher levels of compensation is offset, therefore, by the negative utility which is derived from any extra effort required of the manager to achieve that higher level of compensation. The term 'leisure' in this context is defined as the opposite of any effort that increases the expected value of the firm to its owners. It includes the manager's consumption of so-called 'perquisites' (commonly known as perks), which are benefits relating to the job such as company cars, lavish offices, and so on. The consumption of such perquisites diverts the owners' capital away from what the owners would regard as desirable productive investments and into the manager's own consumption.

Therefore, to summarise, the owners supply capital to the firm and hire managers to act on their behalf. Managers allocate their time at work between productive effort and leisure ('shirking'), and also allocate the firm's resources between productive investments and the consumption of perquisites.

An intuitive solution to the above situation would be for owners to simply monitor the actions of managers to reduce shirking and the over-consumption of perquisites. This, however, can be extremely difficult in practice. There are several reasons why this monitoring is difficult. First, the tasks undertaken by managers are generally considered to be relatively complex and consequently not well understood by the owners, who are not involved in the detailed running of

Figure 10.2 The manager's utility function

the business. Secondly, the decisions made by managers are taken in an uncertain environment, which makes it difficult for owners to judge the appropriateness of managerial actions in any particular set of circumstances. Finally, and perhaps most importantly, information is not evenly distributed between managers and owners. This problem is known as 'information asymmetry' and has two separate, though related elements: moral hazard and adverse selection.

Moral hazard

Moral hazard arises where it is difficult or costly for owners to observe or infer the amount of effort exerted by managers. In such a situation, there is an inevitable temptation for managers to avoid working to the terms of the agreed employment contract, since owners are unable to assess the 'true picture'. Managers may also have the incentive as well as the means to conceal the 'true picture' by misrepresenting the actual outcomes reported to the owners. Accounting provides one such means for misrepresentation through its ability to represent outcomes from any course of action in more than one way.

Adverse selection

Whereas moral hazard relates to the 'post-decision' consequences of information asymmetry, adverse selection is concerned with the 'pre-decision' situation. Since all the information that is available to the manager at the time a decision is made is not also available to the owner, the owner cannot be sure that the manager made the right decision in the circumstances. In addition, the manager has no incentive to reveal what he knows since this will then make it easier for the principal to properly assess his actions in the future. This is known as 'information impactedness'.

The existence of 'information asymmetry' means that for owners to obtain relevant information concerning the manager's effort, they must either rely on the communications received from the managers themselves or must incur monitoring costs. An example of monitoring costs would include the annual audit of the firm's financial statements; indeed, such auditing of financial statements was instituted as a means of safeguarding such investments in firms made by those who had no part in the operational activity of the firm. In the context of the agency relationship between top management and divisional management, such monitoring costs would include the cost of employing head office staff to monitor the performance of divisions. One approach to this problem is to get managers to commit to acting in the best interests of the owners, but in this situation the owners will incur a bonding cost to effect this relationship. Even in this situation, however, since managers may not share the same beliefs and preferences as the owner, there may still be a 'residual loss'.

Information asymmetry can be depicted as shown in Figure 10.3.

Agency theory, as applied in practice, is concerned with the design of employment contracts which reduce shirking and the consumption of perquisites, so

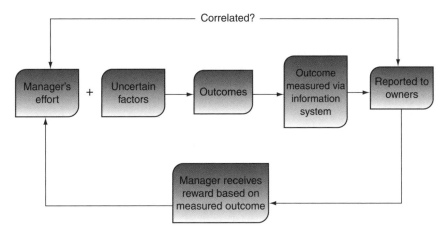

Figure 10.3 Information asymmetry

that instead of managers acting in their own interests they are encouraged to act more in the interests of the owners of the firm. Solutions to agency problems are often described as 'second-best'. This is due to the conflicting implications of the incentive-effect and the risk-sharing aspect of the agency relationship. These should be interrelated, as shown in Figure 10.4.

On the one hand, the optimal contract should achieve optimal risk-sharing. As the owner is able to hold a diversified portfolio of shares, it is usually assumed that he or she is risk-neutral and will not take risk into account in deciding between one course of action and another. The manager, on the other hand, clearly cannot diversify his or her job, and is more likely to be risk-averse and hence to make risk-minimising decisions. In this situation, therefore, optimal risk-sharing would imply that the owner of the firm should bear the most risk, since the manager will require compensation for risk-bearing, whereas the owner will not.

A flat fee paid to the manager irrespective of performance achieves this, since the manager's salary is shielded from the uncertainty which affects expected outcomes. Such a flat fee as remuneration for the manager's effort, however,

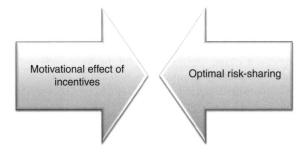

Figure 10.4 Risk sharing

provides no incentive for the manager to exert optimum effort. Due to the fact that the manager's effort cannot realistically be observed, then only if the manager's income is linked to performance will he or she be motivated to contribute more effort. This, in turn, exposes the manager to risk. A double-edged sword is evident. The more a manager's income is dependent upon performance, the greater the incentive effect, yet at the same time, the sharing of risk becomes increasingly sub-optimal.

The 'first-best' solution would be to pay a flat fee to reward 'conscientious' managers who do exert optimum effort. Such a 'first-best' solution is not viable, however, since it is not realistically possible to judge whether or not a manager has acted 'conscientiously' in any particular set of circumstances.

Rating agencies

A rating agency is a company that devises credit rating – assessments of the risk involved – to various financial instruments and their issuers. In some cases, the servicers of the underlying debt are also given ratings. In most cases, the issuers of such securities are companies, state and local governments, not-for-profit organisations and NGOs or national governments issuing debt-like securities (e.g. bonds) that can be traded on a secondary market. A credit rating for an issuer takes into consideration the issuer's creditworthiness (i.e. its ability to pay back a loan), and affects the rate of interest applied to the particular security being issued. In theory, the role of the rating agency is to provide an impartial assessment – based upon its expertise and research – to potential lenders in order to compensate for the inevitable information asymmetry between borrower and lender.

The recent failures of such agencies have been well documented. Too often they gave high ratings to bonds that subsequently defaulted. Their investment grade ratings of many subprime mortgage-backed securities were a primary cause of the recent crisis. Such faulty assessments have allowed companies to raise capital that they later wasted whilst denying more deserving companies capital they could have used to create jobs. The losses borne by bond investors have been huge and the government has absorbed many of these losses to prevent the total collapse of the financial system. More recently, they have been overcompensating for their rash assessments by downgrading – to an extreme extent – their assessed creditworthiness of governments and causing yet more financial chaos.

A credit rating is a statement about the future. An investment grade rating should indicate that a bond is unlikely to default. Since the future is unpredictable, some investment grade bonds will default. However, defaults should be uncommon. Rating agencies have been criticised for having too close a relationship with company management, possibly opening themselves to undue influence or the vulnerability of being misled. Also information about ratings changes from the larger agencies spreads quickly so they charge debt issuers, rather than investors, for their ratings. This has led to accusations that these agencies are plagued by conflicts of interest that might inhibit them from providing accurate and honest ratings.

At the same time, the largest agencies (Moody's and Standard & Poor's) are often seen as agents of market forces, that drive companies to consider how a proposed activity might affect their credit rating, possibly at the expense of employees, the environment, or long-term research and development. The lowering of a credit score by an agency can create a vicious cycle, as not only would interest rates for that company go up, but other contracts with financial institutions may be affected adversely, causing an increase in expenses and ensuing decrease in creditworthiness. This also happens to countries, which is another cause of economic crisis, or prevention of economic recovery. Sadly these agencies have a track record of not just over-rating securities and their lenders in the first instance but overcompensating by downgrading as a reaction. So their actual role in compensating for information asymmetry has been shown to be somewhat questionable.

The limitations of agency theory

Whilst Agency theory offers a number of advantages in the way in which it explains managerial behaviour in organisations, it is necessary to recognise that it also suffers from a number of limitations:

1. It is based on a single-period model. In other words, it is not a dynamic model, and may not be applicable in more realistic multi-period settings.
2. Its assumption that both principal and agent are rational utility maximisers is questionable.
3. The analysis is limited to one principal and one agent, and therefore the results may not be applicable in multi-principal and multi-agent settings.

Managers and business ethics

Business ethics is a subject of considerable importance to any organisation, and accounting information has often been accused of providing an excuse for unethical behaviour. Indeed, this accusation has been extended to accountants and business managers generally, who have been accused of behaving unethically in their search for profits to the exclusion of all else. The unethical ways in which accounting information has been used have been analysed in detail by Smith (1992), who describes the way in which new accounting techniques have been created with the sole purpose of boosting reported profits. These techniques have become known as creative accounting and have been the subject of much media attention. Smith's book, *Accounting for Growth*, makes interesting reading for any prospective business manager.

Other writers, however, have been concerned with highlighting the value of ethical behaviour and have claimed that this actually leads to better business performance. Thus, McCoy (1985) considers that ethics need to be at the core of business behaviour and that effective business management is based upon ethical behaviour. He claims that this recognition, and acting accordingly, actually increases the performance of a business. The UK accounting bodies are also concerned with business ethics and all have a stance in this matter, having incorporated a requirement for ethical behaviour into their codes of conduct. The subject of ethical behaviour among businesses has also had an effect upon auditing practice and upon the financial reporting of businesses.

Any manager operating in a business environment needs to be aware of the importance of ethical behaviour. Equally he or she will experience conflicts, in attempting to behave ethically, between different alternative courses of action, and may find conflicts between the firm's objectives and his or her own personal motivation and objectives. No ready solution to these conflicts is available but a manager should be aware that research has shown ethical behaviour leads to better performance in the longer term, and so should be encouraged to act accordingly.

The Grameen Bank

The Grameen Bank is a community development bank – or microfinance institution – which started in Bangladesh to make small loans (known as micro-credit or *grameencredit*) to the rural poor who could not provide collateral. The word 'Grameen' is derived from the word 'gram' and means rural or village in the Bangla language. The philosophy of this bank is based on the idea that the poor have skills which are under-utilised. A group-based credit approach is applied which makes use of peer pressure within the group to ensure that borrowers follow through their plan and use caution in conducting their financial affairs with strict discipline, ensuring eventual repayment and allowing the borrowers to develop a good credit standing. The bank also accepts deposits, provides other services, and runs several development-oriented businesses including fabric, telephone and energy companies. Another distinctive feature of the bank's credit programme is that a significant majority of its borrowers are women.

The origin of Grameen Bank can be traced back to 1976 when Professor Muhammed Yunus, a Fulbright scholar at Vanderbilt University and Professor at the University of Chittagong, developed a research project to examine the possibility of designing a credit delivery system to provide banking services targeted at the rural poor, which became the Grameen project. In October 1983, the Grameen Bank Project was transformed into an independent bank by government legislation. The organisation and its founder were jointly awarded the Nobel Peace Prize in 2006.

According to UNESCO (UN Educational, Scientific and Cultural Organization), the Grameen Bank has reversed the conventional banking wisdom by removing any collateral requirement and has created a banking system which is based on mutual trust, strict supervision, accountability, participation and creativity. At the Grameen Bank, credit is the entry point and it serves as a catalyst in the overall development process. It sees credit as an empowering agent, an enabling element in the development of socio-economic conditions of the poor, who have been kept outside the banking orbit on the simple ground that they are poor and hence not bankable.

Professor Muhammad Yunus, the founder of Grameen Bank and its Managing Director, reasoned that if financial resources can be made available to the poor people at terms and conditions which are appropriate and reasonable, 'these millions of small people with their millions of small pursuits can add up to create the biggest development wonder'. This conviction of Professor Yunus had its root in the traditional banking structure which has been designed in such a way that it would never help the poor, who constitute the largest segment of the society and are the ones who are desperately in need of credit.

The Grameen Bank has now become a national institution that provides credit to the rural poor in Bangladesh. It is today also owned by the poor, whose paid-up share capital amounts to taka 200 million. Credit provided by Grameen in 1994 exceeded the total amount of all other financial institutions and NGOs (non-governmental organisations) put together in Bangladesh. Grameen is committed to the goal of alleviation of poverty and empowerment of the rural poor. To fulfil its strategic objective, Grameen has grown institutionally, its credit operations have expanded rapidly and its programmes have become more diversified.

The nature of governance

The concept of governance has existed as long as any form of human organisation has existed. The concept itself merely encapsulates the means by which that organisation conducts itself. Recently, however, the term has come to the forefront of public attention and this is probably because of the problems of governance which have been revealed at both a national level and in the economic sphere at the level of the corporation. These problems have caused a concern to re-examine what exactly is meant by governance and, more specifically, just what the features of good governance are. It is here, therefore, that we must start our present examination.

When considering national governance then this has been defined by the World Bank as 'the exercise of political authority and the use of institutional resources to manage society's problems and affairs'.

This is a view of governance which prevails in the present, with its assumption that governance is a top-down process decided by those in power and passed to society at large. In actual fact the concept is originally democratic and consensual, being the process by which any group of people decide to manage their affairs and relate to each other. Such a consensual approach is, however, problematic for any but the smallest of groups and no nation has actually managed to institute governance as a consensual process. With the current trend for supranational organisation[6] then this seems an even more remote possibility; nor is it necessarily desirable. Thus a coercive top-down form of governance enables a society to accept leadership and to make some difficult decisions which would not otherwise be made.[7] Equally, of course, it enables power to be usurped and used dictatorially – possibly beneficially[8] but most probably in a way in which most members of that society do not wish.[9]

This top-down, hierarchical form of governance normally takes place in large monolithic organisations such as the nation state. Conversely, the consensual form tends to be the norm in small organisations such as local clubs. There are, however, other forms of governance which are commonly found. One of these is governance through the market (see Williamson, 1975). The free market is the dominant ideology of economic activity and the argument, of course, is that transaction costs are lowered through this form of organisation. From a governance perspective, however, this is problematic as there is no automatic mechanism and negotiation is used. The effect of this is that governance is decided according to power relationships, which tend to be coercive for the less powerful (e.g. consumers). Consequently, there is a need to impose some form of regulation through governments or supra-national organisations such as the World Trade Organization, which thereby reimposes the eliminated transaction costs. The argument therefore resolves into an ideological argument rather than an economic one.

An increasing number of firms rely upon informal social systems to govern their relationship with each other, and this is the final form of governance. This form is normally known at network governance (Jones, Hesterly and Borgatti, 1997). With this form of governance there are no formal rules – certainly none which is legally binding. Instead, social obligations are recognised and governance exists within the networks because the different organisations continue to engage with each other, most probably in the economic arena. This form of governance can therefore be considered to be predicated in mutual self-interest. Of course, just as with market governance, power relationships are important and this form of governance is most satisfactory when there are no significant power imbalances to distort the governance relationships.

Although in some respects these different forms of governance are interchangeable, they are, in reality, suited to different circumstances. Whichever form of governance is in existence, however, the most important thing is that it can be regarded as good governance by all parties involved – in other words, all stakeholders must be satisfied. For this to be so then it is important that the basic principles of good governance are adhered to.

The principles of governance

There are eight principles which underpin every system of governance. These are shown in Figure 10.5.

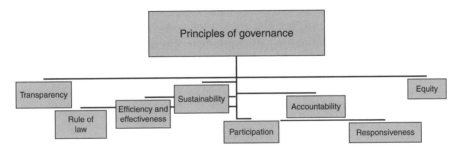

Figure 10.5   The principles of governance

Transparency

Transparency, as a principle, necessitates that information is freely available and directly accessible to those who will be affected by such decisions and their enforcement. Transparency is of particular importance to external users of such information as these users lack the background details and knowledge available to internal users of such information. Equally, therefore, the decisions which are taken and their enforcement are done in a manner that follows rules and regulations. Transparency therefore can be seen to be a part of the process of recognition of responsibility on the part of the organisation for the external effects of its actions and equally part of the process of redistributing power more equitably to all stakeholders.

Rule of law

This is a corollary of the transparency principle. It is apparent that good governance requires a fair framework of rules of operation. Moreover, these rules must be enforced impartially, without regard for power relationships. Thus, the rights of minorities must be protected.[10] Additionally, there must be appeal to an independent body as a means of conflict resolution, and this right of appeal must be known to all stakeholders.[11]

Participation

Although participation by all stakeholders is desirable, of course, this is not an essential principle of good governance. The ability of all to participate if so desired, however, is an essential principle. Participation, of course, includes the freedom of association and of expression that goes along with this. Depending upon the size and structure of the organisation, participation can be either direct or through legitimate intermediate institutions or representatives, as in the case of a national government. Participation would involve everyone, of course, or at least all adults, both male and female.

Responsiveness

This is a corollary of the participation principle and the transparency principle. Responsiveness implies that the governance regulations enable the institutions and processes of governance to serve all stakeholders within a reasonable timeframe.

Equity

This principle involves ensuring that all members of society feel that they have a stake in it and do not feel excluded from the mainstream. This particularly applies to ensuring that the views of minorities are taken into account and that the voices of the most vulnerable in society are heard in decision making. This requires mechanisms to ensure that all stakeholder groups have the opportunity to maintain or improve their well-being.

Efficiency and effectiveness

Efficiency, of course, implies the transaction cost-minimisation referred to earlier, whereas effectiveness must be interpreted in the context of achievement of the desired purpose. Thus, for effectiveness it is necessary that the processes and institutions produce results that meet the needs of the organisation whilst making the best use of resources at their disposal. Naturally, this also means sustainable use of natural resources and the protection of the environment.

Sustainability

This, of course, requires a long-term perspective for sustainable human development and the way to achieve the goals of such development. A growing number of writers over the last quarter of a century have recognised that the activities of an organisation impact upon the external environment. These other stakeholders have not just an interest in the activities of the organisation but also a degree of influence over the shaping of those activities. This influence is so significant that it can be argued the power and influence of these stakeholders is such that it amount to quasi-ownership of the organisation. Central to this is a concern for the future which has become manifest through the term 'sustainability', a term which has become ubiquitous within the discourse of both globalisation and corporate performance. Sustainability is, of course, a controversial issue and there are many definitions of what is meant by the term – as we have discussed in detail in Chapter 6.

Accountability

Accountability is concerned with an organisation recognising that its actions affect the external environment, and therefore assuming responsibility for the effects of its actions. This concept therefore implies a recognition that the organisation is part of a wider societal network and has responsibilities to all of that network rather than just to the owners of the organisation. Alongside this acceptance of responsibility there must therefore be a recognition that those external stakeholders have the power to affect the way in which those actions of the organisation are taken and a role in deciding whether or not such actions can be justified, and if so at what cost to the organisation and to other stakeholders. Inevitably, there is a need for some form of mediation of the different interests in society in order to be able to reach a broad consensus in society on what is in the best interest of the whole community and how this can be achieved. As a general statement, all organisations and institutions are accountable to those who will be affected by decisions or actions and this must be recognised within the governance mechanisms. This accountability must extend to all organisations – both governmental institutions and the private sector and also to civil society organisations – which must all recognise that they are accountable to the public and to their various stakeholders. One significant purpose of this is to ensure that any corruption is eliminated or at the very least minimised.

Developing a framework for corporate governance

In the UK there has been a succession of codes on corporate governance dating back to the Cadbury Report in 1992. Currently, all companies reporting on the London Stock Exchange are required to comply with the Combined Code on Corporate Governance, which came into effect in 2003. It was subsequently revised in 2006 and became known as the UK Corporate Governance Code in 2010. It might be thought, therefore, that a framework for corporate governance has already been developed but the code in the UK has been continually revised whilst problems associated with bad governance have not disappeared. So clearly a framework has not been established in the UK and an international framework looks even more remote.

One of the problems with developing such a framework is the continual rules versus principles debate. The American approach tends to be rules-based whilst the European approach is based more on the development of principles – a slower process. In general, rules are considered to be simpler to follow than principles, demarcating a clear line between acceptable and unacceptable behaviour. Rules also reduce discretion on the part of individual managers or auditors. In practice, however, rules can be more complex than principles. They may be ill-equipped to deal with new types of transactions not covered by the code. Moreover, even if clear rules are followed, one can still find a way to circumvent their underlying purpose – this is harder to achieve if one is bound by a broader principle.

There are, of course, many different models of corporate governance around the world. These differ according to the nature of the system of capitalism in which they are embedded. The liberal model that is common in Anglo-American countries tends to give priority to the interests of shareholders. The coordinated model, which is normally found in Continental Europe and in Japan, recognises in addition the interests of workers, managers, suppliers, customers and the community. Both models have distinct competitive advantages, but in different ways. The liberal model of corporate governance encourages radical innovation and cost competition, whereas the coordinated model of corporate governance facilitates incremental innovation and quality competition. However, there are important differences between the recent approach to governance issues taken in the USA and what has happened in the UK.

In the USA a corporation is governed by a board of directors, which has the power to choose an executive officer, usually known as the chief executive officer (CEO). The CEO has broad powers to manage the corporation on a daily basis, but needs to get board approval for certain major actions, such as hiring his or her immediate subordinates, raising money, acquiring another company, major capital expansions, or other expensive projects. Other duties of the board may include policy setting, decision making, monitoring management's performance, or corporate control. The board of directors is nominally selected by and responsible to the shareholders, but the articles of many companies make it difficult for all but the largest shareholders to have any influence over the makeup of the board. Normally, individual shareholders are not offered a choice of board nominees among which to choose, but are merely asked to rubberstamp the nominees of the sitting board. Perverse incentives have pervaded many corporate boards in the developed world, with board members beholden to the chief executive whose actions they are intended to oversee. Frequently, members of the boards of directors are CEOs of other corporations – in interlocking relationships, which many people see as posing a potential conflict of interest.

The UK, on the other hand, has developed a flexible model of regulation of corporate governance, known as the 'comply or explain' code of governance. This is a principle-based code that lists a number of recommended practices, such as:

- the separation of CEO and Chairman of the Board;
- the introduction of a time limit for CEOs' contracts;
- the introduction of a minimum number of non-executive directors, and of independent directors;
- the designation of a senior non-executive director;
- the formation and composition of remuneration, audit and nomination committees.

Publicly listed companies in the UK have either to apply those principles or, if they choose not to, to explain in a designated part of their annual reports why they decided not to do so. The monitoring of those explanations is left to shareholders themselves. The basic idea of the Code is that one size does not fit all in matters of corporate governance and that instead of a statutory regime like the Sarbanes-Oxley Act in the US, it is best to leave some flexibility to companies so that they can make choices most adapted to their circumstances. If they have good reasons to deviate from the sound rule, they should be able to convincingly explain those to their shareholders. A form of the Code has been in existence since 1992 and has had drastic effects on the way firms are governed in the UK. A recent study shows that in 1993 about 10% of the FTSE 350 companies were fully compliant with all dimensions of the Code whilst by 2003 more than 60% were fully compliant. The same success was not achieved when looking at the explanation part for non-compliant companies. Many deviations are simply not explained and a large majority of explanations fail to identify specific circumstances justifying those deviations. Still, the overall view is that the UK's system works fairly well and in fact is often considered to be a benchmark, and therefore followed by a number of other countries. Nevertheless, it still shows that there is more to be done to develop a global framework of corporate governance.

In East Asian countries, the family-owned company tends to dominate. In countries such as Pakistan, Indonesia and the Philippines, for example, the top 15 families control over 50% of publicly owned corporations through a system of family cross-holdings, thus dominating the capital markets. Family-owned companies also dominate the Latin model of corporate governance, in, for example, Mexico, Italy, Spain, Brazil, Argentina, and other countries in South America.

Corporate governance principles and codes have been developed in different countries and have been issued by stock exchanges, corporations, institutional investors, or associations (institutes) of directors and managers with the support of governments and international organisations. As a rule, compliance with these governance recommendations is not mandated by law, although the codes which are linked to stock exchange listing requirements[12] will tend to have a coercive effect. Thus, for example, companies quoted on the London and Toronto Stock Exchanges formally need not follow the recommendations of their respective national codes, but they must disclose whether they follow the recommendations in those documents and, where not, they should provide explanations concerning divergent practices. Such disclosure requirements exert a significant pressure on listed companies for compliance.

In its 'Global Investor Opinion Survey' of over 200 institutional investors first undertaken in 2000 (and updated in 2002), McKinsey found that 80% of the respondents would pay a premium for well-governed companies. They defined a well-governed company as one that had mostly outside directors, who had no management ties, undertook formal evaluation of its directors, and was responsive to investors' requests for information on governance issues. The size of the premium varied by market, from 11% for Canadian companies to around 40% for companies where the regulatory backdrop was least certain (e.g. those in Morocco, Egypt or Russia). Other studies have similarly linked broad perceptions of the quality of companies to superior share price performance. On the other hand, research into the relationship between specific corporate governance controls and the financial performance of companies has had very mixed results.

Conclusions

Agency theory has been developed from the Organisational Failure Framework of Williamson. It seems to offer some pointers as to how firms can be managed better but has problems as far as practical application is concerned. It is based upon one key assumption – that every party to a transaction acts in a rational manner in order to maximise his or her utility. This assumes, of course, that the evaluation of utility undertaken by every individual can be precisely calculated and thus that the same decision would always be made by the same individual in exactly the same set of circumstances. Nevertheless, it helps us to understand corporate behaviour. So, too, does governance and its principles. Codes of governance have been developed in response to problems which have become apparent in the behaviour of firms and seek to determine that firms behave in a uniform manner towards their investors.

Summary of key points

- Financial misdemeanours have created a concern for CSR which has caused the development of codes of corporate governance.
- Information symmetry is one of the most salient points regarding organisational management and several techniques have evolved to address the issue.
- There are eight principle of good governance.
- Agency theory has developed to explain the relationship between the managers of an organisation and its owners and investors.
- Agency theory therefore recognises that people are unlikely to ignore their own self-interest in making decisions.

Definitions of key terms and theories

Accountability is concerned with an organisation recognising that its actions affect the external environment, and therefore assuming responsibility for the effects of its actions.

The **Combined Code** on Corporate Governance, which came into effect in 2003, sets out standards of good practice in relation to board leadership and effectiveness, remuneration, accountability and relations with shareholders.

Governance encapsulates the means by which that organisation conducts itself.

Information asymmetry means that for owners to obtain relevant information concerning the manager's effort, they must either rely on the communications received from the managers themselves, or must incur monitoring costs.

Moral hazard arises where it is difficult or costly for owners to observe or infer the amount of effort exerted by managers.

The **Rule of law** implies that good governance requires a fair framework of rules of operation.

The **UK Corporate Governance Code** was a renaming of the Combined Code and was introduced in 2010.

Test your understanding

1. What is meant by information asymmetry?
2. What are the principles of good governance?
3. How do rating agencies help to solve information asymmetry?
4. What is the difference between the British approach to governance and the American approach?
5. What is the difference between moral hazard and adverse selection?
6. Why is the rule of law an essential feature of good governance?

Suggestions for further reading

Aluchna, M. 2009. 'Applying Corporate Governance in Europe', in G. Aras and D. Crowther (eds), *Global Perspectives on Corporate Governance and Corporate Social Responsibility*. Farnham: Gower.

Aras, G. and Crowther, D. 2008. 'Exploring Frameworks of Corporate Governance', in G. Aras and D. Crowther (eds), *Culture and Corporate Governance*. Leicester: SRRNet, pp. 3–16.

Joyner, B. E. and Payne, D. 2002. 'Evolution and Implementation: A Study of Values, Business Ethics and Corporate Social Responsibility', *Journal of Business Ethics*, 41: 297–311.

Notes

1. See for example Emmanuel *et al.* (1985).
2. Such owners are, of course, the legal owners of the business, that is the shareholders.
3. See the VBM discourse considered by Cooper *et al.* (2001).
4. For example the discourse surrounding social accounting and the problems of actually measuring the benefit to be distributed.
5. See Rappaport (1986, 1992).
6. Such as the European Community.
7. For example the decision to abolish capital punishment in the UK in 1969 could not have been made consensually; nor could the decision to invade Iraq in 2003.
8. The ancient Greeks favoured beneficial dictatorship as a means of running their city states.
9. Few would argue that, for example, power was usurped in the USSR by Stalin because of a centrally imposed governance; equally few would suggest that this power was used beneficially or in a way which most members of the society were happy about.
10. This, of course, would imply the protection of human rights but could also be taken to imply concern for the environment and its protection.
11. This can be to national courts, trade associations, supra-national courts such the European Court of Human Rights or to an organisation such as the

United Nations. Whatever the body, it needs to be appropriate and not just impartial but also seen to be impartial to all concerned in order to maintain the credibility to adjudicate disputes.

12. Such as, for example, the UK Combined Code referred to earlier.

References

Briers, M. and Hirst, M. 1990. 'The Role of Budgetary Information in Performance Evaluation', *Accounting, Organizations and Society*, 15, 4: 373–98.

Child, J. 1974. 'Managerial and Organisational Factors Associated with Company Performance – Part 1', *Journal of Management Studies*, 11: 73–89.

Child, J. 1975. 'Managerial and Organisational Factors Associated with Company Performance – Part 2', *Journal of Management Studies*, 12: 1227.

Coates, J. B., Davis, E. W., Longden, S. G., Stacey, R. J. and Emmanuel, C. 1993. *Corporate Performance Evaluation in Multinationals*. London: CIMA.

Cooper, S., Crowther, D., Davies, M. and Davis, E. 2001. *Shareholder or Stakeholder Value*. London: CIMA.

Crowther, D. 2004. 'Limited Liability or Limited Responsibility', in D. Crowther and L. Rayman-Bacchus (eds), *Perspectives on Corporate Social Responsibility*. Aldershot: Ashgate, pp. 42–58.

Crowther, D. and Ortiz-Martinez, E. 2007. 'No Principals, No Principles, No Reserves: Shell and the Failure of Agency Theory', *Social Responsibility Journal*, 3, 4: 4–14.

Emmanuel, C. R., Otley, D. T. and Merchant, K. 1985. *Accounting for Management Control*. London: Chapman & Hall.

Fitzgerald, L., Johnston, R., Brignall, S., Silvestro, R. and Voss, C. 1991. *Performance Measurement in Service Businesses*. London: CIMA.

Jones, C., Hesterly, W. S. and Borgatti, S. P. 1997. 'A General Theory of Network Governance: Exchange Conditions and Social Mechanisms', *Academy of Management Review*, 22, 4: 911–45.

McCoy, C. S. 1985. *Management of Values: The Ethical Difference in Corporate Policy and Performance*. Marshfield, MA: Pitman.

Rappaport, A. 1986. *Creating Shareholder Value*. New York: The Free Press.

Rappaport, A. 1992. 'CFO's and Strategists: Forging a Common Framework', *Harvard Business Review*, May/Jun: 84–91.

Scherrer, C. and Greven, T. 2001. *Global Rules for Trade: Codes of Conduct, Social Labelling, Workers' Rights Clauses*. Münster: Verlag Westfälisches Dampfboot.

Smith, T. 1992. *Accounting for Growth*. London: Century Business.

Williamson, O. E. 1975. *Markets and Hierarchies: Analysis and Anti-trust Implications*. New York: The Free Press.

Performance Evaluation and Performance Reporting

11

Learning objectives

After studying this chapter you should be able to:

- Define the various aspects of performance.
- Discuss competing requirements of stakeholders.
- Outline the design of the balanced scorecard and discuss alternatives.
- Discuss the purpose of the reporting of performance.
- Distinguish between financial performance and social performance.
- Explain what is meant by triple bottom line reporting.

I think that Capitalism, wisely managed, can probably be made more efficient for attaining economic ends than any alternative system yet in sight. But that in itself is in many ways extremely objectionable. Our problem is to work out a social organization which shall be as efficient as possible without offending our notions of a satisfactory way of life. (John Maynard Keynes, 1926)

Introduction

For all organisations the question of the management of the organisation depends upon the ability to measure performance and then evaluate and report upon that performance. When we are considering CSR this is equally true, although it becomes more difficult to measure and evaluate that performance. In this chapter, therefore, we will consider some of the issues involved as well as some of the aspects of performance.

What is performance?

It should be clear that the determination of good performance is dependent upon the perspective from which that performance is being considered and that what one stakeholder grouping might consider to be good performance may very well be considered by another grouping to be poor performance (Child, 1984). The evaluation of performance for a business therefore depends not just upon the identification of adequate means for measuring that performance but also upon the determination of what good performance actually consists of.

Just as the determination of standards of performance depends upon the perspective from which it is being evaluated, so too does the measurement of that performance, which needs suitably relevant measures to do so, not absolutely as this has no meaning, but within the context in which performance is being evaluated. From an external perspective, therefore, a very different evaluation of performance might arise, but, moreover, a very different measurement of performance, implying a very different use of accounting in that measurement process, also might arise.

The measurement of stakeholder performance is perhaps even more problematic than the measurement of financial performance. Objective measures of stakeholder performance are not given in the annual reports of companies and therefore we have chosen to consider the subjective measures included within the 'Britain's Most Admired Companies' surveys annually published in *Management Today*. These measures provide a reputation rating, as gathered from 'rivals' perceptions, in nine categories (see Figure 11.1) and these measures are also added to provide a total score. The nine categories are:

(1) quality of management;
(2) quality of goods and services;
(3) capacity to innovate;
(4) quality of marketing;
(5) ability to retain top talent;
(6) community and environmental responsibility;
(7) financial soundness;
(8) value as long-term investment;
(9) use of corporate assets.

Nike

Nike has been criticised for contracting with factories in countries such as China, Vietnam, Indonesia and Mexico. Vietnam Labour Watch, an activist group, has documented that factories contracted by Nike have violated minimum wage and overtime laws in Vietnam as late as 1996, although Nike claims that this practice has been halted. Full details of their expectations from their sub-contracting companies and of their monitoring procedures can be found on their website. The company has been subjected to much critical coverage of the often poor working conditions and exploitation of cheap labour overseas where their goods are typically manufactured; again they have a code of practice.

Nike has been criticised about ads which referred to empowering women in the US whilst engaging in practices in their far eastern factories that some felt disempowered women. During the 1990s, Nike faced criticism for the use of child labour in Cambodia and Pakistan in factories it contracted to manufacture soccer balls. Although Nike took action to curb or at least reduce the practice of child labour, they continue to contract their production out to companies that operate in areas where inadequate regulation and monitoring make it hard to ensure child labour is not being used. In 2001, a BBC documentary showed occurrences of child labour and poor working conditions in a Cambodian factory used by Nike. In the documentary, six girls were featured, all of whom worked seven days a week, often sixteen hours a day. A July 2008 investigation by Australian Channel 7 News found a large number of cases involving forced labour in one of the biggest Nike apparel factories. The factory, located in Malaysia, was filmed by an undercover crew who found instances of squalid living conditions and forced labour. Nike has since stated that it will take corrective action to ensure the continued abuse does not occur.

The constantly growing textile industry faces criticism for the negative effects it has upon the environment. Nike is a large participant in this manufacturing and many of its processes negatively contribute to the environment. One way the expanding textile industry affects the environment is by increasing its water deficit (we have discussed embedded water on page 143), climate change, pollution, and fossil fuel and raw material consumption. In addition to this, today's electronic textile plants use significant amounts of energy, whilst also producing a throw-away mindset due to trends founded upon fast fashion and cheap clothing.

Although these combined effects can negatively alter the environment, Nike tries to counteract their influence with different projects. According to a New England-based environmental organisation, Clean Air-Cool Planet, Nike ranks among the top 3 companies (out of 56) on a survey conducted about climate-friendly companies. Nike has also been praised for its Nike Grind programme by groups like Climate Counts. In addition to this, one campaign that Nike began for Earth Day 2008 was a commercial that featured Steve Nash wearing Nike's Trash Talk Shoe, a shoe that had been constructed in February 2008 from pieces of leather and synthetic leather waste retrieved from the factory floor. The Trash Talk Shoe also featured a sole composed of ground-up rubber from a shoe recycling programme. Nike claims this is the first performance basketball shoe that has been created from manufacturing waste, but it only produced 5 000 pairs for sale.

Nike is an example of a company which has listened to its critics and accepted that practices have not always been ideal and has therefore taken steps to change. As a result it is more popular than ever and the evidence supports other evidence that people do not expect perfection from large companies but do expect honesty in admitting mistakes and an effort to make improvements. This aspect of improvement is one of the defining features of CSR.

Figure 11.1   Objective measures of stakeholder performance

Social accounting

Social accounting first came to prominence during the 1970s when the performance of businesses in a wider arena than the stock market, and its value to shareholders, tended to become of increasing concern. This was first expressed through a concern with social accounting. This can be considered to be an approach to reporting a firm's activities which stresses the need for identification of socially relevant behaviour, the determination of those to whom the company is accountable for its social performance and the development of appropriate measures and reporting techniques.

Thus, social accounting considers a wide range of aspects of corporate performance and encompasses a recognition that different aspects of performance are of interest to different stakeholder groupings. These aspects can include:

- The concerns of investors
- A focus upon community relations
- A concern with ecology

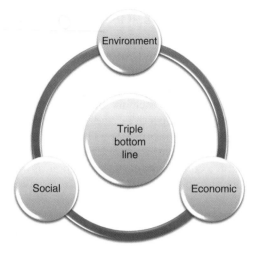

Figure 11.2   The triple bottom line

These factors, of course, equate to the triple bottom line discussed earlier (see Figure 11.2).

Measuring performance in terms of these aspects will include, in addition to the traditional profit-based measures, such things as:

- Consumer surplus
- Economic rent
- Environmental impact
- Non-monetary values

Many writers consider, by implication, that measuring social performance is important without giving reasons for believing so. Solomons (1974), however, considered the reasons for measuring objectively the social performance of a business. He suggests that whilst one reason is to aid rational decision making, another reason is of a defensive nature.

Solomons proposed a model, which seems to provide a reasonable method of reporting upon the effects of the activities of an organisation on its external environment, but failed to provide any suggestions as to the actual measurement of external costs and benefits. Such measurement is much more problematic and this is one of the main problems of any form of social accounting – the fact that the measurement of effects external to the organisation is extremely difficult.

Indeed, it can be argued that this difficulty in measurement is one reason why organisations have concentrated upon the measurement through accounting for their internal activities, which are much more susceptible to measurement.

The measurement and reporting of performance

The evaluation of the performance of an organisation is partly concerned with the measurement of performance and partly with the reporting of that performance. If a greater importance is given to social accountability then changing measurement and reporting needs of an organisation must also be recognised. Social accounting is an attempt to measure and report upon organisational performance from a variety of perspectives, and hence to supply various diverse groups with different needs for information. Thus it has been argued that there is a need for several distinct types of accounting to perform such a function. This argument is based upon a consideration of the limitations of the traditional economic base for accounting; it questions some of the premises of this economic base, such as:

- the desirability of continuing economic growth
- the existence of rational economic man, making rational economic decisions
- the exclusion of altruism from any decision-making process
- the exclusion from consideration of the way in which wealth is distributed

These factors are argued to be such that there is a need for a new paradigm. In this new paradigm the environment is considered as part of the firm rather than as an externality. Thus, the concept of sustainability, together with a consideration of the use of primary resources, is given increased weighting as far as accounting for the actions of a firm is concerned. Indeed, some writers go further and argue that there is a need for a new social contract between a business and the stakeholders to which it is accountable, and a business mission which recognises that some things go beyond accounting.

Accountability and social activity

It is generally recognised that power is an essential component of accountability and greater accountability is recognised towards those stakeholders which have more power. In this respect organisations can be considered as externalising machines suited to self-preservation. Thus, when faced with conflicting pressures a company will act in the interests of self-preservation with smaller risk but less benefit being chosen. It is also argued that the power of businesses is increasingly being consolidated into the hands of the executives, rather than owners, as it is they who have the expertise to assess this risk. One of the problems with this concern with power is that society at large, and the environment in particular, tend not to be powerful stakeholders. It is perhaps for this reason that social accountability tends not to be a feature of organisations.

Research has been undertaken, however, with regard to the relationship between managers and employees and the use made of accounting information in this respect. This research has been concerned with the disclosure of accounting information to trade unions. Different conceptualisations of the relationship between management and employees can generate different conclusions regarding the disclosure of accounting information during industrial relations bargaining. Findings from such research demonstrate that increased disclosure can lead to reduced opposition from employees, greater commitment and loyalty, and increased legitimacy for intended action. This evidence therefore seems to suggest that greater disclosure of information can actually bring about benefits to the organisation as well as to the stakeholders involved. This is in line with the concepts of social and environmental accounting which are concerned with greater disclosure of the activities of an organisation but with an emphasis upon disclosure of actions and the way in which they impact upon the external environment.

Much of this research and argument is undertaken by people who start from the presumption that such accountability, and consequent reporting, is desirable without giving any reasons why this should be so. The benefits which ensue therefore go to the various stakeholders who benefit without any discernable benefit to the organisations themselves. One way to achieve this is through legislation and this is the approach taken by various countries around the world, with mixed results.

Another approach, however, is to demonstrate the benefits to an organisation itself from such social responsibility, and this is the approach taken in this book. These benefits can take place in either the short term or in the long term. Generally speaking they can be in any of the following forms:

- increased information for decision making
- reduced operational costs or increased revenue
- more accurate product or service costing
- improved strategic decision making
- improved image
- market development opportunities

The principles of social accounting

The approach to measuring organisational activity through accounting for the actions of a firm in relation to the external environment, and the impact of those activities of the firm upon external stakeholders, is generally known as environmental accounting. This form of accounting recognises that the actions taken by a firm impact upon its external environment and consequently can be, and should be, accounted for. This is in contrast with the traditional view of accounting, grounded in classical liberalism, that what happens to the firm is of relevance to the firm and should therefore be accounted for, whilst what happens outside the firm, whether affected by the firm or not, is irrelevant to the firm and not therefore a proper subject for accounting as far as the firm is concerned. Forms of accounting which reflect the actions of the firm upon its external environment are generally labelled social accounting, which has been defined as:

> the process of communicating the social and environmental effects of organisations' economic actions to particular interest groups within society and to society at large, beyond the traditional role of providing a financial account to the owners of capital, in particular, shareholders. Such an extension is predicated upon the assumption that companies do have wider responsibilities than simply to make money for their shareholders. (Gray, Owen and Maunders, 1987: ix)

and as:

> Voluntary disclosures of information, both qualitative and quantitative made by organisations to inform or influence a range of audiences. The quantitative disclosures may be in financial or non-financial terms. (Mathews, 1993: 64)

There are some essential features of this form of accounting which distinguish it from traditional accounting. These features are based upon three principles:

1. it is an attempt to report upon the effects of the actions of the firm upon the societal environment which is external to the firm itself;
2. it is aimed at an audience external to the firm, and which has no legal ownership of that firm;
3. it is voluntary in nature.

In this respect it differs from traditional accounting in terms of its audience and its voluntary nature. One consequence of this is that not all firms feel the need for reporting this aspect of their operations and such reporting as does take place is by no means uniform in its approach.

The principles of environmental accounting

One subset of social accounting is that form which is concerned with reporting the actions of the firm insofar as they relate to the environment in a physical rather than social sense. This is collectively known as environmental accounting. Environmental accounting can be defined in the following terms:

> it can be taken as covering all areas of accounting that may be affected by the response to environmental issues, including new areas of eco-accounting. (Gray and Bebbington, 2001: 6)

and

> Environmental accounting can be defined as a sub-area of accounting that deals with activities, methods and systems for recording, analysing and

reporting environmentally induced financial impacts and ecological impacts of a defined economic system. (Schaltegger, Muller and Hinrichsen, 1996: 5)

Just as the definitions of such forms of accounting vary from one person to another, so too does the way in which such accounting is operationalised within different firms. Indeed, this variation can be found not just through inter-firm comparison but also through longitudinal study. Environmental accounting is a relatively recent phenomenon and Mathews (1997) suggests that its roots go back only as far as the 1970s. Since that time, interest in such accounting has grown considerably and the applications, perceived relevance and techniques of environmental accounting have developed extensively. Indeed, the purposes of environmental accounting have also changed. It has been argued that such forms of accounting were used in the past to placate external environmental activists. Now, however, it is regarded as an important source of information for the internal management of the firm. It is also suggested that one of the prime uses of environmental accounting data is for external consumption rather than for internal decision-making purposes.

It must be stated at this point, however, that difficulties surround the nature and purposes of environmental accounting. This is equally true with regard to the nature and purpose of traditional accounting, and the appropriateness of any measures suggested for either. Nevertheless, it is clear that social and environmental accounting is significantly different from traditional accounting because of its attempt to include an accounting for the effects of the actions of the organisation upon the external environment. Thus the organisation, although recognised to be a discrete entity, is only one part of a system which transcends the organisational boundary and negates the internal/external binarism of traditional accounting. This different focus both distinguishes such accounting from its traditional role and leads to the need for different measures of performance.

The measurement of environmental impact

The techniques of environmental accounting have been subject to continual development over the years, and we will consider them in detail in the rest of this book. Growth in the techniques offered for measuring environmental impact, and reporting thereon, has also continued throughout the last twenty-five years during which the concept of environmental accounting has existed. However, the ability to discuss the fact that firms, through their actions, affect their external environment and that this should be accounted for has often exceeded any practical suggestions for measuring such impact. For example, it has been suggested that the concept of social overhead be offset against reported results from traditional measures of income, without suggesting how this might be calculated. Equally, a model for such accounting, based entirely upon non-financial quantification, has been suggested. Other suggestions include a conceptual model for the categorisation of various forms of socially oriented disclosure, which included the separation of socially responsible accounting from total impact accounting. Various models for sustainability accounting have also been suggested.

At the same time as the technical implementation of environmental accounting and reporting has been developing, the philosophical basis for such accounting has also been developed. Thus, the extent to which accountants should be involved in environmental accounting has been the subject of considerable discussion. Similarly, it has been argued that such accounting can be justified by means of the social contract as benefiting society at large. Some have argued that sustainability is the cornerstone of environmental accounting whilst others have stated that environmental auditing should be given prominence.

More critical authors have viewed traditional accounting from a labour process perspective; they view it as a mechanism to support the dominance of capital over labour interests. Such authors have tended to view social and environmental accounting as a mechanism for benefiting non-traditional users of accounting information.[1] Thus it has been argued by some that there is a need to prevent the institutionalisation of such environmental accounting by its adoption and absorption by the accounting profession into normal accounting. Such critical views, however, conflict with the declared aims of environmental accounting – namely of measuring and reporting upon the effect within the external environment of the activities of the firm. In order to do so effectively then environmental accounting needs to be absorbed within mainstream accounting and utilised by practising accountants as a part of their normal activities. Environmental accounting cannot therefore be both a radical vehicle for change as well as a mechanism for incorporating externalities into the reporting of the firm through its accounting.[2]

Environmental accounting can be seen to be a topical issue from a variety of perspectives but to be useful in measuring and reporting upon the impact of the actions of the firm it must necessarily be absorbed into the repertoire of accounting practitioners and into the systems of organisational control and reporting, rather than remaining as a critical external discourse. In other words, to be of use to businesses it is not appropriate to consider environmental accounting as a means of providing a basis for the criticism of organisational activity and behaviour. Such accounting becomes relevant and practical only when its benefits are established and built into organisational accounting. It is the purpose of this book not to show that such accounting provides a vehicle for criticism but rather to demonstrate its practical utility.

The terms 'social accounting' and 'environmental accounting' can therefore be seen to have a variety of meanings and uses which for some people are revolutionary in their implications but for others are merely concerned with the ways in which business performance can be improved. In summary, the terms have two major dimensions to their use:

- they can refer solely to those costs and benefits which directly impact upon the bottom-line profitability of the company; these can be termed private costs and benefits;

- they can refer to the costs and benefits which affect individuals, society and the environment for which a company is not accountable; these can be termed societal costs and benefits.

In this chapter we are concerned primarily with the private costs and benefits, partly because this is where organisations wishing to implement social or environmental accounting typically begin and partly because any justification for the implementation of such accounting must have a demonstrable benefit to that organisation. Much of what we consider, however, will be applicable to societal costs and benefits, and where there are obvious benefits to the organisation these will also be considered.

A primer produced by the Association of Chartered Certified Accountants (ACCA)[3] claims that environmental accounting arises in three distinct contexts:

(1) National Income Accounting: in this context such accounting refers to the consumption of a nation's resources, both renewable and non-renewable.
(2) Financial accounting: in this context the concern is with the disclosure of environmental liabilities and material environmental costs.
(3) Management accounting: in this context the concern is with the identification of costs and benefits which affect the organisation's decision-making processes.

It is this third context that we will concentrate on, although there will be some implications for the other two contexts which will be mentioned.

Triple bottom line reporting

There have been a number of initiatives regarding changed reporting and various descendants of Brundtland,[4] including the concept of the Triple Bottom Line (Aras and Crowther, 2008). This is based on an assumption that addressing the three aspects of economic, social and environmental is all that is necessary in order not just to ensure sustainability but also to enable sustainable development. Indeed, the implicit assumption is one of business as usual – add some information about environmental performance and social performance to conventional financial reporting (the economic performance) and that equates to triple bottom line reporting. And all corporations imply that they have recognised the problems, addressed the issues and thereby ensured sustainable development. This implication is generally accepted without questioning – certainly without any rigorous questioning. Let us look at the concept of the Triple Bottom Line – the three aspects of performance which are illustrated in Figure 11.3.

Sustainable development policies encompass these three general policy areas: *economic, environmental* and *social.* In support of this, several United Nations

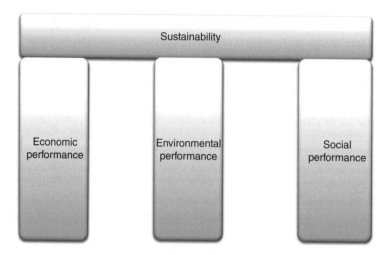

Figure 11.3   The triple bottom line for sustainable performance

texts, including the 2005 World Summit Outcome Document (UN, 2005), refer to the 'interdependent and mutually reinforcing pillars' of sustainable development as economic development, social development, and environmental protection.

This has led many organisations to undertake what they have called Triple Bottom Line reporting. In the main this is conventional financial reporting with some extra information about social and environmental performance – but certainly not the three equal pillars referred to by Brundtland.

The Global Reporting Initiative (GRI)

In 2000 the Global Reporting Initiative (GRI) produced its Sustainability Reporting Guidelines, which have been developed through multi-stakeholder dialogue. The guidelines are claimed to be closely aligned to AA1000, but focus on a specific part of the social and environmental accounting and reporting process, namely reporting. The GRI aims to cover a full range of economic issues, although these are currently at different stages of development. The GRI is an initiative that develops and disseminates voluntary Sustainability Reporting Guidelines. These Guidelines are for voluntary use by organisations for reporting on the economic, environmental and social dimensions of their activities, products, and services. Although originally started by an NGO, GRI has become accepted as a leading model for the way social environmental and economic reporting should take place. It aims to provide a framework that allows comparability between different companies' reports whilst being sufficiently flexible to reflect the different impacts of different business sectors.

The GRI aims to develop and disseminate globally applicable Sustainability Reporting Guidelines. The GRI incorporates the active participation of representatives from business, accountancy, investment, environmental, human rights, research and labour organisations from around the world. Started in 1997, GRI became independent in 2002, is an official collaborating centre of the United Nations Environment Programme (UNEP) and works in cooperation with UN Secretary-General Kofi Annan's Global Compact. The guidelines are under continual development and in January 2006 the draft version of its new Sustainability Reporting Guidelines, named the G3, was produced and made available for feedback. The G3 are the so-called 'Third Generation' of the GRI's Sustainability Reporting Guidelines. They were launched in October 2006 at a large international conference that attracted thousands.

The G3 consist of principles and disclosure items (the latter include performance indicators). The principles help reporters define the report content, the quality of the report, and give guidance on how to set the report boundary. Principles include those such as materiality, stakeholder inclusiveness, comparability and timeliness. Disclosure items include disclosures on management of issues, as well as performance indicators themselves (e.g. 'total water withdrawal by source'). The G3 are the basis of the Reporting Framework. There are other elements such as Sector Supplements and National Annexes that respond to the needs of specific sectors, or national reporting requirements. The Reporting Framework (including the G3) is a free and public good.

There is a 'third generation' because the GRI seeks to continually improve the Guidelines. The G3 build on the G2 (released in 2002), which in turn are an evolution of the initial Guidelines that were released in 2000. The G3 Guidelines provide universal guidance for reporting on sustainability performance. This means they are applicable to small companies, large multinationals, public sector, NGOs and other types of organisations from all around the world. It is the way that the Guidelines are created (through the multi-stakeholder, consensus-seeking approach) that enables them to be so broadly applicable. The GRI pursues its mission through the development and continuous improvement of a reporting framework that can be used by any organisation to report on its economic, environmental and social performance. The GRI has become the popular framework for reporting, on a voluntary basis, for several hundred organisations, mostly for-profit corporations. It claims to be the result of a permanent interaction with many people that supposedly represents a wide variety of stakeholders relative to the impact of the activity of business around the world.

GRI and AA1000 provide a set of tools to help organisations manage, measure and communicate their overall sustainability performance: social, environmental and economic. Together, they draw on a wide range of stakeholders and interests to increase the legitimacy of decision making and improve performance. Individually, each initiative supports the application of the other – at least this is the claim of both organisations concerned; AA1000 provides a rigorous process of stakeholder engagement in support of sustainable development, whilst GRI provides globally applicable guidelines for reporting on sustainable development that stresses stakeholder engagement in both its development and content.

Since January 2009, more than 1,500 organisations from 60 countries have been using the Guidelines to produce their sustainability reports.

Aspects of performance

One factor of importance to all organisations, which comes from its control system, is the factor of performance measurement and evaluation. To evaluate performance it is necessary to measure performance, and Churchman (1967) states that measurement requires the following components:

- Language to express results;
- Specification of objects to which the results will apply;
- Standardisation for transferability between organisations or over time;
- Accuracy and control to permit evaluation.

Kimberley, Norling and Weiss (1983) also make this point and argue that traditional measures do not necessarily even measure some aspects of performance and can certainly lead to inadequate and misleading evaluations of performance. They state that:

> Traditional perspectives on performance tend to ignore the fact that organisations also perform in other, less observable arenas. Their performance in these arenas may in some cases be more powerful shapers of future possibilities than how they measure up on traditional criteria. And, paradoxically competence in the less observable arenas may be interpreted as incompetence by those whose judgements are based solely on traditional criteria. Particularly in the case of organisations serving the interests of more than one group where power is not highly skewed and orientations diverge, the ability to develop and maintain a variety of relationships in the context of diverse and perhaps contradictory pressure is critical yet not necessarily visible to the external observer. (p.251)

In a survey organised by Faversham House Group, four out of every five executives interviewed said that new laws were the most important factor in persuading their companies to spend on the right technology and management to save energy and reduce emissions. More than half the interviewees saw prosecution as the ultimate weapon for forcing responsibility to the top of the agenda at board meetings.

The balanced scorecard

A different perspective upon performance evaluation has been proposed by Kaplan and Norton (1992) with the development of their balanced scorecard approach. They argue that traditional measurement systems in organisations are based upon the finance function and so have a control bias but that the balanced scorecard puts strategy and vision at the centre. They identify four components of the balanced scorecard, each of equal importance, and each having associated goals and measures. The four components are:

(1) Financial perspective – how does the firm look to shareholders?
(2) Customer perspective – how do customers perceive the firm?
(3) Internal business perspective – what must the firm excel at?
(4) Innovation and learning perspective – can the firm continue to improve and create value?

They state (1993) that measurement is an integral part of strategy:

> Today's managers recognise the impact that measures have on performance. But they rarely think of measurement as an essential part of their strategy. For example, executives may introduce new strategies and innovative operating processes intended to achieve breakthrough performance, then continue to use the same short-term financial indicators they have used for decades, measures like return on investment, sales growth, and operating income. (p. 135)

and

> Effective measurement, however, must be an integral part of the management process. (p. 136)

They maintain that the balanced scorecard is a way of evaluating performance which recognises all the factors affecting performance and it is certainly true that an external perspective, in the shape of customers, is included in this framework. The framework they propose is illustrated in Figure 11.4.

The scorecard enables companies to balance their short-run and long-run goals. It also highlights where results have been achieved by trade-off of other objectives.

The scorecard uses four perspectives from which to view the firm. These are:

(1) Financial: How the company is perceived by the shareholders.
(2) Customers: How the company is perceived by its customers.
(3) Internal: What the company must excel at, e.g. core competencies.
(4) Innovation and Learning: How can future value be created.

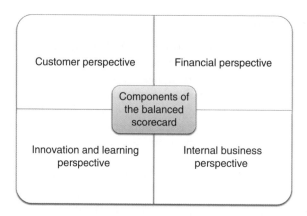

Figure 11.4   The balanced scorecard

Each business that adopts the approach develops its own purpose-built scorecard that reflects its 'mission, strategy, technology and culture'. The strength of the system is that it measures the success in achieving the strategies cascaded down by top management. There is often a divergence among mission statements, strategies and performance measures. The scorecard offers a mechanism to avoid this divergence.

The scorecard could, for example, take a mission statement that has a customer focus and convert generally stated goals into specific objectives and then develop associated performance measures. In this example the measurement system may seek an interface with the customer's management information system. If the customer has a system for capturing data that assess its suppliers, the firm could attempt to capture this information to enable it to judge its own performance through the customer's eyes.

The balanced scorecard system, it is claimed, actually balances the competing needs of an organisation. In its original form (1992) the balanced scorecard was credited with the ability to 'allow managers to look at the business from four important perspectives'. The techniques is claimed to focus upon the needs of the stakeholders of a business. Thus, shareholders and customers are two specific stakeholders mentioned within the balanced scorecard. The focus upon innovation and learning, however, and upon continuous improvement would also indicate the need for employee development, and supplier relations should be incorporated within the internal-business-process perspective (as it was referred to in 1996).

In fact each business is expected to design and adopt its own scorecard to meet its own needs. Kaplan and Norton (1996) explicitly state that they 'don't think that all stakeholders are entitled to a position on a business unit's scorecard. The scorecard outcomes and performance drivers should measure those factors that create competitive advantage and breakthroughs for an organization.' The over-arching objective of the balanced scorecard is to achieve both short-term and long-term financial success and is actually competing with other more explicitly shareholder value-based approaches as a method to enable businesses to achieve this.

The environmental audit

Before the development of any appropriate measures can be considered it is first necessary for the organisation to develop an understanding of the effects of its activities upon the external environment. The starting point for the development of such an understanding therefore is the undertaking of an environmental audit. An environmental audit is merely an investigation and recording of the activities of the organisation in order to develop this understanding (Kinnersley, 1994).

Indeed, ISO14000 is concerned with such audits in the context of the development of environmental management systems. Such an audit will address, *inter alia*, the following issues:

- the extent of compliance with regulations and possible future regulations;
- the extent and effectiveness of pollution control procedures;
- the extent of energy usage and possibilities increasing for energy efficiency;
- the extent of waste produced in the production processes and the possibilities for reducing such waste or finding uses for the waste necessarily produced;
- the extent of usage of sustainable resources and possibilities for the development of renewable resources;
- the extent of usage of recycled materials and possibilities for increasing recycling;
- life cycle analysis of products and processes;
- the possibilities of increasing capital investment to affect these issues;
- the existence of or potential for environmental management procedures to be implemented.

Such an audit will require a detailed understanding of the processes of an organisation and so cannot be undertaken by just the accountants of the organisation. It will also involve other specialists and managers within the organisation who will need to pool their knowledge and expertise to arrive at a full understanding. Indeed, one of the features of environmental accounting is that its operation depends to a significant extent upon the cooperation of the various technical and managerial specialists within the organisation; such accounting cannot be undertaken by the accountants alone.

The objective of such an audit is first to arrive at an understanding of the effects of organisational activity and then to be able to assign costs to such activity. It should also enable the managers of the organisation to consider alternative ways of undertaking the various activities which comprise the operational processes of the organisation, and to consider and evaluate the cost implications, as well as the benefits, of undertaking such processes differently.

Such an audit will probably necessitate the collection of information which has not previously been collected by the organisation, although it may well be in existence somewhere within the organisation's data files. A complete environmental audit is a detailed and time-consuming operation but there is no need for such an exercise to be completed as one operation. Indeed, the review of processes and costs should be a continuous part of any organisation's activity which can lead to the implementation of better processes or control procedures without any regard to environmental implications.

Thus, the way to approach this is to extend the normal routines of the organisation to include a consideration, and quantification, of environmental effects on an ongoing basis.

Once this audit has been completed then it is possible to consider the development of appropriate measures and reporting mechanisms to provide the necessary information for both internal and external consumption. These measures need to be based upon the principles of environmental accounting, as outlined below. It is important to recognise, however, that such an environmental audit, whilst the essential starting point for the development of such accounting and reporting, should not be viewed as a discrete isolated event in the developmental process.

Environmental auditing needs to be carried out on a recurrent basis, much as is financial or systems auditing, in order to both review progress through a comparative analysis and establish where further improvement can be made in the light of progress to date and changing operational procedures.

The measurement of performance

The measurement of performance is central to any consideration of performance evaluation and this resolves into two areas for consideration, namely why measure and what to measure. Measurement theory states that measurement is essentially a comparative process, and comparison provides the purpose for measurement. Measurement enables the comparison of the constituents of performance in the following areas:

- temporally by enabling the comparison of one time period with another;
- geographically by enabling the comparison of one business, sector or nation with another;
- strategically by enabling alternative courses of action and their projected consequences to be compared.

Performance itself is not absolute but rather comparative and it is essential in evaluating performance to be able to assess comparatively in the nature of 'better than expected', 'worse than the competition', etc. It is not possible to assess performance in other than these terms and so a quantitative approach to performance evaluation is essential even if some aspects of performance are qualitative in nature. It is necessary, therefore, that measurement is a constituent of performance evaluation and so it becomes necessary to determine what should be measured in order to evaluate performance.

It is therefore essential to select appropriate measures for the purpose of the evaluation. It is argued, however, that appropriate measures cannot be selected until the purpose of evaluation has been determined. It is therefore again demonstrated that the foundation of performance measurement is the identification of the reasons for the evaluation of performance, and this must now be considered. It is clear from the evaluation of the literature, and a consideration of actual practice, that the evaluation of performance takes place for several reasons:

- for control
- for strategy formulation
- for accountability

The evaluation of performance

A variety of measures exist to measure and evaluate performance, and whilst these have been criticised in their efficiency by some writers, it is nevertheless true that such measures have a role in this function. The efficiency of measures of performance, however, can be determined only by considering their use in the measurement of performance when the purpose of that measurement has been determined. It seems reasonable to argue that different purposes need different measures and that perhaps some, but by no means all, measures are universal in addressing all needs.

Measurements, however, derive their meaning from the use to which they are applied, and mismeasurement by using measures incorrectly can cause conflict and misunderstanding. Once a framework has been developed which identifies and addresses the needs and purposes of evaluation it is then possible to consider the efficiency and effectiveness of existing measures and identify deficiencies in the measurement system. It is then also possible to develop and implement new measures which are appropriate to the purposes identified.

It can readily be seen that the differing needs of different parties in the evaluation process cause tensions within the organisation as it seeks to meet its internal control, strategy formulation and accountability functions, and produce a reporting structure to meet these needs. Whilst the basic information required to satisfy these needs is the same information, or at least derives from the same source data, the way in which it is analysed and used is different, which can lead to conflict within the organisation.

Such conflict is exacerbated when a measure is adapted for one need but only at the expense of a deterioration in its appropriateness for another purpose. Part of the semiotic of corporate reporting, however, is that managers have the ability to manage information provision in such a way that all stakeholders can be satisfied both with the information received and with the performance of the organisation.

One factor of importance in performance evaluation is the concept of the sustainability of performance. It is therefore important for all stakeholders to be able to ascertain, or at least project, not just current performance but its implications for the future. Performance evaluation must therefore necessarily have a future orientation for all evaluations. The appropriate measures developed through this proposed framework are likely to facilitate a better projection of the sustainability of performance levels and the future impact of current performance.

This is because addressing the needs of all stakeholders is likely to reveal factors that will impact upon future performance which might not be considered if a more traditional approach were taken towards performance evaluation. An example might be the degree to which raw materials from renewable resources have become significant to many industries recently but were not considered at all until recently by any stakeholders of an organisation other than community and environmental pressure groups.

Multi-dimensional performance management

Probably the best known of the multi-dimensional performance measurement frameworks is the balanced scorecard, which we have considered. Another example is the service profit chain which specifically considers three stakeholders – namely employees, customers and shareholders. Again this model specifically considers the first two stakeholders as means to achieving superior financial results.

Thus it is argued that satisfied and motivated employees are essential if service quality is to be of a high standard and hence customers are to be satisfied. Further, it is then argued that satisfied customers provide the basis for superior financial results. Both of these models acknowledge the needs of stakeholder groups and thus deem it necessary to measure performance for these groups but still target financial performance as the ultimate goal.

A stakeholder-managed organisation therefore attempts to consider the diverse and conflicting interests of its stakeholders and balance these interests equitably. The motivations for organisations to use stakeholder management may be in order to improve financial performance or social or ethical performance, however these may be measured. In order to be able to manage stakeholder interests adequately it is necessary to measure the organisation's performance to these stakeholders, and this can prove complicated and time-consuming.

Conclusions

Social and environmental accounting has a significant part to play in the management of an organisation and the adoption of the techniques will have the following effects:

- improved decision making within the organisation;
- better cost allocation, leading to improved decision making;

- better use of, and allocation of, resources within the organisation;
- improved operational performance;
- improved operational procedures, based upon greater understanding of the impact of activities;
- improved profitability, through either cost reduction or increased activity;
- greater support of investors and other stakeholders, through increased transparency and disclosure leading to greater confidence.

These effects are based upon the adoption of the principles of social and environmental accounting but these principles need to be translated into action, in terms of the accounting and reporting systems of the organisation. It is to this that we now turn.

Summary of key points

- Good performance is multidimensional.
- Good performance is dependent upon the perspective from which that performance is being considered.
- Both Social and Environmental accounting have developed to address the need for a wider interpretation of performance.
- Environmental audit is necessary to understand environmental impact.
- Triple Bottom Line reporting is an attempt to address the three pillars of sustainable development.
- The balanced scorecard is an attempt to address all aspects of performance.
- The GRI is a generic reporting mechanism to show sustainable performance.

Definitions of key terms and theories

The **balanced scorecard** is a way of evaluating performance which recognises all the factors affecting performance.

Environmental accounting is a sub-area of accounting that deals with environmentally induced financial impacts and ecological impacts of a defined economic system.

Environmental audit is an investigation and recording of the activities of the organisation to understand its environmental impact.

The **Global Reporting Initiative (GRI)** is an initiative that develops and disseminates voluntary Sustainability Reporting Guidelines.

Social accounting considers a wide range of aspects of corporate performance and encompasses a recognition that different aspects of performance are of interest to different stakeholder groupings.

Triple Bottom Line reporting addresses the three aspects of economic, social and environmental performance.

Test your understanding

1. What categories are included for Britain's most admired companies?
2. What factors are included in the balanced scorecard?
3. Why is the measurement of performance important?
4. What is ISO14000 and what factors does it cover?
5. What is the GRI?
6. What is meant by Triple Bottom Line reporting?
7. How does social performance differ from conventional financial performance?

Suggestions for further reading

Gray, R., Dey, C., Owen, D., Evans, R. and Zadek, S. 1997. 'Struggling with the Praxis of Social Accounting: Stakeholders, Accountability, Audits and Procedures', *Accounting, Auditing and Accountability Journal*, 10, 3: 325–64.

Perrini, F. 2006. 'The Practitioner's Perspective on Non-Financial Reporting: Strategies for Corporate Social Responsibility', *California Management Review*, 48, 2: 73–103.

Waddock, S. A. and Graves, S. B. 1997. 'The Corporate Social Performance-Financial Performance Link', *Strategic Management Journal*, 18, 4: 303–19.

Notes

1. In other words, stakeholders other than the professionals for whom external reporting has generally been considered to have been designed.
2. The academic discourse of environmental accounting debates this dilemma to a great extent but this dilemma is not translated into the discourse of corporate reporting. My reading of the academic discourse is that there is general agreement concerning what is desirable in such accounting and the debate is concerned with the means of achieving that outcome – whether incremental change or revolutionary change is the preferred means of securing the desired outcome.
3. *An introduction to environmental accounting as a business tool*, which was a reprint of the primer developed by the United States Environmental Protection Agency in 1995.
4. The Brundtland Report (1987) is referred to in Chapter 2.

References

Aras, G. and Crowther, D. 2008. 'Evaluating Sustainability: A Need for Standards', *International Journal of Social and Environmental Accounting*, 2, 1: 19–35.

Child, J. 1984. *Organisation: A Guide to Problems and Practice*. London: Harper & Row.

Churchman, C. W. 1967. 'Why Measure?', in C. W. Chuchman and P. Ratoosh (eds), *Measurement: Definition and Theories*m London: Wiley, pp. 83–94.

Gray, R. H. and Bebbington, K. J. 2001. *Accounting for the Environment.* London: Sage.

Gray, R., Owen, D. and Maunders, K. 1987. *Corporate Social Reporting: Accounting and Accountability.* London: Prentice Hall.

Kaplan, R. S. and Norton, D. P. 1992. 'The Balanced Scorecard – Measures that Drive Performance', *Harvard Business Review*, Jan/Feb: 71–9.

Kaplan, R. S. and Norton, D. P. 1993. 'Putting the Balanced Scorecard to Work', *Harvard Business Review*, Sept/Oct: 134–47.

Kaplan, R. S. and Norton, D. P. 1996. 'Using the Balanced Scorecard as a Strategic Management System', *Harvard Business Review*, January/February: 75–85.

Keynes, J. M. 1926. *The End of Laissez-Faire*, www.panarchy.org/keynes/laissezfaire.1926.

Kimberley, J., Norling, R. and Weiss, J. A. 1983. 'Pondering the Performance Puzzle: Effectiveness in Interorganizational Settings', in R. H. Hall, and R. E. Quinn (eds), *Organizational Theory and Public Practice*. Beverly Hills: Sage, pp. 249–64.

Kinnersley, D. 1994. *Coming Clean: The Politics of Water and the Environment.* Harmondsworth: Penguin.

Mathews, M. R. 1993. *Socially Responsible Accounting.* London: Chapman & Hall.

Mathews, M. R. 1997. 'Twenty-five Years of Social and Environmental Accounting Research: Is there a Silver Jubilee to Celebrate?' *Accounting, Auditing and Accountability Journal*, 10, 4: 481–531.

Schaltegger, S., Muller, K. and Hindrichsen, H. 1996. *Corporate Environmental Accounting.* Chichester: John Wiley & Sons.

Solomons, D. 1974. 'Corporate Social Performance: A New Dimension in Accounting Reports?', in H. Edey and B. S. Yamey (eds), *Debits, Credits, Finance and Profits.* London; Sweet & Maxwell, pp. 131–41.

CSR in NGOs and Non-Profit Organisations

12

Learning objectives

After studying this chapter you should be able to:

- Describe the distinguishing features of the sector.
- Explain what is meant by an NGO.
- Discuss the particular CSR aspects of such organisations.
- Distinguish the various types and scale of operation of such organisations.
- Explain the benefits of a relationship between an NGO and a commercial organisation.

Introduction

Non-governmental organisations (NGOs) fulfil a vital role in society, filling the gap often left between civic responsibility undertaken through an agency of the government and personal responsibility often undertaken through the family. Indeed, the modern streamlined state very often deliberately relies upon such NGOs to undertake responsibilities previously undertaken by the state, such as health, welfare and educational roles, which can no longer be undertaken due to the twisted logic of privatisation. To fill the gap, states often rely upon NGOs and provide funding accordingly – a state obligation undertaken by proxy. The role and significance of NGOs has risen accordingly; commensurate with this we have seen an explosion in the number of NGOs and a concomitant explosion in the spheres of influence of such organisations and in the roles which they claim for themselves. This is likely to increase further as states all across the developed world reduce their activities to tackle high levels of debt – a legacy from the 2008–10 recession.

In many ways this has been brought about by the retreat of the state, which has caused the number of NGOs to increase to fill the gap left by this retreat (Kajimbwa, 2006). This retreat means that the current situation is reminiscent of the situation in the middle of the nineteenth century, with the rich being expected to donate some surplus to the poor but with a clear distinction between the deserving poor and the undeserving poor, with the distinction, of course, being dependent upon the acceptance by the receivers of the norms of the givers. Any further retreat would take us back to the medieval world of charity being inseparable from religion, but at least such charity was available to everyone as religious organisations tend not to discriminate in this manner! Thus, the role of NGOs has increased very significantly in recent years.

It is uncertain how many NGOs exist in the world but there are many millions. It is estimated, for example, that in India alone there are 2 million such organisations. Some are very large international organisations and there are a few thousand[1] of these whilst many are national organisation or even very local organisations. Some of these are very small indeed and not all are active at a particular point in time. One thing which is certain, however, is that the number continues to grow as new ones are established for new purposes.

The nature of the sector

A *not for profit organisation* is one whose objective is to support or engage in activities of public or private interest without any commercial or monetary profit. In many countries some of these will be charities but there will also be many which are not; they can all be classified as NGOs, however. An NGO is a legally constituted organisation which operates without any participation or representation of any government – or at least without any direct participation.[2] In the cases in which NGOs are funded totally or partially by governments, the NGO maintains its non-governmental status insofar as it excludes government representatives from membership in the organisation.

It is very easy to establish an NGO; almost no regulatory requirements exist and almost no control is exercised. In many countries the establishment of an NGO is completely free of regulation.[3] All that is necessary is to decide a purpose for the NGO. This can be very broad and general such as the Worldwide Fund for Nature (WWF) or Médecins Sans Frontières (MSF). Or it can be very narrow and specific such as Brinsley Animal Rescue,[4] UK or the Temple Trust, Sri Lanka.[5] All that is necessary is that the NGO has a purpose and does not seek to make a profit. Indeed, it is easier to set up a new NGO than it is to close one down. One consequence of this is that the number of NGOs is increasing all the time, arguably at an exponential rate. We can describe this as an inflationary situation and therefore have coined the term *NGO inflation*. In many respects this is laudable as the need is almost infinite for organisations serving charitable purposes or even serving PR or lobbying purposes. In other respects, however, there are, or can be, problems associated with this inflation.

It is important to start by considering the nature of the sector. The not-for-profit (NFP) sector is one which is growing in importance all over the world. Moreover, it is much bigger than people generally realise. In Europe, for example, it is estimated that the sector comprises around 40% of GDP. There is a growing movement within the 'non'-profit and 'non'-government sector to define itself in a more constructive, accurate way. Instead of being defined by 'non' words, organisations are suggesting new terminology to describe the sector. The term 'civil society organization' (CSO) has been used by a growing number of organisations, such as the Center for the Study of Global Governance. The term 'citizen sector organisation' (CSO) has also been advocated to describe the sector — as one of citizens, for citizens. This labels and positions the sector as its own entity, without relying on language used for the government or business sectors. However, some have argued that this is not particularly helpful given that most NGOs are in fact funded by governments and business.

Médecins Sans Frontières

Médecins Sans Frontières (MSF) – which translates as Doctors Without Borders – is a deliberately secular NGO formed to provide humanitarian aid to those in need regardless of race or religion or nationality. It is best known for its projects in war-torn regions and in developing countries facing endemic diseases.

Médecins Sans Frontières was created in 1971 by a small group of French doctors as a consequence of the Biafran War in Nigeria, who believed that all people have the right to medical care regardless of race, religion, creed or political affiliation, and that the needs of these people supersede respect for national borders. The organisation is known in most of the world by its French name or simply as MSF, but in some countries – particularly the United States, Canada, Australia and Ireland – the name 'Doctors Without Borders' is often used instead.

Core documents outlining MSF's principles are the Charter and the Chantilly Principles, along with the later La Mancha Agreement, which in Rules, Section 2 addresses governance. MSF has an associative structure, where operational decisions are made, largely independently, by the five operational centres (Amsterdam, Barcelona, Brussels, Geneva and Paris). Common policies on core issues are coordinated by the International Council, in which each of the 19 sections (national offices) is represented. The International Council meets in Geneva, Switzerland, where the International Office, which coordinates international activities common to the operational centres, is also based.

In 2007 over 26,000, mostly local, doctors, nurses, and other medical professionals, logistical experts, water and sanitation engineers and administrators provided medical aid in over 60 countries. Private donors provide about 80% of the organisation's funding, whilst governmental and corporate donations provide the rest, giving MSF an annual budget of approximately $400 million.

The organisation actively provides preventive health care training and medical training to populations in more than 60 countries, and frequently insists on political responsibility in conflict zones such as Chechnya and Kosovo. Only once in its history, during the 1994 genocide in Rwanda, has the organiation called for military intervention. To be able to speak and act freely, MSF remains independent of any political, religious or economic powers. The majority of all MSF activities are paid for with private donations.

MSF received the Nobel Peace Prize in 1999 in recognition of its members' continuous effort to provide medical care in acute crises, as well as raising international awareness of potential humanitarian disasters. Prior to this, MSF also received the Seoul Peace Prize[6] in 1996. It is a good example of an NGO which is able to do things because it is not connected to any governmental organisation.

Competing for resources

Although NGOs all have a declared purpose which is related to the public good, or at least the founder's perception of the public good, it is nevertheless true that the vast majority of NGOs are formed by a single individual with the drive to do so. Only a relatively small number of NGOs are formed by a group of people. Consequently, we need to consider the motives the individuals have for forming NGOs, and these motives extend beyond the declared purpose of the NGO. In other words, the formation of an NGO is normally not undertaken for altruistic reasons and there is often a hidden agenda.

The first thing we must remember about this sector is that there is no profit motive and decisions must be taken according to different criteria. Instead, the emphasis is upon the provision of a service, which is the essential reason for the existence of such an organisation. Additionally, there is normally a disconnection between the acquisition of resources and their use – in other words the money to provide the services does not normally come from the recipient of those services. Moreover, the need for those services frequently outstrips the ability of the organisation to satisfy those needs and it is forever operating under a situation of resource constrain. This means that there are different motivations operating in the NFP. It also means that the stakeholders are different – something which we will return to as it is important for our consideration of CSR in such organisations.

One important issue for every NGO is the acquisition of resources to enable it to carry out its purpose. For some international NGOs – such as those which deal with natural disasters – this can be a very large requirement. For others it can be a relatively small amount required to keep the organisation functioning. For each one, however, the amount required is significant in the context of the scale of the organisation. Moreover, there needs to be a constant scanning of the environment in order to continually secure the necessary resources. In other words, the acquisition of sufficient resources for this year merely changes the focus to the acquisition of sufficient resources for next year. It is an endless process. With the exception of the very large international NGOs which acquire their resources from governmental funds, there are two sources of funding for an NGO. The first of these is from businesses and the second is from individuals.

As far as organisations are concerned then there are a number of benefits from being associated with NGOs because of the image of the business which is thereby created. A positive image that people share about an organisation can yield positive influence on the quality of the relationships between that organisation and its stakeholders. Chajet (1989) postulates that a company with a good image can more easily attract audiences (including investors, partners, employees, and customers) which will influence the success of the organisation. Similarly, Mackiewicz (1993) outlines research studies which indicate that nine out of ten consumers use the reputation of an organisation in order to decide which product or service they will buy from among those that are available at a similar price and quality. Poiesz (1988) stipulates that without the existence of images, it will not be easy for consumers to decide which products to buy, whilst Bernstein (1986) claims that image affects attitudes, which in turn affect behaviour. The Reputation Institute indicated that those corporations with the best reputations in the USA – the world's major market – also perform significantly better than others in terms of market share and share value (*Wall Street Journal*, 1999). Companies need to protect their reputations in order to ensure growth and even the long-term survival of the company. The building of and maintaining a strong positive reputation depends on establishing strong relationships with the corporate stakeholders.

There are many benefits of a strong corporate reputation, including the improvement of shareholder value as a strong corporate reputation inspires confidence in investors, which in turn leads to a higher stock price for a company[7]; increased customer loyalty to the products of the company as a positive customer perception of a company extends to its products; employee morale and commitment are higher at corporations with a good corporate reputation. At a time of a crisis a good corporate reputation can shield the company from criticism and even blame, and can help it communicate its own point of view more easily to audiences that are willing to listen to its point of view,[8] whilst a company with a solid reputation is more influential on legislative and regulatory governmental decision making. Additionally, of course, a strong corporate reputation is an influential factor for forming partnerships and strategic alliances as the partner company has the potential to improve its own reputation by association. An organisation's reputation is shaped by the 'signals' the organisation gives about its nature – for example, the behaviour of its members, or the type of organisational activities performed. In fact, various businesses focus their efforts on gaining a competitive advantage and a strong positive reputation by demonstrating a commitment to their responsibilities towards the society.

Thus the way organisations behave, are talked about, reported and perceived by their publics greatly influences the management of their reputation. By aligning charitable giving[9] with the corporations' self-interest, in which corporations select suitable recipients of funding not so much according to need, but according to their potential of adding brand value, is one means for improving corporate reputation. In today's global society, organisations are judged not solely on their achievements but on their behaviour too. This is, in fact, an opportunity for corporations if they see CSR as an essential business strategy, as brand value and reputation are widely accepted as a company's most valuable assets and CSR can instil trust and brand loyalty. In principle, CSR can be used to strengthen corporate reputation and profitability by signalling to the various stakeholders with whom the organisation interacts that it is committed to meeting its moral obligations and expectations beyond common regulatory requirements. The argument here is not for a cynical exploitation of a concern in society for socially responsible behaviour; rather it is for a recognition that CSR needs to be part of the strategic planning of the organisation – central to its development rather than an optional add-on. Research has shown that corporations and the civil society have become more tightly interrelated. Business involvement in civil society focuses on charitable giving, corporate philanthropy and community participation. More recently the focus has shifted towards 'strategic philanthropy' (Smith, 1994) and 'cause-related' marketing (Varadarajan and Menon, 1988).

It can be seen, therefore, that there is benefit to a business from an association with an NGO. The important point, however, is that in an environment where there is an increasing number of NGOs then there is equally an increasing number seeking an association with, and funding from, a finite number of businesses. In other words, there is competition for resources and that competition is becoming fiercer as the number of NGOs increases. This is equally true in acquiring resources from individuals – as the number of NGOs increase, so too do the competitions, not just for financial resources but also for the time of individuals. One consequence of this increased competition is that NGOs must spend more time and effort in securing resources for their activities. Resulting from this is that the cost of acquiring each unit or resource increases and the NGOs therefore become less efficient merely because of the increased competition. At the same time overheads as a proportion of total expenditure are increasing, thereby making it harder to acquire further resources and increasing overhead costs and inefficiency still further in a vicious circle of rising overhead costs of operating an NGO. It also means that the large international NGOs benefit disproportionately as the difficulties of competition are not so severe for them because of their international profile. The competition and its consequences are more severe for smaller national and especially local NGOs. In this business, like many others, it pays to be big and not just because of economies of scale. Moreover, as the competition between NGOs continues to increase, this size advantage also continues to increase disproportionately.

Types of NGO

We can classify NGOs into various types, each with a different purpose. Public bodies are related to government in some way and include such things as a local authority and a health authority. These all have the function of providing services

Figure 12.1 Types of NGO

to members of society and receive their funding and powers directly from the national government. Quasi-public body are also often known as Quangos (quasi-autonomous non-governmental organisations) and serve a public or civic purpose without having any direct relationship with the government. Many civic societies are like this and other examples include such things as housing associations. These too often get some funding directly from the government. Other types are shown in Figure 12.1.

It is also possible to classify NGOs according to their purpose – providing assistance in times of need (operations NGOs) and lobbying for change (advocacy NGOs) as represented in Figure 12.2. Many of the larger NGOs, of course, fulfil both functions.

Educational institutions, on the other hand, as the name suggests serve an educational function and include such organisations as schools, further education colleges and universities. These may be publicly owned organisations or privately owned and the norm differs between countries.

Many NGOs take the form of a charity, which is an organisation which exists to fulfil a particular function which involves providing a service. As charities are a significant number of the organisations in the NFP sector then we need to consider their structure in some detail. The first point to make is concerning the

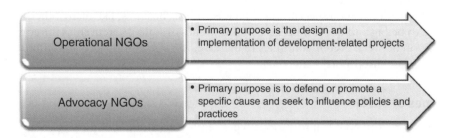

Figure 12.2 Purpose of NGOs

legal environment in which they operate. This can be described *intra vires* rather than *ultra vires*. The difference is that an *ultra vires* organisation[10] has the power to do anything which it is not specifically prevented to do according to either the law or its founding legal articles of association. All commercial organisations are founded like this and can therefore extend and change their operations according to market needs and circumstances. Conversely, an *intra vires* organisation can undertake only those activities which it is specifically empowered to undertake. It is therefore much more difficult for such an organisation to extend or change its activities. All charities are established as *intra vires* organisations. This can be defined as its charitable purpose.

A charity has many tax and regulation advantages but in return there are certain restrictions on what it can do. Thus a charity is not able to act as a pressure group – at least not overtly. Politics are excluded from its sphere of operation. It can engage in fund raising, of course, but it is prevented from trading as a means of raising funds. This might seem surprising given how many charities are visibly engaged in trading. This is done either through a third party or by means of a trading subsidiary which then gifts the proceeds to the charity. Thus these restrictions are legal restrictions to ensure that the benefits of being a charity can only accrue to an organisation with a genuine charitable purpose but these restrictions are interpreted fairly liberally for organisations which are recognised to be charities. The ultimate sanction, of course, is the removal of charitable status from such an organisation.

The final point to make about charities is that they make extensive use of volunteers as well as of paid employees. This keeps their operating costs down, of course but also adds another stakeholder group with an interest in and concern for how the charity operates, manages its performance and services its beneficiaries. Moreover, the relationship between volunteers and paid employees is sometimes a source of conflict. Here too there is more competition as the number of NGOs increases. All rely upon voluntary assistance and too large a number of NGOs mitigates against the ability to find sufficient assistance of this nature. As the alternative is paid assistance then the consequences of competition can again be seen to be increasing inefficiency of operation.

Motivation for starting an NGO

The motivation for the existence of NGOs is important to consider as it tends to be different to profit-seeking organisations and this has implications for CSR. First it should be recognised that a NGO is motivated by some kind of societal concern – as perceived by the founder. Normally this involves the provision of a service to some part of that society but it can act as some kind of pressure group for change. When a service is provided then it is important to note that this service provision is normally unrelated to payment for that service – it is free to the beneficiary and the cost is met by raising funding. One motivation for an NGO, therefore, is the acquisition of resources in order to undertake the provision of those services. Thus there is a concern with the optimising of the utilisation and allocation of what is inevitable scarce and restricted resources. Similarly, there is a concern with transaction cost-minimisation. These issues are similar to those of profit-seeking organisations but the way in which they are decided and the way in which effectiveness is measured tends to be quite different.

Because there is no profit motive then this way of providing motivation to managers and rewarding them for their performance does not exist and alternatives must be sought. Another factor which must be borne in mind is the matter of who decides what constitutes good performance. For a profit-seeking organisation the customer will ultimately decide by choosing to buy or not buy. In a NGO there is no customer and the service beneficiaries do not pay (or at least not full cost) for the service received. Thus the determining of measures of performance is important for these organisations. So too is the setting of standards and the reporting of performance. This is normally done through the development of performance indicators. Often a variety of measures are used including budgetary control and cash flow, performance indicators of a wide variety of types, non-financial measures and inevitably a range of non-numeric qualitative factors. For the evaluation of performance then there is less relevance of accounting measures and a correspondingly greater importance of non-financial measures. This inevitably involves problems of quantification and a necessity for deciding between alternatives. One technique which is particular to this environment is that of cost–benefit analysis.

In an environment in which the number of NGOs is increasing then the ability to comparatively measure and evaluate performance becomes crucial as this is one differentiating factor which can be used to assist in the competition for both funding and for voluntary assistance. The different nature of this kind of organisation, however, makes this more problematic than for a conventional profit-seeking organisation, and more subjective in nature.

Implications for managers

It will be apparent that there are a number of issues facing the founders, the management board and the managers of these organisations. The first is concerned with the acquisition and utilisation of resources. There is considerable uncertainty regarding the acquisition of resources and this makes planning particularly difficult. The planning horizon therefore tends to be short even though the projects which some NGOs are involved in are inevitably long-term in duration. This makes for uncertainty which mitigates against the effective operation of such organisations. This is exacerbated by the increasingly competitive environment which is brought about by the prevalence of NGO inflation.

Other issues which concern managers include the setting of objectives and the measuring of performance. Finance, budgeting and control, of course, are particularly important in this environment. Another factor is concerned with the influence of stakeholders. Without customers and without shareholders and investors there are a range of other stakeholders who are important and have a great deal of influence. These will include such stakeholders as donors, recipients and society at large.

As far as the external environment is concerned there are a number of issues which are important and distinctive. The first is the question of market identification; this is essential for planning but is not necessarily obvious. Then, as we have implied already, there is the fact that service delivery is not evaluated by its beneficiaries who do not pay for its receipt. There are a lot of different stakeholders who all have a view about performance and some influence on its evaluation – a complex situation.

NGOs are – in theory at least – not in competition with each other. Increasingly this is untrue. We have already discussed the increasing competition in the acquisition of resources but it is also becoming true as far as the provision of services and the helping of beneficiaries is concerned. For the provision of services there are often several organisations involved in providing the same services and it might be thought that collaboration – rather than competition – might be an effective way of providing such services. Certainly high-profile disasters always involve several large charities which often collaborate and pool resources. At a more local level collaboration is less common than competition and we argue that the psychological aspects of their formation provide a significant reason for this competitive environment – no founder or manager wants their NGO to fail. It can also be argued that although there are several reasons which lead to the formation of an NGO, once it is founded then the primary motivation changes. Instead of providing the service for which it is nominally founded the primary motivation of an NGO becomes that of perpetuating its own existence and managers become embroiled in activity to achieve this end.

One of the factors in this sector already mentioned, howeveris that the largest NGOs are most able to acquire additional resources. Thus there is competition for market share because this leads to easier resource acquisition. In theory also NGOs exist to fulfil a particular purpose. Once that purpose has been satisfied there is no purpose to their continued existence. For both of these factors, however, the egos of the people managing the NFPs becomes a factor as each strives to extend its life, extend its purpose and extend its size and market share.

Access to available resources

For the small number of large international NGOs the main source of funding comes from the government. This is certainly true for public bodies and for quasi-public bodies. In most countries it is also true for educational institutions. For the largest charities it is also true as governments tend to use these charities to distribute their aid programmes.

Other sources of funding include borrowing but this is only really an option for capital projects when some security can be provided. So for many NGOs the other main source of funding is from fund raising. This can take the form of seeking donations or legacies or trusts. For the larger organisations then raising funds through trading is also a viable possibility and in the UK, for example, the shopping centres have a considerable number of charities represented. Fund raising also has become competitive as the number of NGOs continues to increase.

Accounting issues

We have dealt with a number of accounting issues already in our consideration of planning and budgeting; of the measurement and reporting of performance; and of the evaluation of results. Another important point to make though is concerning the time horizon adopted by these organisations. Many projects are long-term in nature but sources of funds are often short-term in nature. So there is a long-term horizon for expenditure but a short-term horizon for income; this is problematic and a source of difficulty in planning for many of these organisations.

Many of these NGOs engage in fund raising, as we have seen. This itself causes complications for the accounting of such organisations and can affect its operational procedures. Money can be given to one of these organisations either for its general activities or for a specific purpose. For example, the larger charities frequently have appeals for a specific disaster relief operation. When money is given for a specific purpose then it can be used for only that purpose. Thus these organisations tend to have a number of funds for specific purposes. This can be problematic when the need for such money has been completed and there is a surplus – it is difficult to use this for another purpose. A further difficulty is caused by the fact that some funding is needed for general administration. People are willing to give for a specific cause but not for general administration. Thus the accounting for these organisations is geared towards making as much expenditure as possible direct expenditure rather than indirect. These are all actors which make for administrative inefficiency in an NGO and raise their overhead costs. Competition from the increasing number of such organisations serves to make this problem worse.

CSR issues in NGOs

All of these factors have implications as far as CSR is concerned. It is often thought that is an organisation exists for a public or charitable purpose then it must be a socially responsible organisation. Our consideration of issues throughout this book should have enabled you to understand that this is not necessarily the case. CSR is about how an organisation conducts its operations and deals with its stakeholders. For NFPs we can see that there is a different focus and we need to consider this in terms of CSR implications. We can consider this according to a number of different criteria.

First, and perhaps most importantly, there is the question of stakeholders. Instead of customers there are beneficiaries or service users. There are also volunteers and funding providers as well as the normal range of stakeholders. There are different stakeholders for an NGO and the different stakeholder groups have different amounts of power to a profit-seeking organisation. It is inevitable, therefore, that dealing with these stakeholders will be a much more important function for a NGO. Moreover, the sources of conflict might be different and the actions taken in resolution of this might also be different. Inevitably also the decision-making process is likely to be different.

In terms of doing more with fewer resources (see Aras and Crowther, 2009) then this is always an objective for this kind of organisation. In terms of affecting the choices available to future generations then an NGO actually seeks to do this and to redistribute resources more equitably. In terms of seeking a continual existence then really an NGO should strive to make its purpose of existence no longer relevant and should not seek sustainability. Thus sustainability is an equally important issue for these organisations but its implications are very different in terms of both motivation and decision making. NGO inflation makes such sustainability a more difficult problem for these organisations.

Accountability is an even more important issue for this kind of organisation and who it is accountable to can be very different. Without either shareholders or customers then accountability is to donors, beneficiaries and a wide range of other stakeholders. Moreover, it needs to address this accountability – which can be different for different stakeholders – in order to be able to continue with its operations.

With this diverse set of stakeholders groupings which all have considerable interest in the organisation and its activity then there is obviously a great need for transparency and all such organisations will strive for this. This is particularly exacerbated by the need to keep funds for specified restricted purposes. On the other hand, it is in the interest of the NGO to seek to use its accounting system and procedures to classify indirect costs as direct and thereby to minimise the apparent administrative costs incurred. This is contrary to the principle of disclosure but completely understandable!

Increasing disclosure is a feature of corporate reporting as they seek to satisfy stakeholders through increased accountability and transparency. Disclosure has, of course, always been a feature of NGO activity as such disclosure is necessary to seek additional funds as well as to satisfy the diverse but powerful and vociferous stakeholder groupings. In this respect there it might be considered that profit-seeking organisations are becoming more like not-for-profit organisations.

The environment in which NGOs operate is somewhat different to profit-seeking organisations which leads to different problems but there are still CSR implications which are mostly concerned with sustainability and with accountability. Particular features of this environment are: the uncertain resource availability ate its effect on long-term planning; the different extent of stakeholder power and involvement; conflicting priorities; a different legal environment and the problems of managing ambiguity. This makes the NGO environment quite different.

Greenpeace

Greenpeace International is an NGO with member organisations – each country has its own Greenpeace affiliated to Greenpeace International – which has offices in over 42 countries. It has an international coordinating body in Amsterdam. Greenpeace states its goal is to 'ensure the ability of the Earth to nurture life in all its diversity'. On its official website, Greenpeace defines its mission as the following:

> Greenpeace is an independent global campaigning organisation that acts to change attitudes and behaviour, to protect and conserve the environment and to promote peace by:
>
> Catalysing an energy revolution to address the number one threat facing our planet: climate changes.
> Defending our oceans by challenging wasteful and destructive fishing, and creating a global network of marine reserves.
> Protecting the world's remaining ancient forests which are depended on by many animals, plants and people.
> Working for disarmament and peace by reducing dependence on finite resources and calling for the elimination of all nuclear weapons.
> Creating a toxic-free future with safer alternatives to hazardous chemicals in today's products and manufacturing.
> Campaigning for sustainable agriculture by encouraging socially and ecologically responsible farming practices.

Greenpeace makes use of direct action and lobbying as well as undertaking research to achieve its goals. The global organisation does not accept funding from governments, corporations or political parties, relying on more than 2.8 million individual supporters and foundation grants.

Greenpeace evolved from the peace movement and anti-nuclear protests in Vancouver in the early 1970s. On 15 September 1971, the newly founded Don't Make A Wave Committee sent a chartered ship, *Phyllis Cormack*, and renamed it *Greenpeace* for the protest, from Vancouver to oppose the US testing of nuclear weapons in Alaska. This committee subsequently adopted the name Greenpeace. In a few years Greenpeace spread to several countries and started to campaign on other environmental issues such as commercial whaling and toxic waste. In the late 1970s the different regional Greenpeace groups formed Greenpeace International to oversee the goals and operations of the regional organisations globally.

Greenpeace gained international attention during the 1980s when the *Rainbow Warrior*, the most well-known of several vessels operated by Greenpeace, was sunk whilst in harbour in New Zealand by operatives of the French intelligence service on 10 July 1985, killing one of the activists. In the following years, Greenpeace evolved into one of the largest environmental organisations in the world. It gained further notoriety in 1991 by opposing Shell's proposed sinking of the Brent Spar North Sea oil platform in the mid Atlantic – see Chapter 2.

Today, Greenpeace focuses on the worldwide issues mentioned on its web-site. It is known for its direct action approach and has been described as the most visible environmental organisation in the world. Campaigns of Greenpeace have raised environmental issues to public knowledge and influenced both the private and the public sector but Greenpeace has also been a source of controversy. Its motives and methods have received criticism and the organisation's direct actions have sparked legal actions against its activists.

Social values

The idea that an organisation is not formed merely to provide benefit to its shareholders is not a new concept. Some owners of businesses have always recognised a responsibility to other stakeholders and this is evident from the early days of the Industrial Revolution. Thus, for example, Robert Owen (1816; 1991) demonstrated dissatisfaction with the assumption that only the internal effects of actions need be recorded through accounting. Furthermore, he put his beliefs into practice by including within his sphere of industrial operations the provision of housing for his workers at New Lanark. Others went further still and Jedediah Strutt of Belper and his sons, for example, provided farms to ensure that their workers received an adequate supply of milk, as well as building accommodation for their workforce which was of such high standard that these dwellings remain highly desirable in the present.[11] Similarly, the Gregs of Quarry Bank provided education as well as housing for their workforce. Indeed, Salt went further and attempted to provide a complete ecosphere for his workers.[12] Thus there is evidence from throughout the history of modernity[13] that the self-centred approach of concern only with the organisation and its owners was not universally acceptable and was unable to satisfactorily provide a basis for human activity.

Many organisations have always recognised that they exist within society and must at least partly meet the needs of all of that society. Attempting this task of meeting differing requirements is based upon a recognition of their own position in the community and the values upon which they are founded. This was recognised by Selznick (1957: 136), who stated:

Truly accepted valued must infuse the organisation at many levels, affecting the perspective and attitudes of personnel, the relative importance of staff activities, the distribution of authority, relations with outside groups, and many other matters. Thus if a large corporation asserts the wish to change its role in the community from a narrow emphasis on profit-making to a large social responsibility (even though the ultimate goal remains some combination of survival and profit-making ability), it must explore the implications of such a change for decision making in a wide variety of organisational activities.

The ethical implications of a firm's behaviour were considered by McCoy (1985: 87) who considers ethics to be at the core of business behaviour. He states:

> Dealing with values required continual monitoring of the surrounding environment, weighing alternative courses of action, balancing and (when possible) integrating conflicting responsibilities, setting priorities among competing goals, and establishing criteria for defining and evaluating performance. Along with these goes learning ways to bring this ethical reflection directly and fully into the processes by which policy is made, implemented, and evaluated. Increasingly, skills in dealing with values as integral components of performance and policy-making are being recognised as central for effective management in a society and a world undergoing rapid change.

The way in which a business performs in terms of its ethical behaviour and identified place in society as a whole is determined by its relationship with its stakeholder community. It is also to some extent determined by, as well as to some extent determining, the culture of the organisation. Kotter and Heskett (1992) consider corporate culture and show how this can lead to good business performance but also to bad business performance and a lack of ability to change to match changing environmental conditions. They consider that effective leadership is crucial to success. Success, like good performance, is always, of course, a subjective construct depending upon the perspective of the evaluator. When we consider NGOs, of course, that success becomes even more subjective as there are no yardsticks such as profit; consequently different metrics are needed, including qualitative metrics, and it would be useful to research what is needed and what is used.

NGOs reviewed

It is clear that there is a need for NGOs to attempt to bring about change. It is equally clear that there is a need for NGOs to provide operation requirements in many areas. This aspect of need will only increase as the role of the state is shrunk following the economic crisis of 2008–10 and the abandoning of interventionist ideologies. NGOs clearly have some strengths in undertaking these roles but they also have some weaknesses, as described in Figure 12.3.

Conclusions

Although the environment in which an NGO operates is different to a normal profit-seeking organisation, and in many ways more difficult and restrictive, this has not prevented the establishment of an increasing number of NGOs. Indeed, the extent is so great that we have talked about NGO inflation. This has made the environment in which NGOs operate more difficult and more competitive, and has had deleterious effects upon such organisations. Nevertheless, these problems, too have, not prevented this NGO inflation.

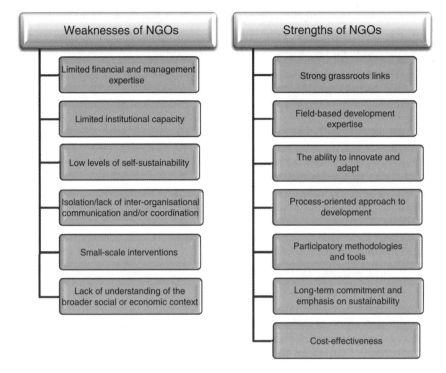

Figure 12.3   Evaluation of merits of NGOs

Summary of key points

The environment in which not-for-profit organisations operate is somewhat different but there are still CSR implications that are mostly concerned with sustainability and with accountability. Particular features of this environment are:

- Uncertain resource availability and its effect on long-term planning.
- Stakeholder power and involvement.
- Conflicting priorities.
- Legal environment.
- Managing ambiguity.

Definitions of key terms and theories

A **not-for-profit organisation** is one whose objective is to support or engage in activities of public or private interest without any commercial or monetary profit. In many countries some will be charities but there will also be many which are not.

A **non-governmental organisation** (**NGO**) is a legally constituted organisation that operates without any participation or representation of any government.

In the cases in which NGOs are funded totally or partially by governments, the NGO maintains its non-governmental status insofar as it excludes government representatives from membership in the organisation.

Test your understanding

1. What is *ultra vires*?
2. What types of NFP exist?
3. How many NGOs exist in the world?
4. What CSR issues exist for NFPs?
5. How is an NGO established?
6. What measures of performance are typically used by these organisations?
7. What differences does a charity have?

Suggestions for further reading

Aras, G. and Crowther, D. (eds) 2010. *NGOs and Social Responsibility*. Bingley: Emerald.

Claver, E., Llopis, J., Gasco, J. L., Molina, H. and Cocna, F. J. 1999. 'Public Administration – from Bureaucratic Culture to Citizen-Oriented Culture', *International Journal of Public Sector Management*, 12, 5: 455–64.

Davis, P. 2001. 'The Governance of Co-operatives under Competitive Conditions: Issues, Processes and Culture', *Corporate Governance*, 1, 4: 28–39.

Notes

1. Wikipedia suggests that there are around 40,000 such international NGOs, although different classifications lead to different numbers. Nevertheless, the number of such large international NGOs is a very small proportion of their total number.
2. Many governments, as part of their retreat from the provision of public services, have utilised NGOs as a means of providing these services and have channelled funding to them accordingly. Thus there may be no direct participation but there certainly is indirect control as a major part of the funding of such NGOs comes directly from governments. Accountability, however, is indirect.
3. There are exceptions. For example, in Turkey there are some general regulations about NGOs. If you want to establish a new association then you have to complete all the necessary paperwork and get permission from the Association board of Turkey. And you have to give a report every year after a general board meeting about managerial and financial aspects. As a sanction it is necessary to pay a very small amount of tax every year if you do not do this but this is a fairly small penalty.
4. Brinsley is a small town in the centre of England and Brinsley Animal Rescue has the purpose of rehoming unwanted pets in the area.

5. The Temple Trust operates from the UK but has the purpose of looking after orphans in a region of Sri Lanka.

6. The Seoul Peace Prize was established in 1990 as a biennial recognition with a monetary award to commemorate the success of the Olympic Games held in Seoul, South Korea. It was established to reflect the wishes of the Korean people and to crystallise their desire for everlasting peace on earth.

7. The Opinion Research Corporation (ORC), which conducts 'Corperceptions', a periodic caravan survey of more than 4 000 business executives in several of the world's major markets concludes that the better the corporate reputation, the higher the stock price (Morley, 2002).

8. A good example is the Pepsi Cola tampering case according to which products on sale were found to contain hypodermic syringes. Pepsi dealt effectively with the crisis by defusing public alarm with a public relations campaign that highlighted the integrity of its manufacturing process and its corporate credibility (Morley, 2002).

9. Charitable giving is perceived to be an indication of social responsibility – see Crowther (2002).

10. A limited company is an example of an *ultra vires* organisation which can undertake anything not specifically excluded by its Articles of Association. As a consequence, such a company can change its basis of operation and its activities without problem. A charity cannot do this. Thus there are many charities which still exist although the purpose for their existence no longer exists.

11. Indeed, the earlier workers' accommodation provided by Richard Arkwright, arguably the instigator of the Industrial Revolution, at Cromford, Derbyshire, remain equally desirable.

12. The illustrations cited here are all from various parts of the UK and all from the late eighteenth and early nineteenth centuries. This is not just because one of the present authors is English but also because the Industrial Revolution commenced in the UK.

13. Examples from pre-modernity also exist primarily in the form of assistance provided by religious institutions to anyone in need. The essential point is that socially responsible behaviour has always existed from among people/organisations who care and has been unrelated to any form of regulation.

References

Aras, G. and Crowther, D. 2009. *The Durable Corporation: Strategies for Sustainable Development*. Aldershot: Gower.

Bernstein, D. 1986. *Company Image and Reality: A Critique of Corporate Communications*. Eastbourne: Holt, Rinehart & Winston.

Chajet, C. 1989. 'The Making of a New Corporate Image', *Journal of Business Strategy*, May/June: 18–20.

Crowther, D. 2002. *A Social Critique of Corporate Reporting*. Aldershot: Ashgate.

Kajimbwa, M. 2006. 'NGOs and their Role in the Global South', *International Journal of Not-for-Profit Law*, 9, 1.

Kotter, J. P. and Heskett, J. L. 1992. *Corporate Culture and Performance*. New York: The Free Press.

Mackiewicz, A. 1993. *Guide to Building a Global Image*. New York: The Economist Intelligence Unit, McGraw-Hill Inc.

McCoy, C. S. 1985. *Management of Values: The Ethical Difference in Corporate Policy and Performance*. Marshfield, MA: Pitman.

Morley, M. 2002. *How to Manage your Global Reputation*. Basingstoke: Palgrave Macmillan.

Owen, R. 1816; 1991. *A New View of Society and other Writings*. Harmondsworth, Penguin.

Poiesz, T. B. C. 1988. 'The Image Concept: Its Place in Consumer Psychology and its Potential for Other Psychological Areas'. Paper presented at the XXIVth International Congress of Psychology, Sydney, Australia.

Selznick, N. 1957. *Leadership in Administration: A Sociological Interpretation*. Evanston, IL: Row, Peterson.

Smith, C. 1994. 'The New Corporate Philanthropy', *Harvard Business Review*. May–June: 105–16.

Varadarajan, P. R. and Menon, A. 1988. 'Cause Related Marketing: A Coalignment of Marketing Strategy and Corporate Philanthropy', *Journal of Marketing*, 52 (July): 58–74.

Globalisation and Regulation

13

Learning objectives

After studying this chapter you should be able to:

- Describe and critique the features of globalisation.
- Understand and explain international organisations and their activity.
- Explain what is meant by Trickle Down theory.
- Discuss the anti-globalisation movement.
- Discuss the problems with regulating global markets and organisations.
- Explain what is meant by arbitrage.
- Explain the causes and effects of contagion.

Introduction

Globalisation is a leading concept which has become the main factor in business life during the last few decades. This phenomenon affects the economy, business life, society and environment in different ways, and almost all corporations have been affected by these changes. We can see these changes mostly related with increasing competition and the rapid changing of technology and information transfer. This issue makes corporations more profit-oriented than a long-term and sustainable company. However, corporations are a vital part of society which needs to be organised properly. Therefore we need some social norms, rules and principles in both society and business life for socially responsible behaviour to be ensured.

Globalisation

Globalisation can be defined as the free movement of goods, services and capital. This definition, however, does not cover all aspects of globalisation or global changes. Globalisation should also be a process that integrates world economies, culture, technology and governance because it also involves the transfer of information, skilled employee mobility, the exchange of technology, flow of financial funds and geographic arbitrage between developed countries and developing countries. Moreover, globalisation has religious, environmental and social dimensions. In order to encompass this broad impact area, globalisation covers all dimensions of the world economy, environment and society. Moreover, it is apparent all over the world and the world is changing dramatically. Every government has a responsibility to protect all of its economy and domestic market from this rapid change.

The question is how a company will adapt to this change. First of all, companies have to understand the different effects of globalisation, which has some opportunities but also threats. A company might have to learn how to protect itself from some negative effects and how to retrieve opportunities from this situation.

Globalisation affects the economy, business life, society and environment in different ways:

- increasing competition
- technological development and technology transfer
- knowledge/information transfer
- portfolio investment (fund transfer between developed countries and emerging markets)
- regulation/deregulation, international standards
- market integration
- intellectual capital mobility
- financial crisis–contagion effect–global crisis

and these can be represented as in Figure 13.1.

Features of globalisation

Globalisation leads to increased competition (that is, increased competition is a consequence of globalisation) This competition can be related to product and service cost and price, target market, technological adaptation, quick response and quick production by companies, etc. When a company produces with less cost and sells cheaper, it will be able to increase its market share.

Customers have too much choice available in the market and they want to acquire goods and services quickly and in a more efficient way. Also they are expecting high quality for which they also expect to pay a cheap price. All these expectations need a response from the company because otherwise company sales will decrease and it will lose profit and also market share. A company must

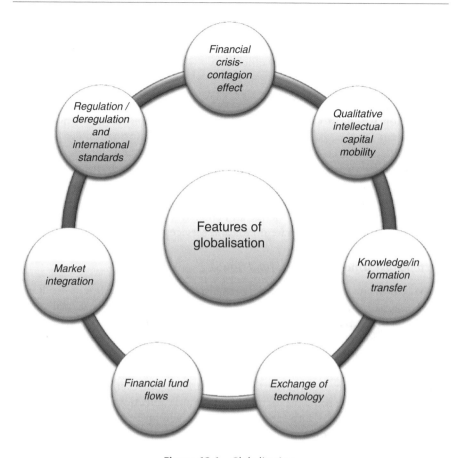

Figure 13.1   Globalisation

always be ready for price, product and service, and customer preferences because all of these are global market requirements.

Exchange of technology

One of the most striking manifestations of globalisation is the use of new technologies by entrepreneurial and internationally oriented firms to exploit new business opportunities. Internet and e-commerce procedures hold particular potential for SMEs seeking to broaden their involvement in new international markets (Wright and Etemad, 2001). Technology is also one of the main tools of competition and the quality of goods and services. On the other hand, it necessitates quite a lot of cost for the company. The company has to use the latest technology for increasing its sales and product quality because globalisation has increased the speed of technology transfer and technological improvement and as a result customer expectations are directing markets. It is mostly companies in capital-intensive markets which are at risk and that is why they need quick/rapid adaptation to customer/market expectations. These companies therefore have to manage technology and R&D efficiently.

Knowledge/information transfer

Information is a most expensive and valuable production factor in the current environment (at time of writing), where exchange of information can be easily and rapidly transferred between countries and is constantly changing. If a company has access to such knowledge and information streams, this enables it to keep ahead in adapting to global changes. This is a similar process to that of technology transfer in global markets. The rapid changing of the market equally requires quick transfer of knowledge and efficient application of that knowledge in the production of appropriate goods and services for global consumption.

Portfolio investment (financial fund flows)

Globalisation encourages increased international portfolio investment. Additionally, financial markets have become increasingly open to international capital flows. For this reason, portfolio investment is one of the major problems facing developing economies because it is almost the only way these emerging countries can increase liquidity of their markets and economies through attracting foreign funds. Significantly, however, this type of short-term investment carries risk of dramatic negative impact on the financial markets. For example, the emerging economies may have some problem in their country affecting their market image or investors may make sufficient profit from their investment and then leave the market. These events would mean that market liquidity would decrease and financial market indicators would plummet immediately.

Regulation/deregulation and international standards

Globalisation requires more regulation of the markets and economy. There are many new and complicated financial instruments and methods in the market and such instruments easily transfer and trade in other countries because of the globalisation effect. Every new system, instrument or tool requires new rules and regulations to determine its impact area. These regulations are also necessary to protect countries against global risks and crises. When a crisis emerges in one country it then influences other countries through trade channels and fund transfers, which we call the contagion effect. On the other hand, during globalisation the shares of big companies are trading in international stock markets and these companies have shareholders and stakeholders in many different countries. International rules and regulations also offer protection to small investors against big scandals and other problems in companies.

International standards also regulate markets and economies by means of international principles and rules such as international accounting standards and international auditing standards. Regulation aims to make corporate reporting standardised and comparable and the multiplicity of organisations in the globalised world means more rules and regulations and more international standards are required than ever before. The financial crisis of 2008–10 has shown why this is very important.

Market integration

In fact, globalisation leads to the conversion of many markets and economies into one market and economy. The aim of international standards and regulations is therefore also to deregulate all these individual markets because the traditional economy needs financial structures capable of handling the higher risk in the new economy. For this reason financial markets must be broad, deep, and liquid and at present only the US financial markets are large enough to provide this financial structure in the world market. Global stock market projection and Pan-European stock market projection are part of this changing economic structure. There are many similar examples in the current situation of market integration which are also the result of increasing competition in the economy. Integration examples are also prominent in company mergers and acquisitions.

Qualitative intellectual capital mobility

Another effect of globalisation is human capital mobility through knowledge and information transfers. One of the reasons for this effect is that international/multinational companies have subsidiaries, partners and agencies in different countries and they need skilled and experienced international employees and rotation of these personnel from country to country to provide appropriate international business practice. This evolutionary process thus also requires more skilled, well-educated and movable employees who can adapt quickly to different market conditions.

Financial crisis–contagion effect–global crisis

Financial crises are mostly determined through globalisation and as a result of the contagious effects of globalisation. In fact, this is quite a true explanation as the financial world has witnessed a number of crises cases. Generally, financial crises emerge from international funds/capital flows (portfolio investments), lack of proper regulations and standards, complex financial instruments, rapid development of financial markets, asymmetric information and information transfers. One country's crisis can turn into a global crisis with systemic risk effect, 'systemic risk' being a risk of a financial crisis spreading from one country to another. In some cases, crises spread even between countries which do not appear to have any common economic fundamentals/problems. Previous global crises have also showed that one of the causes of such crisis is unregulated markets.

How globalisation affects CSR

The question might be how globalisation affects CSR but the answer to this is related to not only the last quarter of the twentieth century but also previous centuries. John Maynard Keynes calculated that the standard of living had increased 100% over 4 000 years. Adam Smith had an important (seminal) idea about the wealth of communities and in 1776 he described conditions which would lead to increasing income and prosperity. Similarly, there is much evidence from economic history to demonstrate the benefit of moral behaviour; for example, Robert Owen in New Lanark, and Jedediah Strutt in Derbyshire – both in the UK – showed the economic benefits of caring for stakeholders. More recently, Friedman has paid attention to the moral impact of the economic growth and development of society.

It is clear that there is nothing new about economic growth, development and globalisation. Economic growth generally brings out some consequences for the community and this is becoming a world phenomenon. One of the most important reasons is that we are not taking into account the moral, ethical and social aspects of this process. Some theorists indicated more than a hundred years ago that the effect of rapid economic growth and development might not be without social and moral consequences and implications.

Another question is who is responsible for this ongoing process and for ensuring the well-being of people and safeguarding their prosperity. Is this the responsibility of governments, the business world (businessman), consumers, shareholders, or all people? Government is part of the system and the regulator of markets and lawmakers. Managers, businessmen and the business world take action concerning the market structure, consumer behaviour or commercial conditions. Moreover, they are responsible to the shareholders for making more profit to keep their interest in the company over the long term and therefore they are taking risk for their own benefit/profit. This risk is not in conflict with the social or moral/ethical principles which they have to apply in the company. There are many reasons for ethical and socially responsible behaviour on the part of the company to be maintained; however, there are many cases of misbehaviour and some illegal operations in some companies, which is evidence that increasing competition makes business more difficult than before in the globalised world.

The good news and our expectations are that competition will no longer have any bad influence on company behaviour. According to international norms (practice) and expectations, companies now have to take into account social, ethical and environmental issues more than they did during in the last two decades. One of the reasons is that more competition does not always mean more profit; another reason is that consumer expectation is related to not only the cost of products but also quality, proper production process and environmental sensitivity.

Moreover, shareholders are more interested in long-term benefit and profit from the company. The key word in this concept is 'long-termism', which also represents a sustainable company. Shareholders want long-term benefit with a sustainable company rather than merely short-term profit, relating to not only the company's profits but also the social and environmental performance of that company – the triple bottom line which we have discussed earlier (see pp. 149, 221). Thus, managers have to make strategic plans for the company concerning all stakeholder expectations which are sustainable and provide long-term benefit for the companies with their investments. However, sustainability can be seen as including the requirement that just values – fair distribution of goods, fair procedures, respect for rights, etc. – are capable of being sustained indefinitely (Aras and Crowther, 2009). Thus, sustainability requires that the values of justice are capable of being continued into the future: if current practices, for instance, reflected only the present point of view but would prevent the same practices from occurring in the future, that would be rejected from the point of view of sustainability (Dower, 2004). So investor or shareholder expectations and all other stakeholder approaches are supporting the socially responsible and ethical company above other companies. Globalisation has had a very sharp effect on company behaviour and yet we can still see many problems, particularly in developing countries. This is one of the realities of the current globalisation process but we can expect to see some different approaches and improvements to this process in the future, with some of them naturally related to international principles, rules and norms. But many of the changes needed are related to ending this flawed system and the inherent problems of capitalism.

The challenge of CSR in a globalising world is to engage in a process of political deliberation which aims at setting and resetting the standards of global business behaviour. Whilst stakeholder management deals with the idea of internalising the demands, values and interests of those actors that affect or are affected by corporate decision making, we argue that political CSR can be understood as a movement of the corporation into environmental and social challenges such as human rights, global warming or deforestation (Scherer and Palazzo, 2008).

Lehman Bros

In 1844, 23-year-old Henry Lehman emigrated from Bavaria to the United States. He settled in Montgomery, Alabama where he opened a dry-goods store, 'H. Lehman'. http://en.wikipedia.org/wiki/Lehman_brothers - cite_note-Wechsberg233-11 In 1847, following the arrival of his brother Emanuel, the firm became 'H. Lehman and Bro.' With the arrival of their youngest brother, Mayer Lehman, in 1850, the firm changed its name again and 'Lehman Brothers' was founded.

During the 1850s, cotton was one of the most important crops in the United States. Capitalising on cotton's high market value, the three brothers began routinely to accept raw cotton from customers in payment for goods purchased, eventually beginning a second business trading in cotton. Within a few years this business grew to become the most significant part of their operation.

→

Following Henry's death in 1855, the remaining brothers continued to focus on their commodities-trading/brokerage operations. The firm continued to grow and prosper for 150 years.

On 15 September 2008, the firm filed for Chapter 11 bankruptcy protection following the massive exodus of most of its clients, drastic losses in its stock, and devaluation of its assets by credit-rating agencies. This was the largest bankruptcy in US history. The following day, Barclays Bank announced its agreement to purchase, subject to regulatory approval, Lehman's North American investment-banking and trading divisions along with its New York headquarters building. During the next week, Nomura Holdings announced that it would acquire Lehman Brothers' franchise in the Asia Pacific region, including Japan, Hong Kong and Australia, as well as Lehman Brothers' investment banking and equities businesses in Europe and the Middle East. The deal became effective on 13 October 2008. Lehman Brothers' investment management business, including Neuberger Berman, was sold to its management on 3 December 2008. Creditors of Lehman Brothers Holdings Inc. retain a 49% common equity interest in the firm, now known as Neuberger Berman Group LLC. It is the fourth largest private employee-controlled asset management firm globally.

A report by the court-appointed examiner published in March 2010 indicated that Lehman executives regularly used cosmetic accounting gimmicks at the end of each quarter to make its finances appear less shaky than they really were. This practice was a type of repurchase that temporarily removed securities from the company's balance sheet. However, unlike typical repurchase agreements, these deals were described by Lehman as the outright sale of securities and created 'a materially misleading picture of the firm's financial condition in late 2007 and 2008'. It seems that nothing has been learned since the Enron debacle.

Globalisation, corporate failures and CSR

Enron, WorldCom, Qwest, Parmalat, Sunkill, ImClone, and various other corporate failures, bring out some governance and CSR issues that have increased attention to the role of business ethics. The managers and CEOs of these companies must be considered responsible for all of these failures and these are cases of 'corporate irresponsibility'. Many people have the opinion that if corporations were to behave responsibly, most probably corporate scandals would stop. This applies particularly to financial corporations after the latest crisis.

CSR protects firms against some long-term loss. When corporations have social responsibilities, they calculate their risk and the cost of failure. First, a company has to have responsibility to shareholders and also all stakeholders, which means that it has responsibility to the whole of society. Corporate failures also have an important impact on the whole society. In particular, big scandals such as Enron have sharply affected the market and the economy. Various stakeholders (e.g. employee, customer, consumer, suppliers, etc.) as well as shareholders and regulators of the firm have a responsibility to ensure good performance. There-fore, CSR is related to not only firms but also to society as a whole. So changing the role of corporate responsibility only shifts the focus from the real problem that society needs to address.

One of the reasons for this outcome is increasing competition between the company and the market. Managers tend to become much more ambitious than before in their behaviour and status in the globalised world and thus we have to focus on corporate and managerial behaviour. The question is how to behave as a socially responsible manager and how to solve this vital problem in business life and in society. In the business world there are always some rules, principles and norms as well as regulations and some legal requirements.

However, to be socially responsible one who has to be capable of acting and being held accountable for decisions and actions must be more than simply law-abiding. The problem is the implication for all of these directions for company and managerial behaviour. On the other hand, one perspective is that a corpo-ration is a 'legal person' and has the rights and duties that go with that status – including social responsibility. In the case of Enron, managers were aware of all the regulations and even though they have known all irresponsible and unethical problems in the company management, they did not change their approach and behaviour.

The conclusion is that it is not always possible to control behaviour and cor-porate activity with regulations, rules and norms. So another question arises in this situation that if people do not know their responsibility and socially respon-sible things to do and if they do not behave socially responsibly then, who will control this problem in business life and in the market. The concern is that the social responsibility implications of the company cannot be controlled through legal means, the only social contract between managers on the one hand and society and stakeholders of the company on the other.

Firms will consciously need to focus on creating value not only in financial terms, but also in ecological and social terms. The challenge facing the business sector is how to set about meeting these expectations. Firms will need to change not only in themselves, but also in the way they interact with their environment (Cramer, 2002).

Failures in regulation

One thing which is apparent is that the recent (2008–10) financial crisis, much as previous ones, has highlighted failures in regulation just as much as failures in governance. Indeed, this has been a focus of much attention and some have argued that the regulators are more culpable even than the perpetrators and should be sanctioned accordingly. Equally, of course, it is the function of govern-ment, in Lockean (1690) tradition, to implement the Social Contract (Rousseau, 1762) and introduce regulation to curb the exercise of power and to protect the less powerful for a better operation of the markets. Clearly this has not worked – not because the principle is flawed but because economic reality has changed, encouraged by the Washington consensus and fostered by such people as Gordon Brown, former Prime Minister of the UK. Indeed, many people hold the policies of Brown, in relaxing regulation to impotence in order to encourage banks into the UK, as being a prime cause of the ensuing financial crisis regarded as inevitable. The situation could be regarded as a house of cards ready to collapse at the slightest breeze. Inevitably this breeze did arrive in the form of the subprime lending scandal in the USA! From this the contamination spread from one country to another as all economies are affected by both the consequences of dubious lending practices and the ensuing crisis of confidence.

So it is wrong to single out regulators for blame. Their overseers must accept responsibility for encouraging profligacy.[1] The crisis is, of course, made much worse by bank lending policy and financial profligacy, with bank lenders being secure in the expectation that there was no risk because governments would step in to rescue them[2] from the dire consequences of their irresponsibility. Indeed, government bodies – with press complicity – have sought to disguise the fact that such lending has been completely irresponsible by falling back on semiotics to create the term 'toxic debt' in order to disguise the reality of complete irresponsibility bordering on lunacy. The language being used by these bodies tends therefore to be used as a device for corrupting thought (Orwell, 1970), that is, used as an instrument to prevent thought about the various alternative realities of bank lending policy.

Of course, such bank managers – encouraged in their lending policies by their governments – failed to recognise that it was possible to lend too much. Indeed, it is scarcely creditable that such a scale of lending was possible but the banks in Iceland succeeded in lending at a level of seven times the country's GDP. It is unsurprising, therefore, that the government was unable to rescue their banks from the credit crisis and had to resort to both seeking to pass liability on to individual citizens in other countries[3] and becoming the first developed European country for over thirty years to need IMF assistance – although not the last as others feel the effects of the crisis. Perhaps the British government protested so strongly about Icelandic behaviour because the UK is also at risk, with bank lending exceeding twice GDP and a distinct possibility of the British economy similarly imploding. Interestingly, the effects of the crisis have led to negative growth in the developed world but not elsewhere.

When considering the antecedents of the 2008 crisis, however, it is our view that this started to go wrong when the concept of limited liability was introduced for corporations – in the UK in the early part of the nineteenth century (Crowther, 2000). The principle of limited liability was introduced to protect investors (i.e. shareholders) from the potential adverse consequences of the actions of the corporations in which they invested. This paved the way for the attraction of many more investors, thereby enabling the growth in size of business enterprises, with those investors secure in the knowledge that they were protected from any loss greater than the sum they had invested in the enterprise. Thus, for relatively small levels of risk they were able to expect potentially great rewards and thereby escape from some of the consequences of the actions of the enterprise. Further actions have been taken since to alleviate corporations (and hence shareholders) from the risk associated with their investments. Buckminster Fuller (1981) describes lucidly the actions of successive US governments during the twentieth century, which had the effects of transferring all risk to society in general through taxation, reduced regulation and through acting to bail out failed enterprises. Examples can be found in the actions of most other governments. So without risk corporations were able increasingly to do whatever they wished – and without responsibility anything became possible, even the lies of the present, because no one was accountable for their actions as long as economic growth – and profitability – continued. Thus we arrive at the present excesses. The link between rights and responsibilities had been severed and forgotten. So it is reasonable to argue that the current state is an inevitable consequence of the increasing laxity regulation of markets just as the Enron debacle was an inevitable consequence of the increasing laxity in accounting and reporting standards. The unfolding of the details regarding bank lending policy[4] and the consequent effects upon the world economy parallel the unfolding of the Enron affair. This time also the casualties are becoming apparent but they are more than banks which are profligate with their lending; countries have also been shown to be profligate and are also paying the cost. Thus not only has Iceland has been shown to be problematic with its banking regulation laxity and has had to seek an IMF rescue but also other European countries have been shown to be similarly lax.

To a certain extent this too is a consequence of the reality that what is becoming more important than governments and nation states is the multinational company, operating in a global environment. Some of these multinationals are very large indeed – larger than many nation states and a good deal more powerful. The exercising of this power, coupled with the desire of politicians to court the favour of these multinationals, is one of the significant causes of the crisis. Many governments throughout the world have behaved as if they recognise this reality and have responded to the veiled threats from these corporations to relocate their operations by granting concessions of various kinds. Even the government of the United States – the most powerful nation on earth – has behaved in this way. For them, however, the problem is that all their politicians are funded by these corporations and so they must behave as if they are on the payroll and must do as they are told. Needless to say, these corporations are concerned with their own interests rather than with altruism and so American domestic and foreign policy is dictated by the needs of multinational corporations. And where America leads others must follow – or suffer the consequences – economic or physical.

The free market system

Although this philosophy of individual freedom was developed as the philosophy of Liberalism, it can be seen that it has been adopted by the conservative governments throughout the world, as led by the UK government of Thatcher and the US government of Reagan in the 1980s, seduced by the arguments of Hayek (1944). This philosophy has led increasingly to the reduction of state involvement in society and the giving of freedom to individuals to pursue their own ends, with regulation providing a mediating mechanism where deemed necessary. It will be apparent, however, that there is a further problem with Liberalism and this is that the mediation of rights between different individuals works satisfactorily only when the power of individuals is roughly equal. Plainly this situation never arises among all individuals and this is the cause of one of the problems with society. A further problem with the legitimisation of the Free Market system is the trick perpetrated by Friedman (1962), the Chicago School of economists and the great myth of Trickle Down theory (Aghion and Bolton, 1997) – a myth based upon wishful thinking rather than any evidence.[5]

Whilst this philosophy of Liberalism was developed to explain the position of individuals in society and the need for government and regulation of that society, the philosophy applies equally to organisations. Indeed, Liberalism considers that organisations arise within society as a mechanism whereby individuals can pursue their individual self-interests more effectively than they can alone. Thus firms exist because it is a more efficient means for individuals to maximise their self-interests through collaboration than is possible through each individual acting alone. This argument provides the basis for the Theory of the Firm (Coase, 1937), which argues that through this combination of individuals the costs of individual transactions are thereby reduced.

Gambling the future

The proposed solutions to the crisis are themselves problematic. First, the Free Market system upon which much of the current economic system is based has been abandoned as governments have sought to support ailing banks, thereby signalling yet again that there is no cost to profligate irresponsibility as far as financial markets are concerned. For institutions, therefore, the cost of irresponsibility must be borne by society at large and particularly by future members of that society who must repay the enormous amount of government borrowings or at best must service that debt. So the cost of irresponsibility now has been conveniently externalised into the future. Whilst this public spending is in accord with the Keynesian economics that are the alternative to the deregulated economics of the Chicago School, Keynes himself actually advocated that the public spending should be utilised on the provision of public goods and infrastructure as an investment in the future. This time the spending has disappeared and the future has been mortgaged without any discernable benefit.

Although there has been much public discussion regarding how the responsibility should be apportioned, this is not really significant, although it is apparent that those responsible are, in the main, avoiding sanction and penalty. Similarly, many people have discussed the failures in the system that have led to the crisis. Significantly, however, there does not seem to be any recognition that this crisis is largely caused by the combination of a global environment with national regulation, and the voices of those calling for a regulatory environment to deal with this global environment are very quiet. But it is certain that this needs to be solved in order to prevent future reoccurrences and until this happens we are gambling with the future for no benefit. More significantly there has been a lot of soul searching but no concrete actions have been taken to prevent future occurrences. Given that such crises have been a feature of the economic situation since at least the beginnings of industrialisation[6] and have become increasingly frequent in recent times, there is every reason to expect more in the near future. This time, however, the governments will not be able to stave off collapse with their investment as they will not have recovered from the 2008–10 crisis. So action is necessary which will prevent such crises happening again. Such action must be more profound than that currently proposed: we must treat the cause rather than the symptoms.

ISO 26000

The International Organization for Standardization (ISO) has published its third series of management system standards in 2010. This series is designated as ISO 26000: Social Responsibility. The previous series, i.e. the quality management standards (ISO 9000) (the first generation), and the environmental management standards (ISO 14000) (the second generation) were based on the Deming PDCA cycle. ISO 26000 is based on the same rules. Despite all the apparent similarities, the new series of ISO management system standards does not assume the customer is king; instead, such attention is extended to the whole range of stakeholders. Also, the new standard series is even expected to influence the existing TQM concepts gathered throughout many years and it is expected that in future all three management standards series will be integrated into only one series of standards. Such an expectation seems to be true since, as claimed by WBCSD, social responsibility, along with economic growth and ecological balance, is the third pillar of sustainable development. If we accept that economic growth is, among other factors, a result of good quality and, at the same time, if we accept that ecological balance is a consequence of environmental protection, we gather that sustainable development is founded on the pillars of quality, environmental, and SR management system standards.

According to the ISO website the standard should:

- assist organisations in addressing their social responsibilities whilst respecting cultural, societal, environmental and legal differences and economic development conditions;
- provide practical guidance related to operationalising social responsibility, identifying and engaging with stakeholders, and enhancing credibility of reports and claims made about social responsibility;
- emphasise performance results and improvement;
- increase confidence and satisfaction in organisations among their customers and other stakeholders;
- be consistent with and not in conflict with existing documents, international treaties and conventions and existing ISO standards;

→

- not be intended to reduce government's authority to address the social responsibility of organisations;
- promote common terminology in the social responsibility field; and
- broaden awareness of social responsibility.

Meanwhilst, as mentioned above, the range of stakeholders related to social responsibility covers a wide range consisting of employees, their families, environment, customers, shareholders, etc. It means that social responsibility standards must respond to those interested in quality and environment as well. So paying respect to social responsibility would imply paying respect to quality and environment.

Adopting ISO 26000 in future is the best and most reliable way to adopt globalisation. Some of the benefits of ISO 26000 for customers might be as follows:

- Enhanced customer access to and choice of products and services provided by companies observing social responsibility.
- Enhanced customer satisfaction through improved link with providers of services and products.
- Access to a unique standardised method to prove claims on social responsibility.

Some of the benefits of ISO 26000 for trade:

- Enhanced customer reliance on global markets resulting in the growth of global trade.
- Improved competitiveness for companies adopting ISO 26000.
- Improved assurance to the companies adopting ISO 26000, as having the basis for customer satisfaction.

Some of the socio-economic benefits of ISO 26000:

- Reduced costs due to development of diverse standards, by application of only one internationally accepted standard.
- Improved reputability for institutions adopting ISO 26000 as a proof of their goodwill.
- Proved commitment to ethics for institutions adopting ISO 26000.

Is globalisation an opportunity or threat for CSR?

We have no certain answer for this question, which depends on where are you are looking from. It is clear that the globalisation has different effects on the social responsibility of the company and the behaviour of managers. Some of these are supporting companies/managers for motivating towards socially responsible behaviour, whilst others are destroying fair business and all principles, norms and regulations which are the result of increasing competition. Globalisation has created bigger companies in terms of turnover, market capitalisation and amount of assets. This causes imperfect competition with other small and medium-size companies, which is a major threat for them. But it might also provide companies with great opportunities for reaching people and customers, and for collaboration with other companies from all over the world. In fact, we have to accept that globalisation is an inevitable phenomenon for which we have no alternative yet. Well-regulated and -controlled markets are not a big problem and constitute little threat, but lack of regulation and norms is the main problem in a developing country, where globalisation has a big influence.

Moreover, CSR implementation is one of the most important issues for globalised economies and markets. CSR requires some rules for the determination of the relationship between the corporation and society, which is still a complicated process. The implication is that CSR is not merely a simple process but also needs a long-term strategic approach by companies which need to learn socially responsible behaviour, and their decision makers must enforce these principles in the company.

When the company takes a long-term perspective it will have benefits concerning profit and stakeholder interests in the company. Some studies show that there is a clear relationship between CSR and corporate financial performance which is an important academic research topic. Research results focus on the existence of slack resources resulting from better financial performance made when companies invest in areas that are related to social actions. Some other results also support the good management approach which states that good management practice resulting from engagement in social actions enhances the relationship with stakeholders, leading to better financial performance. This topic still needs more research for finding better solutions for corporate behaviour.

The duty of corporations is serving their shareholder through providing proper products and services. The purchasing decision of the customer is not only related to price and quality but is also based on a consideration of the social behaviour of the company. Socially responsible investment and behaviour gives some opportunities to the company which is more visible than others and also shows more concern for stakeholders.

In particular, the development of information technology is helpful for the company for trading in any place in the world to any customer. Customers want the corporation to treat its suppliers properly , and its suppliers to treat their labourers fairly even in far distant countries. When the company behaves unethically then people all over the world will get to know about this problem and its effect on company sales and stakeholder interests in the company will be affected accordingly.

So, from this aspect, globalisation has a multidimensional effect relating to socially responsible behaviour. Good and bad behaviour is easily visible around the world and all company stakeholders will be aware of it. A company can use this opportunity both ways, which is that good behaviour affects the company positively but unethical behaviour will undoubtedly have negative effects for them. Companies already know that proper behaviour is the only way they can survive and enhance their commercial interests and thereby increase their profits. So the demands of society will be reflected in corporate behaviour. In summary, a firm has an investment in reputation, including its reputation for being socially responsible. An increase in perceived social responsibility may improve the image of the firm's management and permit it to exchange costly explicit claims for less costly implicit charges. In contrast, a decline in the level of stakeholders' views of a firm's social responsibility may reduce its reputation and result in an increase in costly explicit claims (McGuire, Sundgren and Schneeweis, 1988), We can also confidently say about CSR's impact at the present time is that it benefits some people and some companies in some situations. Consequently thought is being given to the implications of CSR for the developing world (Blowfield and Frynas, 2005).

Conclusion

As we can see, globalisation has an enormous effect on society and business life which can be manifested in a number of different ways. So business life needs more regulation and proper and socially responsible behaviour than before. In this chapter we have shown the relationship between CSR and globalisation. We have pointed out that the relationship between business failure and scandals increased after globalisation, and socially responsible behaviour decreased.

Summary of key points

- Globalisation has many effects; some are beneficial whilst others are less so.
- Financial misdemeanours have created a concern for CSR. This includes reckless behaviour and fraud and theft.
- The free market is a cause of problems.
- Globalisation has created a global marketplace and fostered economic competition.

Definitions of key terms and theories

Arbitrage is profit that can be earned due to price difference in different markets.

Contagion means that problems in one market will spread to other markets.

Portfolio investment is based on investment for returns rather than for development. Consequently it is transient.

Trickle down theory argues that wealth will initially accrue to the rich but eventually permeate down through society. A legitimating theory of the free market, it has no foundation whatsoever.

Test your understanding

1. What is the main indicator of Globalisation?
2. How does globalisation affect CSR?
3. Is globalisation a threat for CSR?
4. What is meant by contagion?
5. What is the problem with regulating financial markets?
6. Is irresponsible management the cause of big corporate scandals?

Suggestions for further reading

Doh, J. P., Rodriguez, P., Uhlenbruck, K., Collins, J. and Eden, L. 2003. 'Coping with Corruption in Foreign Markets', *Academy of Management International Review*, 17, 2: 114–27.

Prahalad, C. K. and Hammond, A. 2002. 'Serving the World's Poor, Profitably', *Harvard Business Review*, 80, 9: 48–57.

Notes

1. Of course, in the UK the 2009 scandal over parliamentary expenses and the misuse – even sometimes criminal fraud – of public money has shown that governments are often not fit to act as overseers and are unable to behave any better than – or even as well as – the managers of financial institutions.
2. Consider for example the British government's nationalisation of Northern Rock before the crisis had really started. Consider also the even more surprising *volte face* of the US government in acquiring stakes in struggling financial institutions – lots of evidence of the risk-free environment in which banks have been operating...
3. The Icelandic government policy seems to have been to indemnify their own citizens while refusing to do so for citizens of other countries – not a popular policy in the UK where many people had accounts with Icelandic banks, although a settlement seems now to have been reached.
4. That is, if indeed there was any lending policy other than greed and a naïve belief that the good times were here forever so that risk could be ignored!
5. Indeed, all the evidence shows that this effect does not take place.
6. Some would trace the beginnings back to the Dutch tulip bulb speculation of the sixteenth century and the UK-based South Sea Bubble of the seventeenth century. Others trace the antecedents back into the Middle Ages. The salient point, however, is their continual recurrence.

References

Aghion, P. and Bolton, P. 1997. 'A Theory of Trickle-Down Growth and Development', *Journal of Economic Studies*, 64, 2: 151–72.

Aras, G. and Crowther, D. 2009. *The Durable Corporation: Strategies for Sustainable Development*. Farnham: Gower.

Blowfield, M. and Frynas, J. G. 2005. 'Setting New Agendas: Critical Perspectives on Corporate Social Responsibility in the Developing World', *International Affairs*, 8, 81 (3): 499–513.

Buckminster Fuller, R. 1981. *Critical Path*. New York: St Martin's Press.

Coase, R. H. 1937. 'The Nature of the Firm', *Economica*, 4, 16: 386–405.

Cramer, J. 2002. 'From Financial to Sustainable Profit', *Corporate Social Responsibility and Environmental Management*, 9: 99–106. Published online by Wiley.

Crowther, D. 2000. 'Corporate Reporting, Stakeholders and the Internet: Mapping the New Corporate Landscape', *Urban Studies*, 37, 10: 1837–48.

Dower, N. 2004. 'Global Economy, Justice and Sustainability', *Ethical Theory and Moral Practice*, 7: 399–415.

Friedman, M. 1962. *Capitalism and Freedom*. Chicago: University of Chicago Press.

Hayek, F. A. 1944. *The Road to Serfdom*. London: Routledge.

Locke, J. 1690. *Two Treatises of Government*. many editions.

McGuire, J. B., Sundgren, A. and Schneeweis, T. 1988. 'Corporate Social Responsibility and Firm Financial Performance', *Academy of Management*, 31, 4: 854–72.

Orwell, G. 1970. *Collected Essays, Journalism and Letters Vol 4*. Harmondsworth: Penguin.

Rousseau, J.-J. 1762. *The Social Contract*. many editions.

Scherer, A. G. and Palazzo, G. 2008. 'Globalization and Corporate Social Responsibility', in A. Crane, A. McWilliams, D. Matten, J. Moon and D. Siegel (eds), *The Oxford Handbook of Corporate Social Responsibility*. Oxford: Oxford University Press

Wright, R. W. and Etemad, H. 2001. 'SMEs and the Global Economy', *Journal of International Management*, 7: 151–4.

Stakeholders and Protest: Challenging Corporate Activity

14

> **Learning objectives**
>
> After studying this chapter you should be able to:
>
> - Describe and classify the types of actions which customers have undertaken in protest.
> - Classify the types of organisations involved in protest according to several classifications.
> - Critique the role of the internet in empowering individuals as customers and as citizens.
> - Identify the main factors which lead to a successful protest.

Introduction

It is easy to think that individual customers have little power when faced with the power of large organisations, from which goods and services must be purchased. Often there is a tendency to think that if we are not happy with those goods or services, or even with the organisation itself, then our only alternative is not to purchase those goods and services. Thus, we must either purchase alternatives from another organisation or manage without. Of course, this is a simplistic view of the relationship between customers and their suppliers as organisations are reluctant to lose customers. In general it costs around six times as much to attract a customer as it does to retain an existing customer, so organisations will inevitably try to retain customers as well as attract new ones.

This view of the power relationship between individuals and organisations is also somewhat simplistic as customers have exerted significant influences upon organisations, particularly when acting in concert. In this chapter, therefore, we are going to consider the ways in which individuals can, and have, influenced organisations through their actions.

Purpose of protest

There have been a number of protests of one sort or another which have taken place concerning organisations and their behaviour or concerning the types of goods and services which they provide. Indeed, the history of such protests is as long as the existence of such organisations themselves. Such protests have taken place for a variety of reasons and one way to categorise these protests is in terms of their purposes. They can be classified as follows.

Price protest

Customers have, of course, always complained about the high price of products and services but high prices by themselves have not tended to be a cause for protest. Instead, the factor which tends to cause a protest is a sudden change in prices to a higher level, and there is a long history of protesting about such price increases. Sometimes such protesting has been spontaneous and sometimes it has been organised. For example, during the latter half of the eighteenth century and the early part of the nineteenth century in the UK there were periods when food prices rose dramatically. At one time this led to the formation of the Anti Corn Law League whose express purpose was to lobby for the repeal of the Corn Laws and thereby to increase the import of foreign corn with a consequent reduction in the price of bread. Other protests against the price of food during this time were less organised and consisted often of riots. Customers in markets protested against the price of food by attacking and destroying the stalls of traders but sometimes these riots were purposeful and, instead of destroying these stalls, customers took them over and sold the food at prices which they considered to be reasonable, instead of the prices being asked, giving this money to the traders.

In the USA, protests against the price of meat were a recurrent feature of the twentieth century. In one particularly successful protest in Washington in 1946 a boycott of all meat cuts which were priced in excess of 60c per pound was organised. This had the effect of forcing sellers to reduce the price of all cuts of meat, as only the cheaper ones were being sold (Stein, 1975). This was an organised boycott of more expensive products but protests with less organised beginnings have been successful. In the UK, during 2000, some people began protesting at the price of petrol after a number of price increases which were caused in part by an increase in the tax on petrol. Initially small in scale, this protest caught the public imagination and became an organised blockade of petrol distribution depots which was sufficiently effective to cause a shortage of petrol in the country. This protest was a national protest which polarised public opinion, as not everyone – especially those who were inconvenienced by the lack of petrol – was in favour of the protest. Nevertheless, the protest was sufficiently effective after a few weeks to cause the government to promise a review of petrol prices as the means of ending this protest.

Ecological protest

Not all protests are against such things as price rises which affect individuals at a personal level. Other protests have been caused by a concern for wider ecological and environmental issues. A good example is the protest concerned with the proposed method of disposal of the Brent Spar North Sea oil platform in 1995 by Shell which we considered earlier. And example of a similar protest which took place during the 1980s was concerned with tuna fishing and the effect that this had upon dolphins. In this protest the objection was to fishing with nets, as opposed to fishing with lines, as dolphins became entangled in the nets and died because they could not surface to breath. In this case, therefore, publicity was organised to boycott firms which made use of net fishing and one of these organisations was Heinz. In this case, rather than boycotting the firm itself the protest took the form of targeting supermarkets which sold Heinz's products and relying upon the supermarkets to pressure Heinz to change their practices. The major supermarket chain chosen was Sainsbury's and mass protests took place outside a number of Sainsbury's supermarkets every weekend to protest about the fishing practices of Heinz and to encourage the boycott of the products of this company. This, of course, seriously damaged the trading of Sainsbury's as well as their image through association and had the effect of making Sainsbury's state their position of wishing to boycott these fishing practices and therefore pressurising the major companies involved to change their practice. In this case, therefore, the protest was effective through indirect action.

One cause of concern in the UK in recent years was the building of new roads and this spawned a new type of protest which is known as 'ecoprotest'. This protest takes the form of occupying land which has been designated for the building of these roads and using every peaceful means possible to prevent the roads from being built. With the exception of one protest – in Derby where the local inhabitants became very much involved and mounted a successful political and legal action – none of these protests has been successful in preventing such road building but they have raised awareness of the issues involved and have seriously delayed, and increased the cost of, such schemes. In this case, of course, there are as many people in favour of the building of new roads as there are opposed to it and the issue is not as clear-cut as in the other protests mentioned. Nevertheless, this kind of protest has created a new kind of occupation – the ecoprotestor – of people who are engaged full-time in this kind of protest and rely upon the sympathetic aid of local inhabitants who will be adversely affected for help. This kind of protest has recently extended into protests about genetically modified (GM) foods and the growing of genetically modified crops. This protest has much broader appeal all across the EC and governments themselves are involved in the debate about such crops. Customer boycotts have succeeded in making some supermarkets withdraw food products containing GM produce from sale and in making governments enact legislation requiring the labelling of all such products. More recently still (2010), there have been protests about the sale of meat from cloned cattle. So, for this kind of protest, the success or failure of any instance would seem to be dependent upon the extent to which popular opinion is mobilised.

The case of ecoprotestors

The ecoprotestor phenomenon, as a form of protest, has been in existence in the UK for a number of years. The phenomenon has been manifested as direct action against the destruction of nature for its replacement by, in most cases, roads, although one particularly high-profile protest was concerned with the extension of Manchester airport. Not all protests of this nature, however, are given such a high profile and many remain merely local phenomena creating effects and news only within their local spatial environment. Thus there are approximately 12–20 such protest sites in existence at any particular time though the majority remain known only to the ecoprotestors themselves, through their highly effective news dissemination network, and to the inhabitants of the local area of any particular protest site.

Despite their profile as direct action protestors these ecoprotestors have received a mostly favourable press. Their impact upon the geographical landscape of the country, however, has been largely ephemeral and has been restricted to the delaying of any proposed developments through raising the profile of the issues concerned. Indeed, in the main they define their success for this form of protest as the length of time by which such developments have been delayed, the increased cost of such developments (brought about by the increased security and eviction costs incurred), and the extent to which the environmental issues involved have been publicly aired. In this respect they realistically adopt a long-term perspective for their form of protest and take the view that each incident, although ultimately ending in defeat, is merely one step upon the road to eventual victory in giving long-term environmental impact precedence over short-term economic gain. These views are openly expressed by many of the ecoprotestors involved in these protests.

Ecoprotestors themselves comprise two types of person: one type is the new age traveller who is involved full-time in either protest or in travelling; the other type of person is a part-time protestor who at other times is involved in the local community which will be affected by a proposed development. It is perhaps significant that in the cases considered in this chapter and in the vast majority of, if not all, other cases the protest has been established by a member of the local community. This person, in order to establish such a protest site, must inevitably be familiar with this form of protest and be in touch with others who are engaged in such protest. Thus, in order for a protest site to become established, it is necessary that it be initiated by a member of the local community who is also a protestor and in contact with other protestors. This contact from the initiator must inevitably include contact with new age travellers as it is essential that a permanent site is established involving people who are permanently resident at the site, and it is only the travellers who are able to enact this role in the protest.

At any particular site, the number of people who are present at any particular time will vary and will comprise a number of permanent residents, travellers, and a number of part-time protestors, local residents. Thus it was possible for the researchers to visit a camp at one time and find only two people present whilst at another time there were 40–50 present. Local inhabitants will naturally tend to be present outside working hours and tend to be staying at the camp only during weekends and holidays. Travellers themselves are, in the main, static at the site for long periods of time and it is common to find that they stay a period of time at one camp before moving on to either another protest site or another traveller site. Very few remain at a site throughout the duration of the protest, although there seem always to be a (very small) number of dedicated protestors who will remain throughout the period of the protest. This is not, however, arranged in any formal manner and it would seem to be reasonable, given the transience of all protestors, to find that at a particular time there may be no one in occupation at a particular protest site.

The traveller community

Whilst the consequences of ecoprotest have a significant impact upon the local community, there is one other community which is involved in the ecoprotest. This community is that of the travellers who, as travellers rather than ecoprotestors, have different objectives and upon whom the protest impacts differently. These objectives are not explicitly stated and have not been arrived at by any overt decision making; rather they have developed over time through an unconscious process. It is argued that this unconscious process is one of the adaptive features of a self organising system which the travellers represent. Nevertheless, these strategic objectives are clearly defined and openly expressed by the travellers who were interviewed during this research. These objectives have been expressed by these travellers as seeking to achieve two distinct objectives, which are:

- learning to live differently,
- developing a community spirit and identity.

By learning to live differently these people mean both that their relationship with nature must be different and that their ability to exist in a peaceable manner must not be driven by the normal societal motives of economic consumption and wealth creation. In this respect, therefore, they refuse to recognise the proprietary ownership mores of mainstream society as a basis for resource utilisation, and this applies in particular to land, which is viewed as a common resource to be used rather than owned (see Crowther and Cooper, 2001; 2002).

Discrimination protest

Other protests have been against discrimination. In the 1950s in the USA racial discrimination was lawful and in the southern states buses were segregated, with black people not being allowed to sit on seats reserved for white people. On 1 December 1955 Rosa Parks refused to give up a seat reserved for white people when a white man demanded the seat, and was consequently arrested. This protest started what became known as the Montgomery Bus Boycott when for nine months black people refused to use the buses and sought alternative means of transport. This event led to the formation of the civil rights movement in America and eventually brought Martin Luther King to national prominence. Events in the civil rights movement have been attested to in films such as *Mississippi Burning*.

Other protests against discrimination have been made by people not directly affected by the discrimination. Thus in the UK during the late 1960s there were protests about apartheid in South Africa. Successful protests prevented the touring of South African sports teams in the country. A less successful protest attempted to boycott Barclays Bank because of its investment interests in the country. It is interesting, therefore, to consider what leads to a successful protest as opposed to one which fails, and we will return to this later in the chapter.

Ethical protest

Other protests have been about ethical issues. For example, there has been a long-running protest in the UK against the exporting of live animals to Europe because of the conditions in which they are kept during transport. This protest has taken the form of marches, vigils and demonstrations but during 2000 these protests became large-scale and involved attempting to block ports where such animals are transported. Mass demonstrations took place and involved direct action. On one occasion it resulted in a person being killed as she was struck by one of the lorries involved. Since then the protest has been lower key but has not ceased. This protest has met with little success, however, and, apart from the mass demonstrations of 2000, has received little media attention. It would appear, therefore, that the receiving of significant media attention is one attribute which helps the success of any protest.

Another example of a long-running protest was that against Huntingdon Life Sciences, a company which uses live animals for experimental purposes in the production of drugs. For many years[1] there has been a campaign to close this company which has worldwide support. The campaign has taken many forms during its life and includes demonstrations outside the company premises and outside the homes of directors of the company. The campaign has also extended to companies which do business with Huntingdon Life Sciences and has had the effect of necessitating the company to change its banker and also resulted in its auditors refusing to serve any longer. There have also been accusations of death threats against some of the senior people involved in the business. This ongoing campaign has seriously affected the viability of the company but has failed to get the company closed down – instead it has moved its operations to Maryland, USA where security can be more effectively maintained. From time to time this campaign gets media attention, some of which is supportive of the campaign and some of which is not. In general terms, the negative press has highlighted such things as the accusations of death threats and this mitigates against the success of the protest but probably the main reason for the lack of success is that this campaign and the issues involved are peripheral for most people.

Political protest

Probably the largest political campaign being waged by ordinary consumers is that which falls under the heading of the anti-globalisation movement. Anti-globalisation is the umbrella term for a group of different protests concerning environmentalism, third world debt, animal rights and opposition to multinationals. The targets of anti-globalisation protests have been meetings of the World Trade Organization (WTO), International Monetary Fund (IMF) and World Bank. Other meetings of national leaders and businesses have also been hit, such as the Summit of the Americas in Quebec, and the World Economic Forum in Davos. Protests have often resulted in violence, e.g. the scenes in Seattle or Quebec, but most of the protesters are supporters of non-violent direct action. Opponents of globalisation say it leads to exploitation of the world's poor, workers and the environment. They say it makes it easier for rich companies to act with less accountability. They also claim that countries' individual cultures are becoming overpowered by Americanisation. Several of the largest US brands (e.g. McDonald's and Starbucks) face particular opposition.

Such protests are against the reduction in the rights of individuals and are partly against companies and partly against governments. Indeed, in the globalisation debate it is often difficult to separate the two. This lack of separation spread over into the anti-Iraq war campaign of 2003 which saw mass protests around the world, partly against the war, partly against the government of the USA, and partly against the spread of corporate America. This kind of protest is overtly political and only indirectly concerned with individuals protesting as consumers.

We can see, therefore, that protest has been a feature of the Western world for a long time and is a manifestation of dissatisfaction resulting from a variety of causes. Some causes affect individuals in their purchasing whilst others are concerned with wider issues. Some have been successful whilst others have not. There are a number of factors involved in the likelihood of success which we need to consider. Before doing so, however, it is important to consider the nature of the protests and to arrive at a categorisation of reasons for protest (see Figure 14.1) and types of protest (see Figure 14.2).

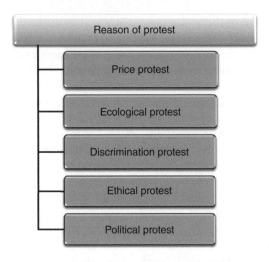

Figure 14.1   Classifications of reasons for protest

Types of protest

It is easy to categorise protests as violent or non-violent but this classification is not helpful as all intend initially to be non-violent. So it is more helpful to classify them in terms of the type of actions undertaken:

- Boycotts: these can be partial or complete and can involve secondary companies. Friedman (1999) gives a more complete classification but this is sufficient for our purposes.
- Direct action: this can involve a variety of types of action including demonstrations, picketing, information dissemination, advertisements, obstruction (a tactic employed by, for example, French farmers), or destruction (for example of GM crops).
- Pressure groups: these are often involved in various forms of protest and the mobilisation of public opinion. See below for details of pressure group action.
- Secondary action: this can involve such activity as legal campaigns, lobbying, gaining media attention, exerting attention or applying political pressure.
- Electronic action: a new form of protest which is considered in detail.

Electronic protest and action

The increasing availability of access to the Internet has instigated a discourse which considers the present and likely future impact of this means of communication upon the construction of society and upon the lives of individual members of that society (Rushkoff, 1997). Much of this discourse is based upon an expectation that the Internet and the World Wide Web will have a significant impact upon the way in which society operates (see, for example, Holmes and Grieco, 1999). Indeed, access to the WWW is starting to be considered in some countries as a fundamental human right. Views are mixed and Sobchack (1996) argues that this technology will be more liberating, participatory and interactive than previous cultural forms, whilst Axford (1995) argues that it will lead to increasing globalisation of politics, culture and social systems. At the time of writing, the equality of access to the whole of the internet seems to be under threat because of Google; it will take time to see the outcome of this. Postmodernist arguments suggest that the technological capability of the Internet will lead to a duality of social structures. This will be manifested in increasing globalisation of social structures and also increased localisation of such structures (Eade, 1997).

Much of this discourse is concerned at a societal level with the effects of Internet technology[2] upon society, and only by implication upon individuals within society. It is, however, only at the level of the individual that these changes can take place. Indeed, access to the internet, and the ability to communicate via this technology to other individuals without regard to time and place, can be considered to be a revolutionary redistribution of power (Russell, 1975). Moreover, the disciplinary practices of society (Foucault, 1977) break down when the internet is used because of the lack of spatial contiguity between communicants and because of the effective anonymity of the communication which prevents the normalising surveillance mechanisms of society (Clegg, 1989) to intercede in that communication. Thus the internet provides a space for resistance to foment (Robins, 1995) but also provides a psychotic space in which all wishes are (or potentially can be) fulfilled (Weibel, 1990).

The Internet provides the ideal environment for a community of resistance to exist: the web-structured organisation of the Internet means that no separate geographical existence is necessary for a web-based community, and the nature of the Internet is such that people are only part of an Internet community when they actually choose to participate in the activities of that community. Thus, an Internet community is a truly postmodern virtual community. The information architecture of the Internet means that it is relatively easy for such a community to establish its existence (Rheingold, 1994) and therefore examples of such communities abound. It is relevant to observe, however, that such communities have existed for a considerable period of time in such areas as academic life and social life. One essential feature of postmodernity, however, is the changing informational architecture of society and this both makes virtual communities more prevalent and provides one possible infrastructure for determining community identity. Thus, both the territorial and temporal constituents of community disappear, or at least assume diminished significance, in a postmodern environment. At the same time, this argument has been extended (Barnett and Crowther, 1998) to the proposition that any community need have neither any discrete geographical existence nor any continuous temporal existence but may exist as a virtual community, having sporadic temporal existence and no territorial existence.

Of particular interest, however, is the way in which accessing the technology to use the internet can change the power relationship between large corporations and individuals. In this respect the changes in these power relationships can be profound and even revolutionary. The technology provides a potential challenge to legitimacy and can give individuals the ability to confront large corporations and to have their voice heard with equal volume within the discourse facilitated by cyberspace. Thus, for example, without access to the internet the trial of Helen Steel and Dave Morris would have been unnoticed by all but a few close friends, and their protest would have been effectively silenced by McDonald's in the way expected when all power accrues to the large corporation rather than the individual. Because of the internet, however, this balance of power has shifted in favour of the individual. Indeed, this power has shifted to such an extent in this particular case that the 'McLibel case' has become world-renowned and although McDonald's eventually partly won the legal case, it is questionable as to whether or not they won the moral and publicity cases.

It is the internet, and the widespread access of individuals to it, which brought this case to prominence and enabled the defendants to communicate with a large number of people scattered throughout the world. Moreover, it enabled these people, whilst spatially disparate and unconnected, to join together in their expressions of support and their publicising of the actions of McDonald's. This would not have been possible without access to the internet, whereas its advent enabled mass individualised communication, together with information dissemination mechanisms in the form of websites related to the trial. Perhaps more significantly, it empowers the people involved through a transformation of their skills (Holmes, 1995), which become more powerful when transferred to this electronic domain. There are many such sites but perhaps one of the more interesting in terms of exploring the power redistribution potential of the technology can be found at <http://McSpotlight.org>. Thus, people who might be excluded from a debate requiring physical presence, either for spatial or temporal reasons, can be included; people who might not be able to speak in public can enter the debate; and age, gender and race provide no barrier to entry. Moreover, in a virtual environment every person has an equal voice, and no one can be silenced. This is one of the liberating aspects of the internet, which allows the redistribution of power within society, in that the new electronic form has provided a mechanism for the forging of a new global solidarity.

The McLibel trial was a high-profile case which provides a good example of the way in which internet technology can be used to change power relationships but there are numerous other examples from around the world. It has also led to another case (McLibel 2) to defend the public's right to challenge multinationals in the European Court of Human Rights.

The world's favourite airline

Until recently this was the slogan of British Airways, the national airline in the UK and formerly the largest carrier in the UK until surpassed by Easyjet. The airline was formed in 1974 and privatised in 1987 at the start of the Thatcherite programme of privatisation. More recently, it has been involved in merger talks and the creation of alliances; like most carriers it has realised that it cannot survive independently. It has also been beset by industrial relations problems as it has sought to modernise its operations in order to remain profitable; these have had a disastrous effect on both morale and its reputation as a reliable carrier.

It is recognised that managing an airline is a complex and costly process and that the containment of costs is at least as crucial to the successful operating of an airline as is the logistics of moving passengers with a degree of reliability. There are many ways in which these costs are contained but excluded from the discourse is a consideration upon shareholder value of the way in which passenger luggage is handled. This, therefore, is the focus of this chapter. The logistical necessities of moving passenger luggage require that this is handled by a variety of people acting as agents of the airline in order for it to be loaded at the airport onto the correct plane and unloaded upon arrival; this is further complicated when it needs to be moved in transit from one flight to another. Mistakes happen and, in the words of a British Airways employee, 'Unfortunately, where there is a mixture of manual and mechanical labour, things can go wrong from time to time' but 'under our Conditions of Carriage we are not liable for any consequential losses'.

It is obviously inconvenient for a passenger to arrive at a destination without luggage but the cost-reduction imperative of airlines means that it is less costly for a plane to depart without all the luggage of the passengers than to suffer delay, even when this necessitates the subsequent use of couriers to reunite a passenger with that luggage. Thus, airlines are quite blatant and unrepentant about such practices as the imperative of cost-minimisation – disguised as scheduling constraints – prevails. The inconvenience of this practice is one of the unfortunate costs which a passenger must bear in order to be transported to another location but it is quite clearly a cost that has been externalised from the airline to the customer and thereby removed from the accounting practices which record value created for shareholders.

Of greater concern, however, is the mechanism which has evolved for dealing with luggage that is mislaid in transit. Briefly, the situation is that dealing with problems in this respect has been removed from the direct control of the airline company itself and is dealt with by a series of agents. One company deals with the details of mislaid luggage and assumes responsibility for locating it; another company provides call centre facilities for a helpline, whilst yet another company provides the courier service which delivers the luggage to the passenger when it is finally relocated. It is presumably structured in this way because of the cost-minimisation imperative but one consequence is that it is very difficult to ascertain which company one is dealing with – or in the case of the call centre – even where the company is located. Thus, any chain of responsibility is effectively obfuscated and when a problem arises the various parts of the chain are able to deny responsibility and attempt to pass that responsibility onto another party. As most people who are involved are not employees of the airline then it is not surprising that they feel no particular loyalty to the airline. Indeed, with the different steps in the chain the customer changes and, whilst

→

the airline's customer is clearly the passenger, for the other companies involved the customer is less certain – some recognition is made that the passenger is at least a significant stakeholder but not necessarily the customer; it is the airline which settles the bills.

Mislaid luggage is a relatively frequent occurrence associated with air travel and procedures have been developed to handle the situation. To a great extent these are common to all airlines in all locations – perhaps inevitably as the same agents act on behalf of a number of different airlines, with the agents employed being determined by location of the airport rather than any other factor. The system adopted by British Airlines differs slightly from that of other airlines, although all claim to make use of 'a worldwide computer baggage tracing system': others enter details directly into this system and can inform passengers there and then of what has happened. British Airways state: 'Your luggage details are entered into a tracing system; however this is usually done when you have completed the form and left the airport.' A set procedure purports to exist for contacting passengers to arrange delivery of the mislaid luggage. According to a BA representative, 'as it is a very busy office, we do not contact passengers. It is our Courier Company who will attempt to call the passenger to inform of the bags arrival.' Alternatively: 'It is not normal policy for our staff to contact you regarding your delayed luggage, it is only when it has been picked up by our Courier Company and is ready for delivery that they should call you to inform you that it is on its way.'

British Airways has had problems regarding lost luggage for many years, possibly resulting from its being based at Heathrow, the busiest airport in the world. A recent survey (June 2010) showed that 1 in 3.8 BA passengers has had checked luggage lost, delayed or damaged in the last five years. The figure for lost or damaged luggage on British Airways was almost 14% higher than any other airline, with the next worst airline (Virgin) showing that 1 in 8.3 passengers had experienced luggage problems. When it comes to lost luggage, only 27% were reunited with their bags within 24 hours. British Airways branded the statistics quoted in the survey as 'ludicrous' and said: 'The claims made in the press release are complete rubbish. There is absolutely no evidence to suggest that a quarter of BA passengers have experienced lost or delayed baggage over the last five years.'

An exploration of the websites of companies shows that they seek to portray inclusion through the possibility of interaction with the company through cyberspace. This interaction is, of course, carefully orchestrated and controlled to give the appearance of concern without any need to respond to any criticisms; indeed, the possibility of criticism is effectively removed through the construction of the dialogic possibilities.

It is possible, therefore, to see that corporations have made use of internet technology to redesign their corporate space and include within their space the virtual environment provided by the internet. At the same time, they have adopted the technology to create themselves as interested in people as customers

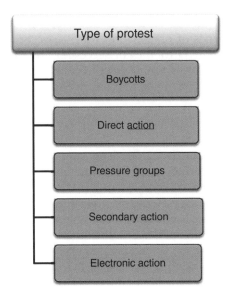

Figure 14.2 Classifications of methods of protest

and investors, or potentially either, to provide a semiotic of being willing and interested to engage in dialogue with such people. This dialogue is, of course, more apparent than real as it is carefully constructed and controlled by the organisations themselves. This raises a question, therefore, as to the liberating effect of technology, and it is to this that we now turn.

What is clear about the internet is that it provides a facility to give a voice to people who would otherwise find difficulty in obtaining that voice (see Grieco, 1996) and as far as the technology is concerned that voice is equal to all other voices. The technology of the internet makes no differentiation between different voices which are present. In other words, it provides a space in which voices can be present and it is clear that it has enabled some voices, such as those of Helen Steel and Dave Morris, to have been heard by a much wider audience than would otherwise have been possible. Equally, however, it is clear that these voices function in much the same way as in normal speech, and in this respect some voices can be heard much more clearly than others. This is, of course, dependent upon the power of the language at one's command and upon access to the microphone. It is in this respect that the internet, rather than providing a vehicle for liberation, in actual fact serves to reinforce the prevailing hegemony, as the more powerful have the louder and more eloquent voices.

Successful targets

The various protests we have considered have shown that some have been successful whilst others have not, so we need to consider at this point what makes a successful protest. Successful protests have been made against governments, end-user companies such as Shell, and against companies supplying end-user companies such as Heinz via supermarkets. Equally, protests have been made against all of these kinds of organisation which have been unsuccessful. So is it possible to identify any attributes of successful protests? To some extent it is determined by luck and by timing (so therefore seemingly random) but the following factors seem to be important constituents of success:

- Leadership: this gives direction to any campaign and therefore makes it more likely to succeed.
- Popular support without alienation: the greater the strength of popular opinion the more likely a protest is to be successful. If popular opinion does not support the issue then it is important that there is no significant opinion against the protest; thus, for example, the issue of fishing's effect upon dolphins probably did not have a great deal of popular opinion but no one was likely to oppose it. Road building, on the other hand, has strong opinions for and against and any protest is therefore less likely to be successful. Campaigns which disrupt other people are also less likely to succeed.
- Media attention: gaining media attention means that an issue is more likely to be successful as the media tend to like a cause which they can rally behind. The only successful anti-road building protest was helped when the local newspaper took it up as a cause. Equally, the McLibel trial succeeded in attracting worldwide media attention, largely through the use of the World Wide Web.
- Targeted action: if the action is targeted it is more likely to succeed. For example, the issue involving dolphins and fishing affected more companies than Heinz but by selecting Heinz and Sainsbury's as the objects of protest the campaigners managed to affect these companies sufficiently to get action taken and thereby effect change for all companies involved. A more general protest would have diluted attention and effect and would have been less likely to be successful.
- Definite objective: a campaign which has a definite and limited objective is more likely to succeed. The anti-globalisation movement is extremely large but has no definite objective. Instead, it is a loose coalition of interest groups without any particular focal point. When these issues coalesced into the anti-war protest it had more impact even though pro-war feelings tended to counterbalance these and prevent success. This can be contrasted with an issue such as the Montgomery Bus Boycott which had a specific objective.

Understanding individual CSR behaviour

The relative power of various stakeholder groupings has changed quite radically in recent years. In particular individuals – as either consumers or customers – have more power and are more willing to use it. This is primarily due to IT and the ability to combine readily with others from different geographical locations around the world. It has taken corporations a long time to realise this and react accordingly.

The illustrations in this chapter show that individuals are not necessarily passive in the reaction towards the corporations which supply them with goods and services. Neither do they necessarily behave from selfish motives as there is ample evidence of altruism and concern for others and for the environment. This, therefore, is a part of the complexity of understanding CSR behaviour. Corporations themselves understand this and act accordingly, and a part of the public relations aspect of corporate behaviour is concerned with understanding and reacting to this aspect of individual behaviour.

Summary of key points

- Customers engage in protest activity for a variety of reasons; some are connected with the company itself – either in terms of the products or services provided or in terms of the activities of the company; others are for a more general societal or political purpose, with a particular company being used as the focal point for the protest.
- Protests can be violent but the most successful ones avoid violence and seek instead to engage popular support.
- There are a number of ways in which protests can be manifested. These can be classified as:

  o boycotts
  o direct action
  o pressure groups
  o secondary action
  o electronic action.

- Actions taken by pressure groups can be:

  o lobbying, of organisations and influential others;
  o attention directing through the seeking of media attention and support;
  o direct action, both legitimate and illegitimate.

- A new form of protest can be considered to be electronic action, based upon the widespread availability of the internet. This enables isolated individuals around the world to join together in protests, thereby increasing the power of individuals.
- The key factors which influence the chance of success of a protest are:

  o Leadership
  o Popular support without alienation
  o Media attention
  o Targeted action
  o Definite objective.

Definitions of key terms and theories

Boycott is the avoidance of the goods or services of a corporation, on either a total or partial basis.

Direct action refers to types of action including demonstrations, picketing, information dissemination, advertisements, obstruction or destruction.

Ecoprotest is a direct action form of protest against the destruction of nature for its replacement by manmade environments.

Electronic action is protest action making use of the internet.

Pressure groups are groups involved in various forms of protest and the mobilisation of public opinion.

Secondary action refers to actions against secondary parties to influence the main focus of a protest.

Test your understanding

1. How has the relationship between corporations and their customers changed in recent years?
2. Explain the purposes of customer protests. How might these be classified?
3. Can you give examples of how customer protests have led to changes in corporate activity?
4. What factors might explain why one protest is successful whilst another is not?
5. How has the internet changed the nature of consumer protest? What are the implications for the power relationship between individuals and corporations?
6. What are the relative merits of boycotts compared with other forms of direct action?
7. There are different types of pressure groups with different objectives. How might these be usefully categorised?

Suggestion for further reading

Friedman, M., 1999, *Consumer Boycotts*. London: Routledge.

Notes

1. In 1982 comments were first made about this company but a serious campaign did not commence until 1997.
2. In using the term 'internet' this is meant to encompass all related electronic communications media such as email and the World Wide Web (WWW). Equally the word 'technology' is used to mean hardware, software and communications mechanisms. It is not the intention of the authors to debate these technologies but rather to consider their use by individuals. Consequently, terms such as the internet, the web and cyberspace are used generically in this chapter, without any attempt to attach specific and separate meanings to each.

References

Axford, B. 1995. *The Global System*. Cambridge: Polity Press.

Barnett, N. J. and Crowther, D. E. A. 1998. 'Community Identity in the 21st Century: A Postmodernist Evaluation of Local Government Structure', *International Journal of Public Sector Management*, 11, 6/7: 425–39.

Clegg, S. R. 1989. *Frameworks of Power*. London: Sage.

Crowther, D. and Cooper, S. 2001. 'Innovation through Postmodern Networks: The Case of Ecoprotestors', in O. Jones, S. Conway and F. Steward (eds), *Social Interaction and Organisational Change*. London: Imperial College Press, pp. 321–48.

Crowther, D. and Cooper, S. 2002. 'Rekindling Community Spirit and Identity: The Case of Ecoprotestors', *Management Decision*, 40, 4: 343–53.

Eade, J. 1997. 'Reconstructing Places: Changing Images of Locality in Docklands and Spitalfields', in J. Eade (ed.), *Living in the Global City*. London: Routledge, pp. 127–45.

Foucault, M. 1977. *Discipline and Punish*. trans. A. Sheridan. Harmondsworth: Penguin.

Friedman, M. 1999. *Consumer Boycotts*. London: Routledge.

Grieco, M. (1996); *Worker's Dilemma: Recruitment, Reliability and Repeated Exchange*. London: Routledge.

Holmes, L. 1995. 'Skills – a Social Perspective', in A. Assiter (ed.), *Transferrable Skills in Higher Education*. London: Kogan Page.

Holmes, L. and Grieco, M. 1999. '*The Power of Transparency: The Internet, e-mail and the Malaysian Political Crisis*', paper presented to Asian Management in Crisis Conference, Association of South east Asian Studies, UNL, June 1999.

Rheingold, H. 1994. *The Virtual Community*. London: Secker & Warburg.

Robins, K. 1995. 'Cyberspace and the World we Live in', in M. Featherstone and R. Burrows (eds); *Cyberspace/Cyberbodies/Cyberpunk*. London: Sage.

Rushkoff, D. 1997. *Children of Chaos*. London: HarperCollins.

Russell, B. 1975. *Power*. London: Routledge.

Sobchack, V. 1996. 'Democratic Franchise and the Electronic Frontier', in Z. Sardar and J. R. Ravetz (eds), *Cyberfutures*. London: Pluto Press.

Stein, A. 1975. 'Post-war Consumer Boycotts', *Radical America*, 9: 156–61.

Weibel, P. 1990. 'Virtual Worlds: The Emperor's New Body', in G. Hattinger (ed.), *Electronica 1990*, vol. 2. Linz: Veritas-Verlag.

CSR and Strategy

15

Learning objectives

After studying this chapter you should be able to:

- Explain the role of a manager.
- Critique the objectives of a business.
- Explain the decision-making process.
- Describe the principal features of a governance system.
- Understand the dimensions of risk and their implications.
- Construct a typology of risk.

Introduction

The development and implementation of strategy is, of course, important for every organisation, and this has always been so. Increasingly in the present, however, CSR is being considered as a crucial part of that strategy with corresponding advantages to the organisation. In this chapter, therefore, we will consider aspects of this in the context of the objectives of the firm and its procedures for governance.

The tasks of a business manager

A manager of any modern business has a difficult job to perform. A crucial part of his or her job is to meet the objectives of the organisation of which he or she is a part and in order to do so he or she must pay attention to a number of important issues. However, the exact nature of a manager's job may vary quite significantly from one organisation or department to another, so that the role of

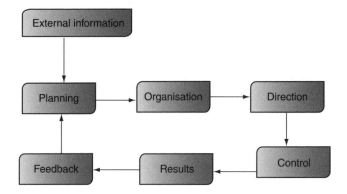

Figure 15.1   The tasks of management

a marketing manager, a production manager or a manager of a supermarket may appear to be quite different. There is, however, considerable similarity in terms of the fundamental tasks to be performed.

These tasks can be categorised as shown in Figure 15.1. Every manager plans his or her work and the work of others as well as organising him- herself and others, directing others as to what to do, motivating them and exercising control over situations and other people. The results are fed back into the planning process in order to modify future plans for the business.

All managers are concerned with working with people: those they work with, those they supervise, those they report to, and those who are the customers for the product or service which is provided by that area of an organisation that the manager is responsible for. All managers are therefore naturally concerned with the output for their particular area of responsibility and so are also concerned with the inputs to their area of responsibility, whether these are raw materials, information or goods to be displayed and sold.

Using the information available, a manager must plan for the future of the business. In this context a manager must decide upon the courses of action which need to be taken in order to achieve the best results, and must consider what alternative courses of action are available, and what the consequences of any particular decision might be.

Thus, the manager of a restaurant, for example, will need to decide what its opening hours need to be and how these might affect possible customers who might want to dine when the restaurant is closed. The manager, however, also needs to decide upon the ingredients of the menu and how much of each to order; in doing so he or she needs to consider what the effect of not ordering enough of a particular item might be in terms of dissatisfied customers and the possible effect this might have upon the future of the business but also what the effects of over-ordering and waste might be upon the profitability of the business. The manager therefore needs to consider alternatives and their con- sequences and decide what course of action to take after this consideration of the facts.

Decision making is a crucial part of the job of any manager, and decisions need to be made between conflicting alternatives. These decisions are often to a large extent conflicting in their possible outcomes and there is a degree of uncertainty surrounding the consequences. Selecting the best possible decision to make is therefore often a difficult and skilful process but it is important that the decisions made are the right ones. Because of this a manager needs tools to help him or her evaluate the consequences of the alternative decisions which he or she might make. These tools will assist him or her in making better decisions.

The objectives of a business

A business manager must be concerned not just with the internal running of the business but also with the external environment in which the business operates – that is with customers and suppliers, with competitors, and with the market for the products or services supplied by the business.

Such concerns of a business manager comprise the strategic element of the job and a manager must therefore be familiar with this aspect of management, and with the way in which decisions affect different aspects of the company. This chapter therefore is concerned with a consideration of the external environment of a business and with the strategic part of a manager's job.

We have discussed the differing objectives that a firm might have in Chapter 1. Any business is likely to seek to pursue a number of these objectives at any point in time. The precise combination of them is likely to vary from one organisation to another and from one time to another, depending upon the individual circumstances of the organisation at any particualar time. The organisation will not view all the objectives which it is pursuing at any particular time as equally important, however, and will have more important ones to follow. These objectives will therefore tend to be viewed as a hierarchy, which may vary from time to time.

None of these conflicts with socially responsible behaviour and there is growing evidence that social responsibility actually enhances the ability to achieve all of these objectives.

Empty words: Aquila Game Reserve, South Africa

Aquila is a game reserve in South Africa, located about two hours' drive from Cape Town. Its business is, of course, to offer safaris to paying customers. It claims to be different from other game reserves, stating that 'Aquila is not yet another luxury game reserve and lodge, its primary purpose is to offer an educational experience to all who visit in the hope that knowledge will enrich our understanding of the importance of living in harmony with Mother Nature'.[1]

Thus Aquila claims to be different to other game reserves in South Africa. It is proud of its ethos, which has always been 'to educate guests on the importance of wildlife conservation, how it affects us all and what we as individuals can do to protect it and indeed the environment'.[2] It is also proud of its social responsibility programmes, claiming to be the proud recipient of an Imvelo Award for its Social Involvement Programme. Further investigation shows that its social responsibility seems to be focused entirely upon the creation of jobs in a disadvantaged area and upon the conservation of wildlife. These are both laudable aims but nevertheless both benefit the organisation – it needs local people to work on its reserve and it needs wildlife for its customers to see. Without either of these there is, of course, no business and so the social responsibility behaviour of the organisation is not really apparent. Depicting this as greenwashing might be somewhat harsh but it is certainly making a virtue out of necessity rather than really engaging with CSR.

A socially responsible organisation, of course, deals with all of its stakeholders in a responsible and equitable manner. It is here, rather than in the promotional material on the website, that an organisation can be assessed. It is here that this organisation fails completely – not only in behaving in a socially responsible manner but also in attaining even the minimal standards that any reputable organisation would be expected to adhere to. We speak with personal experience, based upon our visit during September 2009. Problems happen for every organisation. A responsible organisation apologises and seeks to make amends; and fulfils its promises. Aquila does not – apologies are simply words to get you off the premises. And promises are treated in the same spirit – empty words to be reneged upon later. Its performance is dismal.

Social responsibility must be judged by actions concerning all stakeholders and not just by carefully designed words or even programmes. And a socially responsible organisation must be accountable to all stakeholders as well as transparent in its actions. Only then will a business be sustainable. On this basis Aquila is not socially responsible, and hence not a company to do business with.

The role of a manager

We have seen how the tasks of a manager of a business will vary greatly according to his area of responsibility. We have also seen how the manager needs to help the organisation meet its objectives and that these can vary significantly from one organisation to another. The roles of different managers are therefore very different and the tasks which they undertake to perform their roles are also very different. Nevertheless, we can classify these different tasks into one of several types according to their nature. These are aspects of the role of a manager and can be classified as follows (see also Figure 15.2).

Planning

Managers need to plan for the future in order to decide how best to meet the objectives of the organisation. They need to decide what can be achieved and what inputs are needed to help meet their plans. Planning therefore needs to be not just qualitative but also quantitative in order to evaluate the plan and

Figure 15.2   The role of a manager

determine inputs and outputs to the plan as it evolves. All business processes can be considered as taking a set of inputs and performing operations in order to add value and transform them into outputs. The function of any business can therefore be considered as adding value through the transformations made during its processing, as we discussed in Chapter 7 This can be illustrated as shown in Figure 15.3.

The planning process needs to consider alternatives, not just in terms of alternative targets to set but also in terms of alternative methods of achieving these targets. Planning cannot be done in isolation but needs to take into account what effect the planning has upon the plans of other managers within the organisation. This is especially true when the inputs of this plan come from the outputs of the plan of another manager or when these outputs affect the planning of another manager.

Thus a sales manager cannot plan how much to sell without taking into account the plan of the production manager concerning how much will be produced, and the production manager cannot make plans for production without taking into account the planning of the sales manager regarding how much can be sold. The planning tasks of the manager therefore are important but cannot be made in isolation.

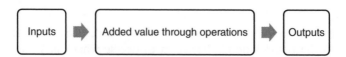

Figure 15.3   The transformational process

Control

Control is concerned with making sure that things happen in accordance with the plan. It therefore involves monitoring the plan, and progress being made in accordance with the plan. It also involves taking action when things are not going in accordance with the plan in order to attempt to change things so that the plan can be achieved. Control is therefore an ongoing activity for a manager and involves comparing actual performance with targets, providing feedback on actual performance and taking action to change performance when it diverges from the plan.

Although the manager may be able to achieve this by physical observation and communication with people, it is likely that this will not be sufficient. He or she will probably need to rely to a large extent upon reports in order to exercise control. The reports which management accounting provides are therefore crucial in assisting a manager to exercise control.

Decision making

One of the key aspects of a manager's job is concerned with making decisions. There is always more than one course of action which a manager can take in any particular situation (even if one of the courses is to do nothing!) and so he or she needs to decide between the alternatives in order to make the decision which is most beneficial. In order to make a decision the manager needs to identify the possible alternative courses of action open to him or her, to gather data about those courses of action and to evaluate the consequences of each particular alternative. The stages in the decision-making process are shown in the diagram in Figure 15.4 below, which illustrates that the decision-making process is not complete when an alternative has been selected and implemented but that the outcomes of the decision need to be followed through into the control process.

In order to make a decision a manager needs information. Management accounting is one tool which exists to help the manager by providing information about the consequences of the alternatives open to him or her.

Performance evaluation

Whilst the performance of organisations is evaluated by such measures as return on capital employed, the organisation in turn needs to evaluate the performance of its units and the managers running these units. The managers in turn need to evaluate the actual performance of their tasks against that which has been planned. In order to evaluate performance there need to be acceptable measures of performance. Measurement needs to be relative to be meaningful – to compare performance with plans and with past performance. Performance measures also need to be quantitative in order to enable comparisons to be made and financial information provides important data for the measurement

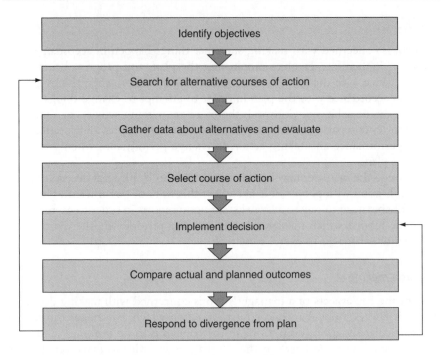

Figure 15.4   The decision making process

of performance. Unless performance can be evaluated, managers have no basis upon which to exercise control, to make decisions and to plan for the future.

Communication

Information available to help managers in their tasks needs to be communicated to them, and managers in turn need to communicate their plans and decisions to others. Communication involves both the sender of information and its recipient, and for the information to be of value it needs to be understood by the recipient as intended by the sender. Any interference which prevents the message being received by the recipient is known as noise and the diagram in Figure 15.5 below shows that two types of noise prevent a message being received as transmitted.

Technical noise is such as occurs on a telephone or radio which is concerned with the technical means of communication. A more crucial type of noise, however, is semantic noise which occurs because a message is not transmitted in a clear and unambiguous manner and so is not correctly understood by the recipient. Quantitative information is less likely to be misunderstood than qualitative information and this is one of the important features of accounting information. Management accounting therefore has an important part to play not just in enabling decisions to be made but also in the communication of this information.

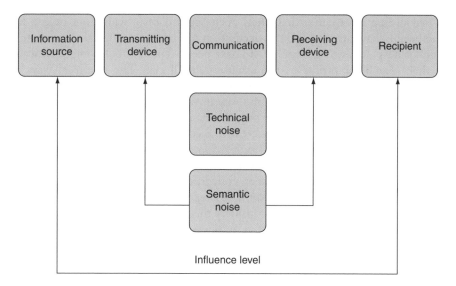

Figure 15.5   The communication of information

The importance of performance measurement

In order for a business to be able to control its operations it is necessary that the managers of that business are able to measure the performance of the business and of individual parts of that business. A significant feature of business management therefore is the need to measure and evaluate performance, both of the business as a whole and of individual parts of that business. Of equal significance is the ability to evaluate the performance of individual managers. This is of importance to the business but particularly to the managers themselves, as their rewards are increasingly based, at least in part, upon an assessment of their performance.

Increasingly also managerial rewards are based upon a variety of aspects of performance and this includes their effect upon the CSR activity of the corporation. This is another reason why CSR is being increasingly linked into the strategic planning process.

Managers and business ethics

Business ethics is a subject of considerable importance to any organisation and we have considered some of the high-profile business failures which have led to the current interest in CSR. Freedom in the markets is, of course, another source of potential abuse and unethical behaviour and the revelations from the recession which took place during 2008–10 provide many examples, ranging from the Madoff ponzi scam to the misbehaviour in the housing lending market – the so-called sub-prime scandal – that led to the serious economic problems in the USA which then spread elsewhere.

Accounting information has often been accused of providing an excuse for unethical behaviour. Indeed, this accusation has been extended to accountants and business managers generally, who have been accused of behaving unethically in their search for profits to the exclusion of all else. The unethical ways in which accounting information has been used have been described in detail by Smith (1992; 1996), who traces the way in which new accounting techniques have been created with the sole purpose of boosting reported profits. These techniques have become known as creative accounting and have been the subject of much media attention. Smith's book *Accounting for Growth* makes interesting reading for any prospective business manager.

Other writers, however, have been concerned with highlighting the value of ethical behaviour and have claimed that this actually leads to better business performance. Thus McCoy (1985) considers that ethics need to be at the core of business behaviour and that effective business management is based upon ethical behaviour. He claims that this recognition, and acting accordingly, actually increases the performance of a business. The UK accounting bodies are also concerned with business ethics and all have a stance on this matter, and have incorporated a requirement for ethical behaviour into their codes of conduct. The subject of ethical behaviour among businesses has also had an effect upon auditing practice and upon the financial reporting of businesses.

Any manager operating in a business environment needs to be aware of the importance of ethical behaviour. Equally he or she will experience conflicts, in attempting to behave ethically, between different alternative courses of action, and may find conflicts between the firm's objectives and his or her own personal motivation and objectives. No ready solution to these conflicts is available but a manager should be aware that research has shown ethical behaviour leads to better performance in the longer term, and so that manager should be encouraged to act accordingly.

Corporate governance

Another important issue which has been exercising the minds of business managers, accountants and auditors, investment managers and government officials – all over the world – is that of corporate governance (Aras, 2008), an extension of the governance which we considered in Chapter 10. Often companies' main target is to became global – whilst at the same time remaining sustainable – as a means to get competitive power. But the most important question is concerned with what will be a firm's route to becoming global and what will be necessary in order to get global competitive power. There is more than one answer to this question and there are a variety of routes for a company to achieve this.

Probably since the mid 1980s, corporate governance has attracted a great deal of attention (Aras and Crowther, 2008). Early impetus was provided by Anglo-American codes of good corporate governance.[3] Stimulated by institutional investors, other countries in the developed as well as in the emerging markets established an adapted version of these codes for their own companies. Supra-national authorities like the OECD and the World Bank did not remain passive and they developed their own set of standard principles and recommendations. This type of self-regulation was chosen above a set of legal standards (Van den Berghe, 2001).

After the various big corporate scandals, corporate governance has become central to most companies. It is understandable that investors' protection has become a much more important issue for all financial markets after the tremendous failures and scandals of firms. Investors are demanding that companies implement rigorous corporate governance principles in order to achieve better returns on their investment and to reduce agency costs. Most of the time, investors are ready to pay more for companies to have good governance standards. Similarly, a company's corporate governance report is one of the main tools for investors' decisions. For these reasons companies cannot ignore the pressure for good governance from shareholders, potential investors and other markets actors.

On the other hand, banking credit risk measurement regulations are requiring new rules for a company's credit evaluations. New international bank capital adequacy assessment methods (Basel II) necessitated that credit evaluation rules are elaborately concerned with operational risk which covers corporate governance principles. These rules were shown to be inadequate during the 2008 financial crisis and are in process of being revised as Basel III. In this respect, corporate governance will be one of the most important indicators for measuring risk. Another issue is related to firm credibility and riskiness. If the firm needs a high rating score then it will have to pay attention to corporate governance rules also.

Credit-rating agencies analyse corporate governance practices along with other corporate indicators. Even though corporate governance principles have always been important for getting good rating scores for large and publicly held companies, they are also becoming much more important for investors, potential investors, creditors and governments. Because of all of these factors, corporate governance receives high priority on the agenda of policymakers, financial institutions, investors, companies and academics. This is one of the main indicators that the link between corporate governance and actual performance is still open for discussion. In the literature a number of studies have investigated the relation between corporate governance mechanisms and performance (e.g. Agrawal and Knoeber, 1996; Millstein and MacAvoy, 2003).

Most of the studies have showed mixed result without a clear-cut relationship. Based on these results, we can say that corporate governance matters to a company's performance, market value and credibility, and therefore that company has to apply corporate governance principles. But the most important point is that corporate governance is the only means for companies to achieve corporate goals and strategies. Therefore companies have to improve their strategy and effective route to implementation of governance principles. So companies have to investigate what their corporate governance policy and practice need to be.

Figure 15.6   The principles of corporate governance

Corporate governance principles

Since corporate governance can be highly influential for a firm's performance, firms must know what the corporate governance principles are and how it will improve strategy to apply these principles. In practice there are four principles of good corporate governance (see Figure 15.6), which are:

(1) Transparency
(2) Accountability
(3) Responsibility
(4) Fairness

All these principles are related to the firm's corporate social responsibility. Corporate governance principles therefore are important for a firm but the real issue is concerned with what corporate governance actually is.

Management can be interpreted as managing a firm for the purpose of creating and maintaining value for shareholders. Corporate governance procedures determine every aspect of the role for management of the firm and try to keep in balance and to develop control mechanisms in order to increase both shareholder value and the satisfaction of other stakeholders. In other words, corporate governance is concerned with creating a balance between the economic and social goals of a company including such aspects as the efficient use of resources, accountability in the use of its power, and the behaviour of the corporation in its social environment.

The definition and measurement of good corporate governance is still subject to debate. However, good corporate governance will address all these main points:

- Creating sustainable value
- Ways of achieving the firm's goals
- Increasing shareholders' satisfaction

- Efficient and effective management
- Increasing credibility
- Ensuring efficient risk management
- Providing an early warning system against all risk
- Ensuring a responsive and accountable corporation
- Describing the role of a firm's units
- Developing control and internal auditing
- Keeping a balance between economic and social benefit
- Ensuring efficient use of resources
- Controlling performance
- Distributing responsibility fairly
- Producing all necessary information for stakeholders
- Keeping the board independent from management
- Facilitating sustainable performance

As can be seen, all of these issues have many ramifications and ensuring their compliance must be thought of as a long term procedure. However, firms naturally expect some tangible benefit from good governance. So good governance offers some long-term benefit for firms, such as:

- Increasing the firm's market value
- Increasing the firm's rating
- Increasing competitive power
- Attracting new investors, shareholders and more equity
- More or higher credibility
- Enhancing flexible borrowing condition/facilities from financial institutions
- Decreasing credit interest rate and cost of capital
- New investment opportunities
- Attracting better personnel/employees
- Reaching new markets

Although corporate governance is primarily considered to be concerned with how a firm conducts itself in relation to its investors, increasingly it is being extended to a consideration of how it conducts itself in relation to all of its stakeholders. This is a part of the current concern for greater accountability. Thus, governance is increasingly being considered to be related to CSR and the concerns of the two are merging (Aras and Crowther, 2010).

Gap Inc.

The Gap Inc. is a clothing and accessories retailer based in San Francisco. On 21 August 1969, Donald and Doris Fisher opened the first Gap store on Ocean Avenue in San Francisco. The store's merchandise consisted of Levis and LP records. The Fishers had raised $63,000 to open the store, and in one year,

→

Gap's sales had reached $2 million. Gap opened its second store in San Jose, California in 1970. Along with this second store, Gap established its first corporate headquarters, employing only four employees. Gap continued to expand rapidly and by 1972–73, had grown to over 25 stores and had expanded to areas outside of California and was entering the East Coast market with its store in New Jersey. In 1974, Gap began to sell private label merchandise in its stores. Currently, Gap has around 140,000 employees and 3 500 stores around the world.

Gap has been involved in various allegations about human rights abuses. In 2003, Gap, along with 21 other companies, was involved in a class action lawsuit filed by sweatshop workers in Saipan. The allegations included workers being required to work unpaid overtime, unsafe working conditions, and forced abortion policies. In May 2006, adult and child employees of Western, a supplier in Jordan, were found to have worked up to 109 hours per week and to have gone six months without being paid. Some employees claimed they had been raped by managers. However, most of these allegations were directed at Wal-Mart (who mostly ignored the claims), whilst Gap immediately looked into the matter to remedy the situation. On 28 October 2007, BBC footage showed child labour being used in Indian Gap factories. Gap has denied that it was aware of such happenings and that it is against its policy to use child labour. The one piece of clothing in question — a smock blouse — was removed from a British store and will be destroyed. Gap also promised to investigate breaches in its ethical policy. This is what they currently say (www.thegap.co.uk):

> As with most other companies that sell apparel, we don't own the garment factories that make our clothes. But we do share responsibility for the conditions under which our clothes are made. Our commitment to safe and fair working conditions extends beyond our employees and stores to include the partners in our supply chain.
>
> We know from firsthand experience that our efforts to improve the lives of people who work on behalf of our company help us run a more successful business. People who work a reasonable number of hours in a safe and healthy environment not only have a better quality of life, but they also tend to be more productive and deliver higher-quality product than those who work in poor conditions.

And:

> At Gap Inc., social responsibility is fundamental to who we are and how we operate as a company. To us, being socially responsible means striving to incorporate our values and ethics into everything we do – from how we run our business, to how we treat our employees, to how we impact the communities where we live and work. Gap Inc. is a leading global specialty retailer offering clothing, accessories and personal care products for men, women, children and babies under the Gap, Banana Republic, Old Navy, Piperlime and Athleta brand names.

Gap actively participates in the 'Joint Initiative on Corporate Accountability and Workers Rights' and is independently assessed by the Social Accountability International (SAI) and Verite. The Gap encourages its vendors to be SA8000 certified. The company also inspects factories for compliance with its internal standards. These standards include requiring suppliers not to employ persons under the age of 14, that wage payment is clear, regular and in accordance with work contracts, and that factories do not permit either physical or non-physical abuse. In 2010, for the fourth year in a row, Gap Inc. was recognised by the Ethisphere Institute as one of the World's Most Ethical Companies for 2010. They stated:

> Gap Inc.'s promotion of a sound ethical environment shines within its industry and shows a clear understanding that operating under the highest standards for business behavior goes beyond goodwill and 'lip-service' and is linked to performance and profitability.

Gap provides a good example of a company facing criticism and responding by taking action. It illustrates the point that social responsibility is not about being perfect but about seeking to improve – for companies just as for people.

Risk management, governance and CSR

Risk management has become an important aspect of business management and CSR has a role to play in this because a full understanding of CSR and its implications can reduce risk. In terms of their attitude to risk, people can be classified into three types, as shown in Figure 15.7.

Risk seeking

A risk seeker is a person who will value a positive outcome more highly than a negative outcome. When faced with two equal possibilities of a profit or a loss arising from a particular decision, a risk-seeking person will choose to proceed because of the possibility of profit.

Risk averse

A risk averter would value the negative outcome more highly than the positive and in the same situation would choose not to proceed because of the possibility of a loss.

Risk neutral

A risk neutral person would value both outcomes equally and would be indifferent about whether to proceed or not in this situation.

Different people have different attitudes to risk and this influences their decision making and how they value possible outcomes. Research has shown,

Figure 15.7   Attitudes to risk

however, that for important business decisions, such as capital expenditure appraisal, managers tend to be risk averse in their decision making. They therefore tend to choose decisions which might have lower expected values than other decisions but which have less risk associated with them. Managers of a business have responsibilities to the owners of that business (i.e. the shareholders) and one of these responsibilities is to act as stewards of that business and to maintain the value of the business and its future viability. This duty will tend to lead managers towards less risky decisions, which they are making on behalf of the owners of the business, than they may perhaps make on their own behalf.

In dealing with risk there are three steps to be considered:

(1) Risk assessment
(2) Risk analysis
(3) Risk management

and these can be considered as separate steps in the treatment of risk. The meaning of each step is as follows.

Risk assessment

This is concerned with the identification of risks that might occur and an identification of which particular risks might occur in the situation with which we are concerned. Once these risks have been identified then it is possible to plan strategies to manage those risks and also to undertake analysis of the possible effects of the risk.

Risk analysis

This is the statistical quantification of the effects of the risks identified through risk assessment. The technique is based upon the probabilistic treatment of risk through the quantification of the effect of any particular risk and its consideration in terms of a probability distribution.

Risk management

This is concerned with the development of strategies for dealing with risk. The development of these strategies is dependent upon the assessment of the types of risk to which the situation is susceptible and the quantification of the possible effects through analysis.

The steps in the treatment of risk can be modelled as shown in Figure 15.8 while the strategies for dealing with risk are shown in Figure 15.9.

From Figure 15.8 it can clearly be seen that feedback and reiteration is a constant part of the risk management process. This is necessary in order to continually reassess the effectiveness of the risk management strategies adopted. Possible strategies are:

Risk avoidance – this would involve not becoming involved in the situation in the first place. For example, a building project in an unstable country might be considered so risky that the company would not tender for the project in the first place.

Risk reduction – this would involve taking steps to reduce the probabilities of certain unfavourable events happening in the assessment. For example, in the building contract in an unstable country it might involve going into partnership with a firm from that country.

Risk protection – this would involve taking steps to limit the risk and in this example might involve setting up security procedures to prevent sabotage to the building works.

Risk managing – this would involve contingency planning to cope with both foreseen and unforeseen situations arising during the course of the contract.

Risk transfer – one strategy for containing risk is to transfer that risk onto another party. Possible ways of doing this include taking out insurance or sub-contracting and passing on the risk in this manner.

In all cases of strategy development the selection of an appropriate strategy depends upon a realistic assessment of the risk and a quantification of possible effects through analysis. It is to risk analysis, therefore, that we now turn.

Figure 15.8   The treatment of risk

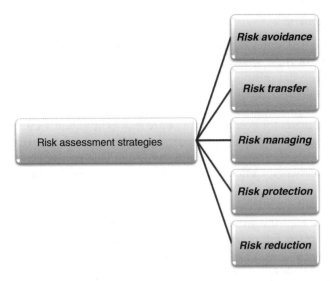

Figure 15.9   Strategies for risk

When a range of possible outcomes for an event exist then obviously the sum of the probabilities for all of the possible outcomes must equal 1 – as one of the outcomes must occur. The assignment of probabilities to each of the outcomes, however, enables us to construct a probability distribution showing the range of possible outcomes and their respective probabilities. Such a distribution may well be important to the analysis because merely selecting the most likely outcome may well not reflect the level of risk involved.

For example, in two projects the best estimate of profitability for each of the projects is identical (see Figure 15.10) but it can be seen from the probability distributions that the risk associated with them is quite different, with one of the projects having a risk of incurring a loss (project B). Without the probability distributions, therefore, a firm would be indifferent as to which project was chosen but with an understanding of the distribution of risk then it can be

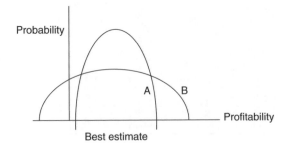

Figure 15.10   Risk probability distributions

seen that project A is the preferable project, providing always that the expected returns for the two projects are similar. Risk analysis can be used to quantify the expected values of the return from each project but assessing the relative relationship between risk and rewards inevitably relies upon managerial judgement and a person's attitude to risk.

A typology of risk

There are a variety of pressures acting upon organisations in terms of risk to which they are subject, and these can be viewed as representing different dimensions of risk. In order to consider the way in which the various aspects of risk affect an organisation and its behaviour in relation to sustainability, it is possible to construct a typology of risks to which a company is exposed (Figure 15.11).

Global risk

As the world has become more integrated – a facet of the globalisation which we considered in the previous chapter – the risk from global competition has naturally increased. Consequently both the nature and scale of the risk have increased.

Environmental risk

An organisation affects its environment and this includes not just the physical environment, in geophysical terms, but also the local environment though such things as pollution, noise or traffic congestion.

Social risk

A firm is, of course, part of society and reacts with that society, both positively and negatively. Risk naturally arises from this interaction.

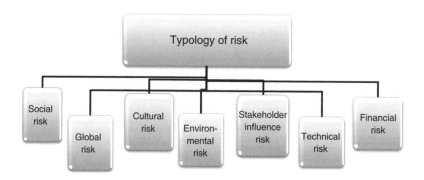

Figure 15.11   A typology of risk

Cultural risk

Much has been written[4] about the relationship between a firm and its employees, which is often negative in nature. This relationship is a source of risk which is particularly significant when the relationship breaks down and litigation or industrial action ensues.

Financial risk

All corporate activity has financial implications. Indeed, the nature of a corporation requires the undertaking of financial risk and the acceptance of the consequences. Ideally, these will result in financial rewards which are commensurate with the level of risk[5] undertaken but sometimes small rewards lead to a high level of exposure to risk.[6]

Stakeholder influence risk

With the increasing accessibility of IT, the power and influence of various stakeholder groups is increasing. This in turn increases the level of risk for the company as the various stakeholder groups are more likely to exert their influence on the company. More effort is therefore needed to manage all the stakeholder groups and the risks which they might pose.

Technical risk

Developments take place for all corporations and these include product or service development and mechanisms for delivery. We will return to this later as this is very significant for our consideration of sustainability; at this point, however, we must recognise that developments have associated risks.

Long-term and short-term effects

Often consequences of corporate activity become manifest in the long term and all decisions are subject to both long- as well as short-term risks. This is of particular significance as some of the long-term risks might not be apparent when decisions are taken and action is commenced. The consequences of the use of asbestos, for example, were not known about in the 1960s when this material was considered beneficial for commercial use.

Some risk therefore might exist which cannot even be recognised at the present time – this is uncertainty. So it must be recognised that in addition to all the identified risks there may well be others which will become apparent with the passage of time.

Risk, CSR and strategy

The identification and management of risk is an important topic for managers at the present time and a great deal of time and effort is being devoted to developing risk management plans. An important point to note, however, is the relationship between corporate governance and the level of risk to which a firm is exposed. Good governance reduces the exposure of a firm to a whole variety of risks. This is clearly recognised by investors and potential investors and so the cost of capital is lower if a firm has good procedures for its governance.

It is clear that the understanding of corporate governance has extended considerably beyond investor relations and encompasses relations with all stakeholders – including the environment. This is essential for the longer-term survival of a firm and is therefore a key component of sustainability. There is evidence that some firms understand this but they are in a minority. So it is possible to say that good corporate governance will address this but that not all firms recognise this. It is equally true to say that the difference between corporate governance and corporate social responsibility is disappearing. Increasingly, they are concerned with the strategic management of the organisation and therefore with its risk management.

It is equally possible to state that a firm which has a more complete understanding of the relationship between social responsibility, sustainability and corporate governance will address these issues more completely. By implication a more complete understanding of the interrelationships will lead to better corporate governance, and therefore to better economic performance. But this is not really the reason why governance has become so important. The reason is that investors are recognising that good governance leads to better financial performance. The relationship is direct and the evidence is overwhelming. The evidence is so great that it is clear investors are increasingly willing to pay a premium to invest in a company with good procedures for its governance. This is because they recognise that this will lead to expected improvements in sustainable performance which will, over time, be reflected in future dividend streams. In other words, it is more profitable for an investor to invest in a well-governed company and the benefits accrue in both the short and long term.

Conclusions

CSR is now generally considered to be an integral part of strategy for any organisation and built into the strategic planning process. There are many perceived benefits to an organisation from this. Governance is also an integral part of this process. Increasingly, these have been built into both the strategic planning process and the risk management systems of an organisation because it is clearly recognised that this will lower exposure to risk and therefore help to improve the performance of the organisation. It is, however, an area which is still developing.

Summary of key points

- There are a number of aspects to the role of a manager; they involve making decisions and interacting with others.
- There are a number of objectives of a business that can be equally as important as maximising profit; which of these takes priority depends upon the business and changes as circumstances change.
- There are a number of steps in the decision-making process.
- Any governance system is based upon the same four principles and will address a range of points.
- There are a number of dimensions of risk and they have significant implications for a company.
- A typology of risk can be constructed which categorises the risks as a precursor to addressing them.

Definitions of key terms and theories

Communication involves both the sender of information and its recipient, and for the information to be of value it needs to be understood by the recipient as intended by the sender.

Corporate governance can be highly influential for firm performance, and is based upon four corporate governance principles.

Risk can be evaluated and therefore planned for; there are three steps in its treatment.

Risk management has become an important aspect of business management and CSR has a role to play in this.

Test your understanding

1. What are the principles of corporate governance?
2. What are the objectives of a business, and which is the most important?
3. What are the tasks of a manager?
4. How many steps are there in the decision-making process, and what are they?
5. How can we classify attitudes to risk?
6. What is the difference between stability and sustainability?
7. What kinds of noise exist in the communication process?
8. How many types of risk can be identified and what are they?

Suggestions for further reading

Burke, L. and Longsdon, J. M. 1996. 'How Corporate Social Responsibility Pays off', *Long Range Planning*, 29, 4: 495–502.
Fombrun, C. and Shanley, M. 1990. 'What's in a Name? Reputation Building and Corporate Strategy', *Academy of Management Journal*, 33, 2: 233–58.

Sethi, S. P. 2002. 'Standards for Corporate Conduct in the International Arena: Challenges and Opportunities for Multinational Corporations', *Business and Society Review*, 107, 1: 20–40.

Notes

1. www.aquilasafari.com.
2. www.aquilasafari.com.
3. An example is the Cadbury Report.
4. See for example Davila Gomez and Crowther (2007).
5. This is, of course, the basis for financial management.
6. Consider for example the financial consequences for Barings Bank of their focus upon short-term financial success.

References

Agrawal, A. and Knoeber, C. R. 1996. 'Firm Performance and Mechanisms to Control Agency Problems between Managers and Shareholders', *Journal of Financial and Quantitative Analysis*, 31, 3: 377–98.

Aras, G. 2008. 'Corporate Governance and the Agency Problem in Financial Markets', in D. Crowther and N. Capaldi (eds), *Ashgate Research Companion to Corporate Social Responsibility*. Aldershot: Ashgate, pp. 87–96.

Aras, G. and Crowther, D. 2008. 'Exploring Frameworks of Corporate Governance', in G. Aras and D. Crowther (eds), *Culture and Corporate Governance*. Leicester SRRNet, pp 3–16.

Aras, G. and Crowther, D. 2010. 'Corporate Social Responsibility: A Broader View of Corporate Governance', in G. Aras and D. Crowther (eds), *Gower Handbook of Corporate Governance and Corporate Social Responsibility*. Aldershot: Gower, pp. 265–80.

McCoy, C. S. 1985. *Management of Values: The Ethical Difference in Corporate Policy and Performance*. Marshfield, MA: Pitman.

Millstein, I. M. and MacAvoy, P. W. 2003. 'The Active Board of Directors and Performance of the Large Publicly Traded Corporation', *Columbia Law Review*, 8, 5: 1283–1322.

Smith, T. 1992; 1996. *Accounting for Growth*. London: Century Business.

Van den Berghe, L. 2001. 'Beyond Corporate Governance', *European Business Forum*, Issue 5, Spring.

CSR and Leadership

16

Learning objectives

After studying this chapter you should be able to:

- Describe the attributes of a good leader.
- Contrast different leadership styles.
- Relate leadership style to organisational culture.
- Describe and contrast various theories of motivation.
- Contrast techniques to analyse power in organisations.
- Relate CSR activity to the strategic planning process.
- Describe the feedback loop and its relationship to systems of rewards.

There are few circumstances among those which make up the present condition of human knowledge, more unlike what might have been expected, or more significant of the backward state in which speculation on the most important subjects still lingers, than the little progress which has been made in the decision of the controversy respecting the criterion of right and wrong. (John Stuart Mill, *Utilitarianism*, 1863)

Introduction

Practical experience demonstrates that if an organisation is to be socially responsible then it needs the commitment of the senior managers of that organisation. All organisations, of course, have leaders but this is not what we are concerned with – rather it is the leadership process which we are going to look at. Effective change management requires leadership to instigate and drive the process and an understanding of this leadership process will help you become a more effective change manager.

Central to a consideration of leadership is the concept of power, and this was highlighted in the previous chapter. Moreover, Rowlinson (1997) has argued that power is central to understanding organisations. We will therefore devote a substantial part of this chapter to a consideration of power in organisations.

The concept of leadership

When we consider the attributes of a good leader it is very common to come up with a list of the qualities which a good leader should have. Such a list might look as follows:

- Integrity
- Judgement
- Energy
- Humour
- Fairness
- Initiative
- Foresight
- Dedication
- Objectivity
- Decisiveness
- Ambition

And, of course, we can also come up with a set of attributes which we consider that a good leader should not have. This might include the following:

- Stubbornness
- Vainness
- Self-centredness
- Ruthlessness
- Unfairness
- Prejudice

The problem with defining a leader through the definition of desirable and undesirable attributes is that what we are seeking is the perfect person. In reality, of course, such a person does not exist – moreover, this kind of definition would exclude both you and me from being considered as a leader – and hence as a manager within an organisation.

A manager in an organisation is, by definition, assigned a role of leadership and every manager would probably claim to be able to exercise leadership in some form. This view would not necessarily be agreed with by the subordinates of that manager. We therefore need to distinguish between the role of a leader and the exercise of leadership. This leadership involves more than the assigning of tasks to subordinates and being accountable for their performance. Such tasks are merely administrative. It is in the way that those administrative tasks are performed that we should look to discover the features of leadership. At that point we will be in a position to consider whether leadership can be exercised by only those with administrative responsibility or whether anyone can be an effective leader.

Leadership itself is more concerned with how a person influences another to carry out various tasks and so it is more concerned with communication and motivation. Leadership is therefore concerned not just with the task in hand but also with relationships between the leader and others involved in the tasks. Hersy and Blanchard (1977) used this notion of the relationship between these two to model leadership styles as shown in Figure 16.1.

According to them, those most concerned with performance of the task in hand will seek to get it done by assigning it to their subordinates – telling. Those with concern for their relationship with their subordinates will seek to persuade them to undertake the task in hand – selling. Those who are more concerned with relationships than with the immediate performance of the task in hand will seek to involve their subordinates in the decision-making and planning process – involving. Those who are not overly concerned with either the completion of the task or their relationship with their subordinates will leave it to them to determine when and how the task should be performed – delegating.

This might make it seem that delegation is a symptom of indifference but in actual fact delegation – leaving the decision as to when and how to carry out a task – is the highest form of trust because in this case the manager keeps responsibility for the performance of the task but cedes control of how it is performed to others. Hersy and Blanchard argue that as managers mature (see Figure 16.2) in their roles and become more familiar with both the tasks required and the people with whom they are working they change their leadership style,

Figure 16.1   Leadership styles

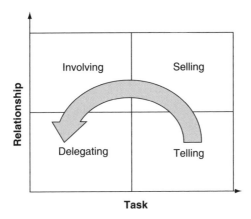

Figure 16.2   Maturing leadership

moving from the telling style through the selling and involving styles to the delegating style. For them, trusting others in this way is the ultimate form of leadership.

Styles of leadership

These ideas suggest that the qualities of leadership are not fixed but rather that they depend upon the people involved, and their respective personalities. This in turn suggests that it is fruitless to study leadership in terms of defining a set of qualities which make a good leader. Good leadership depends upon the interaction between the leader and the led, but it depends upon more than this. It also depends upon the situation. The leadership style for a brand new start-up business would probably need to be very different from that for leading a company which is long established but going through a difficult period. This in turn might be very different to a style needed to reorganise a business after a takeover. The demands of leadership depend, therefore, upon the circumstances as well as the people involved.

We can classify leadership styles into three distinct types:

- Authoritarian
- Laissez-faire
- Democratic

We can relate these back to the styles identified by Hersey and Blanchard (1977) by comparing the authoritarian style to the telling style, the laissez-faire style to the delegating style and the democratic style to the selling and involving styles. What we cannot do, however, is state that any style is necessarily better than any other. This depends upon both the people involved and the situation in which the organisation finds itself. Thus we can state that there are three variables involved in the determination of good leadership. These are:

- the personality of the leader
- the personality of the followers
- the situation at the time

Organisational culture and styles of leadership

There are, of course, other factors which we need to consider, and we have considered one of these in the previous chapter – namely the culture of the organisation. Different styles of leadership will work better in different cultures, so let us spend a whilst considering the relationship between organisational culture and leadership style.

We need to think about this first in terms of the structure of the organisation and it is possible to classify organisations according to their structure in a number of different ways. Thus, Etzioni (Etzioni and Etzioni, 1964) classifies organisational cultures into three types:

- Coercive – where the structure is hierarchical and conformity depends upon the imposition of sanctions for failure to conform. The ultimate example of this kind of structure is the military.
- Utilitarian – where the structure is focused around the completion of the tasks which need to be undertaken. Thus an organisation structured into departments such as Accounting, Production and Marketing would normally be a utilitarian structure.
- Normative – where the culture of the organisation is focused upon a shared vision which all members of the organisation buy into. For this type of culture the structure is largely irrelevant as it is the vision which prevails. Many of the new dot com companies have this type of culture.

A different type of classification was provided by Handy (1983), who classified organisations into four types:

- Hierarchical – where the organisation and the people within it are organised into lines of responsibility reaching upwards and downwards in the organisation.
- Functional – where the organisation is organised according to the functions to be performed. This is similar to the utilitarian structure identified by Etzioni.
- Matrix – where the organisation has a mix of hierarchy and functionality to meet the needs of particular tasks. Thus, a person may have two sets of responsibilities – a functional one depending upon his or her area of specialism (e.g. accounting or IT) and a task one – e.g. the implementation of a new project which requires a multidisciplinary team.

- Individual – where people work largely on their own and only join together in an organisation for administrative convenience. Examples of this type of organisation would be the doctors in a health centre or barristers in a practice.

A third type of classification was provided by Miles and Snow (1978). They classified organisations into the following types, based upon their approach to change and development:

- Defender
- Prospector
- Analyser
- Reactor

Enron employee review policy

Enron is well known for a variety of reasons concerning its governance policies, its accounting policies and, of course, its fraudulent behaviour. It is less well known for its policy towards its employees and the annual reviews that were undergone by these people. In its heyday, Enron recruited constantly and particularly graduates from business schools. And such people were keen to work for such a fast-growing company – the pay was good and the chances of promotion in such a successful company were high. So it was an attractive proposition.

Enron had a set of core values which all employees were expected to adhere to. They were known by the mnemonic RICE – Respect, Integrity, Communication and Excellence. This was widely communicated within the company. Also widely communicated was the Peer Review Committee (PRC), who oversaw the semi-annual review that all employees were required to undergo. Of course, all companies have a review process for employees, although it is normally on an annual basis rather than twice per year. And in many respects the Enron system was similar to many others and could be considered to be quite progressive.

Enron operated a 360-degree review system. This means that feedback is provided on an employee's performance from those above and below and on a par with the employee. Each employee selected five people who they would ask to provide feedback on their performance – an obvious opportunity to manipulate the system through negotiated reciprocity! To combat this, any other person was also able to give unsolicited feedback – an equally obvious opportunity for vindictiveness and the settling of old scores! Once the feedback had been received, each employee was graded by the PRC as between 1 (the best) and 5 (the worst). A fixed amount of people had to be allocated to each grade and 15% of employees, no matter how good, were automatically required to be graded as 5. And those 15% of people were automatically redeployed. This meant that they were removed from their current job and given a few weeks to find another – either within Enron or elsewhere. Effectively, therefore, 15% of people were fired from Enron every six months.

The theory behind this system is that it motivates people to try hard and to be good employees. In reality, it made everyone nervous and insecure, and it meant that a considerable part of their time was spent on a regular basis in defending their record and negotiating with allies for a good review. The automatic 15% cut-off also meant that it was not necessarily poor employees who got fired – just a set number of people. Such a system might motivate people to be not noticed in the company but it does not motivate people to excellent performance. Moreover, the lack of transparency means that it cannot be considered as a socially responsible way to treat employees.

Motivation

We can see that leadership is to a large extent concerned with dealing with people in order to optimise the results achieved. Indeed, all managerial action is concerned with dealing with people. This has been expressed by McGregor (1960: 54) in the following terms:

> Every managerial decision has behavioural consequences. Successful management depends upon the ability to predict and control human behaviour.

McGregor also classified people according to two types, which he labelled as Theory X and Theory Y. According to him, Theory X described the fact that people dislike work and can be persuaded to work by only coercion. His Theory Y on the other hand described the fact that people are conscientious and self-motivated. As far as organisations are concerned, they are often managed on the assumption that Theory Y applies to managers and senior professionals, who are motivated and can be trusted to perform effectively, whilst Theory X applies to other workers who need to be controlled and coerced through sanctions. The ideas of good leadership which we have discussed, however, show this to be problematic. What we should be aiming for as part of good leadership is to motivate people. There are a variety of different theories of motivation, however, which all suggest different thing about what motivates people.

Theories of motivation

The Expectancy Theory of motivation, developed by Vroom and Lawler, suggests that people are motivated by an internal calculation which they do. In this calculation a person works out how difficult a task is to do and how much the rewards for successful completion of the task are worth. The interaction determines the level of motivation. Thus, a person may be motivated to attempt a difficult task if the rewards for success are highly desired but not otherwise. One implication of this theory, however, is that motivation is personal and that the same rewards for successful completion of the same task will motivate different people differently depending upon how hard they consider the task to be and how much they value the rewards on offer. This would suggest a problem with the kind of performance bonuses offered to people.

A different motivation theory was developed by Herzberg (1966) and is known as the Two Factor Theory. For Herzberg there are two types of factor (hence the name), which have different effects upon a person as far as motivation is concerned. These two factors and their effects are:

- Hygiene factors – these do not motivate people if they are present but do de-motivate people if they are absent. For Herzberg, money, above a certain minimal level, is a hygiene factor and does not motivate people.
- Motivators – these motivate people if they are present but do not de-motivate people if they are absent. Motivators are concerned with job enrichment, recognition and praise, and the social aspects of working life.

The Hawthorne studies provide a good example of the difference between hygiene factors and motivators. Initially, Elton Mayo and his team thought that factors such as lighting and speed of work required were the motivating factors but further investigation and chance discovery showed that these did not motivate people but it was the fact that they were being researched (and someone was interested in them) that provided the motivating force.

Another motivation theory is known as the Equity Theory of motivation. This theory argues that motivation is a comparative process and that people will compare what is expected of them and the rewards on offer for success with what they believe is expected of others and their rewards. Moreover, this comparison is not necessarily a realistic one as people will tend to believe that others have to work less hard to achieve the same level of rewards or to gain greater rewards for the same level of effort.

It is important, therefore, to be careful about making assumptions about what will motivate people. The obvious factor is not necessarily the motivating factor, which might be something quite different. It is of equal importance to remember though that motivation is essentially personal. What motivates you will not necessarily motivate someone else; good leaders who are successful in motivating others need to know the people they are trying to motivate in order to understand what it is that will provide the necessary motivation for people as individuals.

Motivation and behaviour

Research into motivation in the 1960s and 1970s showed a variety of things which might be helpful to managers in developing their leadership abilities. First, Williamson (1964) demonstrated that people were motivated by a desire to achieve two sets of goals – those of the organisation and personal goals –

suggesting that leadership should be concerned with the alignment of those two sets of goals. Ronen and Livingstone (1975) found that involvement in the making of decisions and the setting of targets led to higher motivation from those involved. This was supported by the research of Rockness (1977), who found that people would tend to set higher targets for themselves than might otherwise be set and that difficult targets were more highly motivating for people.

There is one danger of this, however, in that if people set difficult targets then there will be a tendency for some to fail to meet those targets. This can have a problem for organisational planning purposes as not all plans will necessarily be achievable. Another problem, particularly in the present, is that many organisations are disapproving of failure and will punish people for failure, often by dismissal. This can have the effect of deterring people from striving to achieve high levels of performance and cause an effect which Schiff and Lewin (1970) observed, namely a tendency for people to create slack in their targets to allow some leeway in case of problems of achievement. Equally, Peters and Waterman (1982) found that those companies which excelled were those which tolerated failure and thereby encouraged people to experiment and take risks in doing so.

Definitions of power

> Power is the capacity to affect organisational outcomes. (Mintzberg, 1983: 85)

> Power is that which enables A to modify the attitudes or behaviour of B. (Handy, 1983: 76).

The ubiquitous nature of power in organisational life is undeniable. This makes it essential that we have an understanding of the nature of power. Bachrach and Baratz (197: 533) state:

> Of course power is exercised when A participates in the making of decisions that affect B. Power is also exercised when A devotes his energies to creating or reinforcing social and political values and institutional practices that limit the scope of the political process to public consideration of only those issues that are comparatively innocuous to A.

Power, or rather the exercise of power, can be recognised by all of us as existing within these definitions. Also existing within these definitions is an implicit assumption that it is observable and therefore measurable. It has been argued that it is an inherent part of the political system of an organisation but Lukes (1974) argues that this kind of definition of power fails as an analytical device as it is incapable of highlighting the way in which power operates 'beneath the surfaces', the way in which it acts in favour of some groups against others.

In spite of this reservation about the theory of power it remains popular within the realm of organisational theory. Indeed, its very weaknesses are also its strengths; it can indicate the outcomes of power plays. In this sense it can provide insights into the tactics of power, which is a point articulated at the level of an individual by French and Raven (1959). Viewing power as being observable when exercised by one party over another, their findings were that individuals may possess power which can be derived from one of the following power bases: reward, coercive, legitimate, referent and expert power. These power bases have proved to be remarkably durable within the discourse of organisational studies in the last forty years. Indeed, more instrumental texts have used them in order to advise 'how power may be gained'.

This dominant view of power regards it as being a possession, i.e. a department has power or a department has lost power. Thus, we can state that power is a commodity at both the level of the individual and at the collective. This is a sentiment that is shared by the strategic contingencies of power literature, which argues that the relative power of a department, in an organisation, can be calculated through an equation. The strategic contingencies perspective links in directly with the issue of organisational resources.

Sources of power

We all have some understanding of what power is, whether or not we agree with the definitions we have considered above. Consequently, we all understand when power is being exercised. What is important to understand, however, is why people are able to exercise power over others in an organisation. For this we need to consider where power comes from – in other words, the sources of power that exist (see Figure 16.3).

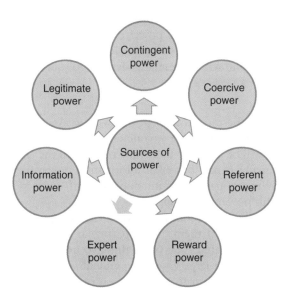

Figure 16.3   Sources of power

We can consider that power comes from a variety of sources and the following are the most common sources of power:

- Legitimate power – a leader has legitimate power if people believe that this leader has the right to give orders which they have an obligation to obey. In most organisations this legitimate power is derived from a person's status and position in the organisation, which carries with it delegated authority.
- Reward power – if a person is able to give or withhold rewards from another (e.g. the giving or not giving of a performance-related bonus) then this gives the person with the authority to grant those rewards power over the other. In a hierarchical organisation this ability to grant rewards exists for all people in the hierarchy who are above you.
- Coercive power – this power exists if the subordinates believe that the leader has the ability to impose penalties which are undesirable. In an organisation these can be social (such as loss of friendship or support), administrative (such as in the way work is allocated) or financial (such as loss of overtime opportunities, performance bonus or promotion). In most respects the ability to bestow rewards and coercive power are opposite sides of the same coin.
- Referent power – this source of power exists depending upon the personality and charisma of the leader. It exists if people believe that the leader has characteristics which are desirable and which command respect.
- Expert power – this exists if a leader has superior knowledge or expertise which is relevant to the task in hand. Expert power exists regardless of a person's role in an organisation and does not depend upon having an assigned leadership role.
- Information power – this is similar to expert power but arises not because of particular skills but rather because of access to a particular knowledge base.
- Contingent power – this form of power exists, as its name suggests, because of the demands of a particular situation. It is very often visible in an emergency where someone will assume a leadership role because of the needs of the situation.

Obviously not all of these sources of power will be available to everyone and will not necessarily be available to anyone all of the time. Thus, for example, contingent power will be available to anyone only when the circumstances make it appropriate. Equally, expert power or information power may be assumed by all of us but only in the particular situations, or with respect to the particular tasks, for which this power is appropriate.

Most people use all of these sources of power at some point or other and very often use more than one of them in any particular situation. We can see that many of them are interrelated. The other thing to note about these sources of power is that they are to a large extent dependent upon the beliefs of people. To a large extent it is a truism to say that each of us has power over others if those others think that we have.

Systems of control

The exercise of power is part of the exercise of control within an organisation. Three different types of control systems have been identified as being used within an organisation (Ouchi, 1979). These are:

- Behavioural control. This involves being able to observe people as they go about their work. Behavioural control works best when cause and effect relationships are well understood.
- Output controls. This form of control involves the collecting and analysing of information about the outcomes of work effort. The most common form of output control in use in an organisation stems from its accounting system. The budgetary system is used to measure performance within the organisation but it is measured entirely in terms of output without regard to the inputs. Indeed, the advantage of this form of control is that it is only necessary to collect information about outputs but this can be a problem in itself in that there may not necessarily be a relationship between effort and results.
- Clan control. This is based upon the creation of a sense of solidarity and commitment towards the organization and its objectives. It is thus strong in the normative type of organization which we considered earlier. It is based upon a shared culture but in its extreme form can be viewed as repressive and as a form of social control.

Starbucks Corporation

Starbucks is the largest coffeehouse company in the world, with over 17,000 stores in 50 countries. From its founding in Seattle as a local coffee-bean roaster and retailer, the company has expanded rapidly. In the 1990s, Starbucks was opening a new store every workday, a pace that continued into the 2000s. The first store outside the United States or Canada opened in the mid 1990s, and overseas stores now constitute almost one third of Starbucks' stores. The company planned to open a net of 900 new stores outside of the United States in 2009, but has announced 900 store closures in the United States since 2008.

Starbucks has been a target of protests on issues such as fair-trade policies, labour relations, environmental impact, political views, and anti-competitive practices. This what the company says, however:

> It's our commitment to do things that are good to people each other and the planet. From the way we buy our coffee, to minimizing our environmental impact, to being involved in local communities. It's doing things the way we always have. And it's using our size for good. And because you support us, Starbucks™ Shared Planet™ is what you are a part of too.

In response to concern about its environmental and human rights policies, Starbucks announced in late 2001 that it would pay a premium for beans grown on environmentally and socially responsible farms, which the company hopes

→

will 'create positive changes within the global coffee market and ultimately result in a fully sustainable coffee production supply chain'. Its new purchasing philosophy developed with the Centre of Environmental Leadership in Business, a division of Conservation International, will be piloted for two years. Its objective is not to replace existing supplier relationships but rather to enlist current suppliers. Going further than Fair Trade Certification, Starbucks argues that it pays above market prices for all of its coffee. According to the company, in 2004 it paid on average $1.42 per pound ($2.64 kg) for high-quality coffee beans. This is in comparison to commodity prices, which were as low as $0.50–$0.60 in 2003–2004. All espresso roast sold in the UK and Ireland is 100% Fairtrade. This means that the coffee in all cappuccinos and lattes are brewed with 100% Fairtrade Espresso.

In 2008, Starbucks announced a volunteer programme in New Orleans, three years after Hurricane Katrina wreaked such damage. It is intended that employees will work on various projects, including houses, planting trees and an urban garden. A volunteer coordinator said that 'I've never seen this magnitude from one corporation before, I'll say that, in terms of the sheer numbers.' In 2004, UNICEF and Starbucks launched SparkHope, a programme in which Starbucks stores in the Philippines provide early childhood care and development for children in a particular community. An area in each store contains a donation box and shows photos of the adopted community and information about UNICEF's programme.

Conversely, Starbucks has been accused by local authorities in the UK of opening several stores in retail premises without the necessary planning permission for a change of use to a restaurant. Starbucks has argued that 'Under current planning law, there is no official classification of coffee shops. Starbucks therefore encounters the difficult scenario whereby local authorities interpret the guidance in different ways. In some instances, coffee shops operate under A1 permission, some as mixed use A1/A3 and some as A3.' In May 2008, a branch of Starbucks was completed in Brighton despite having been refused permission by the local planning authority, Brighton and Hove City Council, who claimed there were too many coffee shops already present on the street. Starbucks appealed the decision by claiming it was a retail store selling bags of coffee, mugs and sandwiches, gaining a six-month extension, but the council ordered Starbucks to remove all tables and chairs from the premises by 20 February 2009, to comply with planning regulations for a retail shop. A Starbucks in Hertford won its appeal in April 2009 after being open for over a year without planning permission. A number of other stores have also been opened without planning permission.

Starbucks also donates a portion of its pre-tax profits to corporate philanthropy as part of its efforts to be more socially responsible. Starbucks makes charitable contributions through the Starbucks Foundation created in 1997 with a direct-giving programme in communities in which it operates and in countries where its coffee is sourced.

Our conclusions must be that all very large and successful corporations arouse suspicions and have examples of bad practice, but they also have examples of good practice. CSR is about working towards improving that practice.

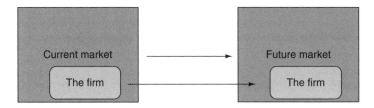

Figure 16.4   Strategic planning and market development

Strategic planning

Strategic planning is concerned with the future of the business and with how the firm can best supply what the market desires. This requires an analysis of the market in which the business is operating in order to decide what the market (i.e. potential customers) wants and what price it is willing to pay for the satisfaction of its wants. This is then followed by an analysis of what the firm is able to produce and supply (and at what price). This determines how the firm will organise its activities in order to provide these goods or services.

Strategic planning is not concerned with the present but rather with the future and is therefore especially concerned with changes to current patterns of demand, and with ensuring that the firm's capabilities change to meet the changes in market demand. Thus, strategic planning is concerned with ensuring the future of the business by ensuring that the firm changes to reflect changed market conditions. This can be modelled as illustrated in Figure 16.4.

Without strategic planning there is a danger that the market would change without the firm being aware of this change and reflecting it in its own changes pattern of operations. Thus the firm would find itself outside the market, as shown in Figure 16.5 and the firm would effectively go out of business.

Strategic planning therefore is concerned with the future direction of the business. This planning, of course, must ensure that the business has the capability of achieving whatever direction and objectives are determined in the planning stage. Thus, the strategic plan must define a set of objectives for the business and the steps necessary to ensure the achievement of these objectives – in other words an implementation plan. Most managers of organisations, at the commencement

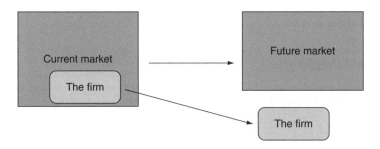

Figure 16.5   Market development without strategic planning

Figure 16.6   The strategic planning process

of their strategy development process, start with a vision of where they see the organisation being in the future. This is known as a 'strategic vision' and is often promulgated throughout the organisation in the form of a Mission Statement, which sets out in very broad terms the reason for the firm's existence.

Thus the strategic planning process can be modelled as shown in Figure 16.6.

The implementation plan will involve the following aspects of planning:
Operations plan: to ensure that the firm has the resources (i.e. manpower, capital investment, working capital) and capabilities to achieve the objectives of the plan. These capabilities include:

• technological capability
• capacity planning
• ability to produce required costings

Marketing plan: to ensure that the firm is able to:

• produce the required amount and maintain adequate stocks
• to price the product correctly

Financial plan: to ensure that the firm has the financial resources to:

• manage operations
• undertake any necessary capital investment

Thus the strategic plan will need to be as shown in Figure 16.7.

Corporate planning

The strategic plan sets out the objectives of the business for the future in outline terms and considers the options available to the business and the capabilities of the business to meet this plan. Once the future direction of the business has been determined by this planning there is a need to change this plan into a more definite one that can be expressed in quantitative terms. This is the function

Figure 16.7   The components of the strategic plan

of the corporate plan, which provides a detailed plan for the organisation, and its component parts, in order to enable the organisation of the firm's future activities and to communicate this planning throughout the firm. This in turn leads to the development of the short-term plan, or budget, of the firm.

The planning stages of organisation are shown in Figure 16.8.

The environmental analysis will enable a firm to develop its strategic plan through an examination of the external environment in which the firm is operating. An examination of the internal environment will enable a firm to translate this plan into a corporate plan for implementation. Part of this analysis will comprise a GAP Analysis which will inform the managers of the firm of its ability to meet the plan and any gaps in resources which need to be addressed. Thus this GAP Analysis will enable the managers of the business to determine what resources are needed in order to implement the plan and this will feed through into both the operating budget and the capital investment budget.

We can see that the business manager needs to be involved at all stages of this planning process and that the accounting techniques which we have discussed have an important part to play in helping at all levels and all stages of the planning process. Thus, management accounting is of importance to a business and its managers, not just operationally but also strategically.

Figure 16.8   Stages in the corporate planning process

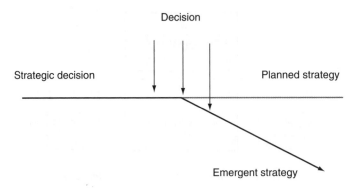

Figure 16.9   Planned and emergent strategies

Planned and emergent strategy

Although an organisation develops its strategy through this planning process, it is often the case that the effects of this strategy do not materialise in the manner intended. Whilst following this strategy the managers of the business will continue making decisions on a day-to-day basis. These decisions will inevitably affect the strategic direction of the organisation and may cause changes in the way the strategy is manifested in the operations of its business. This is known as emergent strategy, and can be modelled as shown in Figure 16.9.

Feedback

An important part of strategic planning is to ensure that the organisation is structured in such a way that the plan can be achieved, and that the control systems of the organisation provide appropriate feedback to managers. This feedback is necessary in order to ensure that managers are able to measure performance against the plan and take corrective action as necessary. Thus, the structure of an organisation needs to be determined by its planning whilst its control systems need to be determined by its structure (see Figure 16.10) and the control systems provide a feedback loop as in Figure 16.11.

Figure 16.10   Planning and control systems

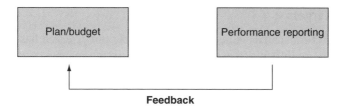

Feedback

Figure 16.11   The feedback loop

Organisational design is therefore dependent upon the planning of the business, and accounting information is used to provide managers with feedback via the control systems in order to measure performance.

Feedback is necessary so that individual managers can be informed of how the business is performing in relation to the planned level of performance and in order to indicate what corrective action needs to be taken in order to correct deviations from the plan. Thus, individual managers need feedback on the performance of that part of the business for which they are responsible. Accounting information from the accounting control system, in the form of reports on current performance, is an important part of that feedback. This feedback needs to be frequent and regular but also needs to be timely so that it is received as soon after the action as possible. This is important in order to ensure that the feedback can be accurately related to the actual decisions made and to ensure that any corrective action can be speedily taken. Detailed feedback given long after the event is of little value in the operations of a business.

Emery and Thorsrud (1963) identify six criteria which a job needs to have in order to maintain the interest of an employee. Such a job must:

- be reasonably demanding in terms other than sheer endurance, yet provide a certain amount of variety;
- allow the person to learn as he or she works;
- give the person an area of decision making or responsibility which can be considered to be his or her own;
- increase the person's respect for the task (s)he is undertaking
- have a meaningful relationship with outside life;
- hold out some sort of desirable future, and not just in terms of promotion, because not everyone can be promoted.

The management of a business therefore needs to take into account the needs of the people working in that business, and this must be reflected in the control system of that business. Specifically, this needs to be reflected in the setting of targets, the recognition of achievements and the reward structure for the level of performance achieved.

Setting of targets

The targets set for managers need to be achievable but research has shown that targets which are difficult to achieve and which stretch managers have a higher motivational effect than those which are relatively easy to achieve. On the other hand, targets which are too difficult to achieve are felt to be unreasonable and therefore also lead to a loss of motivation. Targets are set in the budgeting process, but it is important to recognise here that research has also shown people tend to set harder targets for themselves than those which are set for them by others. This suggests the need for managerial involvement in the budgeting process.

Recognising achievements

Recognition of achievements has a powerful motivational effect not only for the person recognised but also for others who are aware of the recognition given. It is for this reason that firms have tended to introduce achievement recognition systems such as the award of merit certificates, distinctions, 'manager of the month' schemes, and prizes for the best performance.

Rewarding performance

The reward structure for managers needs to be related to their performance in such a way that a manager can relate his or her rewards directly to performance. This performance, however, needs to be measured in such a way that individual managerial performance can be directly translated into company performance. Rewards systems normally operate in the form of bonuses and the payment of a bonus can be related either to the individual manager meeting or exceeding his or her target level of performance or to the performance of the company as a whole. The first method aims to maximise individual performance whilst the second method aims to maximise company performance and stresses the fact that each individual is contributing towards company performance. There is merit in both methods of reward and it is for this reason that managerial rewards and payment tend to be linked to both, with a bonus payable partly for individual performance and partly for company performance.

The operational control systems of a business need to recognise the problems associated with setting standards of performance which are realistic and allow for the revision of standards on a regular basis. The systems also need to recognise that business circumstances can change, and that the economic and competitive climate can also change, thereby making these standards inappropriate. The control systems therefore need to be flexible and to encourage maximum performance rather than merely the achievement of the standards set. This is particularly important in a modern business environment where the emphasis is upon quality and level of service rather than merely the control of the costs identified within the accounting system.

Conclusions

We have covered a lot of ground in this chapter, but leadership is a complex subject and crucial to the understanding of the operation of CSR in an organisation. There are a lot of leadership theories which have some application and relevance.

Summary of key points

- Leadership itself is more concerned with how a person influences another to carry out various tasks and so it is more concerned with communication and motivation.
- Good leadership depends upon the interaction between the leader and the led, but it also depends upon the situation.
- There are a variety of different theories of motivation which all suggest different things about what motivates people.
- There are different definitions of power and there are a number of different sources of power.
- There are various stages in the strategic planning strategy and strategy tends to be emergent.
- Feedback is necessary in order to ensure that managers are able to take corrective action as necessary.
- The control system is necessary for the setting of targets, the recognition of achievements and the reward structure for the level of performance achieved.

Definitions of key terms and theories

Emergent strategy is what actually happens as a deviation from what is planned.

Feedback is necessary in order to ensure that managers are able to measure performance against the plan and take corrective action as necessary.

Leadership is concerned not just with the task in hand but also with relationships between the leader and others involved in the tasks.

Power is the capacity to affect organisational outcomes.

Strategic planning is concerned with the future of the business and with how the firm can best supply what the market desires.

Test your understanding

1. What leadership styles are there?
2. Why is feedback important?
3. What are the sources of power available to a person?
4. What is emergent strategy?
5. What are the four components of the strategic plan?

6. What criteria are necessary for job satisfaction?
7. What is the Two Factor theory of motivation and how does it differ from the Equity Theory?
8. What is the difference between behavioural control and clan control? What third type of control exists?

Suggestions for further reading

Michael, B. and Gross, R. 2004. 'Running Business Like a Government in the New Economy: Lessons for Organizational Design and Corporate Governance', *Corporate Governance*, 4, 3: 32–46.

Paine, L. S. 1994. 'Managing for Organizational Integrity', *Harvard Business Review*, 72, 2: 106–17.

Petrick, J., Scherer, R., Brodzinski, J., Quinn, J. and Ainina, M. F. 1999. 'Global Leadership Skills and Reputational Capital: Intangible Resources for Sustainable Competitive Advantage', *The Academy of Management Executive*, 13, 1: 58–69.

References

Bachrach, P. and Baratz, M. 1974. 'Decisions and Non-decisions: An Analytical Framework', *American Political Science Review*, 57: 532–42.

Emery, F. E. and Thorsrud, E. 1963. *Form and Content in Industrial Democracy*. London: Tavistock.

Etzioni, A. and Etzioni, E. 1964. *Social Change: Sources Patterns and Sequences*. London: Basic Books.

French, J. and Raven, B. 1959. 'The Bases of Social Power', in D. Cartwright (ed.), *Studies in Social Power*. Ann Arbour, MI: Institute of Social Power.

Handy, C. 1983. *Understanding Organizations*. Harmondsworth: Penguin.

Hersey, P. and Blanchard, K. 1977. *Management of Organizational Behaviour: Utilising Human Resources*. Englewood Cliffs, NJ: Prentice Hall.

Herzberg, F. 1966. *Work and the Nature of Man*. London: Staples Press.

Lukes, S. 1974. *Power, a Radical View*. London: Macmillan.

McGregor, D. 1960. *The Human Side of Enterprise*. London: McGraw-Hill.

Miles, R. E. and Snow, C. C. 1978. *Organisational Strategy, Structure and Process*. New York: McGraw-Hill.

Mintzberg, H. 1983. *Power In and Around Organizations*. Englewood Cliffs, NJ: Prentice Hall.

Ouchi, W. G. 1979. 'A Conceptual Framework for the Design of Organisational Control Mechanisms', *Management Science*, 25, 9: 833–48.

Peters, T. and Waterman, R. 1982. *In Search of Excellence*. New York: Harper & Row.

Rockness, H. O. 1977. 'Expectancy Theory in a Budgetary Setting: An Experimental Examination', *The Accounting Review*, 52: 893–903.

Ronen, J. and Livingstone, J. L. 1975. 'An Expectancy Theory Approach to the Motivational Impact of Budgets', *The Accounting Review*, 50: 671–85.

Rowlinson, M. 1997. *Organisations and Institutions: Perspectives in Economics and Sociology*. London: Macmillan.

Schiff, M. and Lewin, A. Y. 1970. 'The Impact of People on Budgets', *The Accounting Review*, 45: 259–68.

Vroom, V. H. 1964. *Work and Motivation*. New York: John Wiley.

Williamson, O. E. 1964. *The Economics of Discretionary Behaviour*. London: Prentice Hall.

Glossary

Accountability
The actions of an organisation affect the external environment in many ways, and accountability means assuming responsibility for the effects of these actions.

The agency problem
There is information asymmetry meaning investors do not have complete information.

Arbitrage
Profit that can be earned due to price difference in different markets.

Archetype
A type of personality present in each of us.

Balanced scorecard
A way of evaluating performance which recognises all the factors affecting performance.

Boycott
The avoidance of the goods or services of a corporation, on either a total or partial basis.

Brundtland Report
The World Commission on Environment and Development (WCED) report, *Our Common Future*, in 1987, which is normally known as the Brundtland Report.

Carbon footprint
The amount of carbon dioxide consumed in the production of a product or the completion of an activity.

Classical liberal theory
States that individuals are rational and seek to pursue their own self-interest, which benefits everyone.

Collective unconscious
Provides a way of acting which is universal in nature and is inherited by all individuals.

Combined Code on Corporate Governance
Came into effect in 2003.

Communication
Involves both the sender of information and its recipient, and for the information to be of value it needs to be understood by the recipient as intended by the sender.

Communitarianism
Based upon the argument that the public good is at the centre of social life.

Contagion
Problems in one market will spread to other markets.

Corporate governance
Can be highly influential for firm performance, and is based upon four corporate governance principles.

Deontological ethics
Holds that there are absolute ethical standards which need to be upheld.

Direct action
Types of action including demonstrations, picketing, information dissemination, advertisements, obstruction or destruction.

Durability
A strong form of sustainability addressing efficiency and equity.

Ecoprotest
A direct action form of protest against the destruction of nature for its replacement by manmade environments.

Electronic action
A protest action making use of the internet.

Embedded water
The amount of water required to manufacture a product.

Emergent strategy
What actually happens as a deviation from what is planned.

Environmental accounting
A sub-area of accounting that deals with environmentally induced financial impacts and ecological impacts of a defined economic system.

Environmental audit
An investigation and recording of the activities of the organisation to understand its environmental impact.

Ethical objectivism
Asserts that some moral principles have universal validity whether or not they are universally recognised.

Ethical relativism
The denial that there are certain universal truths.

Ethics
The natural and structural process of acting in line with moral judgements, standards and rules.

Feedback
Necessary in order to ensure that managers are able to measure performance against the plan and take corrective action as necessary.

Gaia theory
States that the whole of the ecosphere, and all living matter therein, was co-dependent upon its various facets and formed a complete system.

Global Compact
Designed to encourage businesses worldwide to adopt policies regarding sustainable and socially responsible behaviour, and to use a common framework to report on them.

Global Reporting Initiative (GRI)
An initiative that develops and disseminates voluntary Sustainability Reporting Guidelines.

Global village
McLuhan's definition of the modern environment in which economic warfare has replaced physical warfare.

Global warming
Climate change caused by human activity.

Governance
Encapsulates the means by which that organisation conducts itself.

Greenhouse gas
Normally considered to be carbon dioxide but actually a considerable number of gases which contribute to climate change.

Greenwashing
Representing actions as socially responsible without amending practice.

Hubbert's Peak
The point at which maximum production of oil is reached and output cannot be increased by any means.

Individuation
The process of becoming a whole individual self.

Inferiority complex
A deficiency in a physical organ or sense which leads to the deficit being compensated for by action to overcome it.

Information asymmetry
For owners to obtain relevant information concerning the manager's effort, they must either rely on the communications received from the managers themselves or must incur monitoring costs.

Leadership
Concerned not just with the task in hand but also with relationships between the leader and others involved in the tasks.

Legitimacy theory
One of the key theories for CSR, based upon the social contract.

Life cycle analysis
Concerned with all the effects of an activity over the whole of its life, also known as terotechnology.

Moral hazard
Arises where it is difficult or costly for owners to observe or infer the amount of effort exerted by managers.

Not-for-profit organisation
One whose objective is to support or engage in activities of public or private interest without any commercial or monetary profit. In many countries some will be charities but there will also be many which are not.

Non-governmental organisation (**NGO**)
A legally constituted organisation operates without any participation or representation of any government. In the cases in which NGOs are funded totally or partially by governments, the NGO maintains its non-governmental status insofar as it excludes government representatives from membership in the organisation.

Organisation failure framework
Explains that size leads to inefficiencies in a firm.

Political economy theory
One of the key theories for CSR, based upon the work of Adam Smith and John Stuart Mill.

Portfolio investment
Based on investment for returns rather than for development, and consequently transient.

Power
The capacity to affect organisational outcomes.

Pressure groups
Groups involved in various forms of protest and the mobilisation of public opinion.

Resource depletion
A term to describe the increasing rarity of various natural resources, which are therefore harder to acquire and more expensive.

Risk management
Has become an important aspect of business management and CSR has a role to play in this.

Risk
Can be evaluated and therefore planned for; there are three steps in its treatment.

Satisficing
Means making sure that all parties are sufficiently content not to protest.

Secondary action
Actions against secondary parties to influence the main focus of a protest.

Social accounting
Considers a wide range of aspects of corporate performance and encompasses a recognition that different aspects of performance are of interest to different stakeholder groupings.

Social contract theory
Where a contract is made between citizens for the organisation of the society and as a basis for legal and political power within that society.

Social performance
Also recognises externalities in its calculation of benefit.

Spatial externalisation
The way in which costs can be transferred to other entities in the current time period.

Stakeholder
Any group which has an interest in the activities of an organisation; they can be voluntary or involuntary.

Stakeholder management approach
Based upon the idea that all stakeholders are important and their objectives need taking into consideration.

Stakeholder theory
A way of managing an organisation and one of the core theories explaining CSR.

Strategic planning
Concerned with the future of the business and with how the firm can best supply what the market desires.

Superego
One of three parts of the human pyschic apparatus which plays the moralising role and thus acts as a conscience.

Sustainability
This is concerned with the effect which action taken in the present has upon the options available in the future.

Sustainable development
Development that meets the needs of the present without compromising the ability of future generations to meet their own needs.

Teleological ethics
Distinguishes between right and good.

Temporal externalisation
Describes the way in which costs are transferred from the current time period into another.

Transaction cost theory
Explains a firm's behaviour with respect to the market.

Transparency
This means that the external impact of the actions of the organisation can be ascertained from that organisation's reporting and that pertinent facts are not disguised within that reporting.

Trickle down theory
Argues that wealth will initially accrue to the rich but eventually permeate down through society. A legitimating theory of the free market, it has no foundation whatsoever.

Triple bottom line
A form of reporting which recognises social and environmental impacts as well as economic (financial) impacts of a company's performance.

UK Corporate Governance Code
A renaming of the Combined Code, introduced in 2010.

Utilitarianism
A philosophy defining good as the maximum benefit.

Value-based management (VBM)
A technique for managing on behalf of shareholders.

Index